D1229630

# Crop Insurance for Agricultural Development

*This publication is the outcome of collaboration between the International Food Policy Research Institute and the Inter-American Institute for Cooperation on Agriculture.*

# Crop Insurance for Agricultural Development

## Issues and Experience

*Edited by*
Peter Hazell,
Carlos Pomareda,
and Alberto Valdés

*With the assistance of*
Joan Straker Hazell

*Published for the International Food Policy Research Institute*
THE JOHNS HOPKINS UNIVERSITY PRESS
Baltimore and London

Printed in the United States of America

The Johns Hopkins University Press
701 West 40th Street
Baltimore, Maryland 21211
The Johns Hopkins Press Ltd, London

The paper in this book is acid-free and meets the guidelines for permanence and durability of the Committee on Production Guidelines for Book Longevity of the Council on Library Resources.

**Library of Congress Cataloging in Publication Data**
Main entry under title:

Crop insurance for agricultural development

"This publication is the outcome of collaboration between the International Food Policy Research Institute and the Inter-American Institute for Cooperation on Agriculture."
Bibliography: p.
Includes index.
1. Insurance, Agricultural—Crops—Addresses, essays, lectures. 2. Agricultural and state—Addresses, essays, lectures. 3. Agricultural credit—Addresses, essays, lectures. I. Hazell, P.B.R. II. Pomareda, Carlos. III. Valdés, Alberto, 1935– . IV. International Food Policy Research Institute. V. InterAmerican Institute for Cooperation on Agriculture.
HG9968.C76 1985 368.1′22 85-9810
ISBN 0-8018-2673-X (alk. paper)

# Contents

# Figures

# Tables

and reviewed pilot insurance programs in Panama, Bolivia, Ecuador, and Chile.

Selected papers from that conference plus papers commissioned to summarize other countries' experiences are the substance of this volume. It is our hope that it will stimulate debate and research on the important topic of crop insurance and that it will lead to improved policies for coping with agricultural risks.

John W. Mellor
Francisco Morillo

# Foreword

Many countries have ambitious crop insurance programs to assist farmers in coping with risks. On a global basis, several billion dollars are spent each year on public subsidies for such programs. Given the high costs and the alternative uses of these public funds, especially in developing countries, there is a need to take a careful look at the benefits of crop insurance and its alternatives.

The Inter-American Institute for Cooperation on Agriculture (IICA) is involved in many aspects of agricultural development in Latin America and the Caribbean. An important question IICA has tried to answer is how credit insurance might assist farmers and agricultural lending institutions to cope with the risks posed by new agricultural technology. In collaboration with the governments of Panama, Bolivia, and Ecuador, IICA has experimented directly with credit insurance schemes and has provided technical assistance to a number of other Latin American and Caribbean countries. This book draws heavily on IICA's experience.

The International Food Policy Research Institute (IFPRI) has a broad mandate for researching policies to facilitate increased food production in developing countries, with the particular objective of alleviating poverty. IFPRI's research on risk in agriculture has included studies of policies to enhance national food security, price stabilization schemes, and strategies for managing risk at the farm level. This work has provided a useful backdrop against which crop insurance is evaluated in this book.

A conference on crop insurance and agricultural credit, sponsored jointly by IICA and IFPRI, was held at IICA's headquarters in San Jose, Costa Rica, in February 1982. Participants discussed the desirability of government subsidies for insurance, and the impact of insurance on the allocation of farm resources, the stability of farm income, and the lending policies of agricultural banks. They presented detailed evaluations of crop insurance programs in Brazil, Mexico, Costa Rica, and the United States

Acknowledgments

The publication of this book marks the end of a collaborative planning and organizational effort extending over the past four years. We wish to thank all those who contributed to the project, and especially the following individuals.

John Mellor and Francisco Morillo encouraged and supported our efforts throughout and provided financial and institutional support. Mike Gudger and Hector Guerrero were instrumental in organizing and running the conference from which this book evolved, and John Dillon, Brian Wright and Jock Anderson provided perceptive and valued comments on the manuscript.

Our special thanks go to Joan Hazell who bore much of the burden of editing and reworking the papers into a cohesive and more readable entity.

Peter Hazell
Carlos Pomareda
Alberto Valdés

## NOTE ON CURRENCIES

All dollar values in text and tables are in U.S. dollars. The following are the dollar equivalencies for currencies referred to in text.

*Peso*: 22.951 in 1980; 24.515 in 1981; 56.402 in 1982.
*Yen*: 220.54 in 1981.
*Cruzeiros*: 93.12 in 1981; 179.51 in 1982.
*Colones*: 41.094 in 1983.

# Crop Insurance for Agricultural Development

# 1

# Introduction

Peter Hazell
Carlos Pomareda
and Alberto Valdés

Problems associated with risks in agriculture are one of the reasons that many governments intervene directly in agricultural product and factor markets. Risk-related interventions include guaranteed prices, subsidized credit, and publicly provided crop insurance. Such interventions can be expensive, both in their cost to the national exchequer and in their effects on aggregate resource allocation. Even then, they may not be effective in achieving their goals. This book is addressed to the question of whether and how governments should intervene in providing formal risk-sharing institutions to assist farmers. It is particularly concerned with crop insurance and in providing guidance as to when it is a relevant public policy intervention and how it can most effectively be used.

## The Problem

Agricultural production is typically a risky business. Farmers face a variety of price, yield, and resource risks, which make their incomes unstable from year to year. In many cases farmers are also confronted by the risk of catastrophy. Crops and livestock may be destroyed by natural hazards such as hurricanes, floods, fire, and drought. The farmer or his family can also be disabled by accidents, sickness, or death.

The types and severity of the risks confronting farmers vary with the farming system and with the climatological, policy, and institutional setting. Nevertheless, agricultural risks seem to be prevalent throughout most of the world. They are particularly burdensome to small-scale farmers in developing countries. There is also strong evidence that farmers are typically risk-averse (for example, see Binswanger 1980 and Hazell 1982), and that they seek to avoid risk through various managerial and institutional mechanisms. For example, they may diversify their crops, favor traditional techniques over modern technology, and enter into sharecropping arrangements. The incidence of risk and risk-averse behavior in farming is important to policymakers for three reasons.

First, fluctuations in farm incomes, and particularly the risk of catastrophic losses, may present welfare problems for rural people. For the households operating small farms in developing countries, these losses can too easily translate into misery and malnutrition. They can also cause distress sales of farm assets, with deleterious consequences for farm recovery and long-term agricultural growth. Poorer farmers may even lose their land in catastrophic years because of indebtedness to local moneylenders. There are also spillover effects on other rural households. Destroyed crops reduce employment opportunities for the landless and limit sales by agricultural merchants and agroprocessors. Reduced farm incomes also have multiplier effects on the producers and traders of rural consumer goods and services.

Second, because farmers are typically risk-averse and seek to avoid risks through management practices, the average returns to their resources are reduced. This not only reduces average farm incomes, with immediate welfare ramifications, but it also leads to smaller supplies of the riskier agricultural commodities. These may be important food or export crops, and curtailment of their production can affect consumers' welfare directly, as well as reducing foreign exchange earnings. It also leads to a lower national income.

Third, farmers exposed to severe risks are more likely to default on bank loans, particularly in years of natural catastrophes. The provision of subsidized farm credit through agricultural development banks (ADBs) is a cornerstone in the development strategy of many countries. However, the performance and long-term viability of ADBs can be severely impaired by poor loan collection, particularly if many farmers default at the same time because of a common catastrophe. The problem is accentuated when ADBs deliberately target a generous share of their lending portfolio on small-scale farmers, since such farmers are least able to withstand catastrophic losses without defaulting.

Given these concerns, should governments intervene by providing formal risk-sharing institutions to assist farmers? Risk-sharing arrangements aim to reduce the burden of risk for the individual farmer. This can be brought about in two ways. One, by transferring the risk to other individuals or institutions, who are better able to bear the risk or who are less risk-averse. Two, by pooling risks across regions, crops, or other sectors of the economy, to take advantage of less than perfectly covariate risks. Efficient risk pooling reduces the total risk burden to society and may benefit farmers even if they have to pay the full cost of the risk-spreading mechanism.

Risk-sharing institutions are more widely available in developed countries. Farmers can borrow credit for production or consumption purposes to ease the transition from bad years to good. In most cases, they also have access to a variety of privately provided insurance against specific types of risks (such as fire, accident, and theft). They may even be able to trade in commodity futures markets.

In developing countries, these kinds of institutions are usually rudimentary, and they may effectively not exist at all for small-scale farmers. Nevertheless, a range of informal risk-sharing arrangements has often evolved. These include share-tenancy contracts, traditional money lending, and risk sharing within extended family networks. A major limitation to these arrangements is that the participants tend to come from the same region, or even the same village, and hence face much the same risks. The arrangements do not therefore pool risks as efficiently as those that span regions or sectors of the national economy, such as a nationwide crop insurance scheme.

Risk management interventions have proved costly to governments, and they have not always been effective. Before embarking on such interventions, it is desirable to begin with a clear understanding of what is to be achieved, for whom, and of the alternative means available.

In this book we assume that the primary objective of crop insurance is to help stabilize farm incomes, particularly in disaster years. This objective might be justified on welfare grounds, or on the basis of efficient use of resources, or to increase loan recovery rates for ADBs. Stabilizing farmers' incomes will also help stabilize the incomes of other rural households, such as the producers and traders of local consumer goods and services. However, it may do little to help landless workers or agricultural merchants and processors, since the demand for their services will still decline with a decline in farm production. If these groups are to be assisted, then more direct types of intervention may be required, such as food-for-work programs.

Given the objective of stabilizing farm incomes, a government typically has several policy options, depending on the kinds of risks involved. Some risks can be tackled directly. For example, production variability arising from unreliable fertilizer deliveries can often be resolved by consistent import policies and improved transport and storage systems. Likewise, some weather-related risks may be diminished through irrigation, which also contributes to increased production. Many risks lie beyond direct government control and can only be offset by compensating farmers in bad years. If price fluctuations are the primary cause of income fluctuations, then price supports or price stabilization schemes may be the best approach. A well-functioning credit market can also help tide farmers over from poor to good years. Crop insurance works best when yield risks are the primary source of fluctuations in income, and particularly when there is the risk of catastrophic yield failures.

The main purpose of this book is to clarify the role of public risk management policies, particularly of agricultural insurance, to deal with the problem of unstable farm incomes. Since there are usually alternative means of coping with risks, crop insurance is evaluated in this book within the context of its interplay with credit markets and price policies.

The book has three sections. The first discusses the determinants of the demand for insurance by farmers and by suppliers of farm credit. The second section discusses insurance and public policy based on a welfare economics approach. It includes empirical evaluations of programs in Mexico, Japan, and Australia. The third section reviews in depth the crop insurance experiences in the United States, Japan, and Brazil. These experiences and those of other countries provide lessons about the design and management of agricultural insurance programs. The book concludes with an epilogue about the role of crop insurance as a public risk management policy.

## Farmers' Demand for Insurance

The argument for publicly provided crop insurance assumes that existing, privately provided risk-sharing arrangements are inadequate for farmers. If they are not, then publicly provided insurance may simply substitute for existing private arrangements in much the same way that public buffer stocks sometimes displace private storage. It is therefore essential in any economic evaluation of publicly provided insurance to begin with an assessment of the risk-sharing alternatives already available to farmers.

Traditionally, farmers have evolved several ways to deal with disaster: selling part of their assets (such as livestock), using on-farm stocks and family savings, and seasonally migrating to places where there is work, sending money to those who stay on the farm. These are described by Walker and Jodha in chapter 2 for farmers in India, Tanzania, and El Salvador. However, the effectiveness of occupational mobility and access to nonfarm incomes in offsetting farm income losses depends largely on the covariance between agricultural and nonfarm income within and across regions.

The effectiveness of risk adjustment by small-farm households is largely an empirical issue. However, the concern is that the risk/loss management mechanisms available could be very costly in terms of farm survival. Restoring the productive capacity of a farm is a slow process, and the growth and equity implications of severe setbacks should be explicitly considered in the assessment of public policy.

The obvious alternative at the farm level is the use of risk-preventing techniques, which include resource and enterprise diversification and adjustments to husbandry techniques within cropping systems. Crop diversification, intercropping, and flexible input use are the best-known practices to reduce production risk. Walker and Jodha found strong evidence that tenancy has also actively been used in rural south India to spread production risks both within and between cropping years. They also explore the implicit insurance implications of fixed rentals, crop sharing, and other forms of leasing in India.

Because crop diversification is such a dominant strategy in risk prevention, its implications in terms of the demand for insurance are studied in detail. Using farm planning models, the study by Hazell, Bassoco, and Arcia (chapter 3) measures the income forgone due to crop diversification and relates this cost to the premium farmers would be willing to pay for insurance. While their main contribution is the provision of a model to evaluate crop insurance schemes at the farm level, their analysis does provide important empirical results for Mexico and Panama. The study shows the need to evaluate crop insurance schemes simultaneously with the farmer's other decisions and to take formal account of covariances between activities. Both elements turn out to be surprisingly important. In terms of implications for insurance, the results for Mexico show that crop insurance for maize and beans would require a subsidy of two-thirds or more of the total cost to be attractive to farmers in the rain-fed areas. The results for a high-risk region in Panama are more encouraging for insurance. However, results for other regions more representative of Panamanian agriculture suggest that farmers would not pay the full cost of insurance.

## Credit Markets and the Demand for Insurance by Financial Institutions

The case for crop insurance depends not only on the direct benefits of insurance but also on the potential indirect impact on credit markets. In rural areas, credit markets are incomplete. That is, there is credit rationing in the sense that many potential borrowers have little or no access to credit from formal institutions at prevailing interest rates. Most of the restrictions in the capital market grow out of the high degree of uncertainty in agriculture (Johnson 1947, p. 147), and the problem is most serious for the farmer who cannot offer collateral, which is the prevalent situation for many low-income farmers in developing countries. Insurance could lead to an extension of the credit market to these borrowers by acting as a partial substitute for collateral. In fact, Binswanger (chapter 4) argues that a major source of demand for crop insurance may come from financial systems, which are unable to adjust the terms of their credit contracts to the high cost of lending to particular groups.

The extent to which there is a trade-off between crop insurance and collateral for credit (for honest borrowers) in reducing imperfections in the credit market is a central issue. However, whether banks are able to collect collateral in the event of default is an open question. Collection is particularly unlikely if the value of the collateral is automatically reduced by market forces when a catastrophic loss affects a large geographic area. Public banks may also lack the political strength to collect collateral after a widespread catastrophe.

Binswanger conducts a rigorous conceptual analysis of credit markets in rural areas. He concludes that the information and incentive problems plaguing markets for crop insurance are basically the same as those affecting rural credit. The total transaction costs (which include administration costs and losses due to moral hazards) are high in both agricultural credit and insurance operations. To a large extent, this is the result of insufficient information about individual farm risks, which would permit homogeneous grouping of farms and accurate measurement of the risks of each group.

In chapter 5, on credit to small-scale farmers from public institutions, Von Pischke concludes that credit rationing is to a large extent the result of inherent weaknesses in public credit institutions. These official programs usually do not have the flexibility to adequately diversify their loan portfolios across crops, regions, and types of farm. They are also often required to promote development goals through credit programs that do not relate the loan size to a borrower's repayment capacity. Von Pischke concludes that these negative features are common in official credit institutions and that they are likely to apply to official crop insurance schemes as well. This leads him to believe that the potential effect of crop credit insurance on lending institutions may not be large. In fact, in the context of credit projects, there is the risk that credit insurance for crops will be little more than a transfer mechanism, relieving losses for the bank at the expense of the insurer.

Pomareda (chapter 6) examines the effectiveness of crop credit insurance in improving loan recovery and returns, and therefore bank performance. Using a fixed interest rate scenario, he predicts that credit insurance has the potential to improve bank earnings and growth, at least when insured risks are the initial cause of default. The gains from insurance to the banks arise from reduced collection costs, from more prompt repayment and loan turnover, and perhaps from more efficient use of bank staff. Pomareda supports his arguments with an empirical evaluation of the benefits of crop credit insurance to the performance of the Agricultural Development Bank of Panama. Interestingly, though, he also finds that almost identical benefits to this bank could be achieved by simply increasing the interest charge on its loans by 2 percent. This alternative would lead to selection of a different clientele, but it would be less expensive to farmers and the government. In fact the extra 2-percent interest charge is considerably less than the necessary premium rate to cover the administration costs of insurance. While these are results from one case, which cannot be generalized, Pomareda's modeling approach to bank portfolio management could be applied more widely.

## Insurance and Public Policy

Critics of crop insurance programs claim they have two major shortcomings. First, they usually cover only yield variation and not price variation, which limits their contribution to income stability. Second, writing insurance contracts for large numbers of small farms and carrying out inspections is very costly.

The fact is that, with few exceptions, farmers in both developed and developing countries have been unwilling to pay the full cost of all-risk crop insurance. However, there are many examples of farmers paying the full cost of insurance against some specific types of risks, such as fire and theft. Consequently, most all-risk programs remain public sector schemes. Their management is often subject to political pressure regarding premiums and coverage, and the programs are often used as a mechanism to transfer income to farmers. Countries such as the United States, Japan, Brazil, Sri Lanka, Mauritius, and Mexico have several decades of experience with publicly supported crop insurance programs.

The provision of insurance involves real service costs, whether they are met by the insured or by government subsidy. These may be particularly high when the insurer faces difficulties with moral hazard and adverse selection. Both tend to be pervasive in agricultural insurance. Moral hazard arises if farmers become less conscientious in trying to avoid damage because they find it easier to rely on insurance compensation. Adverse selection refers to the phenomenon of attracting mainly farmers who have higher-than-average risks relative to the premiums charged. The problem arises if the insurer cannot easily determine the actuarial risks they are insuring against at a sufficient microlevel and if policies for farmers who face diverse risks are written with the same premiums and indemnities.

Using a welfare economics approach, Siamwalla and Valdés (chapter 7) examine the argument for public intervention in crop insurance. If there is a divergence between social and private returns because of substantial externalities, then private firms may have insufficient incentive to engage in this activity, and crop insurance should be subsidized. After examining several possible externalities, Siamwalla and Valdés conclude that subsidies can more easily be justified during the initial phases of an insurance program. Data for the calculation of premium rates and amount of coverage are difficult to obtain at first, and mistakes are inevitable. Until the insurance program reaches a critical size, it may also be difficult to adequately spread its risks or to build up the necessary reserves to survive a run of bad years. A subsidy in the initial phases can help overcome these problems. The government can also usefully provide the necessary reinsurance, or guarantee, to insure the survival of the program. The danger of course is that a subsidy may prove difficult to remove after its initial purpose has been served. The United States, for example, still subsidizes its crop insurance program after nearly fifty years!

The question of public subsidies for agricultural insurance has been a hotly disputed issue. Of the larger schemes, public subsidies range from a low of 25 percent of indemnities in the United States, to 50 and 80 percent, respectively, in Brazil and Mexico. Siamwalla and Valdés conclude that subsidies of these amounts cannot be justified solely in terms of the risk-reducing advantages of crop insurance.

Empirical evaluation of the social costs and returns of publicly subsidized crop insurance requires measurement of the effect of risk reduction on supply response. That is, insurance supposedly reduces risk for farmers who, being risk-averse, are then willing to expand production because it is then less risky. It is this risk-response effect that leads to the major social gain from crop insurance. There are two possible approaches to measuring this effect, one using mathematical models and the other based on econometric measurement. These approaches are illustrated in a tentative and rather pioneering way in chapters 8 and 9.

Using a sectorwide mathematical model that incorporates risk-averse behavior, the study by Bassoco, Cartas, and Norton (chapter 8) attempts to provide a quantification of the aggregate economic effects of Mexico's crop insurance program. These effects are measured in terms of changes in social welfare, producer income, sector income, employment, output, prices, consumer surplus, distribution of agricultural income, and other variables. The study finds that the social benefits of compulsory crop insurance in Mexico are negative, even before the cost of the subsidy is taken into account. This is because the economic gains from risk sharing are too small to offset the share of the administration costs paid by farmers. In fact, the insurance program leads to a net leftward shift in the aggregate supply. This shift proves beneficial to producers in the short term because of price increases induced by generally inelastic demands. Interestingly, the insurance subsidy worsens the distribution of agricultural income, because the large-scale farmers benefit most. Insurance leads to modest increases in aggregate employment.

Japan is another case where publicly provided crop insurance has been operating for several decades. It is also well documented. In chapter 9, Tsujii estimates an econometric model to provide a social cost/benefit analysis of the Japanese rice insurance program. This program is compulsory for all but the smallest-scale rice growers. However, farmers have some choice in selecting coverage rates per hectare, and therefore a choice in the premium rates they pay. So there is sufficient variation in the data to permit estimating an econometric model incorporating risk-response behavior in the aggregate rice supply.

Tsujii finds that the subsidy of Japan's rice insurance is so large that on the margin it has negligible effects on supply. In fact, if the subsidy rate per hectare were increased by one *yen*, this would lead to only about a 24-metric-ton increase in national rice production. Since about 2.6-million hectares of rice are insured, this means that an increase in the total subsidy of 2.6 million *yen* would lead to a net increase of 24 metric tons of rice.

Tsujii also argues that the insurance program results in large income transfers to farmers. Yet, paradoxically, the family income of paddy farmers is greater than that of urban workers. Tsujii concludes that the program has had a low payoff in terms of aggregate social welfare in recent years. Perhaps the insurance program made sense immediately after the Second World War, when Japan was desperately short of food and the countryside was ravished. However, today, in a highly urban society, the nature of the risk problem has changed.

Australia, another particularly important case, is presented most lucidly by Lloyd and Mauldon in chapter 10. Agriculture is an important sector in the Australian economy, and it is subject to wide output fluctuations. It has a rich institutional setting, which has evolved in the presence of active research and public debate on policy alternatives to deal with risk and rural income fluctuations. Several attempts have been made to introduce commercial multiple-risk insurance schemes to Australia, but with little success. The basic problems are a scarcity of information to determine the relevant risks, the high risk of catastrophy, and problems involved in defining hazards and damage.

Until the mid-1970s, the principal policy approach to stabilizing incomes was to stabilize commodity prices. These schemes provided considerable price assistance to farmers but had little impact on stabilizing their incomes. Since then, there has been a shift in emphasis toward instruments that operate directly on the income and cash flow of individual farmers. Several specific proposals have recently been made by the Australian Industries Assistance Commission, of which rainfall insurance and variable amortization schemes for credit are perhaps the most important (although they have not yet been implemented). An income equalization scheme has been implemented, using the income tax system, but the potential for its use in developing countries is limited given their lack of effective income tax systems for farmers.

The direct use of price policy to tackle the risk resulting from large and frequent price movements is an integral part of risk-management policy. Price schemes can be coordinated with output insurance to reduce income risks. In fact, this coordination is essential if prices and yields are negatively correlated, since stabilizing one alone would increase the variability of farm income.

In developed countries with sophisticated commodity markets, the price risks facing producers can be effectively diffused through forward contracts, futures markets, or a combination of the two. However, in developing countries, such complex markets usually do not exist, and therefore price risks, and the risk premiums that result, must be regarded as an excess burden. Developing risk-diffusing institutions to manage price risks is a slow process, taking decades. Governments therefore have to be concerned with possible shortcuts in institutional innovations during the transition to forward and futures markets.

In chapter 11 Siamwalla proposes interim price intervention to counteract this risk problem. The scheme applies only to annual commodities traded internationally. It consists of a guaranteed price for the crop, announced at planting time and enforced through a variable trade tax or subsidy. Although such proposals have a long history, the novelty of Siamwalla's analysis lies in his discussion of its implementation under different scenarios with respect to fluctuations in world prices.

The best solution to the problem would be to make a supplementary payment or impose a supplementary tax to adjust producers' incomes to what they would be if they faced no price risk. However, given the difficulties of taxing farm incomes in developing countries, Siamwalla concludes that the price risk problem justifies some direct government intervention. While subject to some drawbacks, his proposed scheme is a clear improvement over the ad hoc measures prevailing in most developing countries for reducing agricultural price risks.

## The Experience with Crop Insurance

Countries such as the United States, Japan, Brazil, Sri Lanka, Mauritius, and Mexico have several decades of experience with publicly supported crop insurance programs. Part III includes an evaluation of the programs in the United States, Japan, and Brazil.

The U.S. government became involved in crop insurance in 1938 after several attempts in the private sector failed to provide multiple-peril crop insurance. Gardner and Kramer (chapter 12) pinpoint the main reasons for the failure of private efforts: too broad a coverage of risks, insufficient data for sound actuarial appraisal, group coverage inadequately tailored to the risks confronting individual farmers, and contracts written too late in the growing season.

Two aspects are particularly important in Gardner and Kramer's analysis. The first is the demand for crop insurance in the United States, which they find is related to both the premiums charged and the expected indemnities. They find that it would take quite a large subsidy, probably more than 50 percent of premiums, to get the majority of U.S. acreage enrolled on a voluntary basis. The second aspect is the effects of crop insurance, particularly on alternative risk-reducing activities, such as crop diversification and expansion of farm size. It appears that insurance encourages crop production in marginal areas, but not dramatically. This is true even in areas that had no federal coverage before the disaster payments program established in 1974.

The current Japanese crop insurance program originated in the Agricultural Loss Compensation Law enacted in 1947. (It is reviewed by Yamauchi in chapter 13.) At the time of its introduction, Japan desperately needed to increase cereal production, and this necessitated encouraging the expansion of rice production in riskier areas. Rice production was dominated by small farms, many of whose farmers had become farm owners under the 1947 land reform. Subsidized crop insurance was enacted on a compulsory basis, partly to prevent new owner/farmers from reverting to tenant status in disaster years through distress land sales. Also, the subsidy was biased toward those farms located in the riskier areas. Yamauchi argues that the program was successful in attaining its objectives, though several adjustments had to be made over time.

Originally, insurance coverage was based on the average yields for each village. This failed to adequately protect high-yield farmers, while it overprotected low-yield farmers. In response to widespread criticism, the coverage was changed in 1957 to reflect the average yields of individual plots. Farmers were also offered some flexibility in the amount of coverage they purchased. As Japan prospered in the postwar period, many small farms became part-time holdings, and crop insurance became increasingly irrelevant to their needs. Since the insurance was compulsory, it became necessary to increase each crop's minimum growing area at which insurance had to be purchased.

Brazil's national crop insurance program (PROAGRO) was established in 1973 as a voluntary program to assist farmers in repaying their loans in the event of certain natural disasters. It initially provided coverage of up to 80 percent of the amount of a loan for a standard premium of 1 percent. Loss ratios (indemnities divided by premiums) were high and climbed to 40 in 1975. The program has survived with the aid of large government subsidies. In 1980, the subsidy from the central bank represented 58 percent of PROAGRO's total revenues. In chapter 14, Lopes and Dias attribute PROAGRO's poor performance to three basic causes. First, the low premium rate charged and the high cost of administration. They calculate that the premium should not have been less than 6 percent. Second, because the program was voluntary, it attracted only a few participants, who tended to be high-risk producers. Third, the program was too specialized in wheat and upland rice.

A number of substantial changes have been made to PROAGRO since 1980. The program now is compulsory for all farm production loans.

The premium increases with the proportion of the loan covered, the frequency of claims, and the use of traditional rather than recommended technologies. Finally, farmers can no longer claim indemnities for rice when the crop is undersown with pasture, previously a common source of abuse. Although the loss ratio declined to less than 3 in recent years, it is too soon to determine if the scheme will attain financial solvency. Even so, some variant of the program is likely to continue as part of the government's efforts to assist farmers and as a system for protecting the banking system.

In contrast to PROAGRO is Sao Paulo's successful insurance scheme for cotton, in operation since 1939. The scheme is compulsory and has operated with an average loss ratio of 0.96 for the last seventeen years. One merit of state crop insurance (in Sao Paulo and Minas Gerais) is that it shows the possibility of future transfer of federal programs to state agencies or to private insurance companies.

There are important similarities in the evolution of crop insurance in the United States, Brazil, and Japan. The three have gone through considerable adjustments, learning from their own experiences. After heavy losses in the beginning years, program administrators have introduced new rules, including higher premium rates. Subsidies have been essential, and they are provided by the government on the grounds of broad social objectives. In Brazil, for example, crop insurance to some extent protects the banks that serve agriculture, which allocate credit to farmers at negative real-interest rates. To become self-financing, these programs would have to raise premium rates substantially. However, as shown for the United States and suggested for Brazil, this could cause such a drop in participation that the programs would have to be discontinued.

## Managerial Issues of Agricultural Insurance

In chapter 15, Gudger and Avalos take the view of a practitioner called upon to assist in planning during the initial operation of an agricultural insurer. They use the Costa Rican experience to illustrate what frequently goes wrong in the design and operation of agricultural insurance.

The question of whether crop insurance should be public or private is important to raise, even if only to clarify the objectives and premises of public programs. Gudger and Avalos conclude that the historical experience with multiple-risk insurance in the private sector is not encouraging. There are a number of such programs in Switzerland, Chile, Spain, and other countries. These schemes are characterized by small size, limited clientele, and most critically, an inability to sustain catastrophic losses without concessional reinsurance from the government. A new insurer must usually wait many years before it can purchase reinsurance commercially to protect itself against truly catastrophic losses.

Interesting compromises are mixed-capital ventures, like Ecuador's, and nonprofit, mutual crop insurance, like Bolivia's. In the latter, what began as a government institution is evolving toward a mutual agency, in which the insured themselves are the owners of the company. All three types of programs—private sector, mixed capital, and nonprofit mutuals—have a rather short history, and thus their viability is not certain. However, they bear careful observation to see if they can indeed reach a mass market, or if they will instead remain confined to relatively few large-scale farmers.

In chapter 16, Pomareda explores ways in which improved financial management can help reduce the cost of agricultural insurance. Pomareda's analysis suggests that the premiums needed to cover indemnity and administrative costs for all-risk insurance should be in the order of 20 percent. This is high compared to nonagricultural insurance, and high relative to farmers' demand for insurance. Crucial ways to reduce the cost of agricultural insurance appear to be improvements in actuarial practices, better management of investment portfolios, access to reinsurance, and reductions in administrative costs. For the latter, the homogeneous-area approach is a possibility, and rainfall schemes along the lines suggested by Lloyd and Mauldon in chapter 10 are a logical extension of this approach.

# I

# The Demand for Insurance

# 2

# How Small Farm Households Adapt to Risk

Thomas S. Walker
N. S. Jodha

An evaluation of crop insurance would be incomplete without an assessment of the alternatives available to farm households. Many cropping strategies and farming practices substitute for crop insurance by stabilizing crop revenue. Moreover, the stabilization of crop income does not necessarily imply stabilization of consumption, as many households have opportunities to earn other income. The availability and effectiveness of many of these risk-management alternatives are conditioned by public policy and determine the demand for crop insurance. The effects of public policy on risk management by farm households frequently go unnoticed. Policies that improve access to the land, labor, and credit markets might be more cost effective than crop insurance in strengthening risk management by farm households. So it is important to understand not only how well farm households manage risk without crop insurance but also how competing policies and crop insurance interact with traditional risk-management measures.

Two questions are crucial to an assessment of the efficiency of small-scale farmers' adjustment to risk: (1) do the present risk-management methods protect household consumption stability and preserve farm productive capacity, and (2) does reliance on these options result in sizeable losses in static or dynamic social efficiency? If the answers to these questions are yes and no, respectively, then the scope is limited for a public policy such as crop insurance both to improve farmers' risk adjustment and to contribute to social welfare.

To respond to these questions, we first describe farmers' risk management in three contrasting agroclimatic, socioeconomic, and institutional contexts in South Asia, Central America, and East Africa. Such comparative evidence is illustrative and not definitive; it only maps the boundaries of what farm households do to manage risk. Second, we review the evidence on how well traditional risk-management measures stabilize household income, singling out spatial diversification, intercropping, and

The authors are grateful to Hans Binswanger, Peter Hazell, Bob Willey, and Jere Behrman for preliminary discussions on this topic and to James Ryan and Matthias von Oppen for comments on the paper.

tenancy. Last, we comment on the efficiency costs and the potential adverse effect on equity of traditional risk-adjustment practices. Conceptually, these costs represent potential benefits from a public-sector risk-management policy, such as crop insurance.

We focus on small farm households and yield risk. For farmers in such households, particularly if they are subsistence oriented, yield risk is a greater source of income variability than price risk. Also, crop insurance as a public policy is explicitly but not exclusively directed at reducing yield risk. Because of this orientation, our analysis applies more to rain-fed farming, where yield risk is dominant, than irrigated farming, where price risk is potentially the more important source of farm-income variability (Barah and Binswanger 1982).

## Traditional Methods of Risk Management

Farmers in agriculturally risky environments have evolved several measures to deal with production risk. These measures have been observed with minor variations in several small farming systems in developing countries (Ruthenberg 1976, Collinson 1972, Norman 1974, Haswell 1973, and Navarro 1977).

Traditional methods of handling risk in small farm systems can be divided into (1) routine risk-preventing or risk-minimizing practices, usually adjustments to production and resource use before and during a production season; and (2) risk/loss-management mechanisms, which include farmers' later responses to lower-than-expected crop income caused by natural hazards, such as drought.

### *Loss Management*

When crop income falls short of expectations, farm income can be preserved through the sale of producer durables (livestock and machinery), and through management of on-farm stocks and reserves.

Nonfarm income can also be a powerful force to compensate for lower-than-expected crop revenue. Access to sources of nonfarm incomes, occupational mobility, geographic mobility, and family remittances can help stabilize household income and consumption. Their effectiveness in offsetting farm income losses depends largely on the covariance between agricultural and nonfarm income within and across regions. In Southeast Asia many farm households derive a considerable share of total income from nonfarm sources (World Bank 1982). In Mexico and Central America some small farm households receive remittances from a network of relatives in the United States. Thus they are protected from the highly covariate nature of farm and nonfarm income, characteristic of small regions in developing countries. Such covariance greatly reduces the prospect of finding nonfarm employment in the same region that is afflicted with depressed crop income. Production risks across regions may be less highly correlated; hence temporary migration may be a more rewarding risk-adjustment strategy than occupational mobility within a region.

Potentially important loss-management responses are presented in table 2.1 for small farms in El Salvador, Tanzania, and India. In general, such mechanisms are not as important in Tanzania, where man/land ratios are lower than in India and El Salvador. Absence of a labor market and imperfections in other markets force farmers in Tanzania to rely more heavily on traditional crop-management strategies to cope with production risk.

### *Risk Management*

Risk-management practices embodied in cropping strategies can be subdivided into those that relate primarily to diversification of resources and enterprises and those that relate to adjustments within cropping systems. Potentially important risk-management practices are also presented in table 2.1.[1]

Farmers exploit vertical, horizontal, and temporal dimensions of the natural resource base to reduce production risk. Planting on a toposequence is a mild form of vertical diversification, which allows flexibility in production conditional on the timing and quantity of rainfall at planting.[2]

Spatial scattering offers scope for improving crop income stability to the extent that production risks are not perfectly correlated across microenvironments. Likewise, staggered plantings and sequential diversification reduce variability to the extent that production risks are not perfectly covariate across time.

1. In looking at traditional risk-management strategies and practices, one can seldom distinguish between those where risk and expected profitability are in sharp conflict and those that are characterized by a lower variance in net returns and also higher average returns when compared to other alternatives. A good example of a risk-efficient practice is doubling maize; that is, breaking the stalk below the ear to facilitate field drying. Doubling and field drying are so much more profitable than competing alternatives in El Salvador that they are not included in our set of risk-management practices. If we had perfect information for a decision analysis on the production practices listed in table 2.1, and on alternative courses of action, we would not be surprised to find that for many environments and technology sets, what seem like risk-management strategies and practices are also the most profitable alternatives over time.

2. A more abrupt form is practiced by farmers in the mountain communities of the Andes (Guillet 1981).

TABLE 2.1 Risk/loss-management strategies, rain-fed small farms in northern El Salvador, the Kilosa area of Tanzania, and the semiarid tropics of India

| Loss-management strategies | Risk-management strategies |
|---|---|
| *El Salvador* | |
| Informal mutual aid | Toposequential planting |
| Storage and recycling | Spatially scattered planting |
| Labor market participation and foraging | Temporally diverse planting |
| Public relief | Planting crop with insurance potential |
| Depletion and replenishment of assets[a] | Planting crop insensitive to temporal variability |
| | Mixed cropping and farming |
| | Planting many seeds per hill |
| | Splitting and skipping in input use |
| *Tanzania* | |
| Interlinked consumption and production | Toposequential planting |
| Public relief | Spatially scattered planting |
| Informal mutual aid[a] | Temporally diverse planting |
| Storage and recycling[a] | Planting crop with multiple uses |
| Depletion and replenishment of assets[a] | Planting crop with insurance potential |
| Labor market participation and foraging[a] | Planting crop insensitive to temporal variability |
| | Mixed cropping and farming |
| | Plant spacing (thinning and gap filling) |
| | Planting many seeds per hill |
| | Splitting and skipping in input use |
| *India* | |
| Interlinked consumption and production | Spatially scattered planting |
| Informal mutual aid | Planting crops with multiple uses |
| Storage and recycling | Planting crops with insurance potential |
| Linkages of agricultural factor markets | Planting crops insensitive to temporal variability |
| Depletion and replenishment of assets | Mixed cropping and farming |
| Labor market participation and foraging | Plant spacing (thinning and gap filling) |
| Public relief | Splitting and skipping in input use |
| | Toposequential planting[a] |
| | Temporally diverse planting[a] |

[a]Action partially observed or empirical evidence lacking.

Crop-centered diversification is conditioned through the choice of crops with varying maturity periods, differential sensitivity to environmental fluctuations, and flexible end uses of the main products and by-products. Such diversification is often manifested through intercropping by mixing seed and varying row arrangements.

Manipulation of plant populations in accordance with changing information on soil moisture, and input use dictated by emerging weather conditions also introduces flexibility into management.

*India.* The reliance on spatial diversification and crop diversification is illustrated in table 2.2 for the semiarid tropics of India. The Sholapur villages are located in a high-risk production environment, where cropping primarily takes place after the rainy season on residual moisture. In contrast, the Akola villages are located in a more assured production environment, where rainy-season cropping is practiced. The data suggest that both spatial and crop diversification are more widely employed in the more drought-prone villages near Sholapur.

*Tanzania.* The Kilosa area of Tanzania offers an excellent benchmark of the influence of production risk on cropping decisions. The region is characterized by short, uncertain rains from October to early December and long, more certain rains from late January to the end of April. The differences in cropping decisions clearly reflect greater insurance-oriented practices during the season of short rains (table 2.3). For example, more valley land is planted, and the incidence of intercropping, salvage crops, and cropping near the compound is greater. The share of staggered planting is lower because these rains recede sooner than the long rains.

*El Salvador.* In El Salvador, several studies document the use of risk-management practices by maize farmers. Hybrid maize is more likely to be planted in pure stands in valley land, while local maize varieties, which farmers perceive as more drought-tolerant, are intercropped with sorghum or field beans on hillsides (Cutie 1975, Walker 1981). In northeastern El Salvador, if the May maize planting fails, some farmers, in a rather desperate attempt to salvage something from the cropping year, plant a low-yielding maize crop later in the rainy season (Rodriguez, Alvarado, and

TABLE 2.2 Weather risk and diversification strategies in two semiarid areas of India

| Item | Akola | Sholapur |
|---|---|---|
| *Weather risk* | | |
| Annual average rainfall (millimeters) | 820.00 | 690.00 |
| Probability of favorable soil moisture in rainy season | .66 | .33 |
| *Spatial diversification* | | |
| Scattered land fragments per farm | 2.7 | 5.8 |
| Split plots per farm | 5.0 | 11.2 |
| Fragments per farm by distance from village | | |
| 0 miles | 0.2 | 0.0 |
| 0–0.5 mile | 0.3 | 1.4 |
| 0.5–1.0 mile | 1.1 | 3.4 |
| Over 1 mile | 0.1 | 1.0 |
| *Crop diversification* | | |
| Number of different sole crops observed in area | 20 | 34 |
| Number of different crop mixtures observed in area | 43 | 56 |

*Source*: International Crops Research Institute for the Semi-Arid Tropics.

TABLE 2.3 Farming practices by season in four villages of Kilosa, Tanzania, 1980-81 (percent)

| Farming practice | Oct-Dec.[a] | Jan-May[b] |
|---|---|---|
| | *Share of year's planting* | |
| Lowland planting | 83 | 17 |
| Upland planting | 26 | 74 |
| Planting in compound | 92 | 8 |
| | *Share of season's planting* | |
| Salvage crop planting[c] | 72 | 32 |
| Intercropping | 95 | 79 |
| Staggered planting | 35 | 69 |

*Source*: Jodha (1982)

[a] Season of short, uncertain rains.

[b] Season of long, more certain rains.

[c] Salvage crops can be used before physiological maturity.

Amaya 1978). The renting of cropland for a fixed cash amount increased in El Salvador from 1961 to 1971. Part of this growth can be attributed to the buoyant demand for horizontal diversification (El Salvador 1974). Farmers have consistently rejected the advice to fertilize at planting and prefer to apply fertilizer eight days after planting, when they are assured that the crop has successfully emerged (Alvarado, Walker, and Amaya 1979).

## Effectiveness of Risk Management

Evidence on the effectiveness of risk management by small farm households is scanty. Preliminary results over the five cropping years from 1975 to 1979 in three ICRISAT study villages in the semiarid tropics of peninsular India show that the coefficient of variation of net household income per person averaged 35 percent, and ranged from 15 to 85 percent (Walker and others 1983).[3] Crop income as a share of total income was positively and significantly associated with the coefficient of variation, which suggests that risk-management strategies were not sufficient to protect income.

Some summary evidence from drought areas in India broadly illustrates the size of fluctuations in farm income, the contribution of different adjustment mechanisms, and the multiple consequences of drought on household welfare (table 2.4). Shortfalls in crop and livestock income dur-

3. This estimate refers to nominal income. The results do not change appreciably when calculations are carried out on real income, as village foodgrain price indices showed little variability or trend over the five cropping years (Walker and others 1983).

TABLE 2.4 Changes in economic measures between normal and drought years for farms in various areas of India

| Measure | Drought year change from normal year[a] | |
|---|---|---|
| | Smallest change | Largest change |
| *Current commitments (percent change)* | | |
| Per-household consumption expenditure[b] | −8 | −12 |
| Per-household socioreligious expenditure[b] | −31 | −64 |
| Per-adult foodgrain consumption[b] | −12 | −23 |
| Household postponement of tax payment, etc.[c] | 0 | +27 |
| Household withdrawal of children from school[c] | 0 | +42 |
| *Assets and liabilities (percent change)* | | |
| Asset depletion (sale, mortgage, etc.)[d] | −19 | −60 |
| Outstanding debt[e] | +64 | +192 |
| *Income source (percent change)* | | |
| Crops[b] | −58 | −82 |
| Livestock[b] | −37 | −73 |
| *Migration (percent households)* | | |
| Households with member outmigrating[b] | 37 | 60 |
| Animals outmigrating[b] | 32 | 56 |
| Migrating animals lost or dead[b] | 28 | 53 |
| Nonmigrating animals lost or dead[b] | 59 | 87 |

*Source*: Jodha (1975, 1978) and original data sets of the studies.

[a] Postdrought year for current commitments and income source; predrought year for assets and liabilities.

[b] Three areas.

[c] One area.

[d] Five areas.

[e] Four areas.

ing the drought year were large by any standard. Despite risk-adapting cropping strategies and farming systems, the drought was so severe that crop and livestock income contributed only 5 to 16 percent to total sustenance income in the three areas studied. The shortfall in farm income was to some extent compensated by private borrowing and public relief, which contributed from 44 to 73 percent and 22 to 56 percent, respectively, to household income during the drought year.

In Latin America such detailed microeconomic inquiries (to our knowledge) are not available. What are available are recall surveys such as the one carried out in two villages in northern El Salvador on past and future mechanisms of adjustment to crop loss (table 2.5). Temporary migration to harvest export crops was a leading risk adjustment. This information furnishes some insight but does not allow quantification of the effectiveness of the risk adjustment.

TABLE 2.5 Risk-adjustment strategies of small-scale maize farmers in northern El Salvador (percent)

| Strategy | Farmers using strategy as main adjustment to crop loss in 1977[a] | Farmers who might use strategy as main adjustment to crop loss in future years |
|---|---|---|
| Sale of livestock | 20 | 36 |
| Increased labor market participation[b] | 26 | 62 |
| Draw on family savings | 5 | 2 |
| Receipt of consumption loans in kind | 10 | 0 |

*Source*: Walker (1980).
*Note*: Forty-two farmers in two villages.
[a]Does not add to 100, as 39 percent of farmers did not have to resort to any of these strategies.
[b]Seasonal migration to harvest cotton, coffee, and sugarcane.

### *Trends in Risk Management*

The effectiveness of risk management by farmers is constantly changing in response to changes in resource and institutional environments.

*Tanzania.* In Tanzania the change has been for the worse. Public policy interventions have adversely affected traditional risk-handling methods. State marketing has siphoned off village food reserves. Regulations that compel farmers to plant a fixed acreage in cash crops have eroded production flexibility. The resettlement of villagers into compact communities at selected sites has deprived farmers of access to more diverse lands as well as to diversified farming systems, where tree crops were an important food source (Jodha 1982). Labor market restrictions prohibiting the hiring of agricultural labor and block farming have also reduced farmers' freedom.

*India.* In India many well-intentioned public policies have generated side effects that have made risk management by small-scale farmers less effective in drought-prone areas. Intrayear reserves and intrayear security stocks of food grains and fodder have ceased to be important components in risk adjustment (Jodha 1981b). Group measures such as mutual risk-sharing arrangements, seasonal migration, and informal interlocking of agricultural factor markets are less compatible with new village institutions. Legal provisions regulating credit, labor contracts, mortgage of assets, and tenancy are often insensitive to the specific adjustment problems of drought-prone areas (Jodha 1981b). For these and other reasons, formal public relief has assumed greater significance in drought-prone areas. The enormous public investment in irrigation during the last decade has probably diminished risk for the country as a whole and has at least partially compensated for the deterioration of traditional risk-management measures.

*El Salvador.* In El Salvador the picture is less clear. On the positive side, such technological innovations as hybrid maize and small silos for storage have been accepted by many small-scale farmers. On the negative side, increasing population pressure on land, an inactive land market, and the demise of the traditional *colono* form of tenancy, which though exploitative was risk adjusting, have eroded the effectiveness and availability of traditional risk-management methods.

### *Three Risk-Management Measures*

Village-level studies by ICRISAT provide some evidence on the efficiency of three risk-management actions that have received considerable attention in the literature.

*Spatial diversification.* Spatial diversification of farm plots is a closer substitute for crop insurance than other informal means of risk adjustment. Access to heterogeneous agroclimates, across which production risks are not perfectly correlated, endows farmers with greater flexibility to cope with yield risk.

The incidence of heterogeneity or location specificity may be more common than is generally thought. For example, for the last seven years, monthly July rainfall measured in two gauges located at opposite ends of the 1,400-hectare main experimental station at ICRISAT is correlated at .61, which is far less than what one would expect for such a short distance on flat land.

Even within a village, there may be considerable heterogeneity in yield outcomes. Figure 2.1 shows the correlations between individual farm yields and the average village yield for selected crops. For most crops, yields are positively correlated, but there are a surprising number of cases where the correlations are either low or not statistically significant. This is particularly true for local cotton in the Akola village where from 1975 to 1980 40 percent of the farmers' yields varied inversely with the average village yield. Spatial diversification appears to have been effective in stabilizing local cotton yields in Akola. It is likely, too, that a homogeneous-area approach to compulsory crop insurance would increase instability in crop revenue for many cotton producers in the village.

Still, spatial diversification does not appear to be as strongly associated with net crop income stability as does crop diversification (Walker, Singh, and Jodha 1983). In two regions, crop diversification is negatively and significantly correlated with the coefficient of variation of net crop in-

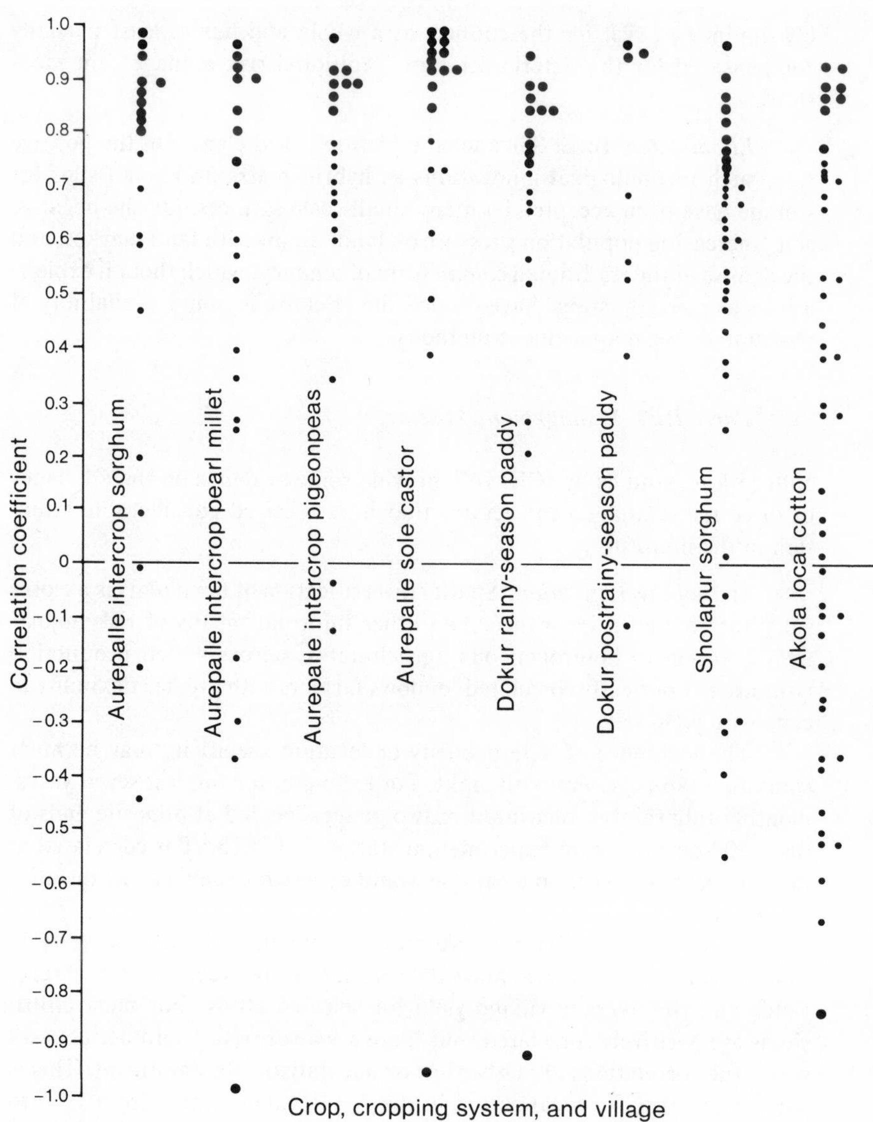


FIGURE 2.1 Correlations between individual-farm yields and average village yield, 1975 to 1979 or 1980

*Note:* ● Statistically significant at the 5 percent level. • Statistically insignificant.

come, while greater spatial diversification is not significantly correlated with the coefficient of variation of net crop income. In the remaining region, greater spatial diversification is inversely associated with the coefficient of variation of net crop income.

*Tenancy.* There are many reasons for tenancy (Newbery 1975, Binswanger and Rosenzweig 1984) and an almost unlimited number of ways to specify a contract. Risk sharing is often cited as an important reason, but what is frequently overlooked is that tenancy affords a means to manage losses incurred in previous cropping years. This is particularly true in areas where the incidence of drought accentuates the importance and extent of tenancy.

The potential for loss management in tenancy contracts is illustrated with data from two ICRISAT studies of villages located in the drought-prone district of Sholapur in India. A severe drought in 1972–73 led to the death or sale of many bullocks, which reduced the capacity of many farm households to reinitiate cultivation in the postdrought year. About 24 percent of all farm households in the two villages had to lease out all their land (Jodha, Asokan, and Ryan, 1977). Tenancy transactions tended to equalize land/bullock ratios. Before the transactions, land area per owned bullock in the two villages was 18.3 and 30.9 hectares for landowners, and 3.4 and 7.2 hectares for tenants. Following tenancy, land area per owned bullock declined to 5.5 and 5.8 hectares for landowners and increased to 7.2 and 8.2 hectares for tenants (Jodha 1981a). Recent evidence also suggests that sharecropping in the Sholapur villages is more common on inferior land that is more susceptible to crop failure (Singh and Walker 1982).

The terms of the tenancy contracts were flexible enough to satisfy the needs of both parties. Table 2.6 presents the risk implications of tenancy according to tenancy arrangements. The arrangements are defined from the perspective of landowners, many of whom lost productive capacity because of drought. Both the payment of a fixed rental independent of the size of the harvest and net output sharing imply risk transfer to tenants. When input and output are shared by both parties, risk is shared. Tenancy arrangements that help manage risk losses are conditioned by the lagged impact of drought-induced losses. They include (1) sharing of all inputs except bullocks (which were lost during the past drought); (2) crop input/output sharing arrangements subject to advance loans to landowners, adjustable against their shares to meet their preharvest resource constraints; (3) land-lease arrangements linked to labor and credit; and (4) other factor and product market contracts between landowners and tenants.

Tenancy arrangements involving the transfer of risk comprised about 29 percent of the tenancy observations. About 57 percent had explicit risk-sharing connotations, and over 60 percent had risk/loss-management implications.

TABLE 2.6 Risk implications to landlord of eleven tenancy arrangements, Sholapur area, India, 1975–78

| Tenancy arrangement (number of farms) | Risk implication |
|---|---|
| Rent essentially fixed but subject to harvest (1) | Implicit risk sharing |
| Rent fixed, independent of harvest (2) | Risk transfer to tenant |
| Advance loan, rent subject to harvest (2) | Implicit risk sharing; risk/loss management |
| Input and output sharing (14) | Explicit risk sharing |
| Input (excluding bullock) and output sharing (28) | Explicit risk sharing; risk/loss management |
| Input and output sharing with adjustable advance loan (30) | Explicit risk sharing; risk/loss management |
| Net output sharing (19) | Risk transfer to tenant |
| Net output sharing with adjustable advance loan (17) | Risk transfer to tenant; risk/loss management |
| Risky plot tenancy with no fixed rental, no advance loan, meager crop share (19) | Implicit risk sharing |
| Midseason leasing with share in output (9) | Risk transfer to tenant |
| Land lease linked to labor and credit contracts (22) | Explicit risk sharing; risk/loss management |

*Source*: Jodha (1981a).

In Sholapur, tenancy clearly helped equalize factor endowments and enabled the sharing of production risk. In Asia, most comparative empirical studies suggest that, once other variables are accounted for, the efficiency cost (in terms of low input intensity or nonadoption) from tenancy is negligible (Binswanger and Rosenzweig 1984). In Latin America, fewer empirical studies are available, but they also point to this conclusion (Colmenares 1975, Cutie 1975, Walker 1980).

*Intercropping*. Perhaps no single feature of small farm agriculture is as striking as the high incidence of intercropping, or mixed cropping (Jodha 1981c, Norman 1974). Intercropping is often praised as a risk-reducing practice in the agronomic and economic literature (Papendick, Sanchez, and Triplett 1976, Bliss 1979). Risk reduction due to diversification has to be separated from the risk-reducing attributes of intercropping by itself, which must be compared to pure stands. This is the perspective most agronomists adopt when they compute land-equivalent ratios of yield in sole-stand and intercropped treatments.[4]

4. Aside from risk reduction, intercropping may be superior to sole cropping in other dimensions (Jodha 1981c, Norman 1974).

Intercropping allows greater yield stability for three reasons (Willey 1981): (1) higher yield in stress conditions, (2) lower incidence of disease and pests, and (3) compensatory yields.

Higher yield under stress has been documented in experimental field trials, where under conditions of moisture stress, intercropping showed a yield advantage over sole cropping (ICRISAT 1980, p. 209). These results probably depended on differences in plant population between intercropping and pure stands.

The second potential source of risk reduction is extremely specific to the host, pest, and parasite (Bhatnagar and Davies 1981). For instance, in pigeonpea crops in India, wilt is reduced when the pigeonpeas are intercropped with sorghum (Willey, Rao, and Natarajan 1980). However, pigeonpeas intercropped with sorghum are subject to pod borer (Bhatnagar and Davies 1981), and there is fragmentary evidence that sterility mosaic is also a greater hazard.

Yield compensation arises from the spatial and chronological responses of species or varieties to the incidence and timing of biological and agroclimatic risk. These risks have a differential effect on crop productivity. Risk reduction in intercropping originates from the ability of at least one crop in the system to compensate for the failure or low yield of another crop. For example, cereals such as millet can partially compensate for low plant stands of other cereals through greater tillering. Compensation is conditioned by a crop's ability to take advantage of sunlight, soil nutrients, or soil moisture "released" by crops that are adversely affected. Compensation would not be possible in pure stands, because all plants would be affected in the same way.[5]

If yield compensation was common, the yield covariance between species planted in a mixed or intercropped system would be less than for proportional areas of the same crops planted in pure stands. In cases of high compensation in high-risk environments, we would expect to see negatively covariate yields. Unfortunately, not enough multiyear and multilocational data are available to compare intercropping and pure stands.[6] A less than ideal but still promising alternative is to evaluate the risk performance of common intercropping systems in farmers' fields. We hypothesize that where compensation is greater, yields between crops are less posi-

5. This is an overstatement for some sources of risk such as insect and disease damage, which may differentially affect plants in pure stands and thus widen the scope for compensation.

6. In one of the few attempts to assemble and analyze such data, Rao and Willey (1980) evaluated yield stability in a sorghum/pigeonpea intercrop. Based on bounded rationality and variance criteria, they found that intercropping provided greater yield stability than sole cropping. However, the nature of their data does not permit the separation of pure time and location effects. That is, yield stability and adaptability are confounded.

tively covariate. We would therefore assign low risk-reducing potential for cropping systems where intercrop yields are significantly and positively correlated over time.

An assessment based on ICRISAT's data provides some estimate of the size of expected compensation effects. Two intercropping systems, one traditional and one somewhat improved, were analyzed. Plot data were available for thirty farming households in each of two villages (Aurepalle and Kanzara) for the six cropping years from 1975 through 1980. The intercropping systems were the most common ones encountered in each village.

The traditional cropping system in Aurepalle consists of row intercropping two medium-duration cereals (local pearl millet and sorghum) with a long-duration grain legume (pigeonpeas). The three crops are grown in a high-risk, low-fertility environment. Sources of risk and crops with a potential for yield compensation are described in table 2.7. We would expect a strong compensatory-yield effect between pearl millet and sorghum only when shootfly inflicts damage on sorghum.[7] There is more scope for compensation between pigeonpeas and the two cereals. A clear implication of table 2.7 is that the later a crop is afflicted, the less chance there is for compensation by another crop.

In order to test the hypotheses suggested by table 2.7, we calculated the yield correlation coefficients for the three crops for the 169 plots in the sample.[8] If compensation effects were strong over many years, we would expect a negative correlation between yields of the two crops. That is, low yields from one crop would be compensated by high yields from the other crop because of reduced competition. Lower correlation coefficients would imply greater risk-buffering capacity. The size of such correlations based on yield data purged of management effects depends on the multivariate distributions of yield risk and their crop-specific interactions. For this particular cropping system, we would expect a positive correlation between sorghum and millet yield and a zero or slightly negative correlation between the yield of either cereal and pigeonpea.

As expected, sorghum and pearl millet yields were significantly and positively correlated at .63 and insignificantly associated with pigeonpea

7. If the initial monsoon rains are late, the incidence of shootfly increases, and farmers respond by planting more castor in fields originally destined for the cereal/pigeonpea mixture. Farmers therefore do not have to rely solely on yield compensation from intercropping.

8. The yield data are adjusted for management effects by regressing yield on farmer and season binary variables using least squares, dummy variable regressions (Maddala 1977). For four farmers, sorghum yields are "corrected" for linear management effects; for pearl millet and pigeonpea there is little evidence of significant differences in technical efficiency among farmers. This is what one would expect with a low-input traditional cropping system. It is important to note that yield variability from plot-specific sources has not been explicitly controlled for in the data.

TABLE 2.7 Sources of risk to traditional sorghum/pearl millet/pigeonpea intercrop systems, and yield compensation relations between crops, Aurepalle village, India

| Source of risk | Affected crop | Effect | Compensatory crop |
|---|---|---|---|
| Shootfly | Sorghum | Poor stand establishment | Pearl millet, pigeonpea[a] |
| Early drought | Sorghum, millet | Poor stand establishment | Pigeonpea[a] |
| Midseason drought | Sorghum, millet | Reduced yield | Pigeonpea[b] |
| Excess late-season rain | Sorghum | Earhead bugs, grain mold | None |
| Late-season drought | Pigeonpea | Reduced yield | None |
| Pod borer | Pigeonpea | Damaged pods | None |

[a]Strong compensation.
[b]Weak compensation.

yields at .06 and .11, respectively. The evidence indirectly suggests that for this cropping system, intercropping provided little risk protection. The same finding applied to the second cropping system, featuring three long-duration crops of local cotton, local sorghum, and pigeonpea cultivated in Kanzara village, which has more assured rainfall. Adjusted yield data for 190 plots show significant correlations (.42, .25, and .15) at the 5-percent level between yields of cotton and sorghum, cotton and pigeonpeas, and sorghum and pigeonpeas. One would expect such a result for crops that mature at about the same time.

## Efficiency Costs and Adverse-Equity Impacts of Risk Management

The risk-management actions of small farm households can entail efficiency costs and adverse-equity impacts. If these households had access to an additional risk-management measure, such as public crop insurance, perhaps the costs could be lowered and the inequities lessened. Any new policy aimed at enhancing risk management by small farm households should augment or make more effective their choices in managing risk. An analogy can be drawn to public price stabilization policies, which can displace traders and speculators and reduce price stability and thus cause little or no stabilization in prices (Peck 1977).

One important consequence of crop insurance could be shifts to cropping patterns that lead to higher average incomes. This issue is addressed at length in chapter 3 and will not be taken up here. Other benefits might be the adoption of technology, and greater use of modern inputs, less depletion of assets during bad years, less shifting of risk adjustment to landless labor, and a decline in land fragmentation.

*Low Input Use and Nonadoption of New Technologies*

Perhaps no risk-management theme has received as much empirical attention as the adverse effect of risk aversion on investment in new agricultural technologies and use of modern inputs. Yet the evidence from positive analyses shows that the potential for intensified farming does not increase by correcting for risk aversion.

Participants in a risk-reducing crop insurance program could capture innovators' rents as early adopters, but they would also be exposed to innovators' losses from unprofitable new technologies (Binswanger and Ryan 1977). A perceived reduction in risk could speed up the adoption cycle. However, unless acceptance by a few precludes adoption by the majority, welfare is determined by ultimate adoption, rather than by early adoption (Gerhart 1975).

Therefore, the more relevant welfare question asks the reasons for nonadoption of mature innovations. Intuitively, the output cost of risk aversion is greater for recommended inputs that are indivisible or are characterized by large financial risk. Recommended inputs are frequently clustered into packages that imply all-or-nothing courses of action. In reality, farmers make adoption decisions on each component of the cluster in a piecemeal, stepwise fashion (Mann 1977). The package approach to the diffusion process greatly accentuates risk and, therefore, the potential for risk aversion as an impediment to adoption. A perhaps biased sampling of positive risk-related research on the adoption of mature innovations in Latin America indicates: (1) that when packages are partitioned into their components, risk aversion is reduced (Gladwin 1977); (2) that the conflict between expected profitability and risk is not as sharp as anticipated (O'Mara 1971); and (3) where risk aversion is the primary reason for nonadoption, moving to a risk-neutral position yields only a marginal increase in expected income (Walker 1981).[9]

It is difficult to forge a consensus; witness adoption research on the Puebla project, where five investigators (Benito 1976, Diaz 1974, Gladwin 1977, Moscardi 1976, and Villa Issa 1976) arrived at quite dissimilar conclusions and policy implications. However, the overriding importance given to on-farm profitability by Perrin and Winkelmann (1976) in their summary of the Centro Internacional de Mejoramiento de Maiz y Trigo (CIMMYT) adoption studies in the 1970s rings as true today as it did to Griliches in 1957.

9. Similar results are reported by Ryan (1972), who assessed the effect of risk aversion on optimal use of fertilizer for potatoes in Peru. He found that the marginal cost (supply) curve for potatoes was only marginally affected when one allowed for risk aversion.

### *Asset Depletion*

Reliance on liquidation of productive assets to even out fluctuations in farm income may have strong implications for economic growth and equity in risk-prone areas. Jodha (1975) has argued that farmers' risk adjustment is conditioned by repeated weather cycles, which translate into asset depletion and replenishment cycles. If governments base risk-management decisions on changes in consumption levels, asset depletion may have already run its course and farm productive capacity may have eroded, perhaps permanently.

In the longer run, such cycles signify stagnating investment in risk-prone regions. Restoring farm productive capacity is a slow, accretionary process, because farmers face a buyers' market in the disaster year and a seller's market in the postdisaster year (Jodha 1975). Asset depletion and replenishment cycles are probably not nearly as severe in most of Latin America as they are in West Africa, East Africa, and South Asia. Nonetheless, their growth and equity implications should not be ignored in the assessment of public policies whose intent is to reduce farmers' risk.[10]

### *Shifting Risk Adjustment to Landless Labor*

Increased participation in the casual-labor market is an important adjustment mechanism for small-scale farmers, particularly in Central America, where basic grains are grown from May through November and export crops such as coffee, sugarcane, and cotton are harvested from December through March. With increased seasonal migration by small-scale farmers, risk adjustment is partially shifted to landless agricultural laborers, who are least able to cope with risk. In any year, the demand for harvesting labor is highly inelastic and is determined by the size of the crop. Increased labor supply translates into decreased real wages or into higher unemployment. Effective crop insurance could therefore indirectly contribute to the income stability of landless laborers. (Of course, a well-timed and flexible public-works program would directly reduce the cost of risk adjustment borne by landless agricultural laborers.)

### *Land Fragmentation*

Efficient crop insurance could also slow land fragmentation of small farms in Latin America. Fields are subdivided and left to heirs in what we suspect

10. Browning (1971) and Durham (1979) contend that low coffee yields and prices forced many small-scale landholders in El Salvador to sell to large haciendas in the 1930s and therefore directly stimulated increasing land concentration.

is an attempt to maintain diverse holdings.[11] Casual empiricism suggests that this is also the case for parts of the semiarid tropics of India. Crop insurance could lessen the use of spatial diversification as a risk-management strategy and create a more favorable environment for consolidation of land holdings in countries where man/land ratios are high. Once again, we need more empirical evidence (in this case on the determinants of the intergenerational transfer of wealth and on the social costs of land fragmentation) before benefits can be quantified.

## Conclusions

It is easier to describe how small farm households adapt to risk than to pass judgement on whether such adaptations are effective. Fluctuations of net household income of about 35 percent over five cropping years, and household food grain consumption shortfalls ranging from 12 to 23 percent during a drought, suggest that risk management is far from perfect for these households.

We found convincing evidence, based on village-level data in rural southern India, that tenancy was actively used to spread production risk within and across cropping years. Crop and spatial diversification even within an area as small as a village may enhance yield stability in some ecological settings. Contrary to expectations, intercropping by itself contributed little to yield stability.

The effectiveness of risk management by small farm households is largely an empirical issue. Household economics that features intertemporal decision making can furnish some insight. However, the most important constraint to understanding farmers' risk adjustment is the paucity of panel data over many years for relatively large samples. For crop insurance, knowledge about the influence of crop revenue on consumption stability is sorely needed. While we may not know as much as we would want, we are sure that when tenancy is banned, mechanization is subsidized, and capital is underpriced in the formal market, risk management by small farm households suffers, and the burden of adjustment falls more heavily on landless laborers. We are less sure that a public program of crop insurance is the cure, or even a step in the right direction.

11. As Roumasset (1976) has pointed out, alternative explanations may underlie what looks like risk-averse behavior. Presumably, if there were enough plots, an owner could take into account land quality and give each heir equitable shares without fragmenting fields.

# 3

# A Model for Evaluating Farmers' Demand for Insurance: Applications in Mexico and Panama

Peter Hazell
Luz María Bassoco,
Gustavo Arcia

Crop insurance has been advocated as a direct way of assisting small-scale farmers confronting production risks, usually with the expectation that such insurance would lead to less risk-averse behavior and to the more efficient use of farm resources. In Mexico, for example, subsidized crop insurance schemes for maize and beans were recently expanded in the rain fed areas as part of the national food plan. The explicit hope was to increase both average farm incomes and the marketed surpluses of these important food crops. In Panama, credit insurance schemes have been introduced for five crops and three kinds of livestock to protect farmers against the vagaries of nature and to encourage more intensive production techniques.

Most crop insurance schemes focus on very specific kinds of risk, like hail insurance for wheat. Such risks can be more readily measured and monitored and are less costly to insure. But it is not widely recognized that such schemes may be ineffective in encouraging farmers to allocate resources in a more profit-maximizing way. For example, farmers growing diversified crops may find that their income is only weakly correlated with the yield of an individual crop. Yield insurance for that crop may have little bearing on the variability of their income, on their ability to repay debt, and on their ability to meet their families' essential living costs.

The purpose of this chapter is to analyze farm-level considerations that determine the kinds of crop insurance that might induce more efficient resource allocation. These considerations are made clear at a general level in the next section and then formalized into a specific mathematical model. This model is then used to analyze the efficiency and potential benefits of crop insurance schemes in Mexico and Panama.

## Objectives and Theory of Crop Insurance

The kinds of crop insurance considered here are concerned with within-year (or within-crop-season) risks between planting, harvesting, and marketing. Though not all are insurable, such risks comprise yield losses arising from natural causes, storage and marketing losses, uncertain product and input prices, and unreliable input supplies. In aggregate, these risks have a direct effect on annual farm income, on the variability of farm income over the years, and therefore on farmers' ability to repay debt each year and to meet essential living costs.

Research suggests that once subsistence is assured, farmers allocate their resources to obtain desired combinations of average income and income risks.[1] Higher average incomes require more risk, and most farmers trade some average income against reduced fluctuation of income.

The intended purposes of crop insurance are twofold: stabilizing income and ensuring enough income each year to repay debts and meet essential living costs.[2] These objectives must be achieved at a lower cost than the cost of risk. If these objectives can be met, farmers will be encouraged to seek higher average profits.

### *Reducing Income Risks*

For single-crop farms, insurance will help reduce income risks if it reduces the variability of net returns for that activity or increases the level of income realized in bad years. Simply compensating farmers for poor yield might not achieve either of these objectives. Consider the simplified case where production costs are not risky, and the objective is to reduce the variability of income as measured by its variance. Let $R$ denote revenue, and let $P$ and $Q$ denote the price and yield of the crop, respectively. Then the variance of income[3] can be approximated (see Anderson, Dillon, and Hardaker 1977, p. 33).

$$V(R) = E(P)^2 V(Q) + E(Q)^2 V(P) + 2E(P)E(Q) \operatorname{Cov}(P, Q). \tag{1}$$

Now if price variations are the major source of risk confronting a farmer, compensating for shortfalls in yield may have little numerical impact on $V(R)$. The second term on the right side of equation 1 would then tend to dominate $V(R)$, but crop insurance would only act on the remaining two terms in the equation. Under these circumstances, price stabilization is likely to be more effective. Further, yield compensation will be less

1. See, for example, Dillon and Scandizzo 1978.

2. Subsistence farmers might benefit more from yield insurance than schemes that attempt to stabilize incomes, particularly when poor yields coincide with high prices. However, such farmers are not likely to participate in insurance schemes that require cash premiums, and family subsistence might be better assured through food subsidies or food-for-work programs. This chapter focuses on crop insurance schemes for farmers with cash incomes.

3. Since income is the difference between revenue and costs, then if the latter are nonstochastic the variance of income is simply the variance of revenue.

effective in reducing $V(R)$ when prices and yields are negatively correlated. High prices will tend to offset low yields and vice versa, and the covariance term will be negative and hence stabilizing for $V(R)$. Poor yields may not even coincide with the worst revenue outcomes if the correlation is strong enough.

In the case of multicrop farms, it is also necessary to take account of the covariances between the returns of different crops. Letting a $j$ subscript denote the $j^{\text{th}}$ crop, then the variance of total farm revenue is

$$V(R) = V(\Sigma_j R_j) = \Sigma_j V(R_j) + \Sigma_{i \neq j} \Sigma_j \operatorname{Cov}(R_i, R_j). \tag{2}$$

Now even if crop insurance for the $j^{\text{th}}$ crop were successful in reducing $V(R_j)$, it still may not stabilize farm income. This depends on how the insurance affects the covariances between the returns of the $j^{\text{th}}$ crop with the returns of all other crops. A good insurance scheme should reduce the positive covariances and increase the absolute value of the negative ones. However it is quite possible for insurance to reduce $V(R_j)$ yet increase the size of positive covariances to the point where $V(R)$ actually increases. We shall encounter such a case in our Mexican data.

An ideal crop insurance scheme would eliminate all income variability. The most direct way of doing this would be to guarantee the farmer his average income each year by collecting premiums in years when income exceeds the average and paying indemnities in all other years. Unfortunately, such a scheme would be very difficult, if not impossible, to operate. Nevertheless, the concept of ideal insurance will prove a useful one in providing a measure of the maximum gain that is attainable from any other insurance scheme.

### *Costs of Insurance*

Risk creates a direct cost to the farmer. It is the amount of income he forgoes on average in order to pursue strategies that reduce his risk to acceptable levels. If insurance is to be effective, it must remove risk at a lower cost than this. Only then will the relative profitability of an insured crop be greater than its uninsured counterpart. However, it is exactly this cost-reducing role of a well-designed insurance scheme that makes it attractive.

Crop insurance is able to reduce risk costs by spreading risks in three ways. First, insurance pools risk among farms. Unless crop risks are perfectly and positively correlated among farms, then such pooling leads to an automatic reduction in the aggregate risk facing the insurance agency. Second, an insurance agency can diffuse crop risks to other sectors of the economy by reinsuring its policies with other institutions or selling stock. If it is a government agency, it can also rely on the ultimate security afforded by the taxpayer. Third, an insurance agency can spread risks over time by accumulating reserves. Since the proportion of farmers requiring indemnities in any one year is largely controllable, an insurer would also have a much better chance than an individual of surviving a run of bad years.

An ideal insurance agency would operate with zero transactions costs and charge farmers a premium that, over a number of years, would be equal to the average indemnities paid. In conjunction with ideal insurance policies, which eliminate income variability, such a scheme could bring about a situation in which farmers were freed from any concerns about risk.[4] Of course, such a scheme is not attainable. The real question is whether realistically designed schemes can provide a cheaper and more effective way of reducing risk costs to farmers than traditional channels of risk sharing.

## A Model for Evaluating Crop Insurance

We have already defined the two objectives of crop insurance as helping to stabilize farm income fluctuations over time and helping to ensure that the farm family has adequate income each year to repay its debts and meet essential living costs. In order to evaluate crop insurance schemes empirically, it is necessary to formulate these objectives more precisely.

Expected utility theory offers a useful way of formalizing a farmer's distaste for fluctuations in income. This theory postulates that each individual has a utility function for money. The shape of this function determines the income distribution parameters that the individual considers when choosing among strategies with risky outcomes. For example, if their utility function for money is quadratic, then farmers will choose among farm plans solely on the basis of their mean and variance of income (Markowitz 1959). In this chapter we assume that farmers behave according to a closely related decision criterion: the mean-income standard-deviation criterion. Specifically, we follow Baumol (1963) and assume that farmers maximize an expected utility function of the form

$$E(u) = E(y) - \phi\sigma_y, \qquad (3)$$

where $\phi$ is a risk-aversion parameter.

This criterion implies that for a given level of mean income, $E(y)$, farmers will always prefer the plan with the smallest standard deviation, $\sigma_y$. Further, they will be willing to sacrifice mean income in order to reduce $\sigma_y$ to the point where the marginal trade-off is exactly $\phi$. Figure 3.1 por-

4. This need not imply that farmers will specialize in only one or two crops. As Roumasset (1978) has argued, there are many possible reasons for diversifying that have nothing to do with risk-averse behavior. For example, bottlenecks due to seasonal labor, requirements of crop rotation, and planting of multiple crops.

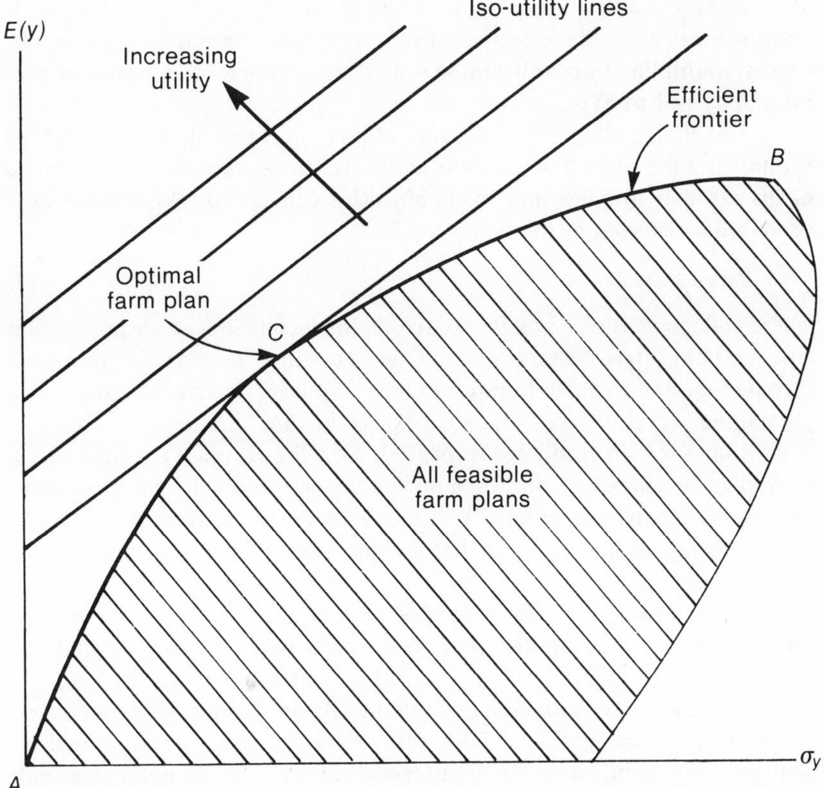


FIGURE 3.1 The optimal mean-income standard-deviation farm plan

trays a set of indifference curves corresponding to equation 3. For any farm planning problem there is also an efficient mean-income standard-deviation set of farm plans. For each of these plans, $\sigma_y$ is as small as possible for the corresponding level of $E(y)$. In figure 3.1, the efficient frontier, $AB$, is the locus of all efficient mean-income standard-deviation plans; all other feasible plans lie to the right of this frontier and are not efficient. Now the optimal plan for farmers is clearly the one that maximizes their utility. This plan will always be a member of the efficient set. In figure 3.1, it is the plan defined by point $C$—the point where the utility surface is tangent to the efficient frontier.

Our chosen decision criterion provides a direct rationale for farmers to purchase crop insurance. Crop insurance should act to reduce $\sigma_y$ for each level of $E(y)$, thereby rotating the efficient frontier to the left in figure 3.1. This will shift the point of tangency with the utility surface upward, allowing farmers to achieve higher levels of expected utility. Of course, if crop insurance is to be effective in this way, then the reduction in $\sigma_y$ obtained, multiplied by $\phi$, must more than compensate for the insurance premium charged to $E(y)$.

The choice of $\sigma_y$ as our measure of risk also happens to be useful for formalizing the second objective of crop insurance, namely the avoidance of disastrously low incomes. This objective can usefully be written as a probability criterion of the form:

$$\Pr(y_t \geq S) \geq 1 - \alpha, \tag{4}$$

where $y_t$ denotes the $t^{\text{th}}$ possible outcome for income net of all production costs and any interest charges on borrowed credit, $S$ denotes the minimum income required by farm families to meet essential living costs, and $\alpha$ is a preassigned level of risk. Since a positive income implies that all input costs financed with credit are recovered, then the criterion requires that a farm plan be chosen so that income is adequate to cover debt repayment and family subsistence at least $1 - \alpha$ proportion of the time. If $\alpha$ is set at 0.05, then equation 4 requires that income exceed $S$ at least 95 percent of the time.

Since farmers are likely to give greater priority to the survival of themselves and their families than to the repayment of debt, we shall assume that when equation 4 is not satisfied, farmers default on loans. On this basis, equation 4 can be interpreted as the probability of default, and $\alpha$ specifies the acceptable default rate. Farmers and lenders, which we shall presume to be banks, may differ about what is an acceptable default risk. However, since bankers' ideas are probably more stringent, and therefore more constraining to farmers, we shall interpret $\alpha$ as the default rate acceptable to banks.[5] With this interpretation in mind, there is no reason why $\alpha$ should bear any relation to $\phi$, since they do not represent risk tolerances for the same individual.

If income, $y$, is normally distributed, equation 4 can be expressed in certainty-equivalent form (Charnes and Cooper 1963). It is equal to

$$\Pr(Z_t \geq S^*) \geq 1 - \alpha,$$

5. Our model does not take into account the fact that subsequent loans may be more difficult to obtain if the farmer defaults in a bad year. Proper treatment of such costs would require a much more sophisticated model, in which all the recourse decisions open to the farmer in the event of a disaster would be considered. The farmer might turn to traditional moneylenders, for example, or adjust his consumption, sell some of his assets, accept government relief, give up farming, and so on. In principle, these options could be formulated in a full stochastic recourse model (Hogan, Morris, and Thompson 1981), but the required data are not available. We have chosen the chance constraint approach as a practical expedient. It is also clear that agricultural development banks do tolerate a certain percentage of bad loans without seeking punitive measures against the offending individuals.

where $Z_t = [y_t - E(y)]/\sigma_y$, and $S^* = [S - E(y)]/\sigma_y$. Here $Z_t$ is a standardized normal (0, 1) variable, and $S^*$ is the value of $Z$ at which $\alpha$ percent of the distribution lies in the tail to the left of $Z$, ($S^*$ is the $\alpha$ percentile). Consequently, by using tables of the cumulative function of the standard normal distribution, one can always find a value of $k_\alpha$, which will be negative for $\alpha < 0.5$, such that

$$E(y) + k_\alpha \sigma_y \geq S \tag{5}$$

is exactly equivalent to equation 4. For example, if $\alpha = 0.05$, then $k_\alpha = -1.65$.

Equation 5 clearly has much in common with the expected utility function defined in equation 3. In fact, maximization of equation 3 will also help farmers comply with equation 5, since the maximization will tend to increase $E(y)$ and reduce $\sigma_y$. Again, crop insurance that reduces $\sigma_y$ and increases expected utility will also serve to reduce the probability of default as defined in equation 5.

We now have the rudiments of a formal model of farmers' planning problems. To complete this model it is necessary to introduce some explicit assumptions about the nature of the production process. Linear programming has proved to be a useful and plausible way of modeling these processes, and we shall adhere to this framework here.

The full farm model can be written as follows:

$$\text{Max } E(u) = E(y) - \phi\sigma_y, \tag{6}$$

where $y = R'x - c'x - ir$, subject to the constraints

$$Ax \leq b, \tag{7}$$

$$w'x - r \leq h, \tag{8}$$

and

$$E(y) + k_\alpha \sigma_y \geq S, \tag{9}$$

where $x$ is a vector of crop areas grown, $R$ is a vector of crop revenues per unit area, $c$ is a vector of direct crop production costs per unit area, $r$ is the amount of bank credit borrowed, $i$ is the interest charge on bank credit, $w$ is a vector of crop credit requirements, $h$ is the amount of funds available from the farm family for on-farm investment, $A$ is a matrix of crop resource requirements, and $b$ is a vector of fixed resource supplies (all other notations have already been defined).

In other words, farmers seek to maximize expected utility subject to a set of constraints on the available resources they can use. Equation 7 requires that the amounts of fixed resources used, $Ax$ (for example, land and labor) do not exceed the available supplies, $b$. The constraint might also include husbandry restrictions such as crop rotation requirements or minimum constraints on the amount of food crops grown for home consumption.

Equation 8 requires that any crop credit requirements, $w'x$, in excess of farmers' own funds, $h$, must be provided by borrowing credit, $r$. Such credit has an interest charge, $i$, which is deducted from income in equation 6. Finally, equation 9 is the debt default risk constraint developed earlier. It limits the amount of credit borrowed to the amount where the probability of default is equal to $\alpha$, the default risk acceptable to the bank. The risk of default will increase with $E(y)$, since the efficient frontier is always an increasing function of $E(y)$ and $\sigma_y$. Equation 9 therefore puts a ceiling on expected income; in some cases it may be lower than the mean income farmers would attain on the basis of their own risk preferences. This feature of the model can lead to some interesting situations, in which farmers are required to be more risk-averse than they prefer in order to obtain desired credit.

The model can even lead to situations where it is quite rational for farmers to purchase crop insurance to reduce $\sigma_y$ even when they are risk-neutral ($\phi = 0$). This result is quite contrary to much of the established theory on insurance. It arises only when banks' risk preferences (as reflected in $\alpha$) are different from farmers' risk preferences (as reflected in $\phi$).

For computational purposes, it is necessary to have an explicit relationship between $\sigma_y$ and $x$. We assume that production costs, $c$, and the interest charge, $i$, are not stochastic,[6] so that income risks arise only from fluctuations in crop revenues. Then letting $\Omega$ denote the covariance matrix of activity revenues, we have the relation

$$\sigma_y = (x'\Omega x)^{1/2}. \tag{10}$$

Since equation 10 is nonlinear, the model can only be solved in its present form with nonlinear programming algorithms, and these are not nearly as convenient as linear programming for large problems. Fortunately, equation 10 can be replaced by a linear estimator of $\sigma_y$ by using the MOTAD approach (Hazell 1971, Hazell and Scandizzo 1974). This method is appropriate when $\sigma_y$ is estimated on the basis of time-series data on crop revenues.

The model can be used to evaluate the effects of alternative insurance schemes on farmers' decisions, including their demand for and repayment of credit. Insurance will affect the model by changing the coefficients of the covariance matrix, $\Omega$, of activity returns. This will lead to changes in $\sigma_y$, thereby affecting both the model maximand and the debt repayment row.

For each crop it is assumed that a time series of revenue data exists corresponding to the uninsured situation. When expressed as deviations

6. Relaxing these assumptions is not difficult, but it does complicate the presentation.

from the mean, these data provide the initial basis for estimating $\Omega$. To simulate the effect of insurance, a new set of revenue deviations must be calculated corresponding to what the initial time series would have been had the crops been insured. These calculations involve the derivation of new series of crop revenues, which differ from the original series in those years in which indemnities would have been paid. The means of the new series are then calculated, the revenue deviations obtained, and the relevant elements of $\Omega$ calculated for the insured crops.

Table 3.1 contains an illustrative set of insurance calculations. The initial uninsured revenue series is based on the product of historical prices and yields. These prices and yields should first be detrended where necessary so that all variability around their means are real elements of risk. The mean of the uninsured revenue series is 1,158.6 and the revenue deviations are calculated around this mean. Now the hypothetical insurance scheme pays an indemnity in those years when the yield is less than 85 percent of the mean yield. This indemnity amounts to the difference between the mean uninsured revenue and actual revenue. The insured revenue series has been calculated on this basis (indemnities are paid in years three and five), and then the revenue deviations are calculated from the new mean of 1,273.2. Note that the insurance scheme reduces the standard deviation of revenue from 268.0 to 112.6 and is therefore quite effective in reducing risk.

Calculations of this kind lead to a new series of revenue deviations which sum to zero. There is no point in deducting a fixed premium from the revenue series, since this will not affect the revenue deviations. The premium minus the average indemnity, and net of any subsidy if relevant, must be subtracted from expected income in the model.

TABLE 3.1 Example of insurance calculations for a five-year period

| | | | Uninsured series | | Insured series | |
|---|---|---|---|---|---|---|
| Year | Price | Yield | Revenue | Revenue deviations | Revenue | Revenue deviations |
| 1 | 5,164 | 0.237 | 1,410 | 251.4 | 1,410 | 136.8 |
| 2 | 5,119 | 0.252 | 1,290 | 131.4 | 1,290 | 16.8 |
| 3[a] | 5,104 | 0.159 | 812 | −346.6 | 1,159 | −114.2 |
| 4 | 5,049 | 0.267 | 1,348 | 189.4 | 1,348 | 74.8 |
| 5[a] | 5,014 | 0.186 | 933 | −225.6 | 1,159 | −114.2 |
| Mean | 5,090 | 0.227 | 1,158.6 | 0.0 | 1,273.2 | 0.0 |
| Standard deviation | 59.1 | 0.054 | | 268.0 | | 112.6 |

[a]Year in which indemnities are paid. An indemnity is paid when the actual yield is less than 85 percent of the mean yield. The indemnity payment is calculated as the difference between actual revenue and mean revenue.

If the variances and covariances of the insured revenues are substituted for the original elements of $\Omega$ in the model, then the ensuing model experiments will correspond to compulsory insurance. If it is desired to evaluate an optional insurance scheme, then rather than modify existing coefficients, simply add additional crop activities and additional covariances to the $\Omega$ matrix in the model. The model is then free to choose between the insured and uninsured alternatives.

## A Mexican Application

### *Description of Model*

Two of the primary objectives of the national food plan in Mexico (the Sistema Alimentario Mexicano, or SAM) were to achieve national self-sufficiency in food and to raise the incomes of farmers operating in rain-fed areas.[7] One component of the SAM policies was an expanded program of crop insurance for these farms. In particular, it was hoped that government risk sharing for maize and beans would lead to an improved allocation of resources to these crops, both in areas planted and in the use of modern inputs.

An aggregate model of the rain-fed areas was obtained from the CHAC model of Mexican agriculture (see chapter 8 for a description of CHAC). This model has recently been updated to a 1976 data base and now has a risk formulation based on the mean-income standard-deviation utility model described in this chapter. With minor changes in the treatment of credit, the model was easily made to conform to the structure defined by equations 6 through 10.

The region portrayed by the model is not contiguous but comprises a set of nonirrigated counties lying at altitudes of 500 to 1,000 meters and having an annual rainfall between 600 and 800 millimeters. The model encompasses about 36,800 farms and about 116,000 hectares of arable land. The principal crops are maize, peanuts, sesame, and sorghum. Small amounts of black beans, lima beans, barley, and wheat are also grown. The region's output of all these crops is only a small share of national production, so all crops are assumed to face perfectly elastic demands in the model.

The model permits the production of all the above crops with a variety of possible planting dates and with two levels of mechanization (basically, mules and tractors). Land and labor constraints are specified

7. The analysis reported here was conducted during the design stages of the SAM risk-sharing policies.

monthly, and labor is provided by hired laborers (at a fixed wage) or by farm family workers (at a zero wage).[8] All crops require credit to purchase chemicals and seeds and to pay for mechanization if used. Credit is available from the national agricultural bank at a 12-percent interest charge. The risk coefficients are for the period 1967 to 1976 after detrending with linear regressions.

Because of varying agroclimatic conditions, not all the available land is suitable for all crops. In the absence of more precise information on these restrictions, two types of constraints are included in the model. The sum of the land areas that can be planted to peanuts, sesame, sorghum, barley, lima beans, and wheat is restricted to be equal or less than the area devoted to the total of these crops in the base year. Also, no one of these individual crops is allowed to exceed 1.25 times the largest area planted to that crop in 1975, 1976, and 1977.

In the model, there are no direct upper limits on the amount of beans and maize that can be grown. However, minimum production of 400 grams per capita per day of maize and 32 grams per capita per day of beans are imposed for farm-family food consumption. Surplus production over these requirements can be sold. The value of the maize and beans consumed is included in the subsistence requirements, $S$, and income is defined so as to include the value of these foods. Since farmers engage in nonfarm employment not included in the model, no cash living expenses are included in $S$. Such expenses are assumed to be met by nonfarm earnings.

### *Basic Model Results*

Table 3.2 contains model results for two levels each of the debt default risk parameter, $\alpha$, and the risk-aversion parameter, $\phi$. The chosen values of $\phi$ correspond to risk-neutral behavior ($\phi = 0$) and reasonable risk-averse behavior ($\phi = 1$). Values of $\phi$ close to 1 have been reported in a number of studies involving direct elicitation of farmers' risk preferences through interview measurement techniques and through less direct inferential approaches (see Hazell 1982 for a recent review).

With a default risk of 0.1 percent, the production pattern is insensitive to changes in the risk-aversion parameter. If farmers are to obtain the amount of credit they can profitably use, they are forced to pursue a risk-averse strategy even when they are risk-neutral. The shadow price on the debt default constraint is substantially larger than the 12-percent interest

8. The original model charged family labor at a reservation wage of 40 percent of the hired laborers' wage. However, since this cost made little difference to the results for this submodel, we deleted it in order to simplify the interpretation of the objective function.

TABLE 3.2 Results under alternative assumptions about risk behavior, with no insurance possibilities, Mexican model

| Item | Debt-default risk 0.1 percent | | Debt-default risk 1.0 percent | |
|---|---|---|---|---|
| | Risk-neutral ($\phi = 0$) | Risk-averse ($\phi = 1$) | Risk-neutral ($\phi = 0$) | Risk-averse ($\phi = 1$) |
| *Income and utility measures* | | | | |
| Expected utility (million *pesos*) | 114.29 | 97.40 | 124.46 | 101.98 |
| Average income (million *pesos*) | 114.29 | 114.29 | 124.46 | 128.85 |
| Standard deviation of income (million *pesos*) | 16.89 | 16.89 | 23.53 | 21.87 |
| Coefficient of variation (percent) | 14.78 | 14.78 | 18.10 | 17.66 |
| *Production ($10^3$ metric tons)*[a] | | | | |
| Beans | 6.54 | 6.54 | 2.10 | 2.10 |
| Maize | 60.27 | 60.27 | 74.54 | 72.22 |
| Peanuts | 9.00 | 9.00 | 9.00 | 9.00 |
| Sesame | 1.35 | 1.35 | 1.35 | 1.35 |
| *Inputs* | | | | |
| Employment ($10^3$ months) | 190.13 | 190.13 | 184.43 | 183.17 |
| Credit (million *pesos*) | 27.64 | 27.64 | 17.26 | 16.85 |
| Agrochemicals (million *pesos*) | 5.12 | 5.12 | 2.19 | 2.19 |
| Machinery ($10^3$ months) | 0.72 | 0.72 | 1.17 | 0.87 |
| Mules ($10^3$ months) | 164.46 | 164.46 | 168.64 | 167.35 |
| *Shadow prices (percent return)* | | | | |
| Credit requirement | 31.53 | 21.36 | 12.00 | 12.00 |
| Debt repayment | 162.74 | 77.98 | 0.0 | 0.0 |

[a] Production of crops not listed (barley, lima beans, sorghum, wheat) is zero in all the model solutions obtained.

charge on credit for both values of $\phi$. When the default risk is relaxed to 1 percent, the default constraint is no longer binding, and differences in risk-averse behavior emerge. More maize is grown under risk-neutral than risk-averse behavior.

Expected utility is always lower with risk-averse rather than risk-neutral behavior. However, for a fixed level of the default risk parameter, differences in risk-averse behavior have little or no cost in terms of the average farm income forgone.

Relaxation of the debt default risk from 0.1 percent to 1.0 percent permits a sizeable increase in expected utility, average income, and maize production, irrespective of the risk-aversion parameter.[9] A well-designed

9. The decline in the use of credit following a reduction in $\alpha$ is surprising. When the default risk is 0.1 percent, much greater weight is given to reducing the standard deviation of income, and this is achieved through a production pattern with greater emphasis on beans. However, beans also have high credit requirements, both for seed and agrochemicals.

insurance scheme, which acts to reduce the standard deviation of income, should therefore usefully contribute to the goals of the SAM.

The maximum gain to farmers that could be attained through an income insurance scheme can be deduced from table 3.2. Suppose farmers actually have risk-aversion parameters of 1.0 and that the acceptable default risk to the bank is 0.1 percent. Then the predicted state of affairs under equilibrium conditions corresponds to the second column of table 3.2. An ideal income insurance scheme, which ironed out all fluctuations in income and which operated at zero cost, would have two effects. First, it would lead farmers to act in a risk-neutral way so that the first column of table 3.2 would more correctly describe their new behavior (that is $\phi = 0$). Expected utility would initially increase by 16.9 million *pesos*.

At the same time, however, the collapse of $\sigma_y$ would reduce the risk of default to zero, and this would be equivalent to a nonbinding debt default constraint. As such, the third column of table 3.2 aptly depicts the final equilibrium attained. The total gain to farmers in expected utility is therefore $124.5 - 97.4 = 27.1$ million *pesos* (or 735 *pesos* per farm). Average income increases by 10.2 million *pesos*, and maize production increases by 14,200 metric tons.

Of course, such an ideal insurance scheme could not be implemented in practice. Even if it could, it would likely cost much more than the gain of 735 *pesos* per farm. Nevertheless, these calculations do demonstrate that there are sizeable gains to be had from more realistically designed insurance schemes. We turn now to an evaluation of some alternative and more practical schemes.

### *The Crop Insurance Option*

As discussed in chapter 8, there is already a national crop insurance scheme in Mexico operated by Aseguradora Nacional Agrícola y Ganadera, S.A. (ANAGSA). This is a credit insurance scheme that assists farmers in repaying bank credit for insured crops in the event of damage from certain natural disasters (for example, hail, flood, and drought).[10] The scheme is not very effective in the temperate, rain-fed areas, and three additional crop insurance schemes were proposed as part of the SAM. A key feature of these proposals was an intent to compensate farmers as well as banks in the event of natural disasters, thereby enabling the government to share more of the risks confronted by farmers. These insurance schemes were specifically targeted for maize and beans.

With the aid of our model, we can proceed to an evaluation of these schemes. The following questions were of particular relevance to the SAM.

10. For more details on ANAGSA, see chapter 8.

Under what circumstances would any of the proposed insurance policies be attractive enough to farmers that they might purchase them on a voluntary basis? Were the schemes likely to have any impact on maize and bean production? Would average farm incomes improve under these schemes? Were there any other policies that might better attain the government's objectives?

In order to undertake the necessary model experiments, revenue deviation series for maize and beans had to be derived for each of the three insurance schemes. These are shown in table 3.3 for traditional maize, and in table 3.4 for beans. Indemnity payments for all three insurance schemes are triggered by the event of certain natural disasters. Because these events are difficult to identify in aggregate time-series data, we made the approximating assumption that a natural disaster occurred whenever the yield was less than 80 percent of the mean yield. In the case of maize, this only happened in one of the ten years, but it happened in three of the ten years for beans.

The first insurance scheme considered modifies the existing ANAGSA scheme. Indemnities are paid for a crop whenever actual yield is less than 80 percent of the mean yield. The indemnity is calculated according to the formula

$$I_{tj} = 1.4(1 - Q_{tj}/Q_j)w_j,$$

TABLE 3.3 Revenue deviations over a ten-year period for traditional maize, four insurance options, Mexican model

| | | | | Revenue deviations from mean (*pesos*/hectare) | | | |
|---|---|---|---|---|---|---|---|
| Year | Price (*pesos*/metric ton) | Yield (tons/hectare) | Revenue (*pesos*/hectare) | Uninsured | Modified ANAGSA insurance | Revenue insurance | Combined insurance |
| 1 | 1,987 | 0.653 | 1,298 | −123.4 | −146.2 | −147.9 | −170.3 |
| 2 | 1,948 | 0.716 | 1,395 | −16.5 | −48.9 | −50.7 | −73.0 |
| 3 | 1,879 | 0.739 | 1,389 | −32.7 | −55.1 | −56.8 | −79.3 |
| 4 | 1,860 | 0.724 | 1,347 | −74.6 | −97.1 | −98.8 | −121.1 |
| 5 | 1,841 | 0.908 | 1,672 | 250.3 | 227.9 | 226.2 | 203.8 |
| 6 | 1,832 | 0.971 | 1,779 | 357.6 | 335.2 | 333.5 | 311.0 |
| 7 | 1,953 | 0.759 | 1,482 | 61.0 | 38.6 | 36.9 | 14.5 |
| 8 | 1,629 | 0.669 | 1,089 | −331.5 | −353.9 | −355.6 | −378.0 |
| 9[a] | 2,070 | 0.570 | 1,180 | −241.4 | −39.7 | −24.1 | 177.6 |
| 10 | 2,001 | 0.791 | 1,583 | 161.5 | 139.1 | 137.4 | 115.0 |
| Mean | 1,900 | 0.750 | 1,421.4 | 0.0 | 0.0 | 0.0 | 0.0 |
| Standard deviation | 122.6 | 0.118 | | 213.7 | 196.7 | 196.4 | 205.9 |

[a]Year in which indemnities are paid.

TABLE 3.4 Revenue deviations over a ten-year period for beans, four insurance options, Mexican model

| Year | Price (*pesos*/ metric ton) | Yield (tons/ hectare) | Revenue (*pesos*/ hectare) | Revenue deviations from mean (*pesos*/hectare) | | | |
|---|---|---|---|---|---|---|---|
| | | | | Unin-sured | Modified ANAGSA insurance | Revenue insurance | Combined insurance |
| 1 | 5,164 | 0.302 | 1,560 | 120.7 | −90.0 | −21.3 | 232.1 |
| 2 | 5,119 | 0.279 | 1,428 | −10.6 | −2214.0 | −152.6 | −363.6 |
| 3 | 5,104 | 0.319 | 1,628 | 189.4 | −1.4 | 47.3 | −163.4 |
| 4 | 5,049 | 0.296 | 1,495 | 55.7 | −155.1 | −86.3 | −297.1 |
| 5[a] | 5,014 | 0.206 | 1,033 | −405.9 | −50.9 | −142.0 | 213.0 |
| 6[a] | 5,159 | 0.183 | 944 | −494.7 | 38.3 | −142.0 | 391.0 |
| 7 | 5,444 | 0.289 | 1,573 | 134.5 | −76.3 | −7.5 | −218.3 |
| 8 | 5,528 | 0.394 | 2,178 | 739.2 | 528.5 | 597.2 | 386.4 |
| 9[a] | 5,223 | 0.176 | 919 | 519.6 | 67.7 | −142.0 | 445.2 |
| 10 | 4,698 | 0.347 | 1,630 | 191.4 | −19.4 | 49.4 | −161.4 |
| Mean | 5,150 | 0.279 | 1,439 | 0.0 | 0.0 | 0.0 | 0.0 |
| Standard deviation | 228.8 | 0.071 | | 385.0 | 204.3 | 224.4 | 319.8 |

[a]Year in which indemnities are paid.

where $Q_{tj}$ and $Q_j$ denote, respectively, actual and mean yields for the $j^{\text{th}}$ crop, and $w_j$ is the maximum amount of credit that can be borrowed from the agricultural bank for that crop. This indemnity is designed to repay a proportion of the credit borrowed (where the proportion is based on the ratio of actual to mean yield) and to assist the farm family directly by adding in an additional indemnity of 40 percent of the amount paid to the bank.

The second scheme considered is a revenue insurance scheme. Again, indemnities are paid if the yield is less than 80 percent of the mean yield, but the indemnity is calculated according to the formula

$$I_{tj} = R_j - R_{tj};$$

that is, the difference between mean revenue and actual revenue.

Finally, a combined insurance scheme is considered, which pays an indemnity amounting to the sum of the above. The proposed schemes are subsidized by the government, but farmers would pay a premium each year to obtain insurance protection. First, we evaluate the gross return to insurance, assuming that the administrative costs of the scheme are fully subsidized, and then explore the effects of reducing the subsidy.

Table 3.3 shows that maize is a moderately risky crop. The standard deviation of uninsured revenues is 213.7 *pesos*, which when divided by the mean revenue gives a coefficient of variation of 15 percent. This is much lower than for beans, which have a coefficient of variation of uninsured revenues of 26.8 percent (table 3.4). Below is a decomposition of the components of the revenue variances using equation 1:

| Crop | $V(R)$ | | $E(P)^2V(Q)$ | | $E(Q)^2V(P)$ | | $2E(P)E(Q)$ Cov$(P, Q)$ | | Residual |
|---|---|---|---|---|---|---|---|---|---|
| Maize | 45,686 | = | 50,266 | + | 8,460 | − | 11,774 | − | 1,266 |
| Beans | 148,254 | = | 133,710 | + | 4,074 | + | 6,110 | + | 4,360 |

In both cases, yield variability is the main source of revenue instability, suggesting that crop insurance may be useful. However, maize has a negative correlation (−0.256) between price and yield, which weakens the revenue-stabilizing role of crop insurance. Notice, too, that the lowest yield does not occur in the same year as the lowest revenue. On the other hand, beans have a small but positive correlation (0.086) between price and yield, which enhances the role of crop insurance.

These expectations are confirmed in tables 3.3 and 3.4. The modified ANAGSA scheme reduces the standard deviation of maize revenues by 8 percent, but it reduces the standard deviation of bean revenues by 47 percent. The revenue insurance scheme has a similar impact, but the combined insurance scheme is not nearly as effective.

On the basis of tables 3.3 and 3.4, it is tempting to exclude the combined insurance scheme from further consideration, but this ignores revenue covariance relations with the other crops (see equation 2). Table 3.5 shows the correlations between the insured revenue series for maize and beans and the revenue series for all other crops in the model. The three types of insurance have different correlations with other crops. For example, the combined insurance series for maize is negatively correlated with peanuts, while the modified ANAGSA and revenue insurance series are positively correlated with peanuts.

### *The Crop Insurance Experiments*

The model was allowed to choose between insuring or not insuring maize and beans and to choose among the three insurance policies or any linear combinations thereof. The experiments were repeated for two values of the risk-aversion parameter, $\phi$, and with the debt default risk set at 0.1 percent. Insurance is offered free of cost in these experiments in the sense that the average indemnity paid is exactly equal to the premium charged. The results are reported in table 3.6.

Bean production is reduced to the minimal level required to meet family consumption in the insured solutions, and insurance is not purchased. Maize insurance is attractive, though, and nearly all the maize crop is insured when policies are available. Maize insurance is even purchased on a voluntary basis when producers are assumed to be risk-

TABLE 3.5 Revenue correlations of maize and beans to other crops, four insurance options, Mexican model

| | Maize | | | | Beans | | | |
|---|---|---|---|---|---|---|---|---|
| Crop | Uninsured | Modified ANAGSA insurance | Revenue insurance | Combined insurance | Uninsured | Modified ANAGSA insurance | Revenue insurance | Combined insurance |
| Barley | 0.76 | 0.70 | 0.69 | 0.54 | −0.37 | −0.16 | −0.29 | 0.13 |
| Beans | −0.47 | −0.66 | 0.67 | −0.79 | 1.00 | 0.41 | 0.76 | −0.29 |
| Lima beans | −0.12 | −0.06 | 0.08 | 0.26 | −0.39 | −0.36 | −0.46 | −0.08 |
| Maize | 1.00 | 0.85 | 0.84 | 0.68 | −0.47 | −0.39 | −0.48 | −0.02 |
| Sorghum | −0.23 | −0.09 | −0.08 | 0.09 | −0.16 | −0.40 | −0.36 | −0.32 |
| Wheat | 0.66 | 0.64 | 0.64 | 0.54 | −0.33 | −0.40 | −0.41 | −0.14 |
| Peanuts | 0.32 | 0.15 | 0.13 | −0.07 | 0.30 | −0.22 | 0.05 | −0.46 |
| Sesame | −0.12 | −0.27 | −0.29 | −0.41 | 0.62 | 0.41 | 0.60 | −0.06 |

TABLE 3.6 Impact of crop insurance under alternative assumptions about risk, debt-default risk 0.1 percent, Mexican model

| | Risk-neutral ($\phi = 0$) | | Risk-averse ($\phi = 1$) | |
|---|---|---|---|---|
| Item | Without insurance | With insurance | Without insurance | With insurance |
| *Income and utility measures* | | | | |
| Expected utility (million *pesos*) | 114.29 | 124.47 | 97.40 | 106.10 |
| Average income (million *pesos*) | 114.29 | 124.47 | 114.29 | 124.27 |
| Standard deviation of income (million *pesos*) | 16.89 | 18.37 | 16.89 | 18.37 |
| Coefficient of variation (percent) | 14.78 | 14.76 | 14.78 | 14.76 |
| *Production ($10^3$ metric tons)*[a] | | | | |
| Beans | 6.54 | 2.10 | 6.54 | 2.10 |
| Maize | 60.27 | 74.54 | 60.27 | 74.54 |
| Peanuts | 9.00 | 9.00 | 9.00 | 9.00 |
| Sesame | 1.35 | 1.35 | 1.35 | 1.35 |
| *Inputs* | | | | |
| Employment ($10^3$ months) | 190.13 | 184.43 | 190.13 | 184.43 |
| Credit (million *pesos*) | 27.64 | 17.26 | 27.64 | 17.26 |
| Agrochemicals (million *pesos*) | 5.12 | 2.19 | 5.12 | 2.19 |
| Machinery ($10^3$ months) | 0.72 | 1.17 | 0.72 | 1.17 |
| Mules ($10^3$ months) | 164.46 | 168.64 | 164.46 | 168.64 |
| *Shadow prices (percent return)* | | | | |
| Credit requirement | 31.53 | 12.00 | 21.36 | 12.00 |
| Debt repayment | 162.74 | 0.0 | 77.98 | 0.0 |
| *Insured maize (percent area)*[b] | | | | |
| Revenue insurance | | 7.2 | | 0.0 |
| Combined insurance | | 92.8 | | 96.5 |

[a]Production of crops not listed (barley, lima beans, sorghum, wheat) is zero in model solutions.

[b]Beans remained uninsured in model solutions.

neutral. This unusual result stems of course from the binding debt default constraint.

Assuming $\phi = 1.0$, then the maize insurance options considered contribute toward meeting the SAM goals. Maize production increases by 14,270 metric tons (or 23.6 percent), expected utility increases by 8.7 million *pesos* (or 236 *pesos* per farm), and average income increases by 10.2 million *pesos* (or 277 *pesos* per farm). Total credit needs also decline sharply as bean production is curtailed (see footnote 9), and the debt default risk falls below 0.1 percent, so that the constraint is no longer binding. The decline in bean production is a minor disappointment, as is a 3 percent decline in total employment.

Another interesting result in table 3.6 lies in the choice of insurance policy. There is a definite preference for the combined insurance policy, even though we found this to be inferior for reducing the standard deviation of maize revenues in table 3.3. This result stems from the more negative correlations between peanuts, sesame, beans, and combined insured maize than between these crops and modified ANAGSA, or revenue insured maize (table 3.5).

The crop insurance options successfully reduce the likelihood of low incomes (figure 3.2). More generally, insurance shifts the efficient mean-income standard-deviation frontier upward, and increases the range of efficient plans that the farmer can consider (figure 3.3).

The potential gains from insurance are sensitive to the level of the maize price assumed. Since the SAM also entailed a major increase in the price of maize from the base-year (1976) price of 1,900 *pesos* per ton, additional model solutions were derived to show the effect of insurance on the supply of maize under different price assumptions. Figure 3.4 summarizes the results obtained with a risk-aversion parameter of 1.0.

The supply function corresponding to no insurance is quite elastic over the price range 1,750 to 2,100 *pesos* per ton but becomes perfectly inelastic at the latter price. At the base-year price of 1,900 *pesos* per ton, a total maize surplus of 33,370 tons is marketed. If the price is increased to 2,100 *pesos* per ton, the surplus jumps to 47,640 tons.

When insurance is introduced, the surplus is also 47,640 tons at the base-year price, and the supply function is totally inelastic at that point. This means that price increases above the base-year price would not increase the supply of maize when crop insurance is available. It is also clear that a price increase of only 200 *pesos* per ton without any insurance schemes provides the same surplus as the introduction of crop insurance options. A simple price increase might therefore be the easiest way to increase maize production. It would also serve to increase the welfare and incomes of farmers. In the absence of any insurance, a 200-*peso*-per-ton increase in the base-year price of maize would increase the expected utility and average income by 530 and 682 *pesos* per farm. These amounts are quite comparable to the gains obtained with ideal insurance at the base-year price.

### *The Net Benefits from Insurance*

So far we have considered only the gross benefits of insurance to farmers, because the models assume that any premium paid is exactly equal to the average indemnity. We now turn to the question of whether insurance would still be desirable if farmers had to pay the administrative costs. We shall also explore the effects of alternative levels of government support.

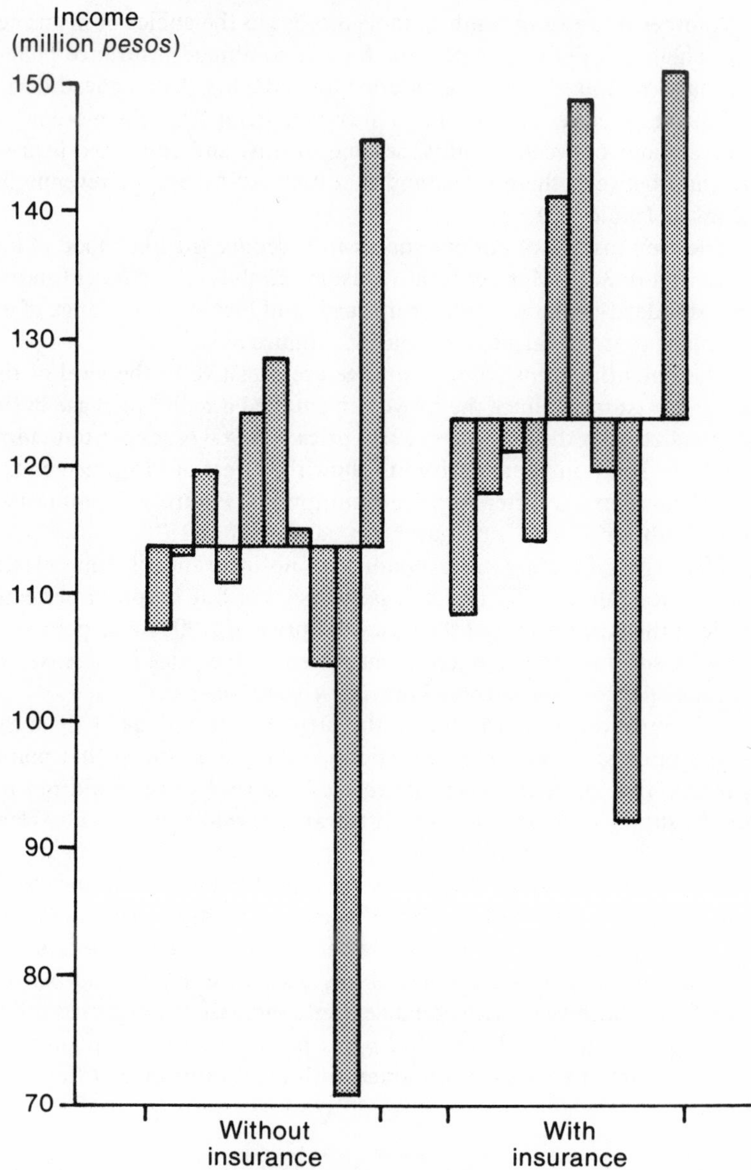


FIGURE 3.2 Fluctuations in income, with and without insurance, Mexican model
*Note:* Default risk 0.1 percent, $\phi = 1.0$.

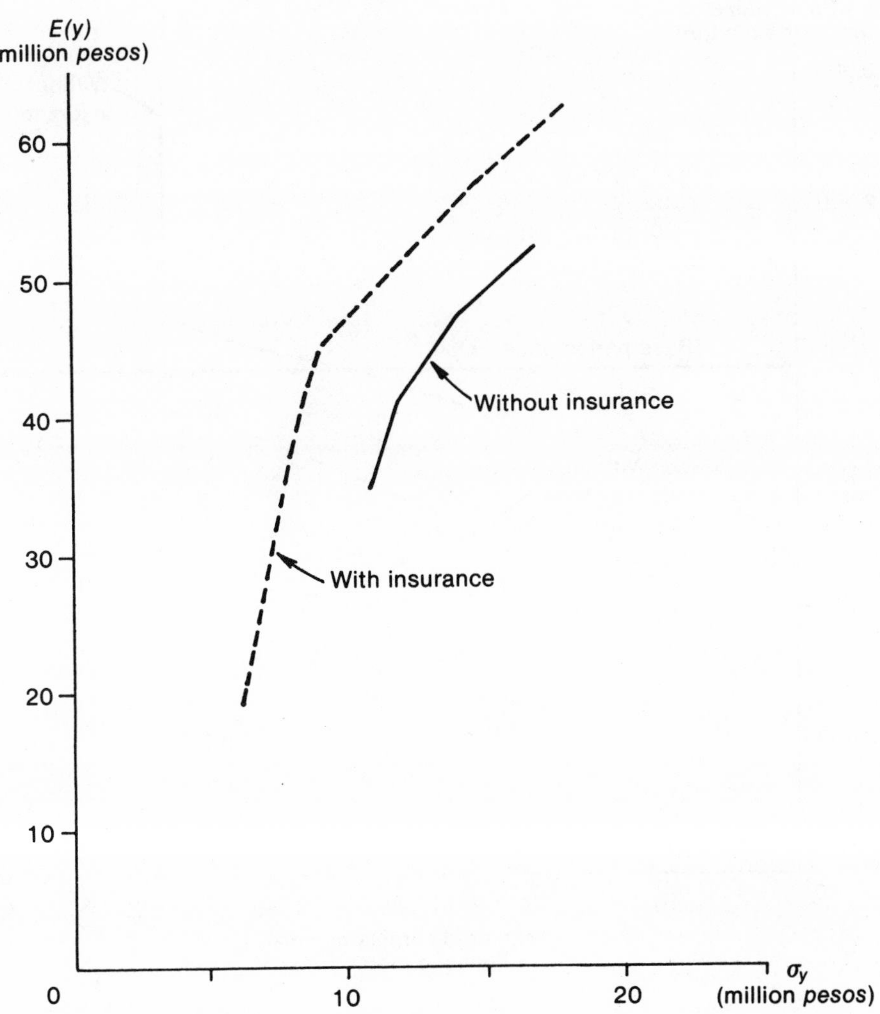


FIGURE 3.3 Efficient mean-income standard-deviation frontiers, with and without insurance, Mexican model
*Note:* Default risk 0.1 percent, $\phi = 1.0$.

For $\phi = 1$, the model predicts a total gain in expected utility to farmers of 8.7 million *pesos*, given the insurance options proposed for SAM (table 3.6). Since insurance is voluntarily purchased for 95,965 hectares of maize, or 96.5 percent of the maize area grown, the gain in expected utility per hectare is about 91 *pesos*. This is a direct measure of the maximum premium that farmers should be willing to pay in order to purchase that amount of insurance without being any worse off than not hav-

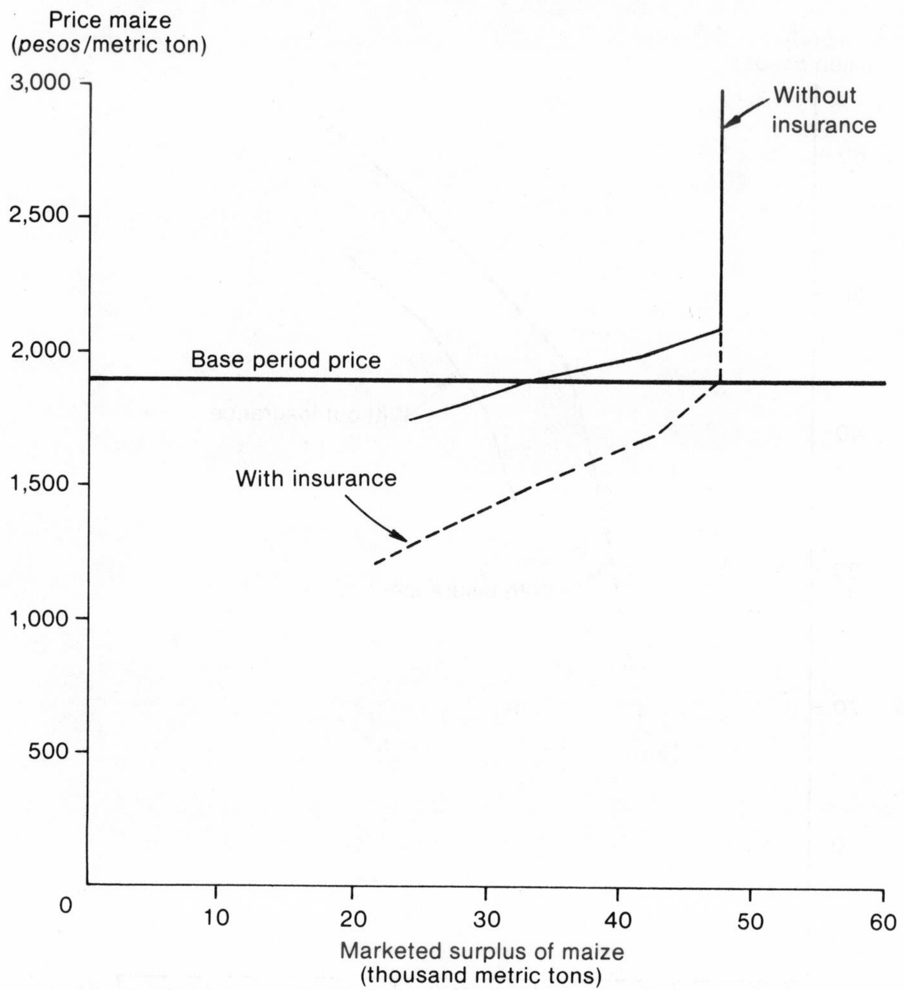


FIGURE 3.4 Supply functions for maize, with and without insurance, Mexican model
*Note:* Default risk 0.1 percent, $\phi = 1.0$.

ing insurance. The gain is clearly inadequate to cover the costs of insurance. Although the full costs of the proposed schemes are not known, they would probably be about 300 to 400 *pesos* per hectare in base-year (1976) prices. In the absence of a substantial subsidy, the amount of insurance purchased would obviously have to be less than the amount in the model solution.

Figure 3.5 shows the model's predictions of what happens with alternative levels of premiums (net of the average indemnity). The percentage

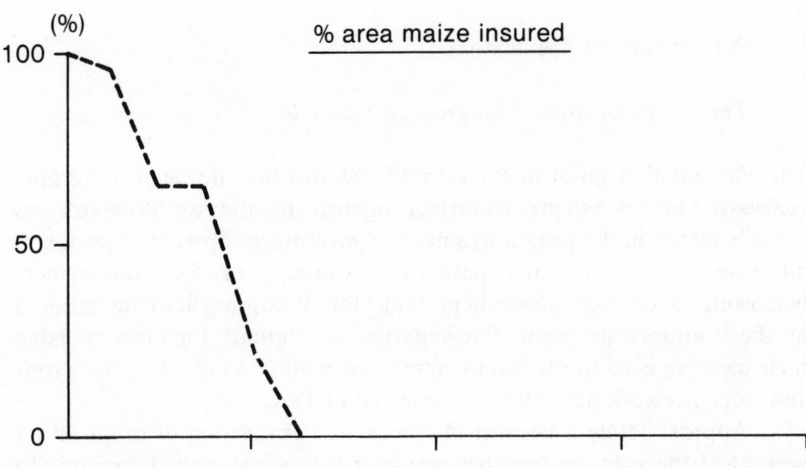


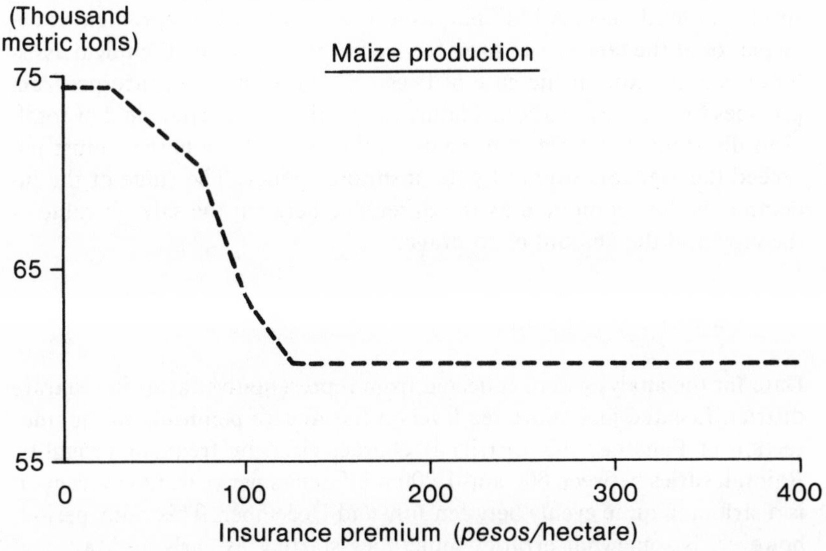


FIGURE 3.5 Effect of increases in the insurance premium on maize production, Mexican model
*Note:* Default risk 0.1 percent, $\phi = 1.0$.

of maize area insured declines rapidly as the net premium is increased from zero, and no insurance is purchased at all when the premium reaches 125 *pesos* per hectare. It seems that the proposed insurance schemes are not at all viable at base-year prices without a substantial subsidy by the Mexican government.

## A Panamanian Application

### *The Credit Insurance Program in Panama*

The Panamanian government created the Instituto de Seguro Agropecuario (ISA) in 1975 to protect farmers against climatic risk. Price risk was not considered in the program, since the government operates a price stabilization mechanism. Participation is now compulsory for those farmers borrowing funds from government banks for all farming activities covered by the insurance program. Participation is voluntary for farmers using their own funds or funds from commercial banks. As of 1981, five crops and three livestock activities were covered by ISA.

Approximately 5 percent of the cost of production of crops and 3 percent of the value of livestock are charged as insurance premium. In return, farmers are covered by an amount roughly equal to 80 percent of the actual costs of production. Each farmer gets his crop or animals inspected at least once. Additional inspections occur when a problem is detected, or at the farmer's request for technical assistance. Technical assistance is automatic in the case of livestock, since the insurance program provides for free vaccination. Claims can be filed for partial-yield or total-yield disasters. For a claim to be paid, the value of the harvest must not exceed the amount covered by the insurance policy. The value of the indemnity is then computed as the difference between the salvage value of the crop and the amount of coverage.

### *Guarare District Data*

Data for the analysis were collected from representative farms in Guarare district. Located just above sea level on the Azuero peninsula in the midsection of Panama, this district is characterized by frequent droughts. Rainfall varies between 800 and 1,200 millimeters per year. On average, it is distributed quite evenly between July and December. This rainy period, however, is somewhat erratic, sometimes starting as early as May, and sometimes ending as late as January. The result is a farming system much riskier than in most areas of Panama, and thus one that should benefit most from the crop insurance program.

The vast majority of Guarare's farms are between 20 and 50 hectares, with livestock activities occupying nearly half of the available land. Corn and sorghum are the main rain-fed crops, and tomatoes, green peppers, plantains, and cassava are the main crops grown under irrigation. Tobacco is also grown, but under allotments by contractual arrangement with the national tobacco company. Farmers who grow tobacco do not generally grow other crops. Livestock are well suited to the region because of the poor land and are raised for both milk and beef. Year-old bull calves are sold to intermediaries for further fattening. Heifers are kept for milk production. Dairy companies send their trucks along fixed routes on a daily basis.

The rain-fed crops, corn and sorghum, are almost totally mechanized. Irrigated horticulture, on the other hand, is labor- and capital-intensive, accounting for most of the labor use in Guarare. Tomatoes are the main irrigated crop, grown by contractual arrangement with a private concern, which buys a predetermined amount at a predetermined price. Unlike tobacco farmers, tomato farmers also engage in other farming activities.

### *The Farm Model*

The model is constructed for a representative 40-hectare farm, and it includes the district's principal production activities—corn, sorghum, tomatoes, green peppers, plantains, cassava, and livestock. Tobacco is not included, since it is grown on specialized farms. Alternative production activities are identified for most crops, reflecting different planting dates, and in the case of corn, different levels of labor, fertilizer, and pesticide use. However, not all the land is suitable for all activities, and three land types are differentiated: 20 hectares are suitable for rain-fed maize and sorghum only; 2 hectares are irrigated and can grow tomatoes, peppers, plantains, and cassava; and 18 hectares are suited only for pasture and livestock. Labor requirements are specified on a bimonthly basis and can be met by the farm family at zero cost or by hiring labor at a fixed wage.

Family food constraints are imposed for corn, cassava, milk, and beef. Beef must be homegrown, but the requirements for corn, cassava, and milk can be met from either home production or through local purchases.

Credit is required in the model to cover the costs of seeds, fertilizers, pesticides, machinery hire, and wage labor. Since very few farmers own machines, all machinery services are assumed to be hired. Farmers are assumed to have $500 of their own funds for on-farm investment. Otherwise, their credit needs must be met by borrowing from commercial or government banks at an interest charge of 14 percent. In the case of tomatoes, sorghum, and input-intensive maize, the model can choose between insured or uninsured loans. However, only uninsured loans are offered for other production activities.

The debt repayment constraint in the model is identical to that described in equation 9. The minimum income requirement, which includes the value of home-consumed foods, is set at $1,800 in 1981 prices. We also assume that farmers maximize mean-income standard-deviation utility, where income is defined to include the value of all homegrown foods but is net of any subsistence foods purchased from local sources.

Since prices are fixed by the government each year, the risk coefficients are calculated to reflect yield risks at 1981 prices. Revenue data per hectare for the years 1977 to 1981 were obtained from six farmers. These were adjusted to 1981 prices and averaged to obtain the series in table 3.7. Time-series data could not be obtained for plantains, cassava, or livestock. Since these activities are known to have very low yield risks, we simply assumed that they had zero risk. Data could not be obtained on uninsured tomatoes, because virtually none are grown, so we did not include this activity in the model.

A drought in 1977 was responsible for a complete yield failure for maize, and only farmers with insurance coverage received any return that year. Similarly, a late rainfall in 1979 was responsible for a sorghum failure, and only insured sorghum had a nonzero return.

The coefficients of variation of the uninsured crops are very large. In the Mexican study, for example, the coefficient of variation of maize revenues was only 15 percent (table 3.3). This is less than one-third of the comparable coefficient in Guarare. Fortunately, the returns from the different crops are not highly correlated, and there is considerable scope to diversify across activities to reduce the coefficient of variation of total farm income. Indeed, as table 3.8 shows, there are very healthy negative correlations between maize and sorghum and between maize and tomatoes. It is also apparent that the insured options for maize and sorghum have quite different patterns of association between themselves and with other crops than do their uninsured counterparts.

TABLE 3.7 Revenue for maize, sorghum, tomatoes, and peppers, Panamanian model, 1977–81 (dollars/hectare)

| Year | Maize | | Insured modern maize | Sorghum | Insured sorghum | Insured tomatoes | Peppers |
|---|---|---|---|---|---|---|---|
| | Traditional | Modern | | | | | |
| 1977 | 0 | 0 | 489 | 581 | 581 | 3,325 | 1,760 |
| 1978 | 378 | 540 | 540 | 465 | 465 | 3,500 | 3,000 |
| 1979 | 427 | 610 | 610 | 0 | 464 | 3,150 | 2,100 |
| 1980 | 469 | 671 | 671 | 768 | 768 | 3,300 | 1,800 |
| 1981 | 436 | 623 | 623 | 505 | 505 | 3,000 | 5,500 |
| Average | 342 | 489 | 587 | 464 | 557 | 3,255 | 2,832 |
| Standard deviation | 194 | 277 | 72 | 284 | 127 | 189 | 1,573 |
| Coefficient of variation (percent) | 56.7 | 56.7 | 12.3 | 61.3 | 22.9 | 5.8 | 55.5 |

*Note*: The insured crop returns are gross of the annual premiums.

TABLE 3.8 Correlation coefficients between revenues for maize, sorghum, tomatoes, and peppers, Panamanian model

| Crop | Maize | Insured maize | Sorghum | Insured sorghum | Insured tomatoes | Peppers |
|---|---|---|---|---|---|---|
| Maize | 1.00 | | | | | |
| Insured maize | 0.86 | 1.00 | | | | |
| Sorghum | −0.17 | 0.06 | 1.00 | | | |
| Insured sorghum | 0.03 | 0.43 | 0.75 | 1.00 | | |
| Insured tomatoes | −0.29 | −0.48 | 0.28 | 0.12 | 1.00 | |
| Peppers | 0.35 | 0.20 | 0.06 | −0.41 | −0.57 | 1.00 |

### *Analysis of the Economics of Insurance*

Basic model results (table 3.9) are obtained by excluding all the insured options for maize and sorghum from the model. As in the Mexican study, we set the debt default risk at 0.1 percent and solved for different values of the risk-aversion parameter, $\phi$.

Under the risk-neutral assumption ($\phi = 0$), the model calls for generous amounts of the high standard-deviation crops to be produced: maize, sorghum, and tomatoes. However, because of the negative correlations between the revenues of these crops (table 3.8), and because of the high average returns from tomatoes, the coefficient of variation of income is only 20 percent. This is considerably less than the coefficients of variation of revenues reported for the individual crops in table 3.7. It is even comparable to the income risk in Mexico (table 3.2). The maize, sorghum, and tomatoes produced declines rapidly as the risk parameter increases, while cassava production increases. These changes lead to a dramatic decline in the standard deviation of income but only at the expense of some sacrifice in average income.

The debt default constraint is binding for $\phi$ values of 0.5 and less. In these cases, farmers are forced by the bank to act in a risk-averse way in order to obtain as much credit as they can profitably use. The amount of uninsured credit borrowed declines significantly between risk-neutral ($\phi = 0$) and reasonable risk-averse ($\phi = 1$) behavior, largely as a reflection of the decline in maize and sorghum production. Insured credit is borrowed exclusively for tomatoes in these model solutions, since the insurance options for maize and sorghum have been deleted.

In all the solutions in table 3.9, maize is produced exclusively with traditional techniques (low fertilizer and low pesticide), rather than with modern (or more input-intensive) techniques. Since one of the objectives of the ISA scheme is to encourage the use of modern technologies, we shall be interested to see if there is a switch in the choice of technique when the insurance options are introduced.

TABLE 3.9 Results under alternative assumptions about risk behavior, debt-default risk 0.1 percent, Panamanian model

| Item | Value of $\phi$ | | | | |
|---|---|---|---|---|---|
| | 0.0 | 0.5 | 1.0 | 1.5 | 2.0 |
| *Income and utility measures* | | | | | |
| Expected utility (dollars) | 4,719.0 | 4,249.0 | 4,057.0 | 4,012.0 | 4,010.0 |
| Average income (dollars) | 4,719.0 | 4,719.0 | 4,234.0 | 4,017.0 | 4,015.0 |
| Standard deviation of income (dollars) | 942.0 | 942.0 | 178.0 | 3.0 | 2.0 |
| Coefficient of variation (percent) | 20.0 | 20.0 | 4.2 | 0.1 | 0.1 |
| *Sales* | | | | | |
| Maize (100 kilograms) | 186.1 | 186.1 | 10.0 | 0.9 | 0.4 |
| Sorghum (100 kilograms) | 35.9 | 35.9 | 0.0 | 0.2 | 0.6 |
| Tomatoes (100 kilograms) | 587.0 | 587.0 | 565.4 | 34.9 | 32.8 |
| Peppers (100 kilograms) | 0.0 | 0.0 | 31.3 | 0.0 | 0.0 |
| Cassava (100 kilograms) | 90.3 | 90.3 | 83.6 | 241.4 | 242.0 |
| Milk (litres) | 25,520.0 | 25,520.0 | 25,520.0 | 25,520.0 | 25,520.0 |
| Beef (kilograms) | 8,700.0 | 8,700.0 | 8,700.0 | 8,700.0 | 8,700.0 |
| *Inputs* | | | | | |
| Employment (days) | 525 | 525 | 452 | 328 | 328 |
| Uninsured credit (dollars) | 4,569 | 4,569 | 3,344 | 3,239 | 3,239 |
| Insured credit (dollars) | 2,163 | 2,163 | 2,083 | 129 | 121 |
| *Technology choice (percent area)* | | | | | |
| Traditional maize | 100.0 | 100.0 | 100.0 | 100.0 | 100.0 |
| Modern maize | 0.0 | 0.0 | 0.0 | 0.0 | 0.0 |
| *Shadow prices (percent return)* | | | | | |
| Credit requirement | 17.38 | 14.57 | 14.0 | 14.0 | 14.0 |
| Debt repayment | 24.12 | 4.10 | 0.0 | 0.0 | 0.0 |

Table 3.10 summarizes the impact of insurance for maize and sorghum. As for Mexico, we only report the results for $\phi$ values of 0 and 1 corresponding to risk-neutral and reasonable risk-averse behavior. These experiments also assume that the administrative costs of insurance are fully subsidized. That is, the average indemnity is assumed to exactly equal the premium paid.

With $\phi = 1$, crop insurance leads to a gain in expected utility of \$256, or \$34.8 per hectare of insured maize. The actual premium charged by ISA is about \$17 per hectare, and this is gross of indemnities paid. Insurance for maize is clearly a viable proposition for Guarare farmers. In fact, additional results confirm that the maize crop would be fully insured on a voluntary basis for premium levels net of indemnities as high as \$50 per hectare. However, the area of maize grown declines rapidly for net premium rates above \$35 per hectare.

TABLE 3.10 Impact of crop insurance under alternative assumptions about risk behavior, debt-default risk 0.1 percent, Panamanian model

| Item | Risk-neutral ($\phi = 0$) | | Risk-averse ($\phi = 1$) | |
|---|---|---|---|---|
| | Without insurance | With insurance | Without insurance | With insurance |
| *Income and utility measures* | | | | |
| Expected utility (dollars) | 4,719.0 | 5,235.0 | 4,057.0 | 4,313.0 |
| Average income (dollars) | 4,719.0 | 5,235.0 | 4,234.0 | 4,685.0 |
| Standard deviation of income (dollars) | 942.0 | 1,108.0 | 178.0 | 373.0 |
| Coefficient of variation (percent) | 20.0 | 21.2 | 4.2 | 8.0 |
| *Sales* | | | | |
| Maize (100 kilograms) | 186.1 | 702.0 | 10.0 | 361.7 |
| Sorghum (100 kilgrams) | 35.9 | 136.1 | 0.0 | 3.1 |
| Tomatoes (100 kilograms) | 587.0 | 337.1 | 565.4 | 584.7 |
| Peppers (100 kilograms) | 0.0 | 0.0 | 31.3 | 5.2 |
| Cassava (100 kilograms) | 90.3 | 158.7 | 83.6 | 88.9 |
| Milk (litres) | 25,520.0 | 25,520.0 | 25,520.0 | 25,520.0 |
| Beef (kilograms) | 8,700.0 | 8,700.0 | 8,700.0 | 8,700.0 |
| *Inputs* | | | | |
| Employment (days) | 525 | 607 | 452 | 548 |
| Uninsured credit (dollars) | 4,569 | 3,165 | 3,344 | 3,178 |
| Insured credit (dollars) | 2,163 | 7,403 | 2,083 | 4,838 |
| *Technology choice (percent area)* | | | | |
| Traditional maize | 100.0 | 0.0 | 100.0 | 0.0 |
| Modern maize | 0.0 | 100.0 | 0.0 | 100.0 |
| *Shadow prices (percent returns)* | | | | |
| Credit requirement | 17.4 | 17.7 | 14.0 | 14.0 |
| Debt repayment | 24.1 | 26.2 | 0.0 | 0.0 |
| *Insurance (percent area)* | | | | |
| Maize | 0.0 | 100.0 | 0.0 | 100.0 |
| Sorghum | 0.0 | 100.0 | 0.0 | 0.0 |

Maize insurance leads to a very significant increase in maize production when $\phi = 1$, and this is accompanied by a complete switch to the more intensive production techniques. This leads to a 21-percent increase in farm employment and a very substantial increase in the amount of credit borrowed, particularly insured loans.

Insurance also leads to a significant reduction in the standard deviation of income for given levels of average income, as shown by the upward rotation of the efficient frontier in figure 3.6. As in Mexico, the range of efficient plans that the farmer can consider is also increased by insurance.

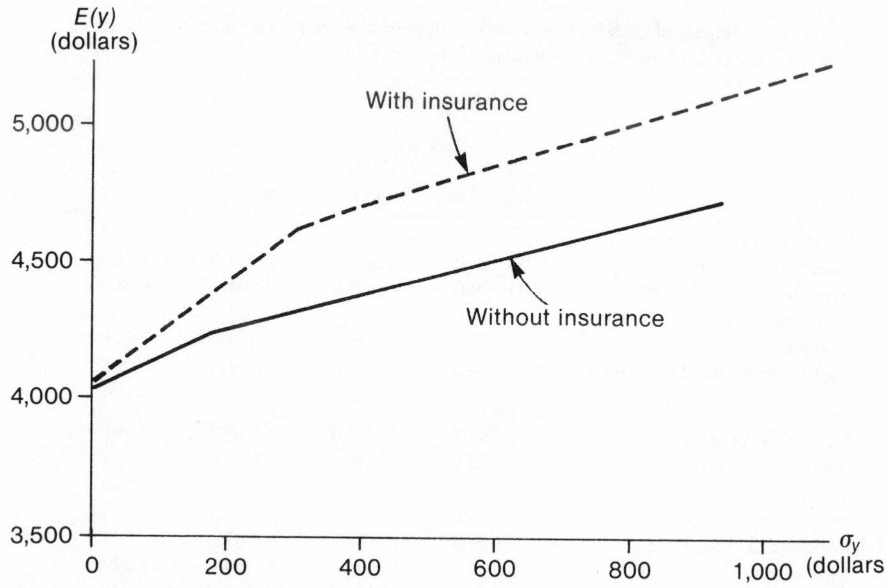


FIGURE 3.6 Efficient mean-income standard-deviation frontiers, with and without insurance, Panamanian model
*Note:* Default risk 0.1 percent, $\phi = 1.0$.

## Conclusions

In this chapter we have used normative planning models to evaluate crop insurance schemes at the farm level. These models assume that farmers make rational economic decisions and, in particular, that they adhere to the behavioral postulates of expected utility theory.

Some may object to this normative approach on the grounds that peasant farmers need to take account of complex socioeconomic considerations not included in the model. Our defense is quite simple. A good insurance scheme should pass the test of rational economic behavior as well as be acceptable to farmers. If an insurance scheme fails to pass the rationality test, then the scheme's proponents should be required to reveal those aspects of farmers' behavior (which might be called irrational) that justify implementation of their scheme.

Two particularly attractive features of our farm modeling approach are its ability to evaluate crop insurance schemes within the context of the whole farm plan and its ability to take formal account of covariances between activity returns in determining income variability. Both features turned out to be surprisingly important in our applications. They often led to very different results from those obtained by evaluating individual crop insurance schemes independently of a farmer's other decisions and independently of his fortunes with respect to other crops.

The Mexican application shows that crop insurance schemes for maize are attractive in the rain-fed areas only if they are heavily subsidized—about two-thirds of the cost of operating the insurance scheme. Insurance for beans is even less attractive, despite the fact that this crop has a higher coefficient of variation of returns than maize.

Subsidized maize insurance could lead to a significant increase in maize production and to a definite improvement in farmers' income and expected utility. Since these outcomes are consistent with the goals of the national food plan (SAM), there is some argument for proceeding with a subsidy. Nevertheless, as is argued in chapter 7, such a subsidy should be carefully evaluated within the context of the national economy. Our results also show that a maize price increase of about 200 *pesos* per ton from the 1976 base price might be just as effective as crop insurance in achieving the SAM goals, but presumably at a considerably lower cost.

These results for Mexico were obtained under the assumption that farmers continue to use traditional techniques for maize production. Another element of the SAM policies was the propagation of more intensive maize technologies. Experimental data show that use of improved seed and more intensive use of agrochemicals could more than double maize yields under rain-fed conditions. If such a technology was widely implemented, the returns to insurance might be much larger than suggested here (see the analysis in Sistema Alimentario Mexicano/IFPRI 1982).

The results from Guarare district in Panama were more encouraging for insurance. We found a very high return to farmers from ISA's maize insurance, sufficiently high in fact that the scheme should be viable without any subsidies. Insurance for sorghum, however, proved to be much less remunerative. It should be remembered that Guarare district is one of the riskiest agroclimatic zones in Panama, and our findings cannot be generalized to Panama as a whole. In fact, in a similar study of insurance in Bugaba district, which is perhaps more representative of Panamanian agriculture, we found that ISA's crop insurance schemes would not be attractive to farmers.

Four caveats are in order. First, the analysis assumes that farmers are equally and reasonably risk-averse. In fact, farmers differ quite widely in their risk attributes (see Binswanger 1980 and Dillon and Scandizzo 1978), which could make an enormous difference in their desire for crop insurance. At best, our results pertain to the representative farmer.

Second, we have had to rely on aggregate data in measuring individual crop variability. In the Mexican case, we used published district-level data, while in Panama we used pooled data obtained from six farmers. The use of aggregate data tends to understate the degree of risk confronted by individual farmers. In fact, a downward bias will always exist so long as the returns from individual crops are not perfectly and positively correlated across farms. Again, while our results may make some sense for the representative farm, the economics of insurance for individual farms could be quite different than reported here.

Third, the time series used were short; ten years for Mexico and only five years for Panama. The results are therefore likely to be sensitive to the outcomes for extreme years (or the lack of extreme years). They may not adequately reflect the true probability distributions of outcomes. This is a data problem rather than a methodology problem, but it is one that is likely to confound any analysis of agricultural insurance, particularly when conducted in the planning stage.

Fourth, our models do not incorporate some of the traditional risk-sharing methods discussed in chapter 2. Seasonal migration, for example, may be a useful way to help stabilize incomes in the two study areas. Omission of these considerations may have led us to overvalue the returns to publicly sponsored crop insurance programs.

4

# Risk Aversion, Collateral Requirements, and the Markets for Credit and Insurance in Rural Areas

Hans P. Binswanger

It has long been recognized that rural credit markets are incomplete. This is because many classes of borrowers have little or no access to credit from formal institutions, and they often borrow small amounts informally at what appear to be excessive interest rates.

It has now also become clear that the market for comprehensive crop yield insurance has, in nearly all cases, failed. While some specific yield insurance (hail, flooding) is provided by private companies in developed countries on a profit-making basis, general yield insurance comes into existence or survives only because of government subsidies.

The failure of crop yield insurance markets does not arise from lack of demand for the stabilization of consumption and income. Recent experimental studies indicate that farmers in developing countries are poor and typically risk-averse.[1] Furthermore, capital markets are also poorly developed, which in principle should increase the demand for insurance on the part of risk-averse farmers. Finally, yield risks are primarily weather related and probability information on weather is not exceptionally difficult to find.

This chapter attempts a systematic exploration of the causes of the serious difficulties of both rural credit and yield insurance markets. I trace these difficulties to an identical set of information, incentive, and management problems that arise in spatially dispersed agricultural production systems.

It is a common observation that people do not freely provide their transaction partners with information. Indeed, people normally attempt to take advantage of lenders' and insurers' information difficulties unless the contracts and information-gathering procedures are structured to preclude such opportunistic behavior. In the insurance literature, these problems are known as moral hazard and adverse selection. They also apply to

1. See in particular Binswanger (1980), Sillers (1980), Walker (1980), Grisley (1980), and Binswanger and Sillers (1983).

a much wider array of economic transactions and will simply be referred to as incentive problems in this chapter.

## The Assumptions

Two sets of assumptions, behavioral and technological, form the basis of the analysis.[2]

### *Behavioral Assumptions*

All individuals are self-interested in their own utility (B-1), they value consumption (B-2), and dislike effort (B-3). They are also risk-averse whenever gains and losses exceed trivial amounts (B-4), though the extent of risk aversion may vary among individuals.

### *Technological Assumptions*

Information is costly to acquire (T-1). Production depends on at least five primary factors (T-2)—land, labor, live capital (livestock and trees), machines, and human capital (management and other skills). Of these, land is immobile (T-3), and this predetermines the peculiar geographic distribution of agricultural production.

Transport and travel costs are high (T-4), though they decline with development. The spatial transmission of information is also costly and time consuming (T-5), particularly in the absence of telephone networks.

There are five sources of risk (T-6). Yield risk, price risk (prices are usually unknown at the time production inputs are committed), uncertainties about the timing of input because of weather, breakdown risk for machines (and animals), and the risk of illness and accident for farmers.

Yield risk and timing uncertainties are weather-induced, and this causes them to be covariate (T-7). If farms in a region grow similar crops, then price risks will be covariate as well. Breakdown risk and the risk of accident and illness are much less covariate except during disastrous events like floods, epidemics, and war.

All of these assumptions could individually apply to nonagricultural pursuits, but their combination is unique to agriculture. The following assumptions are especially important: T-2, the five primary factors; T-3, immobile land, which leads to a spatial pattern of production unique to agri-

2. These assumptions are taken from a larger model, currently in preparation, which is concerned with production relations in agriculture.

culture; T-6, yield and timing risks, which are especially severe for agriculture, and breakdown and life-cycle risks, which are universal; T-7, risk covariance, in small regions especially—for most nonagricultural activities, any risk covariance arises largely from the price or final demand side, not from technological relations.

In exploring the consequences of these assumptions for credit and insurance markets, an important point must be kept in mind. The problems they create for credit and insurance markets are real, but they are often overcome by investments in information, special contracts, or adaptive institutional features. Analyzing them in detail has four purposes. First, it helps explain institutional adaptations to those problems we observe in the real world. Second, for agencies or firms in charge of providing credit or insurance in rural areas it provides a checklist of problems that they should expect and must solve if they are to operate successfully. Third, it directs us to explore technological or institutional solutions that might enable previously infeasible markets or institutions to operate. Fourth, if analysis shows that certain incentive problems cannot be solved at reasonable cost, it directs us to problem solutions beyond the confines of credit or insurance markets.

## General Consequences

Eight general consequences follow from the assumptions. They are discussed in detail below.

### *Asymmetric Information (G-1)*

Information has value and is costly to acquire (T-1). Since individuals are selfish (B-1), they will not part with information they possess unless it is to their advantage. For example, high-quality workers will want employers to have accurate information about workers' quality, while inferior workers would prefer that their employers not know. The same applies to borrowers and the insured. (Problems of asymmetric information arise to some extent in virtually all economic transactions. Sellers of seeds and animals know more about their quality than do buyers, and they may choose to misrepresent this quality.)

### *Incentive Problems (G-2)*

Whenever information is costly (T-1) and asymmetrically distributed (G-1), incentive problems arise in economic transactions.

*Moral hazard.* Daily-paid laborers have no incentive to work hard unless supervised closely, either through direct observation of their effort or inspection of their output. Incentives to work hard may be improved through share contracts, such as piece rates for specific tasks, or crop-sharing tenancy contracts.[3] However, since workers receive only a share of the full marginal product of their effort, they will still not work as hard as if they were owner/farmers, unless they are also supervised or monitored or are penalized in future contracts. Farmers whose crops are insured against all risks relative to a normal level of output also will usually not use as much care, precaution, or inputs as if their crops were uninsured. It is in this context that incentive problems were first called moral hazard problems. Unless the insurance company can stipulate input and care levels and observe or monitor them at low cost, insurance contracts may lead to inefficient resource use. Many contracts anticipate this and include coinsurance clauses; that is, they insure only a fraction of the shortfall in production or of the crop damage. With such clauses, the insured again has a partial incentive to use proper care and input levels, a situation very similar to share contracts or piece-rate payments.

*Adverse selection.* When it is hard for one partner in a transaction to distinguish among potential partners of differing quality, screening problems arise. Insurers call these adverse-selection problems. Among a group of potential insurance clients, those with a high exposure to risk will find insurance most attractive. The insurance company will attempt to distinguish high-risk from low-risk individuals and charge higher premiums to the high-risk ones. If it cannot easily distinguish between them, it will use more easily observed variables such as age, sex, race, caste, and so on, which are perceived to be correlated with risk. If it cannot distinguish among individuals at all, insurers will set the premiums so high that only high-risk individuals find the insurance attractive and apply. The insurance market then fails to exist for low-risk individuals. The presence of high-risk individuals who cannot be identified imposes a cost on low-risk individuals and forces the insurance company to use the terms of the contract to screen individuals into homogenous groups.

*Screening effects.* Similar situations have been hypothesized in other markets. Screening literature contains examples of how employers (Weiss 1980), landlords (Newbery and Stiglitz 1979), and creditors (Stiglitz and Weiss 1981) structure employment, tenancy, and credit contracts so to lead employees (tenants, debtors) to reveal crucial information through their choice of contracts. The most important finding of the screening liter-

3. For a review of the literature on contractual arrangements in agriculture, see Binswanger and Rosenzweig (1984).

ature is the same as for insurance: low-quality applicants impose a cost on high-quality applicants and may lead to the disappearance of the market.

### *Imperfect Enforcement of Property Rights (G-3)*

Where acquisition of information is costly (T-3) and asymmetrically distributed (G-1), property rights cannot be perfectly enforced. There is some positive incentive for theft when it is easy to conceal the identity of the thief; that is, when costs of ascertaining who did it are very high. Many legal and cultural institutions are adaptations to this problem; that is, they reduce costs of information or increase penalties for theft. Furthermore, other things being equal, the cost of information is lower and the penalties in terms of future opportunities higher in small, immobile communities than in large, mobile ones.

### *Desirability of Insurance Contracts and Insurance Substitutes (G-4)*

Given risk (T-6) and risk-averse behavior (B-4), most individuals would be willing to pay some positive amount to reduce their exposure to risk. Where insurance is unavailable, they would be willing, at cost to themselves, to alter their behavior to reduce their exposure to risk. Such behavior includes holding reserves, diversifying prospects, lowering input levels, investing in creditworthiness, and relying on family ties. (Chapter 2 discusses this phenomenon extensively.)

### *Collateral Requirement (G-5)*

A collateral requirement affects borrowers' and lenders' utility in complex ways. First, when borrowers intend to pay back their loans, default can only be a consequence of bad luck. Equation 1 shows that for a given interest rate, $i$, and loan size, $L$, raising the collateral value from zero to some positive amount raises the expected return, $E$, to the lender.

$$E(L) = i(1 - \pi)L + [C - L(1 + i)]\pi. \tag{1}$$

In this equation, $\pi$ denotes the probability of failure of the investment, and $C$ is the value of the collateral to the lender. With zero collateral ($C = 0$), the expected return is equal to the interest earnings, $iL$, multiplied by the probability of repayment $(1 - \pi)$, minus the value of the loan plus interest times the probability of default (assuming that loans are either fully repaid or fully defaulted on).[4] As collateral is added, the second term increases progressively, with only the difference between the collateral and the loan amount plus interest being lost. Note that by raising the collateral value to levels larger than the loan size plus interest, the expected return can be made larger than the rate of interest, a technique that can be used to circumvent the impact of interest rate ceilings.

Thus, from the point of view of expected return, interest and collateral are substitutes. It is feasible to achieve a given expected return on a loan by various combinations of interest rates and collateral values. If lenders are risk-neutral and borrowers are known not to default intentionally, and if both lenders and borrowers have the same information about the probability distribution of the outcomes of the investment financed by the loan, lenders will be indifferent between the two methods of achieving the expected return. If the expected return is sufficiently high, they will make the loan despite the possibility of losing their entire capital in the event of (unintended) default.

Collateral between zero and the amount of the loan shifts a portion of the potential capital loss from lenders to borrowers. If the borrowers are risk-neutral, they do not care whether collateral is or is not required: the expected value of the capital loss in the bad-luck case is offset by the lower expected interest costs in the good-luck case.

Now consider risk-averse borrowers. The fact that the expected value of the capital loss is just equal to the expected value of the interest rate reduction in the good-outcome case is not sufficient to make them indifferent to the imposition of collateral. The large potential capital loss implies a high utility loss. Risk-averse borrowers would therefore rather accept a high-interest contract that allows them to default (involuntarily) in bad-luck cases at no additional cost. With risk-neutral lenders, there should not therefore be a collateral requirement for honest borrowers. Conversely, risk-averse lenders will insist on some collateral, even if they know the borrowers intend to repay. We thus see that collateral is a risk-sharing device,[5] and that the way in which agents view collateral requirements depends on their attitudes toward risk.

The most serious problem facing lenders, whether risk-neutral or risk-averse, is that normally they cannot know borrowers' intentions about

4. A more realistic repayment function is used by Virmani (1981), where partial repayment is made when the borrower's investment yields less than the principal plus interest. Full default would occur only when the project outcome is so bad that partial repayment becomes infeasible. However, a collateral requirement increases the lender's returns in Virmani's case as well.

5. It differs in its risk-sharing dimension from a crop-sharing contract, where the sharing only "insures" the return on the loan of the capital item—land—and not of the capital itself. Since land is not used up in the production process, there is no need to insure it.

paying back their loans. If there is no collateral requirement, utility-maximizing borrowers will default if the utility of their current wealth ($W$) less the loss of future earnings from default ($D$) exceeds the utility of wealth when the loan amount plus interest is repaid. Formally, the default condition is $U(W - D) > U[W - L(1 + i)]$.

Utility cost of default is higher the lower the mobility of the borrowers, who are easier to trace. Their assets can be attached and word of their default transmitted to other potential lenders. The following important implications follow: other things being equal, lenders are more likely to lend without collateral for small loans rather than for large ones, to owners rather than to tenant farmers, and to resident workers rather than to migrant workers.

Some institutions specialize in lending without collateral; some have specialized loan instruments that do not require collateral. These institutions either select customers whose characteristics indicate that they have high repayment incentives or loan small amounts compared to the income of the borrowers.

The utility cost of default on large loans is almost always less than the value of the loan, and collateral makes up for the lack of incentive to repay. The default condition then becomes $U(W - D - C) > U[W - L(1 + i)]$. When the loss of future earnings plus collateral is greater than the loan amount plus interest, $D + C > L(1 + i)$, all incentives for default are removed. Thus when lenders compete and when there are no interest rate ceilings, full collateral for principal plus interest will only be demanded if lenders believe that the loss of future earning opportunities associated with default is negligible. For a given loan size, the incentive effect of the same collateral amount thus varies with the personal characteristics of the borrowers, since these determine $D$. Personal characteristics thus enter into loan transactions in a way irrelevant in the transaction of goods; an impersonal credit market is not feasible.

To summarize, at a given interest rate, collateral has three effects or functions: it increases the expected return for borrowers; it partly or fully shifts the risk of loss of the principal from lenders to borrowers; and it provides those borrowers with low disutility of default with an additional incentive to repay their loans. We now apply these insights to the issue of capital constraints for the owners of small and large farms.

### *Consequences of Collateral for Credit Markets (G-6)*

From the discussion of the collateral problem, it is clear that small-scale farmers who do not own land (or other assets acceptable as collateral) will generally not be able to borrow to invest in fertilizer or other inputs. Rather, they will have to invest out of savings or establish input sharing arrangements with landowners. The credit market does not exist for them. On the other hand, large-scale landowners can obtain credit on favorable interest and collateral terms, since the only reason for collateral in their case would be to shift production risks away from the lender.[6]

Small-scale landowners are eligible for loans, but lenders will usually insist on higher levels of collateral than for large-scale owners, to compensate for the higher risk of intentional default. This shifts risk of capital loss to small-scale landowners and increases the expected cost of the loan as well. Thus these loans are more risky and more expensive than those extended to large-scale farmers, and the utility cost is higher.

Small-scale landowners may of course attempt to shift risk back to the lenders by paying higher interest rates in exchange for a reduction in collateral. However, even risk-neutral lenders will accept such an exchange only if it leaves their expected return as large as that from loans to large-scale landowners and as long as the collateral provides sufficient incentive for repayment. If the disutility cost of the loan is sufficiently high, small-scale landowners may stop borrowing altogether. The credit market for small-scale landowners may disappear because of a lack of demand, despite the fact that they have available collateral.

It is thus clear that the full utility cost of borrowing (relative to other alternatives), including the extra risk, is higher for small-scale landowners than for large-scale ones. The loan market may disappear for small-scale landowners from the demand side if the utility cost of loans exceeds the utility benefits from their investment. The market may also disappear from the supply side for owners who do not own assets in forms acceptable as collateral, or who already have high debt/equity ratios and have used up all this collateral.[7]

### *Insurance as a Partial Collateral Substitute (G-7)*

Can borrowers obtain unsecured loans more easily if they take out insurance that reduces the loss from some disaster and thus reduces the probability of default? Following the same approach as in the previous section, we consider the effects of insurance on the rate of return, the risk of capital loss, and the incentives for repayment.

6. Many government-subsidized rural credit schemes are poorly managed and allow large-scale farmers to use their political power to press the government to accept default on their part. Such systems cannot survive in the long run in the absence of continued government subsidies, and they are not considered here.

7. When insurance markets are poorly developed, an open credit line substitutes for insurance by allowing borrowing after disastrous events. If the collateral value of land has already been fully used to secure credit for production purposes, no further credit lines are available and exposure to risk is substantially increased.

Suppose a loan is to be invested entirely on the borrower's farm, that the loan is a current-account overdraft facility, and that the insurance pays off the loan in the event of hail damage. (Hail insurance circumvents the moral hazard issue of general crop insurance.) The insurance alters the probability distribution of returns from the investment by reducing the probability of one type of loss and by reducing the expected return from the investment by the premium amount. In equation 1, the insurance reduces the probability of default $\pi$. If the insured risk is independent of other risks, then

$$\pi = \pi_H + \pi_O, \tag{2}$$

where $\pi_H$ is the probability of hail damage, and $\pi_O$ is the probability of failure from other causes. If the insurance is also actuarily fair (that is, there are no management costs), the insurance amounts to a mean-preserving reduction in the spread of the distribution of returns to the borrower. It leaves the expected return unchanged but reduces its riskiness. Additional premiums to cover management costs would shift the mean of the distribution of returns downward.

Banks view unsecured loans to insured borrowers (who pay the premiums) as more attractive than loans to uninsured borrowers. In equation 1, with $C = 0$, the expected return of the loan will go up by the sum of the principal plus interest times $\pi_H$, the probability of hail-induced default. Thus insurance, like collateral, increases the expected return of the loan. However, this increase is smaller than that resulting from a collateral requirement, since collateral is realized for all causes of default while insurance is tied to specific risk, such as hail. In addition, hail insurance does not provide borrowers who intend to default, any additional incentive to repay, since their default condition is unaltered. In the event of hail damage, these borrowers will keep the insurance indemnity and default on their loans.

Insurance shifts a portion of the risk of a capital loss due to hail away from the bank and to the insurance company. Risk-averse borrowers will demand insurance (which is not collateral-specific in this case) without compulsion, unless it is very expensive.

We therefore see that insurance is only a partial substitute for collateral. While it increases the rate of return to the bank on an unsecured loan and shifts part of the capital-loss risk away from the bank, it is tied to specific events. Collateral, on the other hand, can be collected in the event of any disaster. From the point of view of an honest, risk-averse borrower, insurance is more desirable than collateral, since it shifts the risk of capital (collateral) loss for the insured risk to the insurance company.

There is, however, a monitoring function that insurance companies perform. If uninsured borrowers are in difficulty because of hail damage and ask for rescheduling of their debts (whether secured by collateral or not), the banks have to assess whether their difficulties are indeed caused by hail (that is, nonintentional) or whether they are under the borrowers' control. For insured borrowers, the insurance company makes the assessment and can provide banks with accurate information that would otherwise be costly to obtain. If the damage assessment requires specialized skills, an insurance company may generate such information more cheaply than a bank could.

In sum, insurance on favorable terms does have some of the same effects as collateral, and in certain circumstances it may even convert nonborrowers into borrowers or increase the size of loans to existing borrowers. Thus efficiency gains may indeed arise in the capital market. However, insurance does not generally solve problems arising from lack of incentive to repay, except when insured disasters occur.

### *Collateral Insurance, Tie-In Sales, and Compulsion (G-8)*

Lenders routinely require or force borrowers to insure houses or motor vehicles that are used as collateral. When the market value of collateral is equal to the loan amount, and the only way lenders can collect is by foreclosure on the collateral, the lenders carry all the investment risk from hazards to the collateral. Thus lenders' expected return can be increased and their risk of capital loss reduced through collateral insurance. If lenders are risk-neutral, they could simply increase the interest charge and, in the case of damage to the collateral, allow default. However, they would have to perform the actuarial calculations and assess the extent and causes of damage. Since banks accept many forms of collateral, this might be expensive. A diversified insurance industry might provide the service more efficiently. Furthermore, banks may lend in small areas where risks to collateral are covariate, such as flood damage to real estate. A specialized insurance company can diffuse such risks over a wider area and therefore reduce their costs. In these cases, banks will insist on collateral insurance even if they are risk-neutral.

One should note that insurance can convert risky assets into secure ones and make them useable as collateral. If automobiles could not be insured against most damages, including owner-caused collision, few wage workers would be able to borrow to purchase automobiles even in developed countries. Similarly, the use of animals as collateral is only possible when animals can be insured against such major risks as theft and accidental death.

In the case just discussed, where the collateral value was equal to the loan amount and there was no recourse for collecting debt other than by foreclosure, even a risk-averse borrower has no incentive to purchase insurance. The entire proceeds of the insurance accrue to the bank, and in the absence of insurance, loss of collateral results in the elimination of debt. Therefore, collateral insurance must be tied to the credit contract and made compulsory.

Partial incentives for the voluntary purchase of collateral insurance by the borrower arise when a personal liability for the loan exists or when the value of the collateral exceeds the value of the principle plus interest. The most common case is the conventional first mortgage, where there is always an incentive to insure one's own equity in a house. Nevertheless, in the absence of compulsion, full incentive to buy insurance will not exist.

In summary, the need for tied sales or compulsion arises in the insurance of collateral-specific risks and in the absence of easily enforced personal liability for the loan amount.[8] Tied sales and compulsion are usually efficiency enhancing. That is, larger loans are made, and more classes of borrowers are eligible.

## Agriculture-Specific Consequences

### *Absence of Crop Insurance (A-1)*

There has been a general failure on the part of private insurers to offer comprehensive coverage of yield risks in agriculture. Such schemes only exist where they are heavily subsidized by government, even in developed countries. Insurance may fail to emerge for three reasons.

*Lack of information.* First, given asymmetric information, the costs of measuring expected yield and its probability distribution and of assessing the yield shortfall in any given year may be excessive. The cost has to be charged as part of the premium. If farmers' utility gain from insurance is less than the information costs of providing that insurance, no market will exist.

In the case of all-risk yield insurance, the information costs are high. Yield risks can vary widely even in small geographic areas, thereby requiring that actuarial data and contracts be drawn up at a very local level. Also, since shortfalls of production from normal yields are frequent, loss assessments (or adjustments) have to be made frequently. Compare this to life insurance, where death has to be ascertained at most once during the duration of the contract, and where probability information accrues cheaply to the insurance firm from many secondary data sources.

8. Another case for compulsion exists in liability insurance, such as for automobile drivers. If drivers have few assets, compulsory liability insurance insures the accident victims rather than the insured themselves.

*Incentive problems.* The second reason for failure of insurance markets is moral hazard and adverse selection. For all-risk yield insurance, or cattle insurance that covers death caused by disease, the insurance contract itself reduces incentives for fertilizer application, feeding, plant or animal husbandry, and for disease prevention. Insuring animals against theft is often difficult, too, because the owner is less likely to invest in guarding the animals and, as an extreme case, may even have incentive to eat or sell the animals and pretend they were stolen. Coinsurance clauses, deductibles, and limitation to specific risks reduce incentive problems but also reduce the potential utility gain to the insured.

*Covariate risk.* Yield risk and incentive problems are essentially problems of information, which is easier for local insurers to obtain than a distant insurance company. Why then do local insurers not create an insurance market? For one reason, information problems may be too severe even for a local insurer. The main reason, however, is high covariance of risks. Because crops of all insured farmers may and often do fail at the same time, local insurers would have to carry high reserves of cash, gold, stocks, or short-term financial assets. In order for local insurers to write credible insurance contracts for their neighbors, their reserves at all times have to equal the total insured value. The insurance arrangement therefore degenerates to a centralized reserve scheme, and each farmer could self-insure at the same cost (as long as the storage costs or returns from short-term financial assets are the same for all individuals). Self-insurance through holding reserves avoids all information and incentive problems and so will usually be preferred.

Insurers who want to provide crop insurance face a trade-off between the information and covariance problems. The more geographically concentrated their operation, the more reserves they must hold, but the more manageable the information problems. The fact that crop insurance schemes in the developed world are organized at the national level with government backing suggests that either the covariance problem remains or information costs and incentive problems are too severe for unassisted crop insurance to emerge.

National all-risk yield insurance is costly in traditional agriculture because information transmission is time consuming and costly (T-5). Hail or typhoon insurance is easier to provide. Even in a country as small as Switzerland, hailstorms are so localized that they affect only a small proportion of farmers in any given year. Therefore, not only information costs but also reserve costs are small. Typhoons are much more widespread and fall into the class of catastrophic risks; that is, risks with high covariance among the insured, but since moral hazard problems are not substantial, pooling risks over a wide geographic area overcomes the problem of covariance. Covariance problems are also less for breakdown and life-cycle risks

(T-6), except for epidemics at regional or village levels. In developed countries, insurance is provided for many such specific risks as cattle accident and theft, life, health, and fire.

### *Insurance Substitutes (A-2)*

We have seen above that a crop insurance scheme for a small region would not be very different from a reserve system. Reserves may be held in the form of cash, gold, financial assets, consumer durables, stocks of food or feed, and as durable factors of production (land, animals) that can be sold in an emergency. Assets differ in their value as reserves. Gold has no positive return, but financial assets and producer durables do. Prices of the latter, however, vary substantially, which reduces their value as reserves (Jodha 1978). Reserves could also be deposits or loans to others.

Conversely, access to credit provides an important substitute for insurance where insurance is absent or costly. Credit can be a low-cost substitute for insurance if borrowing rates in bad years or in emergencies are not much higher than deposit rates or rates of return on financial assets.

The poor development of insurance in agriculture provides a rationale for very conservative debt/equity ratios. Small-scale farmers may not want to tie up all their assets as collateral for production loans. The unused value of collateral is an insurance substitute and ensures access to credit after bad events.

### *Absence of Financial Intermediation (A-3)*

Why do banks enter rural areas only at a very late stage of development? And why do moneylenders not accept deposits but generally lend their own equity? There is no reason that peasant agriculture cannot generate savings for deposit. Why is there not sufficient demand for deposit services to make it attractive to moneylenders to offer them?

Compared to bankers in an urban trading center, who lend to a variety of sectors of the economy, rural moneylenders face fewer information problems. Since they lend primarily to farmers with covariate yield risk, they need knowledge of conditions in only one economic sector rather than several (in addition to knowledge about the borrower's financial condition and other characteristics). However, covariance of yield risk leads to covariance of default risk. Banks, like insurance companies, would have to keep high reserve ratios or require high collateral.[9] In addition, covariance of yield

9. Seasonality of agricultural production is deemphasized here because it is not essential to the arguments that follow. However, seasonality also leads to a covariance between borrowing needs and deposit withdrawals, and it substantially strengthens the arguments.

means covariance of income for both depositors and borrowers: if crops fail, depositors would need to withdraw their deposits but borrowers would not be able to repay their loans. Banks might have to sell the collateral, which in bad crop years may be marketable only at a discount. Moneylenders, on the other hand, lend out of equity and therefore can reschedule loan repayments to a future year and charge interest. The expected return on such loans does not decline because of yield covariance.

If yields were fully insured, the covariance between depositors' incomes and borrowers' default would be sharply reduced. However, in the absence of insurance, banks cannot pay sufficiently high interest rates to attract depositors, because reserve requirements are too high. Nor can they impose sufficiently high collateral requirements on borrowers, because borrowers know that depositors will need their deposits just when the borrowers' loans need rescheduling. Furthermore, if borrowers and depositors are both closely associated with agriculture, banks are not needed (Virmani 1981)—the depositor could lend directly to the borrower. Direct lending lessens the gap between the deposit rate and the lending rate and places a minimum on the deposit rate (usually higher than the rate possible with a high reserve requirement).

Financial intermediaries must operate in a variety of agroclimatic regions, just like insurance companies. This geographic dispersion leads to information problems similar to those of insurance companies: banks must assess yields in order to make rescheduling decisions, and they must evaluate the intentions of borrowers. The late emergence of branch banking for agriculture in rural areas is clearly associated with gradual improvements in information transmission.

The same circumstances that lead to an absence of financial intermediation also make it impossible for farms to issue bonds or bondlike instruments in a local bond market, which could serve as an alternative to deposit banking. Bonds would be very risky instruments, since in bad years both borrowers and lenders would want to sell them, leading to large fluctuations in bond yields and prices. A larger geographic market in bonds issued by farmers would face even higher information and incentive difficulties than a branch network. Thus even the larger agricultural economy is not capable of generating fixed-interest-bearing securities from within, whose yields and prices are not highly correlated with agricultural production conditions. In order for fixed-interest securities to become available in rural areas, they have to be created by borrowers outside of the agricultural system and be marketed in rural areas. The previous discussion also makes clear why deposit banking emerged historically in international trading centers such as Venice, London, and the Hansa towns. A variety of goods arrived from different places at different times, and the borrowing needs of specialized traders and shippers were not covariate.

One further point is clear from this discussion. There is no doubt that, if it were financially feasible, partial or full replacement of local money lenders (based on equity finance) by a regionally diversified branch-banking system (based on deposit banking) would lead to efficiency gains for the rural sector as a whole.

### *Problems with Rural Branches for Banking and Insurance (A-4)*

Because the intentions of borrowers and the insured cannot be known with certainty, banks and crop insurers face common problems. Banks must know the nature of disasters that strike their clients in order to make decisions on rescheduling debts; insurers must assess whether the loss was caused by an insured disaster, and they must measure the extent of the loss. Furthermore, both need information about the returns from the different activities of the farmers they serve. Banks need this information to assess creditworthiness; insurance firms need this information to measure the probability distribution of damages.

Both, therefore, need either a branch or an agent system, which requires that a method exist to measure the performance of managers and agents. Furthermore, managers and agents never have full incentive to behave like the parent company, since their shares in company profits are usually quite small. Indeed, they may often have an incentive to collude with clients against the parent company, as for example when their performance is assessed on the volume of credit or insurance extended. In this case, they have every incentive to extend credit and insurance to more risky clients and to accept bribes from farmers in return for approving payments. While these problems apply to any banking or insurance system, they are particularly severe in agriculture because of the distance between head and branch offices, the absence of cheap telephones in developing countries, and also because of the covariance problem.

If crops fail for most clients, debts have to be rescheduled and indemnities paid at the same time, so that local indicators used in evaluating performance will be small that year. A profit-maximizing strategy for the network implies that the system must be able to accommodate several bad years in a row in a single location. Therefore, local performance may be low for several years in a row, even with an excellent manager or agent. Since there is no perfect way to distinguish between bad managers and agents and bad years, central managers face great difficulties. In some cases, these may be overcome by separating the authority of granting a loan or insurance contract from the authority to reschedule or pay indemnities. However, in a regionally dispersed organization, divorcing these decisions is costly, requiring more people to travel extensively to acquire accurate information about clients.

It is clear that any reduction in the cost of transmitting, storing, and retrieving information to and within the head office will improve the feasibility of branch systems.

### *Risk-Averse Behavior of Rural Branches (A-5)*

The pooling of agricultural banking or insurance over a wide range of agroclimatic zones should allow a company to act in a risk-neutral or profit-maximizing way in writing individual contracts. Nevertheless, local managers or agents must impress the head office with their annual performance and this along with high yield covariance in their areas are likely to induce them to be risk-averse with respect to individual contracts. They will try to reduce the year-to-year fluctuations in their branch's performance by choosing clients with low default risks or low probabilities of damage. Thus, banking and insurance companies may never fully overcome the covariance problem.

## The Demand of Rural Financial Institutions for Agricultural Insurance

### *Collateral-Specific Insurance (C-1)*

From section G-8 it follows that rural financial institutions would find fire, theft, and accident insurance desirable for those assets that have actual or potential collateral value: houses, motor vehicles, pumps, and animals. Innovations that reduce the costs of marketing and damage assessment for such insurance policies should be considered desirable. For example, the marking and registration of animals might reduce theft problems and make animals eligible for accident and theft insurance, which might give animals collateral value. It is also clear from section G-8 that once insurance with fair terms is available, banks should insist through their lending contracts that borrowers buy it.

### *Other Risk-Specific Insurance (C-2)*

According to the discussion under G-7, both farmers and lenders would want to see life insurance and medical insurance extended to rural areas and to have hail or typhoon insurance available for crops. Such insurance acts as an (imperfect) substitute for collateral, thus increasing debt/equity ratios and the extension of the credit market to those who own few assets with collateral value. It is indeed surprising that lending institutions and rural-development experts rarely focus on risk-specific insurance as a means of improving rural financial markets (for an exception, see Lipton 1979). Instead they focus on obtaining government support for compulsory crop insurance.

### *Compulsory Crop-Yield Insurance (C-3)*

Many countries (Japan, Mexico, and Brazil, among others) have instituted compulsory crop yield insurance—most often but not always as a requirement for borrowing formal credit. The discussion under G-8 provides no general justification for such compulsory insurance. The case for tied-in insurance applies only to collateral-specific risks, when extended personal credit liability does not exist or is difficult to enforce. However, crops are not usually used as collateral.

Tying yield insurance to credit may be of some value with loans to small-scale landowners or tenants, who do not have any collateral except for the standing crop.[10] Such insurance can be viewed as insuring the collateral or as a partial substitute for collateral. However, the cost of crop insurance is particularly high for small-scale farmers, and they may prefer not to borrow at all if the insurance premiums reflect the full costs of the insurance.

A case for compulsory yield insurance is often made on the grounds that compulsion eliminates adverse-selection problems and thus may render yield insurance feasible where it would not otherwise have been. This argument is misleading, though, because as long as self-finance or finance from private lenders (who do not impose an insurance requirement) is available, the lowest-risk borrowers will opt out of the government-sponsored credit-with-insurance scheme, and the scheme will be left with the highest-risk borrowers. The adverse-selection problem is simply transferred to the bank. Avoidance of adverse selection therefore calls for compulsory insurance for all farmers regardless of their borrowing behavior.

### *Government Lending Regulations (C-4)*

Lending terms for rural financial institutions are often severely restricted by government fiat. Regulations may restrict collateral to land, for example, which faces fewer risks than other assets. If so, banks are not exposed to other collateral risks, and they will not demand the corresponding insur-

10. Note here that moneylenders and money-lending landlords do regard a standing crop as collateral. In traditional systems, a moneylender may send his bullock cart to the threshing floors, and the landlords (or their agents) usually participate in the harvest to ensure proper division of output.

ance. Even where collateral options are wider, interest rates may be regulated. In order to make profits, banks restrict loans to borrowers with the lowest debt/equity ratio or to loans with high collateral. As we have seen in G-5, both these restrictions lead to higher bank profits at the regulated interest rate.

However, governments may force banks to lend to excluded groups. Since insurance as a partial collateral substitute (G-7) also tends to increase bank profits and reduce risk, banks will attempt to improve their returns on such forced lending (which they perceive as unprofitable) by asking the government to subsidize crop insurance. Crop insurance will partly reduce banks' management problems arising from covariance relations. Furthermore, management costs are reduced when the crop insurer plays a monitoring role, as discussed in section G-7.

Finally, covariate crop losses in disaster years may lead to coalitions of borrowers, who use the legal or political system to prevent the bank from undertaking loan collection and foreclosure. This may drastically reduce the return and insurance value of any collateral the bank might have required. Crop insurance would solve this problem by focusing the actions of the potential coalition on insurance reimbursement.

If moral hazard, information problems, and covariance problems were low, the argument that crop insurance improves rural financial markets would be uncontested. This would be so even where the demand for insurance arose primarily from financial institutions. However, we have seen that the problems of providing crop insurance are precisely the same as the problems facing branch banking. With the exception of its actuarial functions, the crop insurance company needs the same (or more) information to settle claims as the branch banking network does to reschedule loans. Crop insurance simply shifts the cost from one agency to another and would lead to two branch networks where one might have been sufficient.

If farmers wanted crop insurance sufficiently to pay the full costs of providing it, a second network might be warranted, because the insurance coverage purchased would in most cases exceed the amount of the loans. However, farmers have demonstrated that they do not want to carry the full costs of crop insurance (and we have seen in C-3 that the case for compulsion is very weak).

Of course, government subsidy of crop insurance is valuable to farmers and to the banking system, especially if it is sufficiently generous to induce farmers to buy it voluntarily. However, in extreme cases the only demand for crop insurance comes from rural financial institutions as a direct result of government lending regulations. But it may be more appropriate to search for solutions that allow the branch network to self-insure rather than to create a separate institution. This is not to advocate that the bank operate its own insurance subsidiary (which may create serious internal problems) but only that the bank attempt to design rescheduling and monitoring rules to deal with the fundamental covariance problem.

## Conclusions

Crop yield insurance is plagued with problems of information, moral hazard, and adverse selection. These costs, and not the absence of farmers' demand, lie at the root of the universal lack of privately provided crop yield insurance. The information and incentive problems are substantially the same as those affecting rural credit markets, and it may be less difficult to solve these problems by appropriately changing the credit system than by introducing insurance. Also, while a case can be made for tied or compulsory insurance of collateral-specific risks, this does not apply to crop insurance, and especially to subsidized crop insurance. A major source of demand for crop insurance may in fact come not from farmers themselves but from highly regulated financial systems, which are unable to adjust the terms of their credit contracts to the high costs of lending to particular groups.

A strong case can be made for a variety of risk-specific insurance contracts, and it is surprising that the development community has focused so little attention on such alternatives to all-risk crop insurance. Risk-specific insurance contracts are widely available to farmers in developed countries. They include contracts for specific crop risks (hail, flood); accident and theft insurance for livestock and machines; fire insurance for buildings, livestock, and machines; life insurance, and so on. The distinctive feature of these contracts is that they avoid the nearly insurmountable problems of all-risk crop yield insurance. Developing countries might be well advised to concentrate on improving the policy climate for risk-specific insurance on a privately provided basis, possibly with international reinsurance and some government guarantees.

Where pressure arises for crop yield insurance, there is ample reason to limit the contracts to a few specific climatic risks, such as typhoons. The Philippines, for example, provides all-risk crop insurance in Laguna Province, which is blessed with one of the world's best irrigation systems. Except for typhoons, yield risks are quite small, and farmers who buy the insurance contracts are primarily interested in insuring the substantial typhoon risk. There is no reason why the contract should not be limited to this risk.

The case for such risk-specific insurance, as with all insurance, depends not only on the direct benefits of insurance but also on the indirect potential impact on credit markets. Insurance can lead to an extension of the credit market to groups of borrowers who previously could not obtain credit. This may happen if insurance sufficiently lowers the default risk of honest borrowers or if it converts assets that previously had no collateral value into acceptable collateral.

Finally, there is a strong case for institutional and technological innovations and investments that reduce the information and incentive problems lying at the heart of rural market imperfections. Telecommunications, credit bureaus, and computerized data processing and retrieval for branch banking networks are potential alternatives. Also important are institutional innovations, such as a foolproof system of registration and marking of animals, to make risky assets insurable and thus acceptable as collateral.

# 5

# Can Crop Credit Insurance Address Risks in Agricultural Lending?

J. D. Von Pischke

A series of initiatives begun in the late 1970s have resulted in the establishment of government-owned agricultural insurance programs in a number of developing countries. These programs have been stimulated by the United Nations Conference on Trade and Development (UNCTAD) Special Program on Insurance, the Food and Agricultural Organization (FAO), the United States Agency for International Development, and the Inter-American Institute for Cooperation on Agriculture. Some development technicians have advocated agricultural insurance as a financial response to fundamental problems that characterize agriculture and agriculturally based economies. These problems include variability of crop yields and farm income, and the impact of this variability on the welfare of the farm household and on the performance of the rural economy. Possibly of greater interest is the extent to which variability diminishes the ability and willingness of farmers to invest in improved agricultural technology. Such investment is essential to the modernization of agriculture and the enhancement of rural welfare through increased income from viable, commercial farming activities. From this perspective, the potential role of insurance as a means of increasing the debt-servicing capacity of farmers, in effect decreasing the risks of agricultural lenders, has received much attention.

The logical progression from variations in crop yields to concern for debt-servicing capacity involves a number of assumptions that appear to be taken for granted by advocates of agricultural insurance. A critical assumption at the start of this chain—that variations in yields are highly correlated with variations in farm household consumption—is challenged in earlier chapters in this volume. This chapter attempts to deal with several of the subsequent steps in the progression of the argument used by advocates of agricultural insurance.

The views and interpretations in this chapter are those of the author and should not be attributed to the World Bank, to its affiliated organizations, or to any individual acting in their behalf. The author is grateful to the editors, Peter Hazell, Carlos Pomareda, and Alberto Valdés, and to Nelson Maurice, Hans Binswanger, and Richard A. J. Roberts for insights into risk and insurance. However, these individuals bear no responsibility for positions taken or conclusions reached in this chapter.

Crop credit insurance is the agricultural insurance most relevant to the link between credit and the adoption and sustained development of modern technology at the farm level. Crop credit insurance provides protection against events that have an adverse impact on agricultural yields. Its unique feature is that the indemnity is paid to the lender, rather than to the farmer, and cancels the farmer's debt—or some portion of it related to the insured loss. This insurance is expected to protect the liquidity of the lender, so that lending can continue. Continuity is especially important because, to the extent farmers rely on credit, it is most crucial in the period immediately following crop loss. At that time, farmers' own resources are depleted and their creditworthiness may be in doubt as a result of the illiquidity caused by the loss. Equally as important as the restoration of the lender's liquidity, therefore, is the continued creditworthiness of the farmer when the loan is repayed by the insurance indemnity.

In addition to citing the benefits that crop credit insurance can theoretically provide to lender and borrower, advocates cite systems' benefits, which result from the effects on the community of stabilized farm household consumption and credit flows. These benefits include a more stable base for trade, industrial investment, and employment. Also postulated are the benefits that insurance experts can bring to the traditional functions of extension and rural development project design and management through improved consideration of risk-management issues. Government may also benefit from providing an additional useful service.

The following discussion of crop credit insurance is placed in the context primarily of small-farm credit issued by formal lenders.[1] This emphasis is appropriate because crop credit insurance is commonly advocated as a means of increasing credit access for risky borrowers and for those currently outside the portfolio of commercial banks, cooperatives, and other formal lenders. Small-scale farmers are concentrated in these categories.

## Types of Agricultural Lending Risks

Formal agricultural lenders, such as specialized farm credit institutions, cooperatives, and commercial banks, face at least six major risk categories. These include: (1) variability of agricultural production, (2) market risks, (3) managerial risks, (4) character risks, (5) political risks, and (6) strategic risks. These risks create variations in the profitability and cash-flow patterns of agricultural credit institutions, and in their solvency and

1. Small farm credit is broadly discussed in Adams, Douglas, and Von Pischke (1984).

liquidity. As a generalization, production yield risks are the only insurable risks covered by crop credit insurance, although insurance administration and design may help reduce other risks.

### *Variability of Agricultural Production*

Production risks arise from the nature of the production process. Yield variability reflects influences of climate, such as drought, flood, and wind damage, and also damages from fire or pests. These risks are well known, although their impact at the farm level is often not well documented in developing countries. Crop credit insurance responds precisely to this risk by basing indemnities on yields and on variation in yields arising from natural hazards. Crop credit insurance does not provide complete protection against yield variation. For example, the death of the farmer or the illness of members of the farm household may reduce labor and managerial inputs, thus depressing yields. As a result of yield information problems, especially for new technologies, crop credit insurance has in certain cases not met yield risks effectively. It may also impose additional costs on both borrowers and lenders in the form of premium payments and demands on managerial energy.

### *Market Risks*

Market risks arise both from variations in supply and demand for crops not subjected to binding price controls and from the inability of controlled markets to respond efficiently to changes in these conditions. Market risks are reflected primarily in variations in price for produce offered for sale by farmers. In areas where rainfall is high, or where crops are grown under irrigation, the impact of price risks on farm household income generally far exceeds that of yield risks, as elaborated by Barah and Binswanger (1982). Crop credit insurance oriented toward yield would not protect farmers against market risk. It is also superfluous to the extent that yields on insured farms are covariate with yields in given market areas; price increases partially or fully offset the effects of reduced yields on farmer income. In addition, risk-reducing forward sale arrangements linked with informal credit may be available for certain cash crops.

### *Managerial Risks*

Managerial risks confront agricultural lenders at several levels. Innovation at the farm level requires managerial capacity. This capacity is a product of information and of the ability and commitment to act on it. Risk-management services that accompany insurance, such as extension and insurance qualification procedures, may improve information and contribute to better farm management. Pure crop credit insurance appears to have limited relevance to farm-management risk. Bad management decisions should not be underwritten by insurance. It is uneconomical to sustain access to credit in the event of managerial shortcomings reflected in low yields.

Managerial risks in nonfinancial support systems supplying inputs or purchasing produce are generally beyond the scope of insurance programs based on farm yields. They do not directly protect the lender against managerial risk in these activities, which are crucial to the income and debt-servicing capacity of insured farmers. Managerial risks at this level are reflected in failures in the timely supply of inputs and in the inability to absorb produce tendered by farmers or to pay for it promptly. Another risk is the inability to honor stop orders, under which amounts due the lender are to be deducted from the borrower's crop delivery proceeds by the buyer and remitted to the lender. Indirectly, insurance and risk-management activities may make the costs or potential costs of managerial risks more apparent, providing a basis for preventive action.

A third managerial risk is within the lending institutions themselves. Cooperatives and government credit agencies, such as specialized farm credit institutions, have patchy management records. Their management information systems are often inadequate for the timely identification of attractive, new investment opportunities, prompt control of arrears, and determination of portfolio quality. Crop credit insurance may reduce these managerial problems indirectly if liquidity problems caused by the impact of insured events on borrowers divert management attention from the search for new business, the design of new services, and the training of staff. However, the implementation of crop credit insurance demands managerial time and therefore does not necessarily produce a net saving in managerial resources for the credit institution.

### *Character Risks*

Character risks in credit parallel moral hazard in insurance. Character risks are the probability that borrowers will intentionally do things that will diminish the value of loan contracts from the point of view of the lender. Misrepresentation, willful nonrepayment, and diversion of loan proceeds are expressions of character risks. Pure insurance provides no protection against character risks, although advocates of crop credit insurance argue that the additional loan supervision required for generation and administration of insurance contracts reduces opportunistic actions by borrowers.

Also, crop credit insurance may assist in identifying defaulters not having insured losses, providing a basis for managerial follow-up. Character risks vary inversely with the efficiency of credit program implementation and with farmers' perceptions of the dependability of the credit source. Crop credit insurance may increase perceptions of dependability by restoring farmers' creditworthiness in times of distress and by providing liquidity for the lender to fund additional credit to farmers in arrears. However, it remains to be demonstrated that the factors that often inspire farmers to sabotage official credit programs would not also vitiate government insurance programs.

### *Political Risks*

Political risks in agricultural lending are manifested in two forms. The first consists of government intervention in rural credit operations to the detriment of lenders. Interest rates, security rights, and loan allocation and recovery are vulnerable to political risks. The second type of political risk is activities of farmers aimed directly at the credit institution without the intervening factor of government. These include organized default, harassment of credit agency personnel, boycotts and threats, which delay or make impossible the realization of security by the lender, and intervention in the loan allocation process by persons who aspire to political office.

To the extent that arrears caused by yield shortfalls result in activities by the lender that are subject to political modification, a case may be made for crop credit insurance. However, it remains to be demonstrated that political risks would not also compromise the integrity of the crop credit insurance system by merely providing an additional arena for intervention and politically generated inefficiencies. These effects could be reflected in indemnification not related to yield performance and in the politically motivated use of insurance to force lenders to make unsound loans. Therefore it is not clear that crop credit insurance could reduce the political risk to rural financial systems.

### *Strategic Risks*

Strategic risks of three types may be identified in agricultural lending. The first is found in the mechanism by which confidence between borrower and lender is created or destroyed. Confidence is essential for the flow of credit in private markets. However, in government institutions and development projects the issue of confidence is often not accorded much priority or addressed explicitly in project design. It is assumed that extension services or other activities oriented toward the target group, including agricultural insurance, provide a basis for businesslike interaction between borrower and lender. Evidence suggests, however, that this type of confidence is often absent and that official credit portfolios consisting of small-scale farmer loans tend often to self-destruct.

A second strategic issue is the basis by which credit is rationed to small-scale farmers. Two alternative strategies are commonly found, especially where interest rates are subsidized and serve little economic purpose. The first—intensive credit rationing—involves identification of a relatively small target group and provision to them of credit amounts that are large in relation to their existing operations. For example, a farmer with two local cows may be given a loan to buy several higher grade or exotic cows. A small-scale farmer planting local varieties and using only a little organic fertilizer may be issued credit to plant the entire holding with high yielding varieties using chemical fertilizer. Mechanization loans are also often intensively rationed. The size of the loan is such that borrowers could not reasonably be expected to repay from their preloan cash flow; loan repayment must come from the incremental cash flow generated by the loan-supported investment. Credit allocation under these circumstances must be quite selective, and elaborate access mechanisms using farm budgets are frequently employed.

Extensive credit rationing is motivated by considerations of access as well as of production, and access mechanisms are simple. Credit is rationed extensively to large numbers of farmers and broad target groups. For example, all members in good standing of a cooperative may have access to seed and fertilizer loans. All commercial growers of wheat having land titles may be eligible for production loans. Within the budget or balance sheet constraints of lenders, wide access implies relatively small loans to numerous borrowers. Loan limits under extensive rationing are frequently specified in terms of standard amounts based on enterprise budgets. This is in contrast to the more complicated derivation of loan limits from farm budgets used for intensive credit rationing. Extensive rationing is most frequently found in seasonal input credit. Small amounts are issued to each borrower, satisfying the production-oriented bias of program planners and inspiring broad appeal, which is politically desirable.

Each of these varieties of credit rationing contains the seeds of its own financial destruction. The greater the degree of intensive or extensive rationing, the more rapid the self-destruction, other things being equal.

Intensively rationed credit attempts to perform the function of equity or ownership capital in absorbing the impact of uncertainty. Intensively rationed loans and the debt-service burdens that result are relatively large, and they change on-farm factor proportions significantly through the addition of higher levels of technology. Such loans may push the borrower's finances beyond his managerial and risk-bearing capabilities, especially during the initial period of adaptation to credit-supported change. Adversity may be reasonably expected in agriculture and in the implementation of new technology. In periods of adversity, borrowers may find it difficult to meet debt-servicing obligations. Delinquency easily results, because borrowers may have relatively little of their own resources sunk in the loan-supported investment, which tends to reduce their commitment to its successful performance.

Extensive credit rationing can also lead to financial problems. In promoting access, lenders offer credit to some borrowers who are not in a position to use it wisely, and who have little intention of repaying. Others are so exposed to uncertainty, or so close to subsistence, that even small repayment obligations assume major proportions. Input credit often becomes more extensively rationed over time, as inflation raises production costs. Also, the lender's budget constraints, arising partly from nonrepayment by borrowers, do not permit loan limits to keep pace with production costs. Extensively rationed small loans may pose difficulties if prescribed husbandry practices are subject to indivisibility far beyond the average loan size. For example, a loan that is small compared to the financial requirements of improved input packages may lead to incomplete adoption of the package and disappointing results. Access to extensively rationed credit does not necessarily stimulate adoption, and loans may become too trifling to engender commitment to either their productive use or repayment.

Because of the desire to promote development through intensive rationing, or widespread access through extensive rationing, a financial optimum—at which the borrower's repayment capacity is fruitfully related to loan size—is difficult to achieve in official programs. It does not appear that crop credit insurance is a particularly useful device for altering the strategic orientation of government institutions making such loans.

The third strategic risk lies in the types and quality of services that lenders provide. Composition of services is important to the flow of information between borrower and lender, the farmer's value of his relationship with the institution, and the prospects for expanding the relationship between borrower and lender.

Specialized farm credit institutions by definition issue loans but provide relatively few money transfer or deposit facilities. Credit through such a channel is unrelated to savings channels and is usually funded by the national treasury and external donors. Such dependence generally limits the access of specialized farm credit institutions to market information, which can lead to their alienation from the rural community. Rural people do not have the same degree of confidence in such an institution as they would have to have in an integrated financial intermediary to which they entrust their deposits and funds to be transferred. Specialized farm credit institutions, in turn, usually regard rural people not as a market to be developed but rather as poor, exploited, or economically incompetent people requiring assistance. In this environment, institutional management is not in a position to be stimulated by the discipline imposed and opportunities offered by market forces, and it typically develops only limited decision-making expertise.

Crop credit insurance may correct some of the information deficiencies arising from provision of only a narrow range of services. However it is not clear that the greater flexibility provided by crop credit insurance would alter the fundamental strategic problems of government-owned, specialized farm credit institutions, or that it would increase these lenders' incentives to take a more entrepreneurial and information-based approach to their potential clientele. By absorbing certain important risks to lenders, crop credit insurance could in fact diminish their incentive to gather market information.

## Alternative Risk-Accommodation Measures for Lenders

Lenders seek to minimize and accommodate risks through diversification, reserve management, strategies designed to provide a lending cushion, price rationing, measures to increase borrower information flows, and actions that increase the value of the debtor/creditor relationship to the borrower.

### *Diversification*

Portfolio diversification is a straightforward means of accommodating the risk of agricultural lending. However, portfolio diversification across sectors is often difficult for lenders established specifically to lend to agriculture or to small-scale farmers, or where enforced specialization in financial markets is an underlying regulatory strategy. Reducing barriers to diversification is one means of assisting agricultural lenders to accommodate risk.

### *Reserve Management*

Reserve management consists of structuring assets and liabilities to safeguard the liquidity of the lending institution. This involves balancing the maturity structure of loans to borrowers with that of obligations to lenders and ensuring that sufficient additional resources are available to meet unforeseen claims on liquidity. These additional resources include cash, government securities, or similar instruments, which can be used to satisfy liquidity requirements directly or are easily convertible into cash. However, additional resources can also be off-balance-sheet sources of liquidity, such as lines of credit with other financial institutions, the rediscount window of a central bank, and crop credit insurance. By increasing the lender's liquidity, off-balance-sheet resources permit any given level of balance-sheet liquidity reserves to support a larger loan portfolio.

Crop credit insurance could constitute a useful reserve management tool when indemnities are paid quickly—and to the extent that yield losses are a cause of nonrepayment by borrowers. The attractiveness of crop credit insurance for reserve management purposes would depend upon its cost relative to other forms of reserves. How does the opportunity it provides to cancel the borrower's debt compare with the alternative of rescheduling, including automatic conversion of short-term production loans into medium-term loans when yields in a given district fall below expectations?

### *Lending Cushion*

Strategies designed to create a lending cushion include requirements of collateral security and borrower participation in financing the costs of activities partially underwritten by loans. Tying loan decisions to collateral security by making loan size a function of collateral value is generally regarded as not being developmental, because only those with qualifying assets to pledge as collateral can obtain credit. Even where collateral is taken, it may be extremely difficult—for political, social, legal, and institutional reasons—for lenders to foreclose on agricultural land or on other assets, such as cattle and machinery. Probably the most constructive use of collateral security in agricultural lending is as protection against claims by other creditors. Mortgaged land or pledged cattle and machinery cannot easily be used by borrowers as security for other debts, therefore protecting the secured lender's interests.

Increasing the share of investment costs financed by borrower equity results in a smaller debt-servicing obligation and provides the lender with a larger cushion in the form of expected borrower cash flow not required for debt service. High levels of loan financing, often equal to 80, 90, 95, or 100 percent of representative investment costs, are common in lending for agricultural development. This practice is largely convention; the proportion of loan financing specified in agricultural project design is rarely derived from cash-flow projections adjusted for probable adversity.

The approach common to enlightened lending strategy outside agriculture (in sectors where risks are lower!) is to project cash flow for the borrower or for the investment, to make adjustments for reasonably expected adversity, and to determine loan size with reference to both the relevant market interest rate (because interest absorbs a portion of debt-servicing capacity) and the term for which the lender has funds available. The term, like the interest rate, is largely a function of the type of resources available to the lender; commercial banks obtaining resources primarily from demand and short-term deposits are generally reluctant to make long-term loans. Except where loan size is primarily a function of collateral value, as for land purchase, consumer durables, and trade or supplier's credits, loan size normally has no uniform or inherent relation to investment cost. Rather, loan size is tailored to the expected financial performance and characteristics of the investment, or of the borrower, or both.

By contrast, officially funded agricultural development lending generally relates loan size to investment cost, using a rule of thumb. The length of the loan maturity schedule is adjusted within the limits imposed by the cash-flow availability estimated for the investment, using normal-year assumptions. In practice, it is rare for government-owned sources of agricultural credit to negotiate financing proportions to reflect the riskiness of the intended investment or the financial status of the farmer/borrower.

Reducing loan financing proportions under the conventional approach is difficult because of the precedents that have been established, the desire to increase input use at the farm level by those who view credit as an input, the belief that without credit in generous amounts adoption of modern technologies will be retarded, and the appeal of quick-disbursing projects. The "without official credit" situation is virtually never explored in project design. Financial market failure or exploitation by private lenders is almost always assumed. Therefore the nature of interaction between credit and the introduction of new technology under a project is not really known. Until a more refined approach is taken, agricultural credit will continue to be characterized by strategically induced portfolio quality problems, generally regressive subsidies to defaulting borrowers, and institutional maladjustment. In a static sense, whether these problems reside solely in lending institutions or are shared with crop credit insurers is probably not of much economic importance. (Of economic importance, however, is whether sharing would lead to any dynamic changes that would conserve administrative costs and reduce losses. As suggested throughout this chapter, a cost-effective and positive impact seems problematic.)

The function of a crop credit insurer as a residual location for bad debts of government banks might be more effectively performed by agricultural credit trust funds, established as independent financial entities from which funds can be disbursed for projects that are not financially viable in commercial terms. Their institutional format consists of a set of financial accounts maintained by the fund administrator (which would be the agricultural bank), a few perfunctory trustees, and no staff. Funds are disbursed and recovered by the agricultural bank, which is paid a service charge by the fund, but as administrator it bears no risks for its own account from trust fund operations. Through these arrangements, the full, direct financial cost of a program may also be monitored.

Trust funds are highly flexible. They can be established for any purpose, and their performance may be independent of that of the agricultural bank that administers them. After the original purpose of these funds has been served, such as lending under a specific project, disbursement of donor funds, or support for some policy, the trust fund may be allowed to languish or die. Alternatively, it may be replenished if the purpose for which it was established is still attractive.

### *Price Rationing*

Price rationing of credit is another way lenders accommodate risk. In private credit markets, more risky loans are generally characterized by higher interest rates and service charges. (Other factors, such as administrative costs, especially with respect to small loans in agriculture or consumer finance, also contribute to the levels of interest rates and service charges for any given class of loans.) Price rationing of credit is unusual in official agricultural credit programs because of their political nature, which tends to result in unnaturally low interest rates. Within or outside this limitation, it may be difficult politically to charge different farmers different rates for essentially the same activities. Where different classes of loans bear different interest rates, the structure is generally determined in advance in project design; but rates are not a significant rationing mechanism relative to those used to define target groups of borrowers.

### *Information Flows*

Measures to increase information flows may reduce lender's risk. The most common form of technical assistance is extension support for credit programs and their small-scale farmer participants. Technical assistance may also be embodied in loan requirements: minimum-input package programs, prescriptions relating to livestock breeds, and investment in on-farm infrastructure to complement investment in animals.

The efficacy of efforts to link credit and technical assistance is much debated, but there seems to be a broad consensus that technical assistance activities are difficult to target, difficult to administer efficiently, and that results often differ from expectations. In some countries, agricultural lenders have their own extension service or agricultural technicians. However, rather than working with farmers on husbandry practices and farm planning, these technicians are often most useful in identifying good credit risks among the farming community. This function is entirely legitimate but tends to provide credit to farmers who are already progressive.

## *Increasing Value of Loan Contracts*

Making loan contracts more valuable to borrowers reduces lenders' risks. Value is added to relationships by sanctions against willful default but more importantly by the continued prospect of an expanding relationship between the financial intermediary and the client. These prospects are built on expected improvements in the financial situation of the borrower and on the ability of the lender to offer an even wider range of services at competitive prices and conditions through financial innovation. These activities are mutually reinforcing and increase the flow of information between financial intermediary and client, making both more valuable to each other. In contrast to intermediaries interested in extending their financial services' market share through the identification of prospective clients as either depositors or borrowers, agricultural banks perceiving their primary purpose as satisfying credit needs may suffer from a strategic disadvantage.

Crop credit insurance may contribute to the objectives of a competitive financial intermediary oriented toward relationship lending. The extent to which crop credit insurance could be useful would depend upon the efficiency of its administration, its costs to the lender, and the prospects that its implementation would enhance relationships with clients. However, crop credit insurance is most useful in a situation where a lending relationship already exists or is contemplated. The relationship basis for lending puts deposit mobilization first, as this provides information that is useful to the financial intermediary in enhancing services offered through innovation. Where deposit relationships already exist, crop credit insurance may hasten institutions' willingness to lend and may also make institutions willing to provide larger amounts of credit than would otherwise be the case. However, to alter their strategies in this way, lenders would have to have confidence in the insurer.

## Conclusion

The conventional financing approach in agricultural credit projects uses rules of thumb to determine loan size. Conventional practice has proved unwilling to test or consider seriously the without-project alternative—of not providing credit through some official source, such as an agricultural finance institution, or a captive source, such as a cooperative. Poor loan portfolio quality is almost assured by the design of many projects.

Within these inherent but not inevitable limitations, crop credit insurance may have a useful role to play. However, this role has probably been overestimated and oversold by the technicians and agencies that have provided the impetus for the establishment of recent government agricultural insurance programs in developing countries. It is unlikely that crop credit insurance as pure insurance (indemnification against risk, separate from the institutional insurance mechanism and risk management services it may provide) will improve loan decisions. In the context of credit projects, crop credit insurance will be little more than a transfer mechanism, relieving the agricultural lender of embarrassing bad debts but not reducing these losses. Even if the institutional mechanism of insurance were able to improve credit decisions—an untested variable—it may be possible to provide these services without insurance. The costs of three alternatives should be compared: (1) no crop credit insurance, or a continuation of the existing situation in most cases; (2) risk-management services but no crop credit insurance; and (3) crop credit insurance.

Other comparisons should be explored, too. These include the net costs or benefits of improvements in the ways borrowers and lenders accommodate risk, relative to the costs and benefits of crop credit insurance. Improvements in other systems consist of portfolio diversification within and beyond agricultural lending, better reserve management, revision of lending strategies, increased use of price-rationing mechanisms, more efficient means of generating and acting upon information about borrowers, and the development of increasingly valuable relationships between borrowers and lenders. Small-scale farmer credit is at a relatively early stage of development in many of these respects. Considerable gains could be realized from improving these variables. For example, project design could create businesslike relationships between official credit sources and small borrowers, permitting the development of financial market orientations and strategies toward small-scale farmer credit. Whether crop credit insurance would be as fruitful as these other courses remains to be seen. In any event, crop credit insurance should not be seen as a unique measure but as part of a system to enhance the debt repayment capacity of small-scale farmers.

Even if crop credit insurance is useful, its overall impact on the lending institution may not be large. The limitations on its impact stem from: (1) the extent to which yield variations from insured causes are offset at the farm household level by behavior that results in continued creditworthiness, (2) market risks that reduce farmers' income from insured crops, (3) managerial shortcomings on the farm and in rural economic institutions that are not addressed by the risk-management services associated with crop credit insurance, (4) character risks, (5) political actions that lead to nonrepayment of loans by farmers, and (6) shortcomings in the ways lenders structure their relationships with borrowers. In most official projects in which credit is a component, it is likely that these other factors combined are of greater importance to loan recovery and lender liquidity than insured yield variations.

The institutional climate for successful crop credit insurance schemes is probably not materially different from that for successful agricultural credit portfolios. In any financial market involving small-scale farmers, it would not be reasonable to expect wildly better, long-run performance from an official insurer than from an official lender. Given the performance of many of these lenders, the prospects for government insurance are not particularly bright from a financial or institutional point of view. As with small-scale farmer credit experience, the introductory, short-run record is often superior to the long-run record. It would be unfortunate if initial positive signs from official crop credit insurance programs were interpreted prematurely, before the weaknesses and capacities of these systems are demonstrated and their costs more fully known.

6

# An Evaluation of the Impact of Credit Insurance on Bank Performance in Panama

Carlos Pomareda

Many agricultural development banks face poor loan recovery and returns. The problem is sometimes attributed to farm income instability arising from production and market risks. However, as argued in chapters 4 and 5, problems of loan recovery are often related to shortcomings in institutional design and to government policies that restrict the options available to agricultural development banks in managing their lending and financial portfolios.

In chapter 5, Von Pischke argues that crop yield insurance tied to farm credit may not address the more important risks and constraints responsible for the poor performance of most agricultural development banks (ADBs). However, the effectiveness of crop credit insurance in improving loan recovery and returns, and therefore bank performance, is ultimately an empirical issue. This chapter presents an empirical evaluation of the effects of crop credit insurance on the performance of the Agricultural Development Bank of Panama (the Banco de Desarrollo Agropecuario, or BDA). We also explore the extent to which increases in the interest rate charged by the BDA could more cheaply provide the same benefits to the bank as crop credit insurance.

## The Expected Effects of Credit Insurance

The financial performance of ADBs depends critically on interest and loan recovery rates. Interest rates for agricultural lending are often fixed by government, and usually at levels that seriously limit the returns to ADB loans. Fixed low interest rates to agriculture have been advocated for a long time in order to induce technological change and to compensate farmers for low yields, high input costs, and (sometimes artificially) depressed prices of agricultural products. The distortions that such policies introduce are widely documented (Adams, Douglas, and Von Pischke 1984). Many countries are revising their interest rate policies, particularly where inflation has reduced fixed nominal rates to negative real rates.

Galbis (1981) recently documented these changes and recognized this as the means of avoiding further decapitalization of development banks. These policy changes are primarily a political decision, and they require little from the banks themselves in terms of changes in management. However, if interest rates are raised, the ensuing higher returns to banks should motivate them to bear higher risks without requiring farmers to purchase insurance.

The recovery rate is an important determinant of the effective return on bank loans. This rate is reported broadly by banks as the proportion of loaned money that is recovered. However, it is useful to distinguish among various concepts of recovery. *Anticipated late repayment* occurs when, at maturity or before, the farmer and the bank agree on rescheduling the principal and interest payments. However, this is sometimes done using the original rate of interest, which may be lower than the one prevailing at the time of rescheduling, thereby implying an opportunity loss to the bank. *Unanticipated late repayment* occurs when the farmer just shows up late, and the bank then collects the principal without any interest charges during the period beyond the original maturity. The opportunity loss to the bank is larger in this case. A *default* occurs when the farmer never pays back of his own will. Banks often pursue legal action but not always successfully. In many cases, defaults occur when the government for political reasons cancels the debt after a natural disaster or during an economic crisis.

If agricultural disasters are the prime reason for default of debt obligations, they would provide the rationale for agricultural credit insurance. In the event of an insured disaster, the insurer would pay off the farmer's debt for the portion of the crop that is lost or for an animal that dies or loses its function. Therefore, to the extent that repayment problems are due to production risks, credit insurance should increase the average loan recovery. Things are, however, slightly more cumbersome, because it is necessary to distinguish year-to-year fluctuations in loan recovery from chronic low recovery. The first may be due to production risks and to product and capital market risks, which render farm income stochastic. The second may reflect low agricultural productivity, structural problems in the agricultural credit market, or simply the inability of the bank to collect loans.

Agricultural credit insurance might usefully increase the average loan recovery in years of disasters. However, when low loan-recovery rates persist for reasons other than production risks, little can be gained from credit insurance.

The expected effects of credit insurance can be summarized in the following hypotheses: (1) Insurance increases the average loan-recovery rate and reduces its variability through indemnities paid by the insurer to the bank. (2) Insurance reduces the costs to the bank through shorter actual loan maturities and therefore reduces bookkeeping and loan-collection costs. (3) Insurance decreases risk in the bank's loan portfolio. Borrowing from other banks is therefore possible at lower rates because of reduced risk premiums. Indirectly, it affects the leverage position of the bank, as less-risky loans can be considered assets with higher liquidity, therefore increasing the bank's potential for larger holdings of liabilities (see Pomareda 1984).

A less favorable effect is the moral hazard problem. A compulsory program could induce banks to issue loans carelessly, trusting the insurer to reimburse the bank if crops fail. However, the insurer could reject such high-risk loans as not complying with the insurer's standards and provisions.

These hypotheses are tested with the aid of data from Panama. The results are limited by the relatively short period of time (since 1976) that crop credit insurance has been operating in Panama. Nevertheless, they do suggest that the potential benefits from insurance are not inconsequential. The results also highlight some dangers that ought to be kept in mind.

## Agricultural Credit and Insurance in Panama

The BDA is the government-owned bank that specializes in lending to agriculture. However, as shown in table 6.1, it contributes less than a quarter of total institutional (public and private) credit to agriculture. Its financial structure is representative of many specialized agricultural lending institutions in the developing world (Pomareda 1984). Its assets are predominantly held in farm loans, and its liabilities are restricted to direct government subsidies and borrowings from international financial agencies and commercial banks. The latter is made possible by government subsidies

TABLE 6.1 Total outstanding loans to agriculture by source, Panama, 1977/78–1980/81 (millions of dollars)

| Source of credit | 1977 | 1978 | 1979 | 1980 |
|---|---|---|---|---|
| Agricultural Development Bank of Panama | 19.695 | 24.790 | 39.362 | 47.704 |
| National Bank of Panama[a] | 4.320 | 7.206 | 7.250 | . . . |
| Commercial banks[b] | 125.096 | 106.619 | 109.317 | 114.672 |

*Source*: Panama, Comision Bancaria Nacional; Banco de Desarrollo Agropecuario de Panama, *Memoria Anual*, various issues.

*Note*: Loans include crop and livestock loans and investment loans.

[a]Only 2 to 3 percent of the National Bank's loan portfolio is in agricultural loans.

[b]Includes Citibank, Chase Manhattan Bank, Banco Fiduciario, Banco de Colombia, Banco de Santander, Bank of America, Banco de Comercio Exterior, Marine Midland Bank, Sociedad de Bancos Suizos de Panama, and Banco Internacional.

TABLE 6.2 Sources and uses of funds, Agricultural Development Bank of Panama, 1980 (millions of dollars)

| Source of funds | | Use of funds | |
|---|---|---|---|
| *Internal* | | *Operating costs* | |
| Loan recovery[a] | 25.365 | Salaries and honoraria | 3.572 |
| Interest earnings | 4.802 | Other[b] | 1.517 |
| Government subsidy | 6.119 | Capital disbursements | 0.214 |
| Other[c] | 1.535 | | |
| *External* | | *Financial costs* | |
| Borrowing from commercial banks | 22.739 | Amortization | 19.391 |
| | | Interest | 3.802 |
| Borrowing from international agencies[d] | 9.056 | Other | .099 |
| | | *Loans* | 41.021 |
| Total | 69.616 | Total | 69.616 |

[a]Includes insurance indemnities paid by ISA.
[b]Vehicles, maintenance of offices, equipment, and so on.
[c]Sales of property and so on.
[d]Interamerican Development Bank, 8.311; U.S. Agency for International Development, 0.069; World Bank, 0.676.

and guarantees. The composition of its balance sheet is shown in table 6.2, which also reveals the importance of loan recovery to the bank's internal resources. A major proportion of the loan portfolio is committed to production credit (over 90 percent), and of this, 80 percent has an expected maturity of less than a year.[1]

Throughout its history, the BDA has experienced severe problems of loan recovery. The BDA authorities consider that production risks are the main source of poor loan performance (BDA various issues). In response to this belief, the government created the Agricultural Insurance Institute (Instituto de Seguro Agropecuario, or ISA) in 1975.[2] ISA is a public institution that is expected to work in partnership with the BDA. Its rapid growth was made possible by a government subsidy and a grant from the U.S. Agency for International Development, administered by the Inter-American Institute for Cooperation on Agriculture (IICA).[3] These resources provide for the administration costs, while the insurance premiums collected from farmers are expected to pay the indemnities. The premiums are calculated on an actuarial basis, though with limited information because of the short historical data base. Crop premiums vary between

1. The financial year runs from May 1 to April 30.

2. Although the program began insuring in the 1976–77 crop cycle, commercial operations were initiated only in 1977.

3. This latter program also included a strong component of technical assistance.

4 and 7 percent of coverage, and livestock premiums vary between 3 and 4 percent. Between 1976 and 1981, premium income allowed ISA to achieve an average historical loss ratio (indemnities divided by premiums) of less than 1. Because of severe losses in 1982, the average loss ratio increased sharply to around 3 for the period 1976 to 1982. ISA has also been successful in reinsuring its portfolio through the international reinsurance market, though the cost of doing this increased substantially after the severe losses of 1982.

In spite of ISA's rapid growth, it currently covers only approximately 25 percent of BDA's loan portfolio. However, coverage of loans for some individual crops is much larger. Some basic information about the BDA and ISA portfolios is shown in table 6.3. In matching these data, three clarifying comments are necessary. First, approximately 10 percent of

TABLE 6.3 Agricultural Development Bank of Panama (BDA) outstanding loans and Agricultural Insurance Institute of Panama (ISA) insurance coverage, Panama, 1977–82 (thousands of dollars)

| Item | 1977 | 1978 | 1979 | 1980 | 1981 | 1982 |
|---|---|---|---|---|---|---|
| *Loans* | | | | | | |
| Rice | 7,177 | 7,632 | 12,962 | 13,522 | ... | ... |
| Corn and sorghum | 2,477 | 2,432 | 3,457 | 4,622 | ... | ... |
| Industrial tomatoes | 1,038 | 1,068 | 1,063 | 1,806 | ... | ... |
| Vegetables | 1,053 | 1,399 | 2,047 | 2,959 | ... | ... |
| Cattle | 6,261 | 8,254 | 11,249 | 15,446 | ... | ... |
| Other[a] | 1,689 | 4,005 | 8,584 | 9,349 | ... | ... |
| Total | 19,695 | 24,790 | 39,362 | 47,704 | 52,372[b] | ... |
| *Insurance* | | | | | | |
| Rice | 0 | 911 | 2,438 | 3,338 | 5,080 | 8,892 |
| Corn and sorghum | 1,129 | 975 | 1,492 | 2,148 | 2,653 | 3,563 |
| Industrial tomatoes | 0 | 0 | 544 | 1,290 | 689 | 1,142 |
| Cattle | 0 | 748 | 3,556 | 6,307 | 4,605 | 3,563 |
| Other | 0 | 0 | 103 | 31 | 533 | 523 |
| Total | 1,129 | 2,634 | 8,133 | 13,114 | 13,560 | 17,683 |
| *Indemnities paid by ISA* | | | | | | |
| Rice | 0 | 5 | 38 | 68 | 184 | 2,129 |
| Corn and sorghum | 18 | 89 | 57 | 147 | 379 | 813 |
| Industrial tomatoes | 0 | 0 | 22 | 74 | 85 | 40 |
| Cattle | 0 | 8 | 64 | 112 | 214 | 132 |
| Other | 0 | 0 | 13 | 0 | 107 | 57 |
| Total | 18 | 102 | 194 | 401 | 969 | 3,171 |
| ISA loss ratio | 0.30 | 0.90 | 0.59 | 0.74 | 1.27 | 3.0[c] |

[a]Includes crops, other livestock, and investment loans, none of which are insured.
[b]Preliminary.
[c]Whole portfolio. The loss ratio for crops was 4.12.

ISA's portfolio (with some variations between years) are either loans from the National Bank of Panama or investments by individual producers. Second, ISA's coverage as a percentage of the amount lent per hectare increased from 80 percent in 1977 to 95 percent in 1981, but with some variation between crops.[4] Third, the BDA's expected loan recovery in a particular year is the figure to which one should add the indemnities paid by ISA. Unfortunately, this information is not available.

With these clarifications, the most directly observable benefit of ISA's activity is the payment of indemnities to the BDA. Between 80 and 90 percent of ISA's indemnities were paid to the BDA, and they were an important part of loan recovery for the BDA. As shown in table 6.3, these contributions have been quite significant in recent years, but certainly in 1981 and 1982 when serious drought and floods caused major losses. The amount that the bank would have recovered without ISA's program cannot be determined, nor can the extent of loan rescheduling that might have been required be known. In any event, it is clear that the BDA received indemnity income from ISA, and this increased its loan recovery.

Other effects of ISA's insurance on the BDA are observable from a comparison of the performance of a sample of insured and uninsured loans issued between 1974 and 1980 and maturing by June 1981. Loan performance for rice, corn, tomatoes, and vegetables is shown in table 6.4; that of coffee and livestock is in table 6.5. The main conclusions derived from this comparison for different crops are the following:

1. Insured loans on the average have slightly larger net returns than uninsured loans. However, the actual rate of interest is never equal to the agreed rate at issuance time (in nominal terms). This occurs because insured farmers not affected by disasters, or those not receiving indemnities, even if partially affected by disasters, delay some payments.
2. Insured loans have an actual duration nearly equal to their expected duration, and in almost all cases the actual duration for insured loans is significantly shorter than for uninsured loans. This means that by using insurance, the bank can reduce its bookkeeping costs, prosecute fewer overdue loans, and increase the turnover velocity of its capital.
3. Insured loans have more stable returns than uninsured loans (table 6.6).

These results support the arguments offered in the previous section in favor of credit insurance. They imply direct short-term benefits for the bank. However, it is not possible to resolve whether credit insurance encourages the bank to be less careful in its loan analysis and supervision.

4. For the 1981–82 cycle, for example, coverage of rice was 94.7 percent, of corn 96.5 percent, and of sorghum 72.4 percent. Sorghum is historically the crop with the largest loss ratio. Fortunately, however, sorghum represents a small portion of ISA's portfolio.

TABLE 6.4 Loan performance for rice, corn, industrial tomatoes, and vegetables, by size and type of loan, Agricultural Development Bank of Panama, 1974–80

| Item | Rice | | | Corn | | Industrial tomatoes | | Vegetables | |
|---|---|---|---|---|---|---|---|---|---|
| | Small | Medium | Large | Small | Medium | Small | Medium | Small | Medium |
| *Uninsured loans* | | | | | | | | | |
| Amount disbursed (dollars) | 449 | 5,013 | 21,638 | 440 | 1,366 | 433 | 1,619 | 505 | 2,376 |
| Nominal rate of interest (percent) | 9.25 | 9.61 | 9.69 | 8.88 | 8.84 | 8.69 | 9.00 | 8.75 | 9.37 |
| Amount collected (dollars) | 495 | 5,257 | 22,520 | 473 | 1,473 | 457 | 1,704 | 530 | 2,500 |
| Net interest (dollars) | 27 | 235 | 882 | 33 | 106 | 36 | 86 | 24.00 | 153.00 |
| Actual rate of interest (percent) | 6.41 | 5.33 | 5.36 | 7.57 | 6.73 | 5.64 | 7.08 | 5.72 | 6.80 |
| Expected duration (months) | 7.85 | 7.60 | 8.43 | 8.57 | 8.38 | 4.55 | 5.91 | 6.22 | 6.00 |
| Actual duration (months) | 13.20 | 11.74 | 12.06 | 12.81 | 13.50 | 14.17 | 12.80 | 11.70 | 9.96 |
| *Insured loans* | | | | | | | | | |
| Amount disbursed (dollars) | 589 | 4,722 | 22,275 | 748 | 2,286 | 394 | 1,597 | | |
| Nominal rate of interest (percent) | 10.10 | 10.36 | 11.60 | 9.50 | 9.96 | 9.17 | 10.83 | | |
| Amount collected (dollars) | 606 | 4,886 | 23,299 | 799 | 2,387 | 403 | 1,658 | | |
| Net interest (dollars) | 17 | 164 | 1,073 | 51 | 101 | 11 | 61 | | |
| Actual rate of interest (percent) | 8.67 | 5.86 | 6.78 | 9.24 | 8.75 | 8.86 | 9.95 | | |
| Expected duration (months) | 5.83 | 7.69 | 8.01 | 6.50 | 6.79 | 5.06 | 5.67 | | |
| Actual duration (months) | 4.00 | 7.19 | 8.33 | 8.58 | 8.29 | 4.50 | 4.83 | | |

*Source*: Banco de Desarrollo Agropecuario de Panama, "Sample of 900 loans issued between 1974 and 1980." See Pomareda (1984) for a description of the sampling procedure.

*Note*: Small loans, under $1,000; medium loans, $1,000–$10,000; large loans, over $10,000.

TABLE 6.5 Loan performance for coffee, livestock, and other recipients, by size and type of loan, Agricultural Development Bank of Panama, 1974–80

| | Coffee | | Livestock | | Other | | Credit to cooperatives |
|---|---|---|---|---|---|---|---|
| Item | Small | Medium | Small | Medium | Small | Medium | Large |
| *Uninsured loans* | | | | | | | |
| Amount disbursed (dollars) | 490 | 2,447 | 611 | 3,988 | 513 | 2,456 | 36,256 |
| Nominal rate of interest (percent) | 8.59 | 9.13 | 9.17 | 9.16 | 8.97 | 9.26 | 8.44 |
| Amount collected (dollars) | 524 | 2,594 | 704 | 4,574 | 540 | 2,635 | 37,867 |
| Net interest (dollars) | 33 | 147 | 93 | 586 | 28 | 179 | 1,611 |
| Annual rate of interest (percent) | 6.46 | 6.40 | 6.95 | 6.73 | 6.58 | 6.60 | 4.69 |
| Expected duration (months) | 10.81 | 10.51 | 31.33 | 37.36 | 15.57 | 11.36 | 14.10 |
| Actual duration (months) | 12.58 | 12.51 | 28.33 | 33.24 | 15.24 | 13.39 | 13.79 |
| *Insured loans* | | | | | | | |
| Amount disbursed (dollars) | | | | 5,034 | 693 | 3,703 | |
| Nominal rate of interest (percent) | | | | 12.08 | 9.67 | 10.07 | |
| Amount collected (dollars) | | | | 5,633 | 718 | 3,878 | |
| Net interest (dollars) | | | | 599 | 25 | 174 | |
| Actual rate of interest (percent) | | | | 9.42 | 6.58 | 6.49 | |
| Expected duration (months) | | | | 23.66 | 5.08 | 5.24 | |
| Actual duration (months) | | | | 15.08 | 6.67 | 8.85 | |

*Source*: See table 6.4.
*Note*: Small loans, under $1,000; medium loans, $1,000–$10,000; large loans, over $10,000.

TABLE 6.6 Variability of returns by size and type of loan, Agricultural Development Bank of Panama, 1974-80 (dollars)

| Crop or other recipient | Uninsured loans | | | Insured loans | | |
|---|---|---|---|---|---|---|
| | Small | Medium | Large | Small | Medium | Large |
| Rice | 104 | 376 | 1,734 | 10 | 144 | 428 |
| Corn and sorghum | 50 | 210 | [a] | 30 | 194 | [b] |
| Tomatoes | 34 | 160 | [a] | 6 | 26 | [b] |
| Vegetables | [a] | 244 | [a] | [b] | [b] | [b] |
| Coffee | 40 | 268 | [a] | [b] | [b] | [b] |
| Livestock | 130 | 866 | [a] | [b] | 56 | [b] |
| Other loans | 92 | 272 | [a] | 6 | 22 | [b] |
| Credit to cooperatives | [a] | [a] | 3,674 | [b] | [b] | ... |

*Source*: Pomareda (1984)

*Note*: Small loans, under $1,000; medium loans, $1,000–$10,000; large loans, over $10,000. Variability is measured as the sum of the absolute deviations from the mean return.

[a]Not issued by the Agricultural Development Bank.

[b]Not insured by Agricultural Insurance Institute of Panama.

Nor is it known the extent to which at least part of these benefits might have been obtained through better loan appraisal procedures and more diligent efforts to collect outstanding debts.

We turn now to a fuller analysis of the potential benefits of credit insurance on bank credit. Since one of the objectives of the BDA is to provide the largest amounts of credit possible to agriculture over time, it is necessary to consider the effect of insurance on the growth in lending.

## Bank Growth with and without Insurance

Banks are rather complex institutions to manage. Optimization of their asset and liability portfolios would provide a sound basis for bank management (Jessup 1980). In optimizing a bank's portfolio, it is necessary to consider the allocation of physical resources, the riskiness in returns on alternative investments, the need for liquidity, and the intertemporal transfer of funds. The above considerations have been integrated into a multiperiod linear programming model of the BDA. Only a brief summary of this model can be presented here; for a full description see Pomareda (1984).

Annual resource constraints are specified in the model for vehicles, loan officers' time, and collection officers' time. Liquidity requirements are incorporated through an equation that requires a balance of assets and liabilities with different liquidity indices. Risk is included for loan returns only and, as in chapter 3, through use of the mean absolute-deviation measure of variability (Hazell 1971). Intertemporal linkages are established through a multiperiod specification, in which the maturity of loans, securities, and borrowings initiated in year $t$, but maturing in subsequent years, is explicitly modeled. At the end of each year, the available funds are transferred within the model to the next period. Finally, institutional constraints are incorporated, which provide for a minimum of 2,000 small loans (less than $1,000), and a maximum of 2,722 insurance policies issued by ISA in the first year, with both numbers increasing by 5 percent each year thereafter.

Choices among sources and uses of funds in each of the ten years of the planning horizon are specified in considerable detail. Activities are included each year for all the loan classes in tables 6.4 and 6.5. Activities are also included for borrowing from international financial agencies and commercial banks, for savings and checking accounts of different sizes, and for investments in securities with different maturities. The model has a total of 298 equations and 510 activities. Bank management is assumed to be risk-averse, and in particular to behave in accordance with a mean-return standard-deviation utility function of the form $U = E - \phi\sigma$ (Baumol 1963; see also chapter 3). The model's objective function is the maximization of the sum of discounted utility over a ten-year planning horizon, plus the discounted value of terminal wealth. By varying the risk-aversion parameter, $\phi$, in the model's objective function, it is possible to evaluate the effects of insurance given different risk attitudes on the part of management.

The model was used to evaluate the impact of insurance on future bank growth and on other variables of relevance in managing the bank. In the first year of the planning horizon, ISA's coverage is approximately 25 percent of the total BDA portfolio. Since the growth in this coverage is restricted to 5 percent per year, what are being measured as the benefits of insurance do not imply full coverage of the BDA portfolio.

Under risk-neutral behavior ($\phi = 0$), insurance permits an increase in discounted utility from $196.42 million to $226.12 million, or by $29.7 million over ten years (table 6.7). When extreme risk aversion is assumed ($\phi = 3.15$), total utility is necessarily smaller. However, the introduction of insurance under extreme risk aversion increases the value of discounted utility from $181.92 million to $214.21 million, or by $32.3 million over ten years. The size of the utility gain from insurance is not therefore very sensitive to risk aversion. It should be remembered that these benefits are the result of several forces acting in the model as a result of insurance, including cost reductions, increases in loan returns, and a reduction in the riskiness of returns. The discounted sum of the standard deviation of returns (table 6.7) is actually very small relative to the objective function value. This accounts for the apparent unimportance of risk in the results. In other words, the gain in discounted utility in the model as a result of insurance is only marginally due to a reduction in the total riskiness of the loan portfolio.

TABLE 6.7 Results of ten-year crop credit insurance experiments, Agricultural Development Bank of Panama (BDA) model

| Year | With insurance: Risk-neutral ($\phi = 0.0$) | With insurance: Risk-averse ($\phi = 3.15$) | Without insurance: Risk-neutral ($\phi = 0.0$) | Without insurance: Risk-averse ($\phi = 3.15$) |
|---|---|---|---|---|
| | *Discounted sum of expected utility (millions of dollars)* | | | |
| 1-10 | 226.12 | 214.22 | 196.42 | 181.92 |
| | *Discounted sum of standard deviation of returns (millions of dollars)* | | | |
| 1-10 | 3.10 | 2.99 | 4.26 | 3.92 |
| | *Number of small loans*[a] | | | |
| 1-10 | 25,156 | 25,156 | 25,156 | 25,156 |
| | *Number of medium loans* | | | |
| 1-10 | 18,663 | 22,878 | 7,051 | 8,966 |
| | *Number of large loans* | | | |
| 1-10 | 18,331 | 18,161 | 19,127 | 26,063 |
| | *Number of insured loans* | | | |
| 1-10 | 33,566 | 33,566 | 0 | 0 |
| | *Value of BDA loans (millions of dollars)* | | | |
| 1 | 49.79 | 49.79 | 49.60 | 49.63 |
| 2 | 48.94 | 50.41 | 37.94 | 42.54 |
| 3 | 30.96 | 32.14 | 36.51 | 40.20 |
| 4 | 45.32 | 47.18 | 32.90 | 38.77 |
| 5 | 56.20 | 55.46 | 51.18 | 48.87 |
| 6 | 59.70 | 58.98 | 53.79 | 51.56 |
| 7 | 63.53 | 62.86 | 56.63 | 54.49 |
| 8 | 66.20 | 65.25 | 59.23 | 56.82 |
| 9 | 87.26 | 85.97 | 63.70 | 60.90 |
| 10 | 40.74 | 40.07 | 35.70 | 34.22 |
| 1-10 | 548.64 | 548.11 | 477.18 | 478.00 |
| | *Borrowings from commercial banks (millions of dollars)* | | | |
| 1 | 21.40 | 21.40 | 21.40 | 21.40 |
| 2 | 9.90 | 11.71 | 0.61 | 6.07 |
| 3 | 16.07 | 15.52 | 23.12 | 21.42 |
| 4 | 22.38 | 22.05 | 20.50 | 19.47 |
| 5 | 23.87 | 23.55 | 21.63 | 20.63 |
| 6 | 26.68 | 26.37 | 24.07 | 23.10 |
| 7 | 28.54 | 28.25 | 25.46 | 24.54 |
| 8 | 28.89 | 28.50 | 26.51 | 25.29 |
| 9 | 50.90 | 48.35 | 29.48 | 28.09 |
| 1-9 | 228.63 | 225.70 | 192.58 | 190.01 |

*Note*: Small loans, under $1,000; medium loans, $1,000–$10,000; large loans, over $10,000.
[a]The number of small loans is always equal to the minimum requirement of 2,000 loans in the first year, with a growth rate of 5 percent per year thereafter.

Given the bank's leverage requirements for a fixed ratio of liquid assets to outstanding loans, insurance can increase its financial strength and therefore its capacity to acquire more debt. In the risk-averse case, for example, total borrowing over the ten years could increase by $35.6 million, or 18.7 percent, when insurance is enforced. Increased loan recovery and borrowings allow for a faster growth of lending activities. In the risk-averse case, total lending over the ten years would increase by $70 million, or by 14.6 percent.

Insurance allows the issuance of a larger number of loans in both the risk-neutral and the risk-averse case (table 6.7). This is possible because of the increased availability of funds and the more efficient use of the bank's physical resources. The number of insured loans is equal to the maximum allowed within the stipulated growth rate for ISA. Although not reported in the tables, the shadow prices on the permitted number of policies are large, suggesting it would be beneficial to the BDA if ISA were given additional operating resources to issue a larger number of policies each year.

Insurance also enables the BDA to reduce its average administration costs per loan; from $1,135 to $956 in the risk-neutral case. But this savings of $179 per loan is barely larger than ISA's average administration cost per insurance contract (table 6.8). Credit insurance does not seem to be a very cost-effective way of reducing the average administration costs for the BDA.

## Interest Rate Policies as an Alternative to Credit Insurance

Credit insurance does lead to some significant improvements in bank earnings and growth, but the cost of providing it is high (table 6.8). It is perti-

TABLE 6.8 Administration costs of agricultural credit and insurance in Panama, 1976–82

| Source of credit | 1976 | 1977 | 1978 | 1979 | 1980 | 1981 | 1982 |
|---|---|---|---|---|---|---|---|
| *Agricultural Development Bank of Panama* | | | | | | | |
| Total cost (thousands of dollars) | ... | ... | 4,236 | 4,405 | 5,304 | ... | ... |
| Loans issued (number) | ... | ... | 5,473 | 5,556 | 8,020 | ... | ... |
| Loans outstanding (number)[a] | ... | ... | 1,350 | 1,642 | 1,667 | ... | ... |
| Total loans (number) | ... | ... | 6,823 | 7,198 | 9,687 | ... | ... |
| Average cost per loan (dollars) | ... | ... | 621 | 612 | 547 | ... | ... |
| *Agricultural Insurance Institute of Panama* | | | | | | | |
| Total cost (thousands of dollars) | 123 | 188 | 218 | 318 | 463 | 682 | 714 |
| Policies issued (number)[b] | 9 | 351 | 809 | 2,114 | 2,722 | 3,486 | 4,140 |
| Average cost per policy (dollars) | [c] | [c] | 269 | 151 | 167 | 196 | 173 |

*Source*: ISA, *Memoria Anual*, various issues; BDA, *Informe Anual*, various issues.

[a] 30 percent of loans issued in the previous year.

[b] In the case of livestock, includes outstanding policies issued in the previous year.

[c] Pilot years of the program.

nent to inquire whether the benefits of insurance to the BDA might not be more cheaply obtained if the government were simply to allow the bank to charge higher interest rates. To answer this question, additional model experiments were conducted.

Tables 6.9 and 6.10 show the effects on the BDA if all its loan interest rates were increased by 2 percent. The overall impact on bank earnings, lending, and growth is very similar to the changes achieved with credit insurance. However, the average cost of administering loans does not decline with the interest rate increase; in fact it increases by $44, or 3.8 percent. This is because of a modest decline in the average size of the loans issued. On the other hand, the costs of administering ISA are avoided with the interest rate approach, thereby offering the promise of substantial savings to the government in the form of reduced subsidy payments.

## Concluding Comments

Credit insurance has the potential to significantly improve bank earnings and growth. These gains have been demonstrated with empirical data and

TABLE 6.9 Average annual sources and uses of funds under alternative strategies, Agricultural Development Bank of Panama model (millions of dollars)

| Item | Without insurance | With insurance | Without insurance but a 2 percent increase in interest rates |
|---|---|---|---|
| *Source of funds* | | | |
| Internal | | | |
| Loan recovery and interest earnings | 52.62 | 58.89 | 58.91 |
| Government subsidy | 2.99 | 2.99 | 2.99 |
| Other | 0.24 | 0.24 | 0.24 |
| External | | | |
| Borrowings from commercial banks | 19.26 | 22.87 | 22.52 |
| Borrowings from international agencies | 1.79 | 1.79 | 1.79 |
| Total | 76.90 | 86.78 | 86.45 |
| *Use of funds* | | | |
| Operating costs | | | |
| Salaries and honoraria | 5.73 | 6.10 | 6.23 |
| Other operating costs | 0.17 | 0.13 | 0.12 |
| Financial costs | | | |
| Amortization | 20.84 | 24.29 | 24.14 |
| Interest | 2.76 | 3.16 | 3.14 |
| Loans | 47.40 | 53.10 | 52.82 |
| Total | 76.90 | 86.78 | 86.45 |

*Note*: All entries are averaged over the ten-year planning horizon in the model. Bank management is also assumed to be risk-neutral in these experiments.

TABLE 6.10 Effects of alternative strategies, Agricultural Development Bank of Panama model, assuming risk-neutral behavior, $\phi = 0$

| Item | Without insurance | With insurance | Without insurance but a 2 percent increase in interest rates |
|---|---|---|---|
| Discounted sum of expected utility (millions of dollars) | 196.420 | 226.120 | 224.843 |
| Discounted sum of standard deviation of returns (millions of dollars) | 4.264 | 3.100 | 4.547 |
| Small loans (number)[a] | 25,156 | 25,156 | 25,156 |
| Medium loans (number) | 7,051 | 18,663 | 6,995 |
| Large loans (number) | 19,127 | 18,331 | 21,704 |
| Total loans (number) | 51,334 | 62,150 | 53,855 |
| Average size of loans (dollars) | 10,858 | 7,674 | 10,369 |
| Average administration cost per loan (dollars) | 1,135 | 956 | 1,179 |
| Ratio of loan recovery to loan issuance[b] | 1.111 | 1.108 | 1.116 |

*Note*: Small loans, under $1,000; medium loans, $1,000–$10,000; large loans, over $10,000.
[a]The number of small loans is always equal to the minimum requirement of 2,000 loans in the first year, with a growth rate of 5 percent per year thereafter.
[b]Includes interest earnings.

within the context of a normative model of bank portfolio management. Interestingly, most of the gains from insurance to the bank do not arise from reductions in the variability of loan returns but from reduced collection costs, prompter repayment, greater loan turnover, and more efficient use of the bank's staff and other physical resources. Quite possibly, part of these gains might be achieved simply with improved management and better loan approval and supervision procedures. Perhaps the acid test of the value of credit insurance to the BDA is whether the bank would be willing to contribute to its cost, either directly by sharing the farmers' premium payments or through a reduction in the government's subsidy to its own operations.

A 2-percent increase in the interest rate charged on BDA loans would provide benefits to the bank comparable to those from credit insurance—and at a much lower cost to the government. However, increasing interest rates in this way would require an important departure in established government policy toward subsidized loans to farmers.

# II
# Insurance and Public Policy

# 7

# Should Crop Insurance Be Subsidized?

Ammar Siamwalla
Alberto Valdés

Crop insurance programs are promoted with two basic underlying concerns in mind. First, because agricultural production risks are thought to have a substantial effect on resource allocation, crop insurance is promoted as an instrument for reducing the misallocation costs so induced. Second, complemented with other policy instruments, crop insurance is thought to mitigate the ill effects of fluctuations in farmers' income. Thus the broad objectives are to reduce inefficiency and to achieve rural income stabilization, with the underlying premise that the social benefits exceed the costs of crop insurance programs.

In practice, government-supported crop insurance programs are also often used as a permanent income-transfer mechanism to benefit farmers; the cases of Brazil (chapter 14) and Mexico (chapter 8) may be cited as examples. Since the use of crop insurance for this purpose (rather than using more direct and efficient means) has very little intellectual basis other than political expediency, this last objective will not be discussed further in this chapter.

Critics of crop insurance allege two major shortcomings. First, it usually covers only yield variation and not price variation and thus contributes little to income stability. Second, crop insurance usually involves high social costs, due to moral hazard and adverse selection problems, and high administrative costs. With few exceptions, farmers are unwilling to pay the full cost of all-risk crop insurance, and thus they depend on a government subsidy. Farmers do, however, pay full costs of insurance on other important risks, such as hail and fire.

In the literature on risk management for agriculture, issues concerning the welfare economics of crop insurance are rarely discussed. (An exception is Roumasset 1978.) The major question examined in this chapter relates to the concern that a competitive market may not offer farmers adequate opportunities for risk pooling and risk shifting unless there is a subsidy. However, the fact that the insurance market is incomplete does not in itself imply that there is a true inefficiency. The question is whether the lack of crop insurance in developing countries can be attributed to market failure in crop insurance or to the fact that the real costs of insurance exceed its benefits.

## Preliminaries

Farmers cope with the inherent riskiness of agriculture in many ways. First, they may engage in activities by themselves that reduce either the probability of adverse events or the losses that result from such events. Several alternatives are analyzed in chapter 2. Other examples are the use of insecticide, which prevents infestation, or installation of a tube well, which lessens the losses from drought. These activities do not presuppose an effective capital or insurance market.

A second way to cope with risks is to pool them over time by adjusting assets and liabilities. This presupposes a functioning capital market. The costs of using this mode of risk pooling would vary with the efficiency of that market.

Finally there may be risk pooling across individuals, or risk sharing. Landlords and tenants share risks in a sharecropping contract. There is also some risk sharing between borrowers and lenders in the capital market, because of the possibility of default. Governments share some of the farmers' risks when the tax rate (whether for land tax or income tax) varies with the farmers' income. These types of risk sharing are really by-products of contracts and rules that have other purposes. Formal crop insurance is a unique institutional device whose sole function is to share farmers' risks with individuals who may include nonfarmers.

### *Price Risk, Yield Risk, and Income Risk*

If public policy is to be directed at risk reduction, its primary objective should be to lessen income risk. Broadly speaking, income is a product of output price and quantity from all income sources.[1] With some exceptions, public policy has addressed the price and quantity risks separately, simply because the instruments used to reduce them are different. Price risks are usually tackled through price stabilization schemes involving forward prices, or a variable trade tax, or a subsidy. The conventional market approach to quantity risks is crop insurance. A different approach, representing a direct attack on income risk, has been used in Australia in the form of a farm income stabilization scheme (see chapter 10). However, mitigating the effect of rural income fluctuations still requires more than one stabilization instrument.

1. As agriculture is modernized, the rising share of cash input costs may substantially increase the coefficient of variation of the net crop revenue. Input availability risk is also quite significant for many developing countries. The solution to this should be on the marketing and distribution side. Where this is not physically possible (as in the case of irrigation water), it may be regarded as another hazard to be insured.

In many instances, price will be more important than yield as a source of year-to-year variation in income. This was the case in the United States during the 1930s and 1940s (Johnson 1947). Under these conditions, the first and best solution is to reduce the amount of uncertainty through price policy. Crop insurance would then be supplemented when significant yield uncertainty exists.

Discussion of risk management recognizes that price and yield do not vary independently. The general presumption is that prices and quantities move in opposite directions, because it is thought that the major cause of variability comes from supply rather than demand. However, this presupposes that the product is not traded in the world market, or if so, the domestic price is insulated from the world price by policy. Usually, domestic prices are influenced by shifts in world prices, and unless a country accounts for a large share of the world market, price shifts need not be strongly correlated with fluctuations in domestic production.

Given also that individual farm yields are not always highly correlated with regional or national aggregates (see, for example, the evidence in chapter 2), then individual farm yields are only likely to be weakly correlated with prices. Therefore the conventional approach of treating price stabilization and crop insurance as parallel devices for solving the income risk problem of the farmer is justifiable. Additionally, most crops are in any case already subject to some form of government price intervention, in the form of either directly administered prices or indirect controls through trade measures. We recognize that some of these measures unintentionally destabilize prices further, but this additional price risk falls outside of the predictable risk situation for which actuarial calculations can be made.

If farm yields and prices are not weakly related, then providing crop insurance and price stability through separate policy instruments can present difficulties. If prices and quantities are negatively correlated, then provision of either price stabilization or crop insurance, by itself, would destabilize income. In such a case, the correct policy is to provide neither or both. Where covariation between individual farm yields and prices is positive, either price stabilization or crop insurance by itself would be at least partially beneficial. Obviously, the first item on the research agenda before a crop insurance program is launched should be an analysis of these covariations.

In those countries where a large proportion of farmers are subject to income taxes, probably the most efficient way to stabilize farm incomes is to build an insurance element into the tax system through such well-tried devices as income averaging. After thorough examination of the problem of rural income fluctuations, an Australian government commission recommended this method as the most effective means of income stabilization (see chapter 10). Elegant as this solution is, we shall ignore this possibility because most farmers in developing countries do not pay income taxes.

### *Risk Coverage*

If crop insurance primarily reduces yield risk, is the insurance to be provided against general risks or specific risks? If the insurance coverage is specific, then the precise set of events that will trigger an indemnity payment will be listed; for example, hailstorm, typhoon, or fire. If all yield risks are covered, then a realized yield below some specified level will trigger an indemnity payment regardless of cause. Obviously the latter type of coverage is more ambitious, and it is more difficult for the insuring agency because it is more susceptible to moral hazard. We believe this problem is so acute as to make general coverage insurance very expensive, if not practically infeasible, for most developing countries.

Concentration on insurance against specific and measurable risks tends to underplay the role of the public sector in reducing farmers' risks. It causes us to overlook one very important class of situations or uncertainties, for which there may be an important role for the public sector. These situations arise from the introduction of new technologies, in particular those that are the outcomes of public research activities.

When farmers are introduced to a new technology, they are being asked to take something of a leap into the dark. Their response to reduce that uncertainty has been to undertake certain information-gathering activities. Most frequently they start an experimental plot of their own, allocating only a portion of their land to the modern method (for example, a new variety), or they wait to see the results of a neighboring farm's experiment. Now this privately rational action can be socially quite wasteful, as many farmers are engaged in obtaining a better estimate of a single object—a yield distribution function.

A faster and more socially economical method may well be through a centralized research network. It could obtain not only a point estimate of the yield under a new technology but the whole yield distribution under the variety of hazards faced by the farmers. The research network would then disseminate the information to the farmers or to private insurance companies. In some countries farmers might not trust such information, in which case the public authorities might use the information to provide insurance coverage to farmers, at least for a few years after a new technology is introduced.

When a private firm such as a seed company introduces a new technology, the government could require that it introduce crop insurance along with it. This could dampen exaggerated claims for a particular input. However, if the risk is transferred from farmer to research or development agency, the latter may become risk-averse, delaying the introduction of new technology until they are absolutely certain about it. Even if the government takes up the risk burden through insurance, it imposes an excessive cost on research agencies. It would also be extremely difficult to assess the potential impact or true value of a new technology, given the likelihood of moral hazard by farmers.

## Potential Social Benefits of Crop Insurance

An argument for government-subsidized crop insurance is the possibility that a divergence between social and private returns would generate substantial externalities. If so, private firms may have insufficient incentive to provide insurance, and a subsidy would be necessary to bring the economy back to an optimum welfare position.

The key externality pinpointed by some advocates of crop insurance is the spillover effect on consumers. Hazell (1981) has argued that with the reduction in risk made possible by crop insurance, production of many crops will increase. "Increases in production induced by crop insurance will benefit consumers as well as producers. If demand is inelastic, average farm incomes may actually decline, and consumers will reap all the benefits. These distributional effects may require that governments, rather than private companies, establish crop insurance programs. Private insurance companies can only collect premiums from farmers. But governments, acting in the interest of society at large, could subsidize insurance for farmers when the cost can justifiably be recouped from consumers."

We attach particular importance to clarification of the logic for a subsidy, because public funds spent on crop insurance could be drawn from other worthwhile activities, such as primary education and physical infrastructure.[2] Thus the need exists for a cost-and-returns calculation to establish the case for public support of crop insurance.

Consider first a commodity market in a world without crop insurance. The supply curve for the commodity is given by $S_0$ in figure 7.1. Included in this supply curve is a risk premium component, for which the farmers have to be compensated because of production risks that cannot be shifted. In cases where farmers diversify into other safe crops at some cost to their average return, that cost is also included in the risk premium. Now suppose that a crop insurance system is introduced for which farmers pay the full cost. The insurance reduces the farmers' risk premium. Consequently, the new supply $S_1$ is below $S_0$. To simplify the exposition, we assume that both $S_0$ and $S_1$ refer to the supply in normal years, to abstract from short-run shifts around $S_0$ and $S_1$ due to random factors affecting

2. Judging from crop insurance programs in Japan, the United States, Brazil, and Mexico, public subsidies may have to equal two or three times the value of premiums collected. For example, in Brazil the federal budget covers 50 percent of the cost of the program (chapter 14). The national insurance program in Mexico (chapter 8) receives more than 80 percent of its total payments from government.

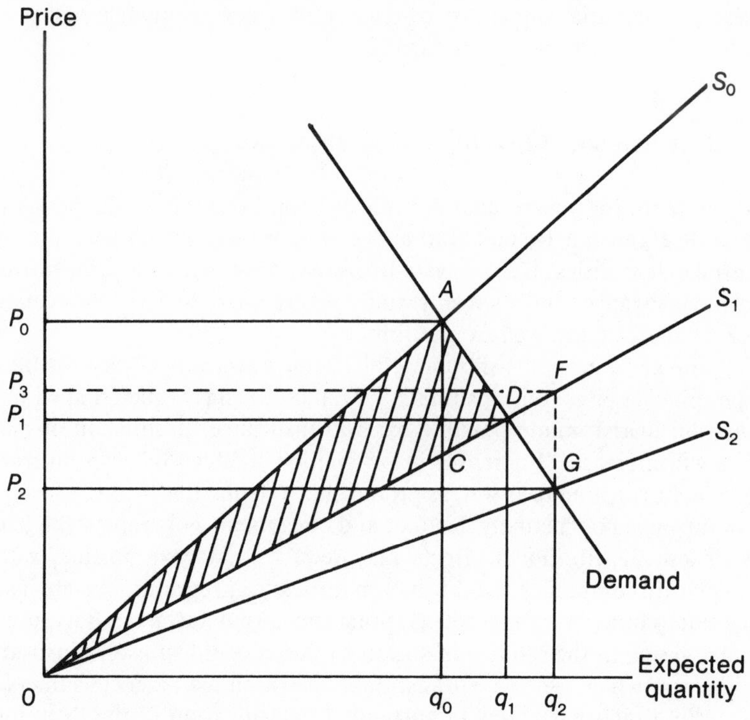


FIGURE 7.1 Welfare gains to consumers and producers from insurance

yields. We also assume that these supply curves correspond to an undistorted capital market situation. To the extent that demand is not perfectly elastic, there will be a fall in price from $P_0$ to $P_1$, with consumers capturing $P_0ADP_1$ as extra surplus.[3]

Initially, the cost to farmers of producing $q_0$ is reduced by $AC$, with a net savings of $OAC$. This cost savings is a sufficient incentive for farmers to buy crop insurance without any subsidy. Once crop insurance is generally adopted, the price will drop as mentioned. So the net welfare gain for producers will be $P_1DO$ less $P_0AO$, which may be positive or negative. Consumers will gain $P_0ADP_1$. For society as a whole, the net welfare gains are represented by the area $OAD$. The amount of the gain will depend on the magnitude of the shift of supply from $S_0$ to $S_1$, resulting from the adoption of insurance and the relevant demand and supply elasticities. Since the insurance premiums paid are included in $S_1$, the welfare gain depicted by the area $OAD$ measures the social value of the introduction of insurance

3. If demand is perfectly elastic, farmers will capture all the benefits of the innovation, and thus the case for a subsidy disappears.

net of its full cost.[4] This social return depends upon the farmers adopting the innovation, but this they will individually do, even if they end up collectively being the losers.

Is it possible that with the leakage of benefits to consumers, there is too little insurance provided, and hence the government should return that surplus to farmers by subsidizing crop insurance? Such a subsidy would in effect shift the supply curve further to some level such as $S_2$, causing the equilibrium production to shift from $q_1$ to $q_2$ and output price to come down further, from $P_1$ to $P_2$. It can be easily shown that the gain in consumers' and producers' surpluses consequent on such a subsidy is *ODG*, and this is always less than the subsidy cost $P_2P_3FG$. As the level of subsidy is arbitrary, there will always be a net social loss regardless of how much subsidy is provided.[5] There are therefore no grounds to believe leakages to consumers have to be corrected by a subsidy to either insurers or farmers.

The introduction of crop insurance can be regarded as a cost-reducing institutional innovation. If it is an economically viable innovation, it generates an increase in social welfare, or a "free lunch," some or all of which accrues to consumers. If demand is inelastic, there is a further transfer from producer to consumer, so that the farmers end up with a loss. This leakage to consumers, however, will not in any way prevent its adoption. As long as the cost of the insurance is fully paid by the farmers, there is no reason to suppose that a suboptimal amount of insurance will be provided.

It is instructive to compare crop insurance with new technologies produced by agricultural research. On the face of it, there are many similarities, even though one is a technological innovation and the other an institutional innovation. Both can generate social surplus. In the case of agricultural research, this has been demonstrably very large, but it is not entirely captured by the producers. Economists (even those highly skeptical about the value of government intervention) have generally pressed for strong public support of agricultural research (Schultz 1979). Would not the same arguments apply to crop insurance?

4. Potential profits to the providers of insurance are not considered; thus we assume implicitly a constant cost function for insurance over the relevant range. Also, the diagram shows the effect of insurance as a rotation of the supply curve, but the conclusion remains unchanged for a parallel, or any other, uniformly downward shift.

5. The gain to producers and consumers, *ODG*, can be expressed as:

$$\tfrac{1}{2} P_1 q_1 + P_1(q_2 - q_1) - \tfrac{1}{2} P_2 q_2 - \tfrac{1}{2}(P_1 - P_2)(q_2 - q_1).$$

This reduces to $\tfrac{1}{2} P_1 q_2 - \tfrac{1}{2} P_2 q_1$. The cost of the subsidy is $P_2P_3FG$, or $(P_3 - P_2)q_2$. Let the supply function be denoted by $P = \lambda\, q$, where $\lambda$ is the slope coefficient, then $P_1 = \lambda_1 q_1$, $P_2 = \lambda_2 q_2$, and $P_3 = \lambda_1 q_2$. Substituting into the above and taking the net social gain as $ODG - P_2P_3FG$, this reduces to $(\lambda_1 - \lambda_2)(\tfrac{1}{2} q_1 q_2 - q_2^2)$. Since $\lambda_1 > \lambda_2$, and $q_1 < q_2$, then the net social gain is always negative. The authors are grateful to Peter Hazell for this proof.

The key difference emerges if we examine the nature of the product of agricultural research. Agricultural research generates knowledge, which is a public commodity. One person's utilization of that knowledge will not in any way detract from another person's capacity to do so. If left to their own devices, private firms will not engage in the production of such knowledge, because there is no way that its output can be sold individually to each user.

Some research results, such as self-pollinated seed and agronomic practices, cannot be patented. Even when patenting is possible, charging for the use of that knowledge may cause underutilization, relative to the optimum, because the social marginal cost of its use is zero. Government support is therefore required for the production and distribution of such knowledge. Note that if the basic knowledge is used in the production of private commodities, such as hybrid seeds and pesticides, the arguments for public subsidy at this later stage disappear. Seed firms can recover the cost of seed production (including its development cost) from the farmers.

The picture for crop insurance is quite different. It is clear that crop insurance itself is not a public commodity. Firms can sell coverage to individual farmers and recover their costs from them. In this respect, their situation is analogous to the seed companies rather than to those engaged in basic agricultural research. However, it may be argued that the institutional innovation of crop insurance does require basic research, like the basic genetics that led to hybrid maize. There is considerable ignorance about the actuarial questions of crop insurance, which adds considerably to the risks facing private insurers. Farmers, too, lack information on how crop insurance would affect the distribution of their net income. This fact implies that the research activity rather than the crop insurance itself should be subsidized.

If learning by doing is less costly or more productive than learning by research, then the subsidy for crop insurance may be justified in its early stages. In that case, the objective of the subsidy should be narrowly specified and the subsidy withdrawn once the lesson has been learned. Such promotional pricing of crop insurance in the early years must be based on the premise that insurance pays in the long run. The Japanese case is quite instructive. They launched their crop insurance program in 1939. Despite the high quality of data Japan possessed even then, the actuarial basis for insurance was rather poor until about 1954 (Ahsan 1981).

There are two other social arguments for subsidized insurance that deserve discussion. First, small-scale farmers are particularly vulnerable to income fluctuations arising from production risks, but they are poorly placed to pay the full price of insurance. In order to avoid the decapitalization or destitution of these households in bad years, subsidized crop insurance may seem justified. However, subsidized insurance should be targeted only on this group, and it is by no means clear that insurance is the most efficient way of attaining this equity goal.[6]

Another argument for subsidized crop insurance arises from the spillover effects crop losses may have if factors of production, particularly labor, are immobile or if factor prices are rigid. Then the income losses originating from crop shortfalls affect nonfarmers through the multiplier process. In this case, normal crop insurance would provide an automatic stabilization mechanism. This is a valid and possibly even powerful argument for subsidizing crop insurance. However, research is needed on how the effects of crop losses percolate through to nonfarmers in the affected region. If these later losses are the economically more significant, then compensating farmers for crop losses would be insufficient, and public-works programs might be needed to reverse the fall in factor demand. Farmers could be compensated through these programs instead of through crop insurance.

Public-works programs and other relief measures, however, tend to be short term and discretionary. They do not provide the certainty of crop insurance. A significant advantage of crop insurance is that the recipient receives compensation as a right and not as a handout.

## Conclusions

This chapter explores the welfare economics of crop yield insurance, weighing arguments in favor of government intervention. Our conclusion is that the benefit of crop insurance is one of institutional innovation and must be weighed against the cost of inducing such an innovation. Any simple across-the-board subsidy of crop insurance is ruled out except perhaps as an infant industry. We have pinpointed the inadequacy of data and information as the major barrier to the development of a crop insurance industry. As these are classic examples of public commodities, the government's role in its provision is clear. We also favor other emergency relief measures rather than crop insurance to alleviate hardships that follow crop losses. The impact of such losses tends to fall on a much broader class than cultivators, the group normally covered by crop insurance.

6. This targeted approach would take care of Roumasset's valid objection (1978, pp. 99–100) that an across-the-board subsidy would not necessarily aid poor farmers more than wealthy ones.

# 8 Sectoral Analysis of the Benefits of Subsidized Insurance in Mexico

Luz María Bassoco
Celso Cartas
Roger D. Norton

Public crop insurance in Mexico has a history of only about twenty years, although private agricultural credit insurance has existed for a longer time. The public insurance agency (Aseguradora Nacional Agrícola y Ganadera, S.A., or ANAGSA) now insures more than a dozen annual crops. The area covered by ANAGSA programs has expanded by about 5 percent per year, and recently even more rapidly. ANAGSA now insures over eight-million hectares (table 8.1), or about half the total area in Mexico sown with annual crops.

In the two-year period 1981–82, maize alone accounted for about 43 percent of the insured area, followed by beans with 16 percent, sorghum with 15 percent, wheat with 8 percent, and soybeans, safflower, and cotton each with 3 percent. The emphasis on basic food crops has increased sharply in recent years, as witnessed by the following statistics on the percentage of the insured area sown in maize and beans: 1976, 45 percent; 1977, 42 percent; 1978, 40 percent; 1979, 41 percent; 1980, 56 percent; 1981, 60 percent; 1982, 57 percent. This new policy emphasis was part of the program orientation of the national food plan (Sistema Alimentario Mexicano, or SAM).

Nevertheless, from its inception Mexico's crop insurance program has contained an important redistributional element. The beneficiaries of the agrarian reform (*ejidatarios*) pay much lower premiums than private farmers do. These variations in premiums do not, and are not intended to, reflect differences in average levels of compensation. On the other hand, increased production efficiency is also one of the motivations of the ANAGSA programs. The SAM programs increased the subsidy element in the insurance premiums, with the explicit aim of providing incentives for increased production of basic crops.

These comments indicate that, from the viewpoint of the Mexican government, the crop insurance program should not be evaluated in terms of any single social goal, but rather it has to be reviewed in the light of multiple policy preferences. This is consistent with Mexico's agricultural

The research reported here does not necessarily reflect the official views of the Mexican government.

TABLE 8.1 Cropping area insured by ANAGSA, Mexico, 1976–82 (thousand hectares)

| Crop | 1976 | 1977 | 1978 | 1979 | 1980 | 1981 | 1982 |
|---|---|---|---|---|---|---|---|
| Sesame | 55 | 65 | 84 | 118 | 145 | 69 | 135 |
| Alfalfa | 0 | 0 | 4 | a | 0 | 10 | 19 |
| Cotton | 146 | 232 | 199 | 205 | 212 | 225 | 240 |
| Rice | 47 | 69 | 42 | 68 | 94 | 136 | 172 |
| Safflower | 105 | 123 | 158 | 164 | 155 | 275 | 198 |
| Barley | 0 | 0 | 0 | 0 | 0 | 69 | 65 |
| Soybeans | 74 | 140 | 100 | 0 | 69 | 204 | 254 |
| Beans | 471 | 331 | 248 | 269 | 767 | 1,163 | 1,307 |
| Maize | 1,028 | 1,160 | 1,017 | 924 | 2,107 | 3,259 | 3,459 |
| Maize, beans[b] | 0 | 0 | 0 | 20 | 4 | 0 | 0 |
| Potatoes | 0 | 0 | 4 | 5 | 2 | 0 | 3 |
| Sorghum | 564 | 514 | 517 | 495 | 830 | 1,062 | 1,229 |
| Wheat | 348 | 348 | 318 | 206 | 294 | 512 | 675 |
| Others | 477 | 541 | 455 | 504 | 486 | 435 | 570 |
| Total | 3,315 | 3,523 | 3,146 | 2,978 | 5,165 | 7,419 | 8,326 |

*Source*: ANAGSA, *Annual Report*, various issues.
[a]Less than 500 hectares.
[b]Intercropped.

policy formation in general, for at least the past three presidential administrations (Mexico, Ministry of the Presidency 1973; Sistema Alimentario Mexicano 1979).

Given these circumstances, this chapter attempts to provide a quantification of the effects of Mexico's crop insurance. These effects are measured in a multivariate way, including changes in producer income, sector income, employment, consumer surplus, agricultural income distribution, and other variables. The analysis is carried out via parametric solution of the Mexican agricultural model, CHAC, with varying assumptions about the riskiness of production decisions and the degree of insurance coverage extended to farmers.[1]

## Mexican Approaches to Crop Insurance

Until recently agricultural insurance in Mexico operated along the following principles:

1. It indemnified the producer for all his cultivation costs when these were totally or partially lost because of drought, frost, hailstorms, hurricane-

1. For a detailed description of CHAC see Duloy and Norton (1975), Bassoco and Rendon (1973), Bassoco and Norton (1983), and Norton and Solis (1983).

force winds, fire, crop disease and infestations, or excessive rainfall or floods.

2. The insurance coverage was calculated per hectare and did not exceed the total costs incurred through the harvest stage. Nor could it exceed 70 percent of the value of the anticipated harvest.
3. The insurance coverage began from the day that the crop germinated or took root after transplanting.

In 1980, several important changes were made in these provisions and in other elements of the operation of the insurance program. The coverage was raised from 70 to 80 percent of the anticipated harvest, and changes were made in the types of risks covered. Risks now covered include exceptionally hot and cold spells, failure of the seed to germinate, inability of the farmer to carry out planting because of poor weather, and other problems beyond the control of the farmer. Insurance protection is now in effect from the date of land preparation to the end of the harvest. (Previously, protection came into force when the plants germinated.)

In addition to the new, regular insurance programs of ANAGSA, some farmers now receive more extensive coverage under the program of shared risk (*riesgo compartido*). This program was spelled out in the Law of Agricultural Insurance and Peasant Livelihood enacted on December 29, 1980. This law provides for indemnification of farmers for 100 percent of their cultivation costs that are totally or partially lost owing to risks adumbrated in the legislation. The new definition of cultivation costs for purposes of insurance coverage now includes labor costs, interest due on agricultural credit, and the insurance premium itself, as long as total costs do not exceed the total anticipated value of the harvest. The shared-risk program departs from previous practices in that it insures participating farmers against variations in income and not just against variations in yields. However, this program has remained quite small relative to the regular insurance program (table 8.2).

TABLE 8.2 Insurance coverage under the shared-risk program, Mexico, 1980–82 (thousand hectares insured)

| Crop | 1980 | 1981 | 1982 |
|---|---|---|---|
| Beans | 13 | 30 | 2 |
| Maize | 6 | 43 | 19 |
| Maize, beans[a] | [b] | 0 | 0 |
| Wheat | 2 | 5 | 1 |
| Total | 21 | 78 | 22 |

*Source*: ANAGSA.
[a] Intercropped.
[b] Less than 500 hectares.

ANAGSA now subsidizes most of the insurance premiums. (Premiums for each crop, by district, are shown in table 8.3. A description of the rain-fed districts—rainfall and altitude—is given in table 8.4.) The total subsidy outlay rose sharply in 1980 and 1981, to a level of about 15-billion *pesos* (The figure for 1982 is for planned operations.)

| Year | Million *pesos* |
|---|---|
| 1970 | 129.3 |
| 1971 | 161.8 |
| 1972 | 172.2 |
| 1973 | 233.0 |
| 1974 | 493.8 |
| 1975 | 783.0 |
| 1976 | 899.4 |
| 1977 | 627.9 |
| 1978 | 877.7 |
| 1979 | 1,295.9 |
| 1980 | 5,224.8 |
| 1981 | 15,188.5 |
| 1982 | 17,305.4 |

## The Design of the Model Experiments

The analyses of the insurance programs were carried out via the solutions of the Mexican national agricultural model, CHAC. It is a static equilibrium model, covering all the major short-cycle crops in Mexico. On product markets, it generates market clearing prices and quantities in the face of downward-sloping demand curves and price-responsive supply sets. In each of the producing regions there are numerous alternative crops and technologies, so the model's response to a price change is governed implicitly by cross-price elasticities of supply as well as by own-price elasticities. The price (return) for farm labor also is endogenous, and possibilities are specified for interdistrict and interregional migration of field labor. Resource constraints are defined on a monthly basis in each district for land, labor, and water, in order to incorporate the major determinants of crop rotation patterns.

The deterministic part of the model's objective function is the maximization of consumer and producer surplus in all product markets. Following Samuelson (1952), this leads to simulations of the behavior of an atomistic market, in which no one producer can influence the market price with his own production. Some kinds of market imperfections have been incorporated into the model. Differing degrees of access to marketing channels and permanent differences in product quality (owing to differ-

TABLE 8.3 Mexican crop insurance premiums with subsidy and without subsidy, 1981 (*pesos* per hectare)

| District and crops | Premium without subsidy | Premium with subsidy |
|---|---|---|
| ***Irrigated*** | | |
| Río Colorado | | |
| cotton | 915 | 346 |
| sorghum | 692 | 278 |
| Hermosillo | | |
| wheat | 374 | 185 |
| Río Yaqui | | |
| safflower | 418 | 227 |
| maize | 365 | 195 |
| soybeans | 382 | 165 |
| wheat | 374 | 185 |
| Culiacán-Humaya | | |
| soybeans | 584 | 251 |
| wheat | 412 | 167 |
| El Fuerte | | |
| rice | 429 | 163 |
| beans | 387 | 119 |
| soybeans | 584 | 251 |
| wheat | 412 | 167 |
| El Bajío | | |
| barley | 272 | 105 |
| beans | 506 | 207 |
| maize | 600 | 239 |
| Other Northwest districts | | |
| cotton | 660 | 339 |
| rice | 429 | 173 |
| cucumbers | 750 | 363 |
| sorghum | 308 | 156 |
| wheat | 412 | 167 |
| Northeast districts (including La Laguna) | | |
| cotton | 693 | 274 |
| safflower | 389 | 163 |
| maize | 368 | 152 |
| Chihuahua and Durango | | |
| cotton | 693 | 274 |
| safflower | 158 | 146 |
| wheat | 415 | 188 |
| Other Central districts | | |
| barley | 377 | 130 |
| beans | 566 | 283 |
| chickpeas | 150 | 67 |
| Southern districts | | |
| green chiles | 470 | 223 |
| beans | 302 | 97 |
| watermelon | 917 | 416 |

TABLE 8.3 *Continued*

| District and crops | Premium without subsidy | Premium with subsidy |
|---|---|---|
| *Rain-fed* | | |
| District B | | |
| sorghum | 178 | 80 |
| District C | | |
| safflower | 414 | 164 |
| maize | 316 | 121 |
| District E | | |
| safflower | 414 | 164 |
| maize | 316 | 121 |
| sorghum | 260 | 114 |
| District G | | |
| safflower | 145 | 62 |
| maize | 157 | 62 |
| sorghum | 191 | 72 |
| District 5 | | |
| maize | 157 | 62 |
| sorghum | 191 | 72 |
| District 6 | | |
| maize | 400 | 154 |
| District 7 | | |
| maize | 400 | 154 |
| wheat | 299 | 100 |
| District 8 | | |
| maize | 396 | 147 |
| District 9 | | |
| maize | 129 | 45 |
| sesame | 283 | 108 |
| sorghum | 182 | 73 |
| District 10 | | |
| maize | 532 | 177 |
| District 11 | | |
| maize | 398 | 96 |
| District 12 | | |
| maize | 450 | 163 |
| District 13 | | |
| rice | 546 | 241 |
| maize | 511 | 224 |
| sorghum | 448 | 187 |
| District 14 | | |
| soybeans | 470 | 197 |
| maize | 446 | 125 |
| District 15 | | |
| sesame | 316 | 132 |
| maize | 511 | 224 |

*Source*: ANAGSA.

*Note*: These premiums were aggregated to the CHAC spatial definitions on the basis of data supplied by ANAGSA. Geographical locations of rain-fed districts: Northwest, B, C, E; North Central and Northeast, G, 5, 6, 7; Central Plateau, 8, 9, 10, 11, 12; South, 13, 14, 15. Their precipitation and altitude are given in table 8.4.

TABLE 8.4 Annual precipitation and altitude, rain-fed agricultural districts, Mexico

| Rain-fed district | Annual precipitation (millimeters) | Altitude (meters) |
|---|---|---|
| B | 200-400 | 0-500 |
| C | 600-800 | 0-500 |
| E | 800-1,000 | 0-500 |
| G | 400-600 | 0-500 |
| 5 | 600-800 | 0-500 |
| 6 | 400-600 | 1,500-2,000 |
| 7 | 600-800 | over 2,000 |
| 8 | over 1,000 | 500-1,000 |
| 9 | 600-800 | 500-1,000 |
| 10 | 800-1,000 | 1,000-1,500 |
| 11 | 400-600 | 1,500-2,000 |
| 12 | 600-800 | 1,500-2,000 |
| 13 | 400-600 | 1,500-2,000 |
| 14 | over 1,000 | 0-500 |
| 15 | over 1,000 | over 2,000 |

ences in soils, climate, and so on) are reflected in constant interregional price differentials. These differentials are added to the national market clearing price in order to obtain the spatial prices that affect producer behavior. Existing input subsidies (including the implicit subsidy on irrigation water) are incorporated in the input-cost coefficients, so that the model simulations are conducted in as realistic a manner as possible. The tendency of subsistence farmers to rely on retention of basic foods is reflected in basic food consumption constraints (for some farm groups) plus parameters that change the wholesale/retail price differentials, which are associated with use of the market rather than home retentions, to meet these constraints. Finally, the technological dualism of agriculture is reflected in the much narrower range of production choices and lower yields faced by subsistence farmers, as opposed to commercial farmers.

Risk considerations for producers are specified in two components: (1) matrices that generate, as part of the solution, measures of the income variability for farmers associated with the endogenous cropping patterns; and (2) risk-aversion parameters in the objective function. As in chapter 3, the latter are based on local linearizations of $(E, V)$ utility functions (Baumol 1963; Markowitz 1959), so that they are expressed in terms of expected income and its standard deviation. The procedure for developing an endogenous measure of income variability (that is, its standard deviation) was developed by Hazell (1971), and it has been adapted to the sector-wide context by Hazell and Scandizzo (1974).

Thus the total objective function is a risk-modified measure of consumer and producer surplus over all agricultural product markets. In nonlinear form it may be written

$$\text{Max } Z = x'M(A - 0.5BMx) - C'x - \phi(x'\Omega x)^{1/2}, \tag{1}$$

where

- $x$ is a vector of cropping activity levels (in *hectares*);
- $M$ is a diagonal matrix of average yields per *hectare*;
- $C$ is a vector of cost coefficients;
- $A, B$ are coefficient matrices of a linear-demand structure, and $B$ is assumed to be diagonal;
- $\phi$ is a risk-aversion parameter;
- $\Omega$ is an aggregate of individual farm covariance matrices of activity revenues. (See Hazell and Scandizzo 1974; Hazell, Norton, Parthasarathy, and Pomareda 1983).

A set of resource constraints is also added to the model in the form

$$Dx \leq r. \tag{2}$$

Forming the relevant Lagrangian function, $L$, then, apart from the feasibility conditions, the necessary first-order conditions of the model are the following:

$$\frac{\partial L}{\partial x_j} = m_j(a_j - b_j m_j x_j) - c_j - \phi(x'\Omega x)^{-1/2}\Sigma_i \omega_{ij} x_i$$

$$- \Sigma_k d_{kj} \lambda_k \leq 0, \tag{3}$$

$$\frac{\partial L}{\partial x_j} \cdot x_j = 0. \tag{4}$$

where the $\lambda_k$ are the dual variables associated with equation 2, and where $a_j$, $b_j$, $c_j$, $m_j$, $d_{kj}$ and $\omega_{ij}$ are elements of the matrices $A$, $B$, $C$, $M$, $D$ and $\Omega$, respectively.

For each cropping activity that is nonzero in the optimal solution, the term $(a_j - b_j m_j x_j)$ equals the expected value of price, so

$$E(P_j) = \frac{1}{m_j}(c_j + \Sigma_k d_{kj} \lambda_k + \phi(x'\Omega x)^{-1/2}\Sigma_i \omega_{ij} x_i). \tag{5}$$

Equation 5 may be interpreted as saying that the expected value of price equals the expected value of the marginal cost of production, where the three terms in marginal cost represent the cost of purchased inputs, the opportunity cost of fixed resources, and a risk-cost term. The sign of the marginal risk-cost term $\Sigma_i \omega_{ij} x_i$ affects the value of $x_j$ in the optimal solution. Products with large variances of income or revenues, which are positively correlated with the revenues of most other products, will tend to have a positive risk-cost term, and hence lower output under risk-averse behavior. For further aspects of the methodology see Hazell and Scandizzo (1974).

This kind of model is used in a comparative statics manner. That is, it does not give information regarding the time path of the variables, but rather it simulates a new equilibrium conditional on changes in parameter values or resource endowments. Such analysis is reported extensively in Bassoco and Norton (1983).

The role of crop insurance can be reflected in the model in two ways: in terms of effects on attitudes toward risk (risk preferences) and in terms of the objective variability of farm incomes. We employ both methods and hence generate two sets of numerical insurance experiments. One set computes estimates of the effects of a "perfect" insurance program, which totally eliminates risk considerations from the farmer's decision function. The other set simulates as closely as possible the consequences of recent alternative formulations of the ANAGSA insurance program.

To implement the initial set of experiments, parametric variations are conducted on the risk-aversion parameter, $\phi$. Clearly, it is not possible to associate intermediate values of $\phi$ ($0 \leq \phi \leq \phi^*$, where $\phi^*$ is the base value) with degrees of effectiveness of the insurance programs, since insurance does not change behavioral attitudes to given levels of risk. However, it is possible to say that $\phi = 0$ corresponds to the case in which risk concerns are totally absent; that is, the insurance program removes all variability in farm incomes. The implicit assumptions are that the insurance scheme is actuarially fair and administrative costs are fully subsidized. The case of $\phi = 1$ is the base for comparative purposes and corresponds to a reasonable level of risk aversion (see chapter 3).

In the second experiment, which simulates the ANAGSA program that prevailed until recently, farmers are compensated if their yields fall below 80 percent of the normal yield for each crop and region, taking into account the production technology used. The model is solved under two different assumptions about the subsidy content of the premiums: without subsidy and with subsidy at prevailing rates. (The shared-risk program under which farmers are compensated for variations in gross revenue rather than just yields is not analyzed here. The government does not intend to expand this scheme much beyond the rain-fed areas currently covered, hence its impact on sectoral aggregates will remain tiny. Anyway, a detailed analysis of the scheme within the rain-fed areas is reported in chapter 3.)

For the last experiments, the objective risk parameters of the model are modified as described in chapter 3—the time series of past values of gross revenues by crop and district are modified as if the revised insurance program had been operative in those years. This corresponds to a new evaluation on the part of farmers of how the revised insurance program would affect income fluctuations over time, assuming that their perceptions of the insurance program are correct.

Before reviewing the model solutions proper, it is useful to examine the variability of crop returns in Mexico. Tables 8.5 and 8.6 contain measures of the variability in prices, yields, and incomes based on a ten-year time series of yields and prices by locality (from 1970 to 1979). Table 8.5 illustrates two facts: that farm incomes in Mexico are unstable and that the degree of their instability varies over crops and locations. The coefficient of variation (the standard deviation divided by the mean) ranges from 0.12 (maize in Río Yaqui) to 1.38 (oats in the north-central irrigated districts).

The coefficient of variation of income usually is greater than each of the component coefficients of variation of prices and yields. Interestingly, prices tend to be more unstable than yields.

TABLE 8.5 Coefficients of variation for price, yield, and income, and optimal cropping patterns under alternative assumptions about risk behavior, Mexico, 1970–79

| | Coefficient of variation | | | Production[a] | |
|---|---|---|---|---|---|
| District and crop | Price | Yield | Income | $\phi = 1$ | $\phi = 0$ |
| *Irrigated* | | | | | |
| Río Colorado | | | | | |
| cotton | 0.64 | 0.22 | 0.79 | 276.7 | 42.7 |
| alfalfa | 0.40 | 0.17 | 0.46 | 1,052.0 | 1,052.0 |
| wheat | 0.31 | 0.16 | 0.48 | 0.0 | 437.1 |
| Hermosillo | | | | | |
| wheat | 0.38 | 0.11 | 0.49 | 485.0 | 480.4 |
| beans | 0.44 | 0.22 | 0.35 | 8.2 | 0.0 |
| sorghum | 0.45 | 0.17 | 0.65 | 0.0 | 33.6 |
| Río Yaqui | | | | | |
| safflower | 0.41 | 0.24 | 0.50 | 7.7 | 0.0 |
| flaxseed | 0.50 | 0.13 | 0.55 | 14.2 | 14.2 |
| soybeans | 0.41 | 0.13 | 0.47 | 178.2 | 0.0 |
| wheat | 0.39 | 0.18 | 0.56 | 1,002.8 | 765.8 |
| maize | 0.37 | 0.12 | 0.12 | 0.0 | 73.4 |
| watermelons | 0.40 | 0.79 | 0.63 | 0.0 | 418.6 |
| Culiacán-Humaya | | | | | |
| rice | 0.56 | 0.21 | 0.70 | 257.3 | 261.6 |
| chiles | 0.48 | 0.36 | 0.67 | 42.2 | 0.0 |
| tomatoes | 0.30 | 0.37 | 0.53 | 383.9 | 649.9 |
| melon | 1.07 | 0.31 | 1.19 | 202.3 | 277.2 |
| soybeans | 0.42 | 0.18 | 0.49 | 35.1 | 0.0 |
| wheat | 0.34 | 0.19 | 0.48 | 40.3 | 0.0 |
| El Fuerte | | | | | |
| alfalfa | 0.32 | 0.18 | 0.46 | 68.0 | 68.0 |
| rice | 0.57 | 0.18 | 0.58 | 58.6 | 64.8 |
| chiles | 0.52 | 0.53 | 0.78 | 2.5 | 0.0 |
| chickpeas | 0.47 | 0.23 | 0.53 | 0.2 | 0.0 |
| tomatoes | 0.51 | 0.36 | 0.43 | 65.4 | 17.3 |
| potatoes | 0.52 | 0.21 | 0.65 | 25.8 | 0.0 |
| wheat | 0.35 | 0.17 | 0.54 | 960.1 | 982.3 |

TABLE 8.5 *Continued*

| District and crop | Coefficient of variation | | | Production[a] | |
|---|---|---|---|---|---|
| | Price | Yield | Income | $\phi = 1$ | $\phi = 0$ |
| El Bajío | | | | | |
| garlic | 0.38 | 0.17 | 0.42 | 24.3 | 0.0 |
| alfalfa | 0.67 | 0.37 | 0.55 | 244.0 | 244.0 |
| peanuts | 0.42 | 0.29 | 0.46 | 53.0 | 10.2 |
| onions | 0.30 | 0.21 | 0.50 | 18.4 | 0.0 |
| barley | 0.28 | 0.12 | 0.31 | 15.7 | 18.4 |
| beans | 0.49 | 0.31 | 0.58 | 30.4 | 89.8 |
| chickpeas | 0.38 | 0.23 | 0.43 | 52.4 | 16.8 |
| sorghum | 0.44 | 0.15 | 0.54 | 206.9 | 34.6 |
| cucumbers | 0.69 | 0.11 | 0.66 | 0.0 | 106.2 |
| Other Northwest districts | | | | | |
| rice | 0.67 | 0.16 | 0.78 | 142.8 | 61.6 |
| beans | 0.51 | 0.27 | 0.52 | 119.5 | 210.2 |
| cucumbers | 0.45 | 0.32 | 0.81 | 40.4 | 0.9 |
| watermelons | 0.33 | 0.22 | 0.45 | 55.2 | 0.0 |
| wheat | 0.38 | 0.19 | 0.54 | 823.4 | 751.0 |
| alfalfa | 0.39 | 0.27 | 0.61 | 514.0 | 514.0 |
| tomatoes | 0.34 | 0.17 | 0.39 | 0.0 | 63.5 |
| sorghum | 0.45 | 0.15 | 0.38 | 0.0 | 84.4 |
| Northeast districts (including La Laguna) | | | | | |
| alfalfa | 0.52 | 0.35 | 0.24 | 771.0 | 771.0 |
| cotton | 0.73 | 0.29 | 0.84 | 248.9 | 385.3 |
| safflower | 0.42 | 0.19 | 0.57 | 167.2 | 45.5 |
| maize | 0.40 | 0.21 | 0.48 | 369.6 | 531.0 |
| sorghum | 0.32 | 0.15 | 0.29 | 89.4 | 0.0 |
| Chihuahua and Durango | | | | | |
| cotton | 0.66 | 0.22 | 0.61 | 383.9 | 264.5 |
| alfalfa | 0.33 | 0.06 | 0.34 | 687.0 | 687.0 |
| safflower | 0.42 | 0.19 | 0.57 | 59.8 | 0.0 |
| onions | 0.39 | 0.53 | 0.81 | 14.3 | 312.1 |
| oats | 1.03 | 0.41 | 1.38 | 0.0 | 52.5 |
| peanuts | 1.02 | 0.24 | 0.58 | 0.0 | 6.7 |
| Other Central districts | | | | | |
| alfalfa | 0.26 | 0.50 | 0.45 | 10,624.2 | 10,642.2 |
| sugarcane | 0.41 | 0.14 | 0.55 | 8,747.5 | 6,252.3 |
| barley | 0.33 | 0.09 | 0.40 | 586.1 | 583.4 |
| chiles | 0.54 | 0.32 | 0.48 | 76.9 | 226.5 |
| strawberries | 0.42 | 0.28 | 0.53 | 96.3 | 96.3 |
| beans | 0.43 | 0.18 | 0.54 | 390.9 | 300.3 |
| lima beans | 0.60 | 0.47 | 0.65 | 19.5 | 0.0 |
| tomatoes | 0.42 | 0.21 | 0.51 | 348.4 | 0.0 |
| maize | 0.33 | 0.12 | 0.45 | 736.5 | 1,261.9 |
| sorghum | 0.40 | 0.21 | 0.47 | 205.1 | 0.0 |
| wheat | 0.35 | 0.28 | 0.50 | 94.3 | 0.0 |
| garlic | 0.46 | 0.28 | 0.43 | 0.0 | 24.1 |
| chickpeas | 0.39 | 0.27 | 0.46 | 0.0 | 28.9 |
| safflower | 0.38 | 0.33 | 0.54 | 0.0 | 179.4 |

TABLE 8.5 *Continued*

| District and crop | Coefficient of variation | | | Production[a] | |
|---|---|---|---|---|---|
| | Price | Yield | Income | $\phi = 1$ | $\phi = 0$ |
| Southern districts | | | | | |
| chiles | 0.24 | 0.27 | 0.34 | 214.3 | 119.8 |
| beans | 0.54 | 0.13 | 0.52 | 124.4 | 147.2 |
| watermelons | 0.38 | 0.25 | 0.59 | 43.5 | 52.1 |
| *Rain-fed* | | | | | |
| District B | | | | | |
| sesame | 0.44 | 0.78 | 1.17 | 0.4 | 6.1 |
| maize | 0.40 | 0.39 | 0.42 | 4.4 | 12.4 |
| District C | | | | | |
| safflower | 0.42 | 0.31 | 0.31 | 9.2 | 0.0 |
| beans | 0.53 | 0.29 | 0.37 | 1.5 | 0.0 |
| sesame | 0.44 | 0.22 | 0.44 | 2.3 | 0.0 |
| maize | 0.36 | 0.29 | 0.27 | 73.1 | 104.3 |
| sorghum | 0.44 | 0.74 | 0.98 | 16.9 | 0.0 |
| District E | | | | | |
| safflower | 0.42 | 0.32 | 0.30 | 8.2 | 0.0 |
| beans | 0.54 | 0.31 | 0.36 | 10.1 | 0.0 |
| maize | 0.36 | 0.31 | 0.29 | 37.4 | 68.4 |
| sorghum | 0.44 | 0.78 | 1.03 | 28.0 | 0.0 |
| District G | | | | | |
| safflower | 0.49 | 0.34 | 0.59 | 4.6 | 31.8 |
| maize | 0.38 | 0.25 | 0.53 | 244.9 | 244.9 |
| District 5 | | | | | |
| beans | 0.54 | 0.69 | 0.51 | 58.1 | 49.5 |
| maize | 0.39 | 0.50 | 0.52 | 348.5 | 420.5 |
| soybeans | 0.45 | 0.15 | 0.45 | 87.1 | 0.0 |
| sorghum | 0.45 | 0.22 | 0.54 | 0.0 | 6.8 |
| District 6 | | | | | |
| maize | 0.38 | 0.13 | 0.39 | 39.2 | 39.2 |
| District 7 | | | | | |
| oats | 0.74 | 0.32 | 1.03 | 0.4 | 0.0 |
| maize | 0.40 | 0.36 | 0.49 | 3.2 | 9.2 |
| wheat | 0.31 | 0.68 | 0.56 | 0.7 | 26.6 |
| District 8 | | | | | |
| cotton | 0.49 | 0.17 | 0.49 | 45.8 | 324.8 |
| maize | 0.39 | 0.14 | 0.48 | 601.6 | 380.2 |
| District 9 | | | | | |
| sesame | 0.33 | 0.09 | 0.34 | 92.6 | 89.3 |
| maize | 0.38 | 0.11 | 0.38 | 12.9 | 12.9 |
| sorghum | 0.32 | 0.16 | 0.35 | 0.0 | 86.9 |
| wheat | 0.32 | 0.25 | 0.39 | 0.0 | 16.7 |
| District 10 | | | | | |
| chickpeas | 0.36 | 0.34 | 0.52 | 136.5 | 143.1 |
| maize | 0.38 | 0.10 | 0.39 | 2,256.2 | 2,246.2 |
| tomatoes | 0.41 | 0.36 | 0.72 | 0.0 | 95.8 |

TABLE 8.5 *Continued*

| District and crop | Coefficient of variation | | | Production[a] | |
|---|---|---|---|---|---|
| | Price | Yield | Income | $\phi = 1$ | $\phi = 0$ |
| District 11 | | | | | |
| onions | 0.37 | 0.13 | 0.47 | 271.0 | 0.0 |
| maize | 0.39 | 0.15 | 0.43 | 41.9 | 41.9 |
| sorghum | 0.28 | 0.12 | 0.33 | 818.1 | 2,614.0 |
| soybeans | 0.42 | 0.16 | 0.51 | 96.8 | 0.0 |
| District 12 | | | | | |
| oats | 0.74 | 0.33 | 1.04 | 49.8 | 0.0 |
| maize | 0.40 | 0.17 | 0.50 | 1,104.0 | 1,720.1 |
| sorghum | 0.41 | 0.19 | 0.52 | 1,705.8 | 394.8 |
| District 13 | | | | | |
| sugarcane | 0.43 | 0.06 | 0.41 | 23,530.8 | 26,025.9 |
| maize | 0.40 | 0.18 | 0.40 | 2.148.1 | 1,680.8 |
| potatoes | 0.25 | 0.29 | 0.52 | 607.0 | 679.1 |
| sorghum | 0.39 | 0.15 | 0.43 | 1,344.7 | 893.4 |
| soybeans | 0.45 | 0.14 | 0.58 | 297.1 | 756.4 |
| tobacco | 0.33 | 0.11 | 0.28 | 31.8 | 8.6 |
| peanuts | 0.59 | 0.16 | 0.67 | 0.0 | 38.1 |
| District 14 | | | | | |
| maize | 0.40 | 0.09 | 0.36 | 7.3 | 7.3 |
| District 15 | | | | | |
| rice | 0.43 | 0.10 | 0.49 | 20.8 | 91.5 |
| beans | 0.53 | 0.15 | 0.55 | 20.4 | 0.0 |
| lima beans | 0.73 | 0.47 | 0.38 | 23.7 | 46.8 |
| maize | 0.39 | 0.27 | 0.43 | 158.6 | 140.2 |
| potatoes | 0.30 | 0.25 | 0.59 | 14.0 | 0.0 |

*Note*: Geographical locations of rain-fed districts are given in table 8.3, note; precipitation and altitude in table 8.4

[a] 1,000 metric tons. Production figures are taken from solutions to the Mexican model.

Table 8.6 presents aggregations over localities of the income coefficients, using as weights the production levels in the base solution ($\phi = 1$). With these aggregations, clearer patterns begin to emerge. First, the coefficients generally do not differ by more than a factor of two across crops, although at the extreme the coefficient for irrigated oats is about three and a half times the coefficient for irrigated barley. Second, the conventional wisdom that vegetables are riskier than grains does not appear to hold up. Under irrigation, leaving aside the extreme cases of oats, melons, and cucumbers (with coefficients of variation of 1.38, 1.19 and 0.81, respectively), the range of values for the coefficient of variation is 0.40 to 0.71 for maize, wheat, sorghum, barley, and rice. It is 0.42 to 0.65 for beans, chiles, onions, garlic, tomatoes, lima beans, chickpeas, strawberries, and watermelons. A similar pattern holds in rain-fed areas, although fewer vegetables are grown there. Third, irrigated and rain-fed areas appear to

TABLE 8.6 Coefficients of variation for income, selected crops, Mexico, 1970–79

| Crop | Irrigated districts | Rain-fed districts |
|---|---|---|
| Maize | 0.46 | 0.42 |
| Wheat | 0.54 | 0.56 |
| Sorghum | 0.47 | 0.45 |
| Barley | 0.40 | ... |
| Oats | 1.38 | 1.04 |
| Alfalfa | 0.44 | ... |
| Cotton | 0.73 | 0.49 |
| Rice | 0.71 | 0.49 |
| Safflower | 0.57 | 0.36 |
| Soybeans | 0.47 | 0.54 |
| Sesame | ... | 0.35 |
| Beans | 0.53 | 0.50 |
| Chiles | 0.42 | ... |
| Onions | 0.64 | 0.47 |
| Garlic | 0.42 | ... |
| Tomatoes | 0.51 | 0.72 |
| Cucumbers | 0.81 | ... |
| Lima beans | 0.65 | 0.38 |
| Chickpeas | 0.43 | 0.52 |
| Strawberries | 0.53 | ... |
| Watermelons | 0.51 | ... |
| Peanuts | 0.46 | 0.67 |
| Melons | 1.19 | ... |
| Sugarcane | 0.55 | 0.41 |
| Tobacco | ... | 0.28 |

*Note*: Aggregation based on weights in the Mexican model solution with $\phi = 1$; see table 8.5.

be comparable in relative riskiness, as measured by the coefficient of variation.

However, this last fact is offset by the consideration that incomes in rain-fed areas are much lower than those in irrigated areas, on the average, so the absolute riskiness of farming, as measured by the standard deviation (or variance) of income, is much higher in irrigated areas. Bassoco and Norton (1983, p. 165) report that for the sector as a whole, annual income per hectare is over four times higher in irrigated areas as it is in nonirrigated areas.

Turning to the solutions of CHAC, complete risk elimination (simulated by setting $\phi = 0$) would have clearly positive effects on social welfare, as measured by the change in the sum of producer and consumer surplus from the base solution (table 8.7). However, consumers are the beneficiaries, and owing to output increases and price responses, producers are the losers. Shifts in demand schedules over time would mitigate these effects, but nevertheless the static consequences for producers are negative. On the

TABLE 8.7 Welfare effects of risk elimination, Mexican model

| Item | Risk-averse ($\phi = 1$) | Risk-neutral ($\phi = 0$) |
|---|---|---|
| Objective function (10 million *pesos*)[a] | 17,962.2 | 18,951.6 |
| Producer surplus (10 million *pesos*) | 2,798.8 | 2,215.9 |
| Consumer surplus (10 million *pesos*) | 15,163.4 | 16,735.7 |
| Sector income (10 million *pesos*) | 3,674.9 | 3,179.8 |
| Gini coefficient | .3386 | .2966 |
| Employment (thousand man years) | 1,561.9 | 1,704.3 |
| Production (index) | 100.0 | 105.0 |
| Maize production (thousand metric tons) | 8,180.0 | 8,995.0 |
| Imports (10 million *pesos*) | 182.0 | 22.8 |

[a]Sum of the producer and consumer surplus.

other hand, landless workers are beneficiaries of this hypothetical change, because employment rises significantly. This leads to an increase in net income for this group, and so the decline in sector income is less than the decline in farmers' income. Maize production would be proportionately more responsive than total production to an elimination of the risk factor.

Risk elimination increases the variability of farm income before the stabilizing indemnities are added in; there are a few exceptions on a spatial basis (table 8.8). From a policy planning viewpoint, this result implies that insurance programs in general may well decrease the level of national food security in some years, because of the greater variance of production caused by the shift toward riskier crops. Of course, the variance of production is likely to be less than the variance of income (see table 8.5), but an increase in the latter is likely to mean an increase in the former. At the macro level, insurance appears to be a double-edged instrument: it leads to higher expected production levels and improves the rural income distribution, but it leads to greater instability of national food supplies. Therefore, a crop insurance program may have to be accompanied either by greater investments in storage facilities or by a policy of holding higher levels of foreign exchange reserves.

The actual Mexican crop insurance program has effects that are rather different from those associated with the hypothetical case of complete risk elimination. One of the differences is that actual programs do not completely eliminate risk. Another difference is that farmers pay insurance premiums that are not equal to the average indemnity received. As noted above, in order to simulate the effects of the actual programs, the risk time series (time series of gross revenue by crop) have been modified to reflect insurance operations. This procedure effectively alters the basis on which farmers form their perceptions of the riskiness of crops and crop combinations. One important departure from reality is that the program is

TABLE 8.8 Standard deviation of income per hectare, by district, Mexican model

| District | Risk-averse ($\phi = 1$) | Risk-neutral ($\phi = 0$) |
|---|---|---|
| *Irrigated* | | |
| Río Colorado | 0.70 | 0.52 |
| Hermosillo | 0.14 | 0.16 |
| Río Yaqui | 0.16 | 0.29 |
| Culiacán-Humaya | 0.58 | 0.74 |
| El Fuerte | 0.09 | 0.12 |
| El Bajío | 0.17 | 0.28 |
| Other Northwest districts | 0.14 | 0.22 |
| Other Northeast districts including La Laguna | 0.24 | 0.28 |
| Chihuahua and Durango | 0.28 | 0.39 |
| Other Central districts | 0.12 | 0.13 |
| Southern districts | 0.10 | 0.11 |
| *Rain-fed* | | |
| District B | 0.08 | 0.08 |
| District C | 0.01 | 0.03 |
| District E | 0.02 | 0.03 |
| District G | 0.04 | 0.05 |
| District 5 | 0.06 | 0.06 |
| District 6 | 0.02 | 0.02 |
| District 7 | 0.03 | 0.06 |
| District 8 | 0.06 | 0.31 |
| District 9 | 0.03 | 0.04 |
| District 10 | 0.04 | 0.04 |
| District 11 | 0.06 | 0.08 |
| District 12 | 0.04 | 0.04 |
| District 13 | 0.04 | 0.06 |
| District 14 | 0.01 | 0.02 |
| District 15 | 0.03 | 0.03 |

*Note*: Geographical locations of rain-fed districts are given in table 8.3, note; precipitation and altitude in table 8.4.

assumed to apply to the entire sector; that is, to the entire area in annual crops. Insurance is also treated as compulsory for all farmers.

Table 8.9 presents the aggregative results of the insurance program simulations. The salient features of these simulations are the following. Measuring social welfare as the sum of the producer and consumer surplus, the actual subsidized insurance program leads to an increase of 1,190-million *pesos* in aggregate welfare. This increase is gross of the cost of the subsidy. In 1980 (the model's base year), the cost of the subsidy amounted to 5,225-million *pesos*. This estimate is lower than the cost implicit in the model solution,[2] but even so it is clear that there is a sizeable

2. The subsidy cost implicit in the model is larger because all farmers are assumed to purchase crop insurance, even if they do not borrow official credit.

TABLE 8.9 Welfare effects of crop yield insurance, Mexican model, assuming risk-averse behavior, $\phi = 1$

| Item | Without insurance | With insurance | |
|---|---|---|---|
| | | No subsidy | Subsidy |
| Objective function (10 million *pesos*)[a] | 17,962.2 | 17,269.0 | 18,081.0 |
| Producer surplus (10 million *pesos*) | 2,798.8 | 3,100.2 | 3,194.9 |
| Consumer surplus (10 million *pesos*) | 15,163.4 | 14,168.8 | 14,886.1 |
| Sector income (10 million *pesos*) | 3,674.9 | 4,079.8 | 4,136.6 |
| Gini coefficient | .3386 | .3327 | .3449 |
| Employment (thousand man years) | 1,561.9 | 1,607.2 | 1,636.6 |
| Production (index) | 100.0 | 98.7 | 100.5 |
| Maize (thousand metric tons) | 8,180.0 | 7,948.0 | 8,179.0 |
| Imports (10 million *pesos*) | 182.0 | 183.5 | 182.5 |

[a]Sum of the producer and consumer surplus.

net social loss as a result of the subsidized insurance. On the other hand, the subsidized insurance does have a beneficial impact on farmers; both producer surplus and sector income are larger than in the no-insurance situation. There is also a favorable impact on employment because of changes in the mix of crops grown. However, because commercial farmers receive a disproportionate share of the subsidy, the distribution of income within agriculture worsens somewhat, as shown by the increase in the Gini coefficient.[3]

If the crop insurance program were not subsidized, there would still be a loss in net social welfare compared to the no-insurance situation. This loss arises because the insurance is compulsory, and in aggregate the administration costs exceed the value of the risk-reduction benefits conferred by the program. In fact, farmers' costs are sufficiently increased by the unsubsidized insurance that aggregate production declines by 1.3 percent. However, because of the generally inelastic nature of the demand for agricultural products, the decline in output leads to price increases that increase producer surplus and sector income beyond the levels attained if crop insurance were not introduced.[4]

In sum, while the crop insurance program in Mexico does lead to a loss in net social welfare, it increases incomes and employment in the farm sector and prevents a decline in aggregate production. Perhaps these effects might more simply be attained through price policy.

3. The Gini coefficient reported in table 8.9 is a measure of the distribution of average farm income across districts.

4. This is a very interesting case, where compulsory insurance turns out to be beneficial to the average farmer, but not because it provides a cost-effective way of reducing risk costs. The gain arises entirely from the price increases induced by the leftward shift in the aggregate supply. A farm-management analysis of the insurance program (like that in chapter 3) would have failed to capture these effects.

# 9

# An Economic Analysis of Rice Insurance in Japan

Hiroshi Tsujii

Multiple-risk crop insurance has been criticized because it is sufficiently costly relative to its benefits that it only exists when subsidized by government. Yet, as Siamwalla and Valdés show in chapter 7, subsidies that increase the amount of insurance purchased beyond that which farmers would purchase voluntarily on a full-cost basis necessarily lead to a net social loss. An important empirical question arises as to how costly crop insurance subsidies really are to society.

Japan has had a heavily subsidized rice insurance program since 1947 (see chapter 13 for details). The major objectives of this scheme were to encourage increased rice production and to help stabilize farm incomes. However, is crop insurance a cost-effective way of achieving these goals? This chapter evaluates the effect of the insurance subsidy on national rice production and calculates a benefit/cost ratio for the government expenditure on the insurance program. The analysis uses the estimation of an econometric model of Japanese rice production. Key features of the model are incorporation of farmers' risk-response behavior and their expectations about the per-hectare income transfer embodied in the subsidy.

## The Cost of Rice Insurance

Japanese rice insurance is part of the crop insurance program established in 1947 by the government. Rice insurance is compulsory for all farmers growing more than 0.3 hectares of paddy. Before 1957, this minimum area was 0.1 hectares.

The author wishes to thank Seiichi Fukui, Peter Hazell, Kenzo Hemmi, Shinichi Ichimura, Ulrich Koester, Nelson Maurice, Marc Nerlove, James Roumasset, Ammar Siamwalla, Suthad Setboonsarn, and Alberto Valdés for their helpful comments and discussions on this chapter. The author would also like to thank Minoru Toda for his kind assistance in gathering relevant data, and Lauren Farnsworth for her accurate assistance in setting up the data bank and in using the SAS package for estimating the model for this study. The major part of this research was done when the author was affiliated with the International Food Policy Research Institute in Washington, D.C.

The rice insurance scheme provides multiple-risk coverage against natural yield risks. Although the insurance is compulsory, farmers do have some flexibility in determining the value of the coverage they purchase and therefore in the premium rate they pay. The key decision variable is the price agreed to at the beginning of each season, which is used to value subsequent crop damage. This price may be any of five specified ratios of the government procurement price for rice. This flexibility in coverage was one of several reforms of the insurance program introduced in 1957.

The government subsidizes over 50 percent of the premiums that farmers pay for crop insurance. In addition, the government bears a substantial part of the administrative costs of the program. It also provides a generous reinsurance facility to the insurer, which often amounts to giving grants in disaster years. In fact, farmers in general receive a net income transfer from the program, because the premiums they pay are less than the indemnities they receive.

The total cost of the crop insurance program to the government is substantial. Table 9.1 provides a breakdown of these costs and shows how they have increased over time. In the late 1970s, the insurance program cost the government about 150-billion *yen* per year. About half of this subsidized premiums, about a sixth went to reinsurance subsidies, and the rest went toward the cost of administering the program. The government's contribution to the insurance program is about twice that paid by farmers. The cost to the government has grown rapidly since the early 1970s, but it has fallen as a share (to less than 5 percent) of the total budget of the Ministry of Agriculture, Forestry, and Fisheries.

Are such high levels of government support for the rice insurance program justified? To evaluate the social returns from the program, it is necessary to measure the effect of the program on the aggregate supply of rice. To this end, we turn to the construction of an econometric model of the Japanese rice sector.

## A Model of Japanese Rice Production Incorporating Insurance

Two behavioral features in the area and yield equations are critical to the evaluation of crop insurance. One is farmers' expectations about the per-hectare returns from growing rice, which are assumed to be based on past returns. They include a revenue component that is the expected difference between the insurance indemnities received per hectare and the premium paid. Where positive, this difference measures the income transfer per hectare embodied in the heavily subsidized crop insurance program. This variable can be used to simulate the effect of changes in the insurance subsidy on rice production. The second behavioral feature is a proxy variable measuring the disutility cost of risk to growers, allowing changes in yield and price risks to affect supply. This feature enables the model to simulate changes in rice production arising from changes in risk bearing induced by the insurance program.

The complete set of equations in the model are set out below.

$$S_t \equiv A_t \cdot YA_t \equiv A_t \cdot (YN_t + u_{3t}). \tag{1}$$

$$A_t = a_0 + \gamma R1_t^* + \delta R2_t^* + a_4 PX_t/PAP_t + a_5 ROT_t + a_6 CF_t. \tag{2}$$

$$YN_t = c_0 + c_1 CF_t + c_2 R1_t^{**} + c_3 R2_t^{**} + c_4 ROT_t + c_5 T. \tag{3}$$

$$CF_t = b_0 + \epsilon R1_t^* + \mu R2_t^* + b_4 V_{t-1}(N) + b_5 PIMAX_t + b_6 OY_t. \tag{4}$$

$$R1_t^* - R1_{t-1}^* = \alpha(R1_{t-1} - R1_{t-1}^*). \tag{5}$$

$$R2_t^* - R2_{t-1}^* = \alpha(R2_{t-1} - R2_{t-1}^*). \tag{6}$$

$$R1_t^{**} - R1_{t-1}. \tag{7}$$

$$R2_t^{**} = R2_{t-1}. \tag{8}$$

The following notation is used:

$S_t$ is total rice production in year $t$ in metric tons of brown rice;
$A_t$ is the total wet-paddy area planted in year $t$ (1,000 hectares);
$YA_t$ is the actual yield in year $t$ (kilograms/hectare);
$YN_t$ is the normal or expected rice yield for year $t$ (kilograms/hectare);
$u_{3t}$ is a stochastic yield term with zero mean (kilograms/hectare);
$PAP_t$ is a farm-gate price index of agricultural products (1970 = 100);[1]
$PX_t$ is an index of the government procurement price of second-grade brown rice (1970 = 100);[2]
$R1_t$ is the realized gross revenue in *yen* per hectare of planted paddy in year $t$ deflated by the price index $PAP_t$; $R1_t$ is therefore $P_t \cdot YA_t/PAP_t$, where $P_t$ is the average government procurement price for rice calculated as $P_t = PX_t \cdot P_{1970}$;
$R1_t^*$ and $R1_t^{**}$ denote producers' expectations or forecasts about $R1_t$ for year $t$;
$R2_t$ is the net return in *yen* per hectare from participating in rice insurance; it is the per-hectare difference between the indem-

1. Rice is included in the price index, but it has a relatively low weight (29.4 percent in 1980).

2. The government procurement price is a guaranteed price announced at the beginning of the production year. Since the government keeps tight control of Japanese rice trade, the guaranteed price virtually determines prices at all levels of the rice market.

TABLE 9.1 Cost of Japanese crop insurance program borne by farmers and government, 1947–81 (million *yen*)

| Year | Premium paid by farmers A | Premium subsidy B | Reinsurance subsidy C | Administrative cost paid by government D | Administrative cost paid by farmers E | Total insurance subsidy F (B + C + D) | Total insurance cost paid by farmers G (A + E) | Ratio of subsidy to farmers' cost (percent) F/G | Share of insurance subsidy in total MAFF expenditure (percent) |
|---|---|---|---|---|---|---|---|---|---|
| 1947 | 719 | 537 | ... | 123 | ... | ... | ... | ... | ... |
| 1948 | 1,243 | 841 | ... | 409 | ... | ... | ... | ... | ... |
| 1949 | 3,079 | 2,253 | 4,612 | 761 | ... | ... | ... | ... | ... |
| 1950 | 3,565 | 2,536 | 6,066 | 761 | 1,398 | 9,363 | 4,963 | 1.89 | 19.29 |
| 1951 | 5,797 | 4,246 | 6,685 | 1,565 | 2,109 | 12,496 | 7,906 | 1.58 | 15.01 |
| 1952 | 6,433 | 6,291 | 4,081 | 2,130 | 2,448 | 12,502 | 8,881 | 1.41 | 8.62 |
| 1953 | 6,788 | 8,444 | 25,449 | 2,513 | 3,032 | 36,406 | 9,820 | 3.71 | 24.42 |
| 1954 | 6,946 | 8,860 | 10,745 | 2,482 | 3,030 | 22,087 | 9,976 | 2.21 | 19.77 |
| 1955 | 7,571 | 8,904 | 2,557 | 2,445 | 3,868 | 13,906 | 11,439 | 1.22 | 14.45 |
| 1956 | 7,780 | 8,839 | 9,160 | 2,421 | 4,098 | 20,420 | 11,878 | 1.72 | 22.58 |
| 1957 | 7,818 | 8,825 | 5,274 | 2,221 | 4,243 | 16,320 | 12,061 | 1.35 | 13.37 |
| 1958 | 6,955 | 8,754 | 6,778 | 2,292 | 4,369 | 17,824 | 11,324 | 1.57 | 17.70 |
| 1959 | 7,184 | 9,174 | 5,863 | 2,352 | 4,331 | 17,389 | 11,515 | 1.51 | 15.10 |
| 1960 | 7,463 | 9,587 | 3,237 | 2,621 | 4,235 | 15,445 | 11,688 | 1.32 | 9.45 |
| 1961 | 7,727 | 9,800 | 8,016 | 3,704 | 4,006 | 21,520 | 11,733 | 1.83 | 9.97 |

| | | | | | | | | | |
|---|---|---|---|---|---|---|---|---|---|
| 1962 | 8,134 | 9,812 | 5,698 | 4,363 | 4,239 | 19,873 | 12,373 | 1.61 | 8.13 |
| 1963 | 8,828 | 10,950 | 10,368 | 5,151 | 4,254 | 38,469 | 13,082 | 2.56 | 11.39 |
| 1964 | 10,472 | 12,721 | 15,808 | 6,162 | 4,549 | 34,691 | 15,021 | 2.31 | 10.08 |
| 1965 | 12,510 | 15,528 | 15,565 | 7,264 | 4,819 | 38,357 | 17,329 | 2.21 | 9.67 |
| 1966 | 14,390 | 17,434 | 17,262 | 8,050 | 5,170 | 42,746 | 19,560 | 2.19 | 7.67 |
| 1967 | 16,584 | 22,201 | 9,580 | 9,025 | 7,494 | 40,806 | 24,078 | 1.69 | 6.62 |
| 1968 | 19,281 | 26,151 | 7,778 | 10,338 | 8,232 | 44,267 | 27,513 | 1.61 | 6.33 |
| 1969 | 21,579 | 29,813 | 12,959 | 11,986 | 8,730 | 54,758 | 30,309 | 1.81 | 6.45 |
| 1970 | 19,676 | 25,236 | 13,299 | 14,523 | 8,591 | 53,058 | 28,267 | 1.88 | 5.08 |
| 1971 | 19,646 | 24,942 | 28,845 | 17,367 | 8,202 | 71,154 | 27,848 | 2.56 | 6.17 |
| 1972 | 20,854 | 26,428 | 10,572 | 20,479 | 8,751 | 57,479 | 29,605 | 1.94 | 4.13 |
| 1973 | 24,190 | 28,773 | 12,042 | 24,432 | 9,925 | 65,247 | 34,115 | 1.91 | 3.61 |
| 1974 | 28,862 | 35,024 | 18,305 | 32,586 | 11,496 | 85,915 | 40,358 | 2.13 | 3.81 |
| 1975 | 38,597 | 47,429 | 21,071 | 36,621 | 13,489 | 105,121 | 52,086 | 2.02 | 4.65 |
| 1976 | 44,669 | 56,484 | 117,218 | 40,144 | 14,267 | 213,846 | 58,936 | 3.63 | 8.59 |
| 1977 | 52,517 | 65,534 | 26,297 | 43,478 | 16,023 | 135,309 | 68,540 | 1.97 | 4.82 |
| 1978 | 57,244 | 71,847 | 27,473 | 46,723 | 16,916 | 146,043 | 74,160 | 1.97 | 4.55 |
| 1979 | 64,781 | 81,481 | 27,859 | 50,065 | 18,401 | 159,405 | 83,182 | 1.92 | 4.46 |
| 1980 | 66,615 | 83,449 | ... | 52,822 | 19,012 | ... | 85,627 | ... | ... |
| 1981 | ... | 87,984 | 118,269 | ... | ... | ... | ... | ... | ... |

*Source*: *Annual Report of Agricultural Damages Compensation Institution*, various issues (Tokyo: Ministry of Agriculture, Forestry, and Fisheries); *An Outline of Agricultural Damages Compensation Institution* (Tokyo: Ministry of Agriculture, Forestry and Fisheries, 1982).

nities received in year $t$, $IND_t$, and the premium paid, $CF_t$, deflated by the agricultural price index, $PAP_t$;

$R2^*_t$ and $R2^{**}_t$ denote producers' expectations about $R2_t$ for year $t$;

$ROT_t$ is the ratio of average off-farm income to average farm income for paddy grower households in year $t$;

$CF_t$ is the part of the per-hectare rice insurance premium paid by farmers in year $t$ deflated by the agricultural price index, $PAP_t$;

$V_t(N)$ denotes a moving variance of per-hectare rice revenues, calculated for the previous $N$ years;

$PIMAX_t$ is a variable designed to capture the effects of institutional change in the rice insurance program; the program has been modified since it was structured in 1947 (see chapter 13), changing the calculation of the maximum rice price ($PIMAX_t$) to be used in the valuation of any subsequent insured damage; given the government procurement price, $P_t$, then $PIMAX_t = aP_t$, and $a = 0.7$ before 1962, 0.9 during 1963–75, and 1 thereafter;

$OY_t$ is the average nonpaddy income for paddy growers in year $t$ deflated by the agricultural price index $PAP_t$; and

$T$ denotes a time-trend variable.

Equation 1 is a production identity; the supply of rice in year $t$ equals area, $A_t$, times actual yield, $YA_t$. Actual yield is the sum of the normal (or expected) yield for that year, $YN_t$, and a random component, $u_{3t}$. Equations 2 and 3 are behavioral relations determining, respectively, the aggregate area of paddy planted in year $t$ and the normal yield to be expected that year.

The paddy area planted is determined by farmers' expectations about per-hectare revenues, $R1^*_t$ and $R2^*_t$, by the government's procurement price for rice, $PX_t$, by the importance of off-farm income relative to farm income for paddy growers, $ROT_t$, and by the cost of rice insurance to farmers, $CF_t$. All monetary variables are deflated by a price index of agricultural commodities, $PAP_t$.

Farmers' expectations about the per-hectare revenue from paddy are broken into two parts: the expected gross value of rice production, $R1^*_t$, and the net income transfer inherent in the insurance program, $R2^*_t$. Although both variables should be positively related to the planted area, they need not be symmetrical (that is, $\gamma$ and $\delta$ may be different). The revenue from rice sales can only be realized after harvest, whereas indemnities, if paid, occur earlier in the season. Further, the crop damage associated with indemnities may preempt the need to incur further production costs. These differences may lead farmers to view the two types of income quite differently. Following Nerlove (1958), farmers' revenue expectations are assumed to be formed adaptively, as defined by equations 5 and 6.

The normal yield each year is determined by farmers' revenue expectations, by the relative importance of off-farm income to farm income, and by the cost of rice insurance. In addition, a time trend, $T$, is included to capture the effect of technological change.

The revenue expectations in the yield function are assumed to be formed differently from the expectations in the area function. This is denoted by the use of double asterisks, and the behavioral rules for determining $R1_t^{**}$ and $R2_t^{**}$ are given in equations 7 and 8. These expectations are simply forward projections of the previous year's revenue. The reasons for having different revenue expectations in the area and yield functions are twofold. First, Japanese rice farmers face more difficult and complex constraints in changing their paddy area than they do in adjusting variable inputs, such as fertilizers, which affect yields. There are strong communal and cultural constraints on the area sown to paddy, and changes are often difficult within the existing infrastructure for water control. Second, if the revenue expectations in the yield function are also given by equations 5 and 6, then serious multicollinearity problems arise in the estimation of the model.

The inclusion of a measure of off-farm income in the area and yield functions is designed to capture the effect on rice production of a strong shift toward part-time farming in Japan in recent decades. As the ratio of off-farm to farm income, $ROT_t$, increases, less effort and labor will be allocated to rice farming, so that $ROT_t$ can be expected to be negatively related to both area and yield.

The cost of insurance, $CF_t$, enters both the area and yield functions. This variable is the average per-hectare premium paid by the farmer for rice insurance, deflated by the agricultural price index, $PAP_t$. Since farmers have some choice in the selection of insurance coverage, and therefore in the premium they pay, $CF_t$ is a rough measure of the aggregate disutility cost of risk to farmers. It is tainted in that it includes not only the cost of participation in a risk-reduction scheme, but it is also the entry price to participating in government handouts in the form of crop-insurance subsidies. This transfer component is also included directly in the area and yield functions through the variable $R2$, but clearly there is not a clean separation of the risk and subsidy effects. This is not a serious limitation for present purposes, though, since the objective is to measure the impact of the insurance subsidy on rice production, and a pure measure of the risk effect is incidental to the analysis.

Previous studies that attempt to incorporate risk-response behavior in aggregate supply functions have either been based on a normative mathematical programming approach (for example, see Hazell and Scandizzo

1974, or chapter 8), or they have included adaptive expectations about the variances and covariance of price and yield (Just 1975, Behrman 1968). The Just approach is compatible with the rice supply model developed here but was rejected on the grounds that it leads to model specifications that are very difficult to estimate. The use of the cost of insurance to the farmer as a proxy for risk behavior is a much simpler approach. Other things being equal, greater risk aversion will lead to the purchase of larger amounts of coverage, and therefore greater values of $CF_t$. Also, the more risk-averse farmers are, the less willing they will be to allocate resources to rice production, hence I hypothesize that the area and normal yield of paddy will be negatively related to $CF_t$ (that is, $a_6$ and $c_1 < 0$).

Farmers' choice of insurance coverage will not only depend on their degree of risk aversion but also on their expectations about the returns and risks involved in paddy growing. These relationships are formalized in equation 4 of the model.[3] Here $CF_t$ is determined by expectations about the returns from paddy, $R1_t^*$, and the size of the income transfer inherent in the insurance scheme, $R2_t^*$, by expectations about the riskiness of paddy returns as captured in a moving variance over $N$ years of past returns, $V_{t-1}(N)$, by the average amount of nonpaddy income earned by paddy growers, $OY_t$, and by a variable, $PIMAX_t$, designed to capture institutional changes in the insurance program. The coefficient on $V_{t-1}(N)$ should be positive; more risky returns should lead farmers to opt for higher levels of insurance coverage. On the other hand, the larger the value of nonpaddy income, the less farmers need be concerned about the risks in paddy farming. The coefficient on $OY_t$ should therefore be negative.

The variable $PIMAX_t$ is designed to capture institutional change in the insurance program. It indicates the maximum price that the farmer can choose for evaluating crop damage at the time of signing the insurance contract. This price has been increased on several occasions since the insurance scheme was established in 1947, and so the coefficient on $PIMAX_t$ should be positive in equation 4.

## Estimation of the Model

As formulated, the model cannot be directly estimated because it contains unobservable variables for farmers' revenue expectations. Following Nerlove (1958), a multiple equation reduction technique was used to derive the following reduced forms of the area and risk premium equations:

3. Pratt (1964) has developed a theoretical relation between the insurance premium an individual is willing to pay, his degree of risk aversion, his level of wealth, and the mean and variance of returns from a risky investment. Equation 4 can be viewed as an empirical statement of this relation.

$$A_t = a_0 + \gamma\alpha R1_{t-1} + \delta\alpha R2_{t-1} + (1 - \alpha)A_{t-1} + a_4 PX_t/PAP_t + a_5 ROT_t + a_6 CF_t + u_{1t}. \quad (9)$$

$$CF_t = b_0 + \epsilon\alpha R1_{t-1} + \mu\alpha R2_{t-1} + b_4 V_{t-1}(N) + b_5 PIMAX_t + b_6 OY_t + (1 - \alpha)CF_{t-1} + u_{2t}. \quad (10)$$

The stochastic residuals have been added to allow for discrepancies between the predicted and actual values of $A_t$ and $CF_t$.

The yield equation to be estimated is obtained by substituting equations 7 and 8 into equation 3, and adding a stochastic residual. This leads to the actual yield equation

$$YA_t = c_0 + c_1 CF_t + c_2 R1_{t-1} + c_3 R2_{t-1} + c_4 ROT_t + c_5 T + u_{3t}. \quad (11)$$

Normal yield, $YN_t$, is then obtained from equation 11 by setting $u_{3t} = 0$.

Equations 9, 10, and 11 define a recursive system that can be estimated by ordinary least squares (OLS) regression. Once these equations are estimated, it is clear from comparison of the coefficients in equations 9 through 11 with those in equations 1 through 6 that all the coefficients of the original model can easily be calculated. The estimated parameters will be consistent, but they may be biased (Nerlove 1958, Goldberger 1964). To explore the biases inherent in the model, the equations were also estimated by a three-stage least squares estimation. However, the resultant parameter estimates were sufficiently close to the OLS estimates that only the latter are reported in this chapter.

The model was estimated using data for the years 1956 to 1979. The estimated equations are as follows (the $t$ statistics for the respective zero null hypotheses are shown in parentheses below the coefficient):

$$\begin{aligned} A_t = {} & \underset{(2.12)}{681.9} + \underset{(2.14)}{0.00087}\, R1_{t-1} + \underset{(1.79)}{0.00530}\, R2_{t-1} + \underset{(6.74)}{0.62109}\, A_{t-1} \\ & + \underset{(1.90)}{666.1}\, PX_t/PAP_t - \underset{(-3.27)}{829.1}\, ROT_t - \underset{(-3.43)}{0.07009}\, CF_t \\ & (\bar{R}^2 = 0.92). \end{aligned} \quad (12)$$

$$\begin{aligned} CF_t = {} & \underset{(-3.54)}{-2787.2} + \underset{(1.94)}{0.00417}\, R1_{t-1} + \underset{(2.73)}{0.03839}\, R2_{t-1} \\ & + \underset{(4.33)}{0.59662}\, CF_{t-1} + \underset{(1.23)}{8.49730(10^{-8})}\, V_{t-1}(5) \\ & + \underset{(2.49)}{15.37684}\, PIMAX_t + \underset{(0.44)}{0.00017}\, OY_t \\ & (\bar{R}^2 = 0.95). \end{aligned} \quad (13)$$

$$YN_t = -196705.0 - \underset{(-1.70)}{0.14400\, CF_t} + \underset{(1.10)}{0.00152\, R1_{t-1}}$$

$$+ \underset{(0.92)}{0.00986\, R2_{t-1}} - \underset{(-1.6)}{2865.0\, ROT_t} + \underset{(2.50)}{102.8\, T}$$

$$(\bar{R}^2 = 0.74). \tag{14}$$

The equations fit well, with satisfactory values for the adjusted coefficients of variation $\bar{R}^2$. The signs of the estimated parameters are consistent with expectations, and most of the coefficients are significant at the 5 percent confidence level or better.

In the risk premium equation 13, estimations were undertaken for alternative values of $N$, the number of years over which the moving variance is calculated. Values of 3, 5, 7, and 10 were tried, but $N = 5$ gave the best statistical results and was therefore chosen.

A particularly encouraging feature of equations 12 through 14 is the results for the risk premium variable $CF$. Not only are the statistical results in equation 13 satisfactory, but $CF$ also enters the equations on area and yield as a statistically significant variable with the correct negative sign.

Given the estimated parameters in equations 12 through 14, the estimated parameters of the original structural model can be derived. Many coefficients are not transformed, but for those that are, the calculations proceed as follows. From equations 12 and 13, $\hat{\alpha}$ is obtained as 1.0 minus the coefficients on $A_{t-1}$ or $CF_{t-1}$, respectively. This gives

$$\hat{\alpha} = 1.0 - 0.62109 = 0.37891$$

or

$$\hat{\alpha} = 1.0 - 0.59662 = 0.40338.$$

Strictly speaking, $\hat{\alpha}$ is overidentified, but since the two values are very similar, I use the average value; that is, $\hat{\alpha} = 0.39114$. Other parameters are then

$$\hat{\gamma} = \widehat{\gamma\alpha}/\hat{\alpha} = 0.00087 \div 0.39114 = 0.00224,$$

$$\hat{\delta} = \widehat{\delta\alpha}/\hat{\alpha} = 0.00530 \div 0.39114 = 0.01355,$$

$$\hat{\epsilon} = \widehat{\epsilon\alpha}/\hat{\alpha} = 0.00417 \div 0.39114 = 0.01066,$$

and

$$\hat{\mu} = \mu\alpha/\hat{\alpha} = 0.03839 \div 0.39114 = 0.09815.$$

## An Economic Analysis

One of the major objectives of the rice insurance program in Japan was to increase national self-sufficiency in rice. Although this objective is less important today, increased rice production is still one of the major payoffs claimed for the insurance program. It is therefore pertinent to examine how cost effective the program is in achieving this goal.

The subsidy is captured in the model in the variable $R2$. This variable measures the difference between the premium a farmer pays and the average indemnity received over time on one hectare of paddy land. The derivative

$$\begin{aligned}\frac{\partial S}{\partial R2^*} &= \frac{\partial A}{\partial R2^*}\overline{YA} + \frac{\partial YN}{\partial R2^*}\bar{A}\\ &= \left(\frac{\partial A}{\partial R2^*} + \frac{\partial A}{\partial CF}\frac{\partial CF}{\partial R2^*}\right)\overline{YA}\\ &\quad + \left(\frac{\partial YN}{\partial R2^{**}}\frac{\partial R2^{**}}{\partial R2^*} + \frac{\partial YN}{\partial CF}\frac{\partial CF}{\partial R2^*}\right)\bar{A},\end{aligned}$$

where $\bar{A}$ and $\overline{YA}$ denote the sample mean area and yield, respectively, measures the long-term change in rice production (in metric tons) induced by a change of one *yen* per hectare in the insurance subsidy. The change is long term in the sense that, on average, farmers' expectations about per-hectare returns are assumed to have converged to values appropriate to a new equilibrium in the market.

When parameterized to the empirical model, the change evaluates at:

$$\begin{aligned}\frac{\partial S}{\partial R2^*} &= (\hat{\delta} + \hat{a}_6\hat{\mu})\overline{YA} + (\hat{c}_3/\hat{\alpha} + \hat{c}_1\hat{\mu})\bar{A}\\ &= 60.8 \text{ tons}/\textit{yen}.\end{aligned}$$

That is, an increase (decrease) of one *yen* per hectare in the subsidy for all the insured paddy land in Japan will lead to a long-term increase (decrease) of 60.8 tons per year in national rice production. This change in production is partly due to changes in the average per-hectare returns (an income effect), but also because the change in the subsidy affects the amount of insurance coverage that farmers are willing to buy (a risk effect).

Given this supply response to the subsidy, a long-term benefit/cost ratio for the insurance program can be calculated. Let $\bar{P}$ denote the landed Thai export price of rice, let $\bar{A}$ denote the average paddy area insured, and let $\overline{R2}$ denote the average net subsidy per hectare. Then the total value of the extra rice production induced by the subsidy can be approximated by

$$B = \frac{\partial S}{\partial R2^*} \cdot \overline{R2} \cdot \bar{P}.$$

The total cost of the insurance program to the government is the sum of the subsidies paid on premiums, the net cost of reinsurance, and the subsidy on administration. Letting $C$ denote the average value of this total cost, the benefit/cost ratio is $B/C$.

If $\bar{P}$ is converted to *yen* at the official exchange rate, the benefit/cost ratio evaluates at 0.39 for the period 1956–79. This implies that each *yen* of the government's financial contribution to the insurance program only produced 0.39-*yen* worth of rice each year at world prices. Put another way, each *yen* of the insurance subsidy could have been used instead to import 2.5 times more rice than it induced in domestic production through the insurance program.

If instead of using the world price of rice, the government's domestic procurement price is used, then the benefit/cost ratio increases to 1.04. Even at this highly distorted price, the government is only just recouping the value of its expenditure on the insurance program.

The model also provides an estimate of the short-term changes that would be induced by a change in the insurance subsidy:

$$\frac{\partial S_t}{\partial R2_{t-1}} = \left(\frac{\partial A_t}{\partial R2_{t-1}} + \frac{\partial A_t}{\partial CF_t} \cdot \frac{\partial CF_t}{\partial R2_{t-1}}\right)\overline{YA} + \left(\frac{\partial YN_t}{\partial R2_{t-1}} + \frac{\partial YN_t}{\partial CF_t} \cdot \frac{\partial CF_t}{\partial R2_{t-1}}\right)\bar{A}$$
$$= (\hat{\delta}\hat{\alpha} + a_6\hat{\mu}\hat{\alpha})\overline{YA} + (\hat{c}_3 + \hat{c}_1\hat{\mu}\hat{\alpha})\bar{A}.$$

This evaluates at 23.8 tons/*yen*.

Again, using the Thai export price for rice, the short-term benefit/cost ratio is only 0.1509 for the period 1957–79. Thus each seven *yen* of subsidy produced one *yen* of rice at world market prices. Even when rice is valued at the government price, the short-term benefit/cost ratio is still only 0.4.

## Conclusions

As a policy to increase national rice production, the subsidy of Japan's rice insurance program does not seem to be efficient. At world market prices, the long-term benefit/cost ratio of the government's contribution to the insurance program is only 0.39. The benefit/cost ratio is even lower in the short run (0.15), and it is still not attractive even if the extra rice is valued at the domestic procurement price.

The objective of increasing domestic rice production was crucial in the immediate postwar period. During the last decade, though, Japan has moved to a situation of rice surpluses (Tsujii 1982), and the production objective is becoming increasingly irrelevant. Government subsidies to the insurance program may well add about 71,000 tons of rice to total supply each year. This additional production aggravates the cost to government of surplus disposal and production reduction programs.

Government insurance subsidies affect rice production mostly through their income transfer effect. In this respect, they reinforce the large income transfers already embodied in the price support policy for rice (Ootsuka and Hayami 1982). Since average farm household incomes are now higher than the incomes of suburban families in Japan, the value of continued subsidy transfers is questionable.

Given the economic inefficiencies of the existing rice insurance program, what changes could usefully be made? First, the program should be made voluntary rather than compulsory. This would greatly reduce the administrative cost subsidy required and would allow the insurance market to operate more efficiently. Second, the income transfer inherent in the insurance subsidies should be reduced. Transfer of income to farmers in the event of major disasters can probably be done more efficiently through relief schemes not connected with the insurance program.

# 10

# Agricultural Instability and Alternative Government Policies: The Australian Experience

Alan G. Lloyd
Roger G. Mauldon

In 1978 the Australian Industries Assistance Commission (IAC) published a report to the Australian government on rural income fluctuations. In setting the terms of reference for the inquiry, the government had sought advice on: "1. whether, to give effect to the objectives in Section 22(1) of the Industries Assistance Commission Act 1973, assistance should be given to reduce fluctuations in the incomes of rural producers; and 2. if so, the nature and extent of such assistance" (Industries Assistance Commission 1978, p. 64).

These objectives toward which IAC advice was to be directed included (1) improving the efficiency of resource use; (2) facilitating adjustment to changes in the economic environment; (3) ensuring that industry assistance measures be integrated with overall national economic policy; and (4) providing adequate scope for public scrutiny and evaluation of commission reports.

The first sections of this chapter give some background information on the IAC role and on the instability of Australian agriculture. The second section provides a summary of relevant sections of the IAC *Report on Rural Income Fluctuations*.[1] The third provides an outline and discussion of subsequent government policy actions on the issues raised in the report.

## Background

The IAC advises the Australian government on matters affecting assistance to industries throughout the Australian economy. It was created in 1974 to replace the Tariff Board, which had operated for over fifty years in the field of tariff protection. The IAC subsumed the functions of the board in offering advice on tariff assistance for import-replacing industries, most

1. The authors of this chapter were the commissioners of the IAC who presided over the inquiry.

of which are in the Australian manufacturing sector. However, it also was given the wider responsibility of examining all forms of assistance, including assistance to the export-oriented industries, which are predominantly mining and agricultural.

In introducing the legislation that established the IAC, Prime Minister Whitlam stated that the government had inherited a complex, confusing, and inconsistent collection of assistance measures, which discriminated among individual industries—particularly between the agricultural and manufacturing sectors of the economy. The IAC was to develop a rational and consistent approach toward all industries, with particular regard to efficient utilization of community resources.

A major initial task for the IAC was to develop criteria for industry assistance, which would be generally applicable. Protection policy for manufacturing and assistance policy for agriculture had developed in Australia largely in isolation from each other. Each had to take the other more or less as given. Even within the field of agriculture, assistance policies had been developed largely on a commodity-by-commodity basis.

Australian industry assistance policies have generally been protectionist. They have resulted in resources being retained within, or attracted into, heavily protected activities in which Australia has a low comparative advantage. Within both farming and manufacturing sectors, assistance to particular industries ranges from zero to very high (sometimes in excess of 100 percent in terms of effective rates of protection). As in many countries, high levels of assistance have usually originated as a temporary cushion to absorb shocks. In fact, the activity given temporary assistance often gradually loses its comparative advantage, and as the shocks persist and worsen, the "needed" level of assistance has grown. The IAC has consistently recommended policies that facilitate adjustment to changes in demand, in technology, and in international competition (rather than policies that defend the status quo) to increase the flow of resources toward more efficient uses. It has also consistently sought to make levels of assistance to industries more uniform, preferably by reducing high levels rather than raising low ones.

One of the central issues of Australian agricultural policy has been the instability of farmers' incomes. Income instability has been particularly apparent among industries that make efficient use of Australia's resource structure. This is not surprising, since these are the industries that export a large part of their production. Over two-thirds of Australia's farm output is sold on volatile world markets. Furthermore, most of this output is subject to great climatic uncertainty. Yield instability probably is greater in Australian agriculture than in any other commercial agricultural sector in the world. The problem of unstable rural incomes seems to be worsening, mainly because of the rising proportion of farm output sold on export markets and the increasing volatility of those markets.

Agricultural stabilization policy has been composed of a patchwork of measures, which were not always consistent with some of their stated objectives. These objectives have included the reduction of risks in relation to price and yield, the smoothing of incomes over time, the mitigation of low incomes faced by some farmers during industry slumps, the stabilization of prices to consumers, and the provision of some degree of assistance to particular industries. This has been done mainly through domestic price supports at the expense of consumers, sometimes augmented by government subventions at the expense of taxpayers. Some of the measures used have clearly served diverse and overlapping functions and have contributed toward misallocation of resources.

Stabilization has been the avowed objective for much of the government intervention in Australian agriculture since federation. As a slogan, stabilization has had considerable political appeal, especially when used in defense of "the family farm," and in tandem with "orderly marketing." Not surprisingly, it has often served as an effective camouflage for "upward stabilization." However, this perhaps cynical observation should not be allowed to obscure the genuine significance of stabilization as a major objective of Australian agriculture.

## The IAC Report

The IAC report contains only a few specific recommendations. Its main conclusions are in the form of broad principles, which provide the framework for a consistent and general stabilization policy. Summaries of sections of the report follow.

### *Risk and Efficiency*

Most farmers are averse to risk and adopt risk-reducing strategies—flexibility, liquidity, diversification, caution in adopting new techniques, levels of inputs that yield less than maximum expected net returns, and so on. This results in output levels and product combinations inconsistent with those for which expected net returns are maximized. By this criterion, there is underinvestment in high-risk activities. For the individual, this could be a rational and efficient choice between income and stability. However, from society's viewpoint the outcome is inefficient, and it has been argued that government should intervene by subsidy or other means to correct this distortion. Government could encourage change in the use of resources through incentives to engage in riskier enterprises or through a general protection of the producer against risk. An early and influential exposition of this view as applied to agriculture was advanced by Johnson (1947).

Such arguments imply at least one of the following assumptions. (1) Even though individuals may be risk-averse, society is or should be risk-neutral. (2) Competitive markets do not offer producers adequate opportunities for risk shifting or risk sharing, through, for example, insurance, futures trading, common stocks, and cost-plus contracts.

These questions have been discussed by Demsetz (1969), Pauly (1968), Arrow (1962, 1963, 1974), Arrow and Lind (1970, 1972), and Pasour and Bullock (1975).

Clearly, individual farmers cannot be regarded as inefficient if they organize their farms to take account of uncertainty. In effect, risk reduction is an economic benefit that should be incorporated into any assessment of efficiency. An analogy might be drawn between stability and leisure. Both are preferences arising from people's attitudes. Both are pursued by producers at the expense of income, which means that the producer has weighed the extra cost, work, and risk involved in extra output against the valuation consumers would place on that output. A system of taxes and subsidies imposed to move producers away from their preferred positions in relation to leisure and stability would raise national output but would not necessarily mean that the community was better off.

National welfare might be increased if society as a whole, through government, were less concerned with risks associated with individual investments than were individual producers. Some risk could be shifted to government in various ways, and depending on the costs involved, this might improve social well-being. The view that society should be less averse to risk than individuals has taken several somewhat related forms. The first is the notion that society, through government, can take a longer-term view than individuals, so that it should be concerned only with maximizing the expected return to the community's scarce productive resources. Second, there is the view that government is better able to pool risks because of its large and diversified portfolio of activities. Finally there is the notion that the total cost of risk bearing is negligible when spread over all taxpayers. An alternative view is that government reflects the attitudes and aspirations of the individuals to whom it is ultimately responsible. Thus it reflects an amalgamation of all individual attitudes to risk. These complex issues have not been fully resolved in the economic and social literature.

The IAC was also unable to resolve these questions. However, it considered that, even if it could be established that governments should encourage risky investments, the conceptual and practical problems involved in applying such a policy would make it infeasible. Some element of uncertainty attaches to every area of economic life, which suggests that it would be desirable to relate the amount of subsidy (or whatever form intervention might take) to the amount of uncertainty. Thus it would be desirable to obtain some ordering of degrees of risk across all possible ventures and across all sectors. Besides the large conceptual problems involved, such a rating would be extremely difficult to obtain in practical terms. Further, it is not only the degree of risk that is relevant but also the effects of that risk on resource allocation in particular cases. This would also be very difficult to measure, as producers would have already taken some actions to reduce both the levels and effects of the risk they face.

The IAC concluded that there is no sound basis for endorsing a general policy of assistance to high-risk activities. This general conclusion does not mean that a case-by-case examination would not identify specific high-risk activities where government involvement might improve resource use and thus general community well-being. This might be expected if government could remove any barriers or impediments that inhibit producers from coping more effectively with variable and uncertain returns. In this regard, the IAC was particularly interested in the performance of commercial markets for risk-reduction services, financial services, and information.

### *Insurance and Efficiency*

Comparisons of production efficiency in situations of risk versus no risk (or risk aversion versus risk neutrality) generally assume that marginal costs are the same in each case. This assumption ignores certain costs incurred in producing relatively stable returns in an uncertain environment.

A risk-averse farmer who fully insures against risk incurs the costs of insurance premiums. His costs will be raised (on average and in the long run) by premiums less claims paid; that is, by the administration costs of insurance including profit. Thus, even if all of the risk facing a producer were insurable, and he fully insures, his output would be suboptimal in the sense that it would be lower than it would have been had he faced no risk. Only if the administration cost of insurance were zero would output be optimal. However, such costs are real social costs, whether they are met by the insured or by government subsidy.

Where insurance is available, it enables some risk-averse producers to achieve preferred risk-income combinations and a higher value of output from physical resources employed. However, risk-averse producers may decide not to adopt insurance but to operate at a lower level of output. They may also combine a mix of activities, which they expect to be less profitable than that chosen by risk-neutral producers. It is not clear that inefficient resource use results from such decisions (unless, as discussed above, it can be shown that society should ignore risk and uncertainty in evaluating efficiency).

It has been argued by Arrow (1962) that the economic system has only limited and imperfect devices for sharing and shifting risks. Arrow considered that it would be worthwhile to increase the variety of such devices but that potential for doing so is limited by the problem of moral hazard. Thus such devices for improving efficiency with respect to risk bearing may worsen technical efficiency.

In a critique of Arrow's analysis, Demsetz (1969) pointed out that the economic system does in fact produce a considerable number of what Arrow terms commodity options, and that Arrow seemed to be assuming that the cost of providing them was zero. He also attacked Arrow's contention that the government should undertake insurance in those cases where the market, for whatever reason, has failed to emerge (Arrow 1963).

In particular, Demsetz disagreed with Arrow's treatment of moral hazard. "The moral hazard problem is no different than the problem posed by any cost. Some iron ore is left unearthed because it is too costly to bring to the surface. But we do not claim ore mining is inefficient merely because mining is not 'complete.' Some risks are left uninsured because the cost of moral hazard is too great. . . . While it may cost nothing to insure risky enterprises in the world of the ideal norm, it does in this world, if for no other reason than the proclivity of some to commit moral hazards" (Demsetz 1969, p. 167).

The notion that markets to handle risks develop as the need arises is dependent on the view that individuals are always well informed, always know their own best interests, and always act accordingly. If such were the case, individuals would certainly be able to calculate the costs and benefits of extra information. Market mechanisms could then be expected to emerge, if enough individuals considered that the benefits of sharing or shifting risks exceeded the costs. From Demsetz's viewpoint, this is a sufficiently adequate representation of the real world.

In this vein, Stigler (1967) writes, "There is no 'imperfection' in a market possessing incomplete knowledge if it would not be remunerative to acquire (produce) complete knowledge: information costs are the costs of transportation from ignorance to omniscience, and seldom can a trader afford to take the entire trip" (p. 291).

In contrast, Arrow bases his argument on the view that it is impossible for individuals to become adequately informed before the establishment of markets. Some other writers take similar views. Pearce (1975), writing in relation to resource conservation, states, "A theory which says that the market would work if operators in the market knew the facts is not sufficient grounds for arguing that it is all right to leave everything to the market when the facts, in the nature of the case, cannot be known" (p. 202).

Mishan (1975) also writes, "By extending the concept of transaction cost to encompass any inertia or lack of initiative in society, one comes uncomfortably close to the thesis that, in economics, whatever is, is best" (p. 699).

The approach of Demsetz and others has been associated with some recent developments in the theory of information, property rights, bargaining, and transactions costs. Their argument has exposed some of the weaknesses in the conventional view of risk and efficiency, which has largely ignored the costs of information and of transactions. However, there may sometimes be occasions when a government should intervene to provide information or to regulate market prices. This is a pragmatic problem, which should be evaluated case by case. Alternative viewpoints on this issue probably will continue to compete, if only because they touch upon broad social goals and values.

### *Crop Insurance*

The predominant form of agricultural insurance offered in Australia is against risk of hail and fire. It has involved cumulative loss ratios of around 0.7 (that is, around 70 cents of each premium dollar was paid to farmers for losses), which is in excess of levels regarded by the industry as desirable for commercial insurance. Generally, this insurance is written by large insurance bodies that avoid offering crop insurance in isolation from other insurance; usually, insured farmers must give all their other insurance business to the same company.

Several attempts have been made to introduce commercial multiple-risk schemes to Australia but with little success, judged on participation rates, scheme costs, and period of survival. Experience suggests that important reasons for the frequently high cost and therefore limited availability of private insurance are the high risk that damage would be of catastrophic proportions, the scarcity of information to determine the relevant risks, and the problems in defining hazards and damage.

Government action can also restrict the provision of insurance. Significant constraints imposed on the conduct of the Australian insurance industry might affect the ability and incentives of insurers to increase coverage in high-risk areas. For example, entry to the industry is restricted, insurers are required to hold a proportion of their assets in government securities, and there are restrictions on the types and nature of business activities that insurers can undertake. While these restrictions have been introduced to meet specific objectives (such as the protection of consumers), their potential to affect incentives to undertake riskier business may be considerable.

Australian governments have also provided significant assistance to rural producers and communities affected by natural disasters, such as droughts, fires, and floods. The assistance has largely been in the form of grants, concessional loans, and freight and taxation concessions. This assistance may be highly desirable for social or welfare reasons, but the effects on individual incentives are not clear. To the extent that it reduces individual incentives to insure, it may be a further reason that agricultural insurance is not more generally available and used.

Crop insurance offered by grower-controlled state marketing boards has sometimes been compulsory. Compulsion usually results in the cross subsidization of high-risk farmers by low-risk farmers, causing inequity and inefficiency. The main arguments usually advanced for compulsion are that it provides economies of scale, and therefore cheaper insurance, and that it spreads risk. Compulsory insurance ensures the participation of those farmers who otherwise would not participate because they are not risk-averse, or they are in a low-risk situation relative to the premium they would have to pay. This conflict might be met by setting more realistic rate structures, though this might be expensive.

Some farmers face little risk, and a proportion of those who face considerable risk are not greatly concerned by it. Of those farmers who are averse to risk, many have other forms of risk reduction available, which they may prefer if left to do their own risk management. Therefore, the use of compulsion, involving the abandonment of the market-place test of voluntary consent, may result in inefficiencies as well as interference with the freedom of choice. This is so regardless of whether the full cost of the insurance is met by the participants or by a public subsidy.

Subsidized insurance as a method of government intervention to offset risk has some important advantages. It is direct in effect, in that it would operate on the income of individual farmers, and the amount of assistance would be related to the degree of risk. Furthermore, it could be and usually is voluntary (in contrast with, say, buffer funds) and does not interfere with the operation of market forces in the product market (in contrast with guaranteed prices). On the other hand, there is the disadvantage that offering insurance below its real cost will distort the choices farmers make between insurance and the many other unsubsidized methods of minimizing or coping with risk and income instability. Furthermore, for many farmers, conventional, multiple-risk insurance may not be as cost effective as some alternatives that the IAC believed should be investigated. For these reasons, the IAC did not recommend subsidized farm insurance as a preferred method of implementing any government decision to subsidize the offsetting of risk and the stabilizing of rural incomes.

The IAC felt that there was a need for investigation of new forms of agricultural insurance, which may offer a higher ratio of benefits to costs than conventional forms of insurance. Such alternatives may be rainfall insurance or, possibly, farm income insurance based on regional-income movements. In Australia, no single factor is more highly correlated to crop or pasture yields than rainfall. Rainfall insurance could reduce the risk of financial loss caused by the effects of excessive or inadequate rainfall. Some types of rainfall insurance are commercially available (for example, for sporting events), but no rainfall insurance schemes seem to have been developed specifically for agriculture. Official statistics would provide some actuarial basis for the determination of premiums.

Such insurance would provide only partial coverage for the production process: rainfall, though important, is only one of a number of factors affecting production levels. Also, coverage would be effective only to the extent that rainfall on an individual's farm corresponds with rainfall at a designated recording station. Additional recording stations might be necessary in some areas. However, individual farmers could avoid the risk of being completely dependent on what happens at one recording station by spreading their hedge over several nearby stations.

Insurance coverage could be offered for a specific calendar period (six months or twelve months) or for specific cropping operations within a particular region (preparation and sowing, or growing and harvesting). Critical periods for livestock production could also be covered. In effect, the producer could hedge against excessive or inadequate rainfall in a specified period by placing a "bet" on the adverse situation against which he is seeking to hedge. The bet would have to be placed sufficiently in advance to prevent advantage being gained from weather forecasts.

There would appear to be no need for the provision of information by the farmer nor the checking of such information by costly farm visits. This factor, together with the avoidance of problems of moral hazard and adverse selection, suggests that administration costs might be very low. However, it would be necessary to devise an accurate and fraud-proof method of recording rainfall.

The type of rainfall insurance proposed by the IAC differs from conventional insurance in that it would be against a particular natural event and not against an assessed loss by the insured resulting from that event. However, rather than being a speculative gamble, it would be a hedge against an undesired occurrence (drought or flood) and would have the effect of reducing the inevitable element of gambling in farming.

Both price-stabilization schemes and multiple-risk crop insurance have major disadvantages as methods of stabilizing the incomes of individual producers. An alternative approach is a voluntary, regionally based income-stabilization plan. The farm income stabilization plan proposed by Lloyd (1977) and discussed by the IAC (1978) is similar in some ways to the plan put forward by Dandekar (1977) and discussed in chapter 16. As a simple illustration of the plan, assume that the regional income per hectare (or per animal) from a product was $x$ percent higher or lower than normal in a particular year. All insured farmers in the region would then receive payouts of $x$ percent (or some proportion thereof) of the region's normal per hectare income from that product on each hectare they had insured. The contribution that such a plan could make toward stabilizing the incomes of individual farmers within a region would depend on the extent to which the variation of individual incomes was attributable to regionwide fluctuations.

A major advantage of the regional approach is that it substantially reduces or avoids problems of moral hazard and adverse selection. If premiums and payouts are determined by movement in regional yields and prices, they are not dependent on events within the control of the individual farmer or on risk characteristics of the individual farm.

Apart from providing probably cheaper insurance, a regionally based farm income stabilization plan has the advantages that it would be comprehensive, covering price fluctuations as well as yield fluctuations and livestock products as well as crops; it would be multiproduct, aimed at stabilizing aggregate income from all enterprises on the individual farm; and it would not interfere with the role of prices in guiding resource use. The IAC recommended that Lloyd's plan be further investigated.

### *Price Stabilization*

The Australian history of price stabilization dates from the 1920s. Since then, various schemes have been applied to wheat, wool, dairy products, sugar, various fruits, rice, eggs, and tobacco.

Price-stabilization schemes in Australia have generally included one or more of the following mechanisms: price discrimination, buffer stocks, buffer funds and pooling arrangements, and guaranteed prices supported by buffer funds or deficiency payments contributions by government. Deficiency payments have also been made as temporary emergency measures.

The issue of price stabilization is especially important in relation to income stabilization. Several witnesses who gave evidence to the IAC, including representatives of farmer organizations and state departments of agriculture, saw price stabilization as a means of reducing the level of risk borne by producers and improving farmers' production planning decisions. Better planning was seen to result from the stabilized price, which is a more reliable guide to market prospects than the price expectations of individual producers.

For many rural commodities, especially crops, output fluctuations account for a larger degree of gross income variability than fluctuations in price. Furthermore, for many commodities, changes in prices and production have been predominantly in opposite directions, tending to offset each other to some degree. Where this tendency is marked, price stabilization (as through a buffer fund) could destabilize industry revenue from that commodity.

For a particular product, much of the variation in yields at the regional level or at the individual farm level is offsetting and is concealed in the aggregate or average figure for the industry. That is, a good season on one group of farms can be balanced by poor seasons elsewhere. Furthermore, most farms produce more than one product, which provides scope for offsetting income variations among products.

As a result of these factors, price stabilization can sometimes destabilize the income of individual producers. For example, under a buffer-funds scheme (a stabilization fund), an export tax is imposed when prices are high; in some cases this will be a deduction from an income that is already low, because a producer has had either a low yield of the product concerned or low earnings from other enterprises. Similarly, payments out of the fund will be destabilizing for some individuals.

When the decisions of farmers (and other producers) are analyzed after they have produced and sold their output, it usually appears that resources have been misdirected. That is, some resources committed to particular activities on the basis of farmers' expectations of prices, yields, and so on, could, as things turned out, have been used more profitably (in terms of realized prices and yields) in other activities. Where these costs of being wrong are large, hindsight has suggested to some people that some form of price stabilization was needed. However, the significance of these costs largely depends on the extent to which information could have been obtained about production and marketing outcomes at the time the relevant decisions were made.

Government involvement to improve farmers' decisions could be justified if it has better market information than farmers or could obtain it more cheaply. For example, government may be privy to information about decisions likely to be made by foreign governments, and they would be more informed about their own actions. Also there may be greater economies of scale in collection (production), analysis, and dissemination of information than the economies of scale available to private operators. However, as governments have often acknowledged, their provision of market information is hazardous. Political pressure could be applied on governments to provide and support optimistic forecasts. Also, governments, like farmers, can be wrong, and errors in official forecasts may lead to claims for redress.

If superior information is available to public authorities, there may be more effective means of disseminating it than through price stabilization. If superior information is not available, the stabilized price would be unlikely to be any more correct than the price expectations of producers and thus might distort market-price signals. Where public forecasting is not better than that of farmers, and the government financially supports the stabilized price (like a guaranteed minimum price), the costs of errors in planning are not reduced but simply subsidized by taxpayers.

In Australia, price discrimination (that is, charging different prices for the same commodity in separate markets) has been practiced for many commodities. To achieve this, the marketing authority must control at least one market. Price discrimination between export markets and domestic markets, with administered home-consumption prices, has been quite common (for example, for wheat, dairy products, sugar, and various fruits). Also, prices have discriminated between end uses for some commodities (for example, animal feed wheat and human-consumption wheat, fresh milk and milk for manufactured products). A major purpose of price discrimination between markets has been to increase total sales revenue, and a considerable part of the total assistance received by Australian agriculture has been from this source. Price discrimination also has had a stabilizing effect by reducing price variability in the controlled market, which tends to stabilize the average return. However, for those commodities for which the controlled market is relatively small (wheat, for example), the stabilizing effect on average returns has been relatively minor, as is the effect on levels of assistance.

The administered domestic price could be set in relation to the export price so as to provide countercyclical assistance for the industry. To some extent, this occurs—when export prices rise to high levels, the domestic price is sometimes held at levels lower than export parity. In this situation, producers are subsidizing consumers, as happened in the case of wheat and sugar in the early to mid-1970s. When export prices fall to low levels, this is often taken into account in setting a domestic price that results in a higher subsidy from consumers to producers.

Since the one product is receiving at least two prices, a problem of price discrimination is the allocation of market shares among producers. The common solution in Australia has been to equalize returns; that is, pay producers a pooled return from the various markets. However, this approach may lead to producers receiving the wrong price signals. This is because the real return to additional production is the price for which that production is sold, not the average price. Thus equalizing prices may encourage overproduction when export prices are low and underproduction when export prices are high, with consequent resource misallocation costs. Also, if, as has often been the case with Australian home-price schemes, domestic prices are above export prices, there may be consumption losses resulting from the higher retail prices. Conversely, there are production and consumption distortions when the home price is set below export levels.

Production distortions may be avoided where each producer is allocated a quota, or market entitlement, covering that part of his total output that supplies the generally higher-price markets. The generally lower price is then paid for any excess production, and therefore, at the margin, the price received by producers reflects its market value.

A buffer stock can be used to reduce price variability through a marketing authority, which buys and holds stocks of a commodity when prices fall and sells these stocks when prices rise. The reserve price scheme for wool uses a buffer stock partly to maintain a minimum (floor) price and to stabilize prices. It has sometimes been suggested that the reserve price scheme also aims at raising prices received for wool. Buffer stocks have also operated in international stabilization arrangements.

In operating the buffer stock, the authority may make speculative profits or losses, depending on the prices and quantities of purchases and sales and the costs of stockholding and administration. In addition, producers may make hidden gains or losses compared with returns they would have received in the absence of the scheme: prices to producers tend to be raised by the authority's purchases and lowered by the authority's sales. These gains or losses are generally independent of the speculative gains or losses made by the authority. They depend on the responsiveness of demand to price changes when the commodity is bought and sold and on the quantities traded by the authority. To the extent that there are either speculative or hidden gains from buffer stocks, the benefits of price stability are reinforced. Similarly, any losses can be thought of as the costs of increased price stability. The potential gains from a buffer-stock scheme would be limited for commodities where storage and handling costs are high, due to factors such as interest costs, perishability, and product heterogeneity (difficulties in grading and standardization).

Several price-stabilization schemes in Australia and overseas have involved governments setting in advance guaranteed minimum prices for commodities. As a stabilization tool, forward prices are designed to provide price information and reduce uncertainty, although they can also be used as a means of price support. To reduce uncertainty and affect production decisions, forward prices must be announced well in advance of the production period. (This has rarely been done in Australia.) If market prices fall below the forward price, the difference must be made up by a government subsidy, or from a buffer fund, or through some similar arrangements to include producer contributions.

Among its general conclusions, the IAC advised the government that income-stabilization objectives should preferably be achieved by measures that do not interfere with the function of prices in conveying market information and incentives. Industrywide stabilization measures, such as price stabilization, are unlikely to contribute greatly to the stabilizing of individual incomes. Price stabilization also can lead to inefficient use of resources by discouraging profitable adjustments.

### *Credit*

The financial system as a repository for savings and a source of credit has a significant role in enabling farmers (and others) to cope with variable returns. In fact, reliance on savings and borrowing is a substitute stabilizing measure for many of the risk-reducing strategies mentioned earlier (see also chapter 4).

There are some government-imposed constraints on the conduct of the Australian banking industry that could limit the flow of funds to risky activities. Government-prescribed maximum rates of interest for the main types of borrowing and lending by banks are examples of constraints that could lead to a credit gap. Without such constraints, credit would probably be sought and made available over a wide range of repayment conditions and interest rates. With interest rates fixed, lenders might use non-price methods, such as specified equity requirements and refusal of risky proposals, to allocate funds. This tendency may have been compounded for the agricultural sector in the period 1956–73 by a further government requirement that banks charge a concessional interest rate on farmers' overdrafts. Restrictions on entry to the banking industry and requirements that some banks' assets be held in low-return deposits may also have reduced the amount of funds available for risky activities.

Some witnesses before the IAC suggested that the problem of servicing large long-term loans from a fluctuating income stream may be reduced by a variable amortization scheme (VAS) such as that proposed by Baker (1974). Under a VAS, borrowers would be wholly or partially relieved of debt repayments in low-income years in return for making larger payments in high-income years.

In evidence before the IAC, bankers said that VAS was unnecessary since variable amortization already existed on an informal basis. It is true that trading banks commonly relax the repayment obligations of farmers in financial difficulties. However, this informal assistance is somewhat uncertain. It may depend on the decision of the local bank manager as well as on the bank's lending policy and the government monetary policy at the time. A VAS may eliminate this uncertainty for risk-averse borrowers whose loan repayment commitment is high relative to their expected cash surplus. Lender risk may also be reduced under some types of VAS, such as those involving a debt reserve.

In recent research by Kent and Lloyd (1983), two forms of VAS were investigated, the debt reserve and the equity credit reserve, each in optional combination with option loans. Under the debt reserve VAS originally proposed by Baker, borrowers undertake to deposit money in prosperous times to be used solely for the purpose of making debt payments in years of depressed income. Under the debt reserve VAS modelled in the Kent/Lloyd study, three-quarters of the disposable cash surplus in any one year is deposited in the reserve, which accumulates up to a maximum of three times the annual repayment commitment on the loan.

Under the equity credit reserve scheme, risk-averse farmers borrow less than the maximum the lender would advance. They thus retain a reserve of borrowing power based on their overall equity, which adds to their farms' liquidity. At the other extreme is the maximum loan, under which the marginal dollar borrowed brings the borrower's equity ratio down to some critical minimum level as regards lender risk. For such maximum loans, the loan commences with a zero equity credit reserve. However, with progressive annual repayments, the increase in the borrower's equity creates a growing equity credit reserve, which under inflation may be further increased by the rising value of the assets forming the loan collateral.

This contingency credit exists regardless of any VAS arrangements: if the prime lender refuses to advance credit in an emergency, the borrower may have sufficient equity for outside borrowing on a second mortgage. However, this could involve significantly higher costs, reflecting the cost of additional information and the legal and administration costs of arranging the new loan. Thus, from the borrower's viewpoint, a formalized equity credit reserve VAS, depending on its cost, may be preferred to temporary outside borrowing. It would be an assured form of contingency credit for meeting loan repayments and it could provide more contingency credit than outside borrowing. Repayment of arrears and interest thereon would be a first claim on the borrower's first subsequent surplus.

Most defaults occur early in the loan period, when insufficient time has elapsed to build up reserves. The Kent/Lloyd study suggests that for a maximum loan, half or more of defaults can be expected to occur in the first three years of a twenty-year loan term. In the early years, neither the equity credit reserve VAS nor the debt reserve VAS can by themselves be effective safeguards against default. Only if the loan is for an amount significantly less than the maximum would there be adequate borrowing power in reserve. To meet this problem, option loans were postulated under which a borrower can purchase an option over additional funds to be used solely for one annual loan repayment. Such funds would be advanced only if the borrower's farm income fell below some specified level during any of the first three years of the loan and if there were insufficient equity credit reserve or debt reserve available to prevent default. An annual fee would be charged until the option was taken up. At that point, the interest rate charged on advanced funds would apply. This rate would be related to some specified benchmark (for example, the long-term bond rate) plus some risk rate agreed upon in the initial loan contract. For year one of a maximum loan, this risk rate could be quite considerable, since the bank would be undertaking a contingent obligation to advance additional credit without additional collateral.

In a quantitative analysis of these proposals, Kent and Lloyd calculated income flows disaggregated to the individual farmer for the high-risk Mallee region in Victoria. They did this by stochastically combining the yields and price of cereals and wool over recent decades. The variance of expected income facing the individual wheat or sheep farmer (and his creditors) was found to be extremely high, with a coefficient of variation of taxable income of 143 percent. Repayment of a twenty-year loan was then simulated under the above-mentioned income flows over a range of earning rates, equity ratios, interest and inflation rates, marginal propensities to save, and so on. The simulation incorporated outside borrowing of up to 80 percent of unused borrowing capacity where necessary, together with some deferment of machinery replacement. Default was considered to have occurred when the annual loan repayment could not be made after resort to accumulated savings, including interest, maximum permitted deferral of machinery replacement, contingency credit from VAS, and maximum outside borrowing. The simulated incidence of default under VAS, compared with default under the conventional loan repayment program, using the conventional amortization formula (equal annual nominal repayments), is shown in table 10.1.

For the maximum (that is, high-risk) loan, VAS arrangements can reduce the probability of default by approximately one-third to one-half. Whether or not this is enough to induce a demand for VAS arrangements sufficient to justify their provision depends on the cost to the borrower of such arrangements. It seems likely that this can be determined only by implementing a VAS scheme on a limited, trial basis, as suggested by the IAC.

A significant conclusion to be drawn from the data in table 10.1 is that the probability of loan default is greatly increased by inflation. This occurs because of the continued and apparently irrational use of the conventional amortization formula for repayment of term loans. The formula belongs to preinflationary days, since it yields equal annual payments in

TABLE 10.1 Defaults on agricultural loans by loan arrangement, loan size, and inflation rate, Australia

| | Defaults per 1,000 loans[a] | | | | | |
|---|---|---|---|---|---|---|
| | 0% inflation | | 5% inflation | | 10% inflation | |
| Loan arrangement | $100,000 loan | $140,000 loan | $100,000 loan | $140,000 loan | $100,000 loan | $140,000 loan |
| Conventional | 12 | 111 | 33 | 216 | 53 | 462 |
| Equity-credit reserve VAS | 8 | 105 | 12 | 194 | 28 | 385 |
| Equity-credit reserve plus 3-year option | 4 | 70 | 8 | 114 | 23 | 265 |
| Debt-reserve VAS | 12 | 107 | 21 | 203 | 50 | 428 |
| Debt reserve plus 3-year option | | 74 | | 153 | | 373 |

[a]Assumptions: real interest rate, 2.5 percent; nominal rates, 2.5, 7.5, and 12.5 percent; loan period, 20 years; earning rate on capital, 4.9 percent; propensity to save, 0.75; outside-borrowing fraction, 0.8; 1,000 replications.

TABLE 10.2 Effect of inflation on real burden of agricultural loan repayment, Australia

| Item | 0% inflation | 10% inflation | | | | |
|---|---|---|---|---|---|---|
| | years 1-20 | Year 1 | Year 2 | Year 3 | Year 10 | Year 20 |
| Interest rate (percent)[a] | 2.5 | 12.5 | 12.5 | 12.5 | 12.5 | 12.5 |
| Annual income (dollars) | 23,215 | 23,215 | 25,537 | 28,090 | 54,740 | 141,981 |
| Annual repayment commitment (dollars) | 6,420 | 13,810 | 13,810 | 13,810 | 13,810 | 13,810 |
| Real burden of repayment[b] | 0.28 | 0.59 | 0.54 | 0.49 | 0.25 | 0.10 |

*Note*: Assumptions: $100,000 loan, conventional amortization over 20 years.
[a]The real interest rate is held constant at 2.5%.
[b]Annual repayment commitment divided by income.

money terms over the loan period. Its continued use under high rates of inflation and interest distorts the time pattern of loan repayment, concentrating the real burden of repayment into the early years of the loan (table 10.2).

By adjusting the loan repayment arrangements to provide annual repayments approximately equal in real terms, rather than in nominal terms (that is, an indexed mortgage), the probability of default can be reduced by more than three-quarters with 10-percent inflation. The simulation study showed that the combination of VAS with full indexation has a dramatic effect: for the $100 thousand loan, defaults fall from 53 per thousand loans to 4, comparing the conventional loan plan under 10-percent inflation with an equity credit reserve VAS plus option loan under zero inflation.

### *Welfare*

In recent years, several studies have investigated the nature and incidence of poverty among Australian farmers and their families (Vincent 1976). These studies have identified two groups of farm families that merit concern. First, a small group that have chronically low incomes; typically these are elderly farmers operating small farms and having little commercial output. Second, a larger group that have low incomes only in some periods. The size of the second group upholds the view that Australian farm poverty fluctuates and is more a product of agricultural instability than of small or nonviable farms.

The welfare implications of rural income fluctuations are considerable. As a general rule, output-based assistance like price stabilization and input-based assistance like freight concessions on fodder are unlikely to meet these welfare needs, since the largest benefits tend to go to the largest farmers. Nevertheless, welfare problems have often been tackled with measures of this kind. The provision of direct income support to farm families and other self-employed groups is quite recent. Product-based assistance was and still is widely used, partly because of its administrative advantages: it is relatively simple to design, quick in effect, and cheap to administer.

In the past, income support did not cover farmers and other self-employed persons, despite the recognition that family incomes in these groups sometimes fall very low. Unemployment benefits require that the recipient be available for full-time work; they also involve a means test on income, but not on net worth. Farmers and other self-employed people meeting the work and means tests were made eligible for unemployment benefits in 1976. However, there are special problems for farmers who do not live within reasonable commuting distance of alternative employment.

There are practical difficulties in determining the monthly or even the annual income of a self-employed person. Also, considerable scope exists for manipulation of income and costs. Extended periods of very low income are often preceded and followed by periods of quite high income. Furthermore, farm families in short-term difficulties often possess considerable wealth, though admittedly not in liquid form.

Provision of household support and short-term carry-on credit was recommended by the IAC. Carry-on finance was recommended for farmers whose properties were considered by the adjustment authority to be viable in the long run but who lacked liquidity in the short term. The essential feature of the recommended household support assistance was payment at the same level of unemployment benefits, for a period of up to one year, to farmers remaining on their farm who were judged to earn inadequate income over that period. Because of the difficulty of accurately estimating income, it was recommended that the payments be included in taxable income. On that basis, tax payments would be made only when the estimate of income proved to be too low.

The federal government in consultation with the state governments accepted the IAC recommended scheme in principle, but the details of operation have differed from the IAC proposals. The rural adjustment authority in each state provides loans to eligible farmers sufficient to raise the applicants' estimated future incomes to the level of their notional entitlement under unemployment benefits.

In the IAC view, income is a better basis for welfare assistance than other indicators of need frequently used, such as produce price or seasonal conditions. Many measurement difficulties remain, such as the determination of equitable ways of accounting for wealth, overcoming any incentives to manipulate revenues and costs so that income in a particular period satisfies specified means tests, and accounting for the significance of nonpecuniary income.

### *Taxation*

Australian governments since early in this century have modified the income tax system to offset some of the adverse consequences of farmers' fluctuating incomes. This has been done by taxing income in the current year at the rate applicable to the average income of the current and preceding four years. The theory behind tax averaging is that, under a progressive income tax system, those whose incomes fluctuate widely from year to year pay more tax over time than those who have a comparable stable income. The purpose of tax averaging is to remove this anomaly, not to stabilize income. In fact, the effect of this long-standing system, which averages only the rate of tax, is to cause posttax income to fluctuate rather more than it would if the taxpayer did not average, though this effect is not large.

In 1976 the Australian government introduced a scheme called income equalization deposits, which would supplement tax-rate averaging along the lines proposed by the IAC by allowing farmers to invest surplus income into an interest-bearing deposit lodged with the federal treasury. Only when the deposit is cashed are the proceeds taxed. Thus, although the tax-averaging system that has operated for many years involves backward averaging of all income to determine the rate at which tax is paid, the newer system involves forward averaging (or adjustment) of some income (determined by the farmer) to determine the income on which tax is paid.

In pure form, these arrangements are instruments of tax equity and income stability for farmers. The IAC proposed that they operate in such a neutral way. However, both of these arrangements can be used to discriminate in favor of farmers, and in practice, elements of positive assistance have been built into both sets of measures. In particular, changes were made to the averaging scheme in 1978, under which averaging applies only where current taxable income exceeds average income. In this case, tax on current income is still levied at the average rate that would apply to a taxable income equal to average income of the current year and the four preceding years. However, where current taxable income is less than average income, tax is levied in the same way as for ordinary taxpayers—on current taxable income without regard to average income. Thus under the new system, a farmer has the benefit of paying tax on his current taxable income at either (1) the rate applicable to his average income or (2) the rate under the ordinary tax scale, whichever is lower.

The IAC considered that the objective of stabilizing individual income would most efficiently be achieved by encouraging farmers to manage their own income and expenditure flows through time. The income equalization deposit scheme was particularly appropriate for this purpose, since it was designed to be tax-neutral. However, the new averaging arrangements, which were criticized by the IAC, make these deposits unattractive to some farmers. Under the new rules, some taxpayers incur a lower marginal rate of tax in high-income years than in low-income years. Thus the extra tax paid when a deposit is cashed in a low-income year can exceed the tax saving made when the income was deposited.

### *Summary*

The IAC report suggested that methods to stabilize the incomes of individual farmers have three characteristics. First, they should directly affect individual incomes, as each farmer's income variability is unique. Second, to ensure neutrality among agricultural activities, regions, and so on, and to avoid the diminution of market signals and incentives, they should not be specific to particular inputs or outputs. Last, their use should be voluntary and allow farmers to choose their own degree of income smoothing. If governments wish to encourage income smoothing, they should make income equalization deposits or similar financial services more attractive to farmers. In the case of the deposits, neutrality of the tax-averaging provisions could be restored and a higher rate of interest be paid.

## Recent Changes in Stabilization Policy

The most positive change in Australian agricultural stabilization policy has been a shift toward measures operating directly through income. Accompanying this, there has been a clearer recognition of separable welfare and efficiency objectives and a greater emphasis on individual choice by participating farmers.

The principal role of government in the Australian farm credit market until the early 1970s had been to provide (or induce the commercial banks to provide) cheap credit to farmers to encourage farm investment. However, since then there has been a shift toward assistance through finance for farm adjustment and, to a lesser extent, for farm income stabilization.

Changes in credit policies and social security policies have enabled the efficiency and welfare objectives of stabilization policies to be met more effectively. There has been a greater opportunity for individual choice by farmers and for assessment of individual needs by program administrators. Paralleling these changes has been a downplaying of the role of prices in stabilization policy and less reliance on industrywide compulsory measures. These changes have usually followed individual commodity reviews, in which the IAC has played a central role.

Until the mid-1970s, the principal policy instruments of stabilization for Australian farmers were a number of commodity price-stabilization schemes. The archetypal scheme was that for wheat. The IAC reviewed the Australian wheat industry's assistance arrangements shortly after it completed its *Report on Rural Income Fluctuations* (1978). Although wheat stabilization plans had periodically provided considerable price assistance to wheat farmers, the IAC concluded that they had little impact on stabilizing incomes. Furthermore, the plans had several inequitable and inefficient features. Through buffer-fund arrangements, income was compulsorily transferred among growers and, on occasion, farmers' funds were tied up for long periods. Thus the plans imposed one price insurance pattern on all wheat farmers, even though each farmer's price risk preference was unique, and the opportunity costs of farmers' funds were diverse. For long periods, the plans stabilized prices above world prices, leading to wastefully high levels of production. At other times, incentives to produce were depressed although more wheat could have been profitably produced.

This did not lead the IAC to reject buffering wheat growers' returns against large and rapid falls in export prices. The wheat industry in Australia has been lightly assisted and makes efficient use of the community's resources. The IAC concluded that to remove the government's commitment to provide backstop support would not improve the efficiency of resource use. It recommended, and the government subsequently accepted, that the traditional price-stabilization arrangements be replaced by a government commitment to underwrite prices to growers in each year at a level equal to a percentage of a moving average of market prices in recent years.

Since the IAC's wheat report, this type of price underwriting has tended to replace the older-style price stabilization schemes for a number of other exported commodities, including manufactured dairy products, apples and pears, and dried vine fruits. When prices fall rapidly, market prices are supplemented by a deficiency payment for a limited period. Assistance is provided only rarely, so that the industries do not develop in an environment of continual assistance. The assistance provided is self-terminating after a short period, since lower market prices quickly become built into the price average against which later prices are underwritten. No buffer funds are used, so that there are no transfers among farmers or among years. In most years, farmers receive returns from actual market realizations.

An underwritten price for wool, supported largely by a producer-financed fund and a buffer stock managed by the Australian Wool Corporation, has operated since the early 1970s. Because of Australia's dominant role in the world wool market, the mechanism can support world prices rather than follow them.

For those commodities having separate domestic-pricing arrangements, moves have been made to ensure that domestic prices move with world price trends. The current wheat marketing arrangement has a mechanism designed to maintain domestic prices for milling wheat at about 20 percent above the trend level of export prices. A less formal arrangement with the same objective operates for manufactured dairy products.

Thus Australia has been moving away from pricing policies designed both to isolate domestic prices of exported commodities from world price movements and to smooth returns from export sales by finely tuned annual adjustments. Buffer funds have been terminated, and policy has been modified to allow domestic prices to follow general world price trends, while export returns are buffered only against sudden and large price falls.

These changes can be interpreted as a downplaying of the role of prices in stabilization policy and an upgrading of the efficiency with which price support is provided. Thus any economic analysis of the policy change should rely less on pure stabilization theory, and more on assistance theory. The IAC concluded that there is no sound basis for endorsing a general policy of assistance to high-risk activities. However, if assistance to an industry is justified for any reason in order to increase resources committed to it, then intervention to reduce risk (or price or revenue fluctuations) may be the most efficient means of doing so. This was the conclusion drawn by the IAC in the case of wheat, but strictly in the context of it being an efficient, lightly assisted, export-oriented industry. Yet even from the viewpoint of stabilization theory, there is reason to believe that fine tuning of stabilized prices may not be welfare-efficient, while a fairly blunt approach, which operates with respect to lower trigger prices, may be welfare-efficient (Quiggin and Anderson 1981).

A shift of emphasis in stabilization policy, away from instruments that operate through prices and toward instruments that operate directly on income and cash flow, is fully in accord with the principles enunciated in the IAC report. However, several of the specific proposals have not been acted upon—for example, rainfall insurance and VAS. The fact that these types of arrangements have not developed independently of government encouragement may reflect in part the regulated structure of the Australian financial system. However, a recent report commissioned by the Australian government on the overall Australian financial system (Campbell Committee 1981) has recommended a considerable relaxation of regulation. If the government accepts these recommendations, it could be expected that a wider variety of commercial instruments would be developed to offset farming risks and income instability.

# 11

# Approaches to Price Insurance for Farmers

Ammar Siamwalla

This chapter addresses the problem faced by small and medium-sized countries attempting to make use of their comparative advantage in production in the face of uncertain and volatile international markets for agricultural commodities. For such countries, it is sometimes possible for governments to use the market to provide price insurance. Such price insurance will, in many circumstances, alleviate the income risks faced by farmers even if the government finds it impossible to provide yield insurance.

## Price Variability and Price Risks

There is a crucial distinction between price variability and price risks. Price variability means that prices may move from year to year on account of shocks to supply and demand. It is conceptually possible, although practically improbable, that the exact time path of the commodity price be known. In any case, the definition is silent concerning the probability distribution of that time path. That distribution may even be nonexistent in the Knightian sense of uncertainty (Knight 1921).

Much of the literature on price stabilization following Waugh (1944), Oi (1961), and Massell (1969) tackles the problem of price variability.[1] The policy instrument to attain price stability discussed, namely buffer stocking, is assumed to be costless. Given this assumption, there is a unanimity of view that buffer stocking confers a net social benefit. However, depending on the assumptions made, results differ as to whether producers and consumers, as groups, gain or lose. This literature stresses the gains to be had from intertemporal arbitrage; that is, moving stocks from years of low prices to years of high prices.

The more realistic case of positive storage costs leads us naturally to the optimal storage literature pioneered by Gustafson (1958).[2] The main

1. For a survey of the literature see Turnovsky (1978) and Newbery and Stiglitz (1981).

2. See also Gardner (1979).

result of this line of work is that there exists a storage rule such that the benefits from the increased stabilization net of storage cost are maximized. At this optimal rate of storage, prices will not be perfectly stabilized. A second result is that, given the usual competitive market assumptions, private storage will be at the optimal level. Whether one believes in the competitive market assumptions or advocates public storage on market failure grounds, the key assumption remains that the optimal storage rule uses the best information available on current market situations. Obviously, more accurate information on the market will yield a different level of optimal stock and will increase the benefits. However, this different level of stock can be reached only by an injection or withdrawal from the market and thus would imply a change in price. Thus an optimal storage policy clearly does not eliminate price variability. However, it can be presumed that the intertemporal arbitrage central to the storage concept would lessen price variability.

The concept of price risks tackled in this chapter is quite different. Price risks occur because farmers and other individuals in the economy have to commit resources before the returns can be known. Even though the output price is unknown, it can be supposed that in the minds of farmers there is a subjective probability distribution of this price. If farmers are risk-averse, then a risk premium would have to be added to the cost of producing the output. By contrast, if the markets within the country are complex and sophisticated enough, the price risks facing the producers can be effectively diffused through forward contracts and future markets. In the limit, the added cost due to the risk premium can be reduced almost to zero, without removing price variability from what it would be if there were a competitive storage industry.

This chapter is concerned with developing countries, where it can hardly be assumed that such complex markets exist or that they can be quickly and costlessly brought into existence. Therefore, the price risks and the premiums that accompany them must be regarded as an excess burden, a result of market failure. What follows assumes that the development level of the country under consideration makes it unrealistic to induce a system of forward contracts and futures markets for agricultural commodities. The evolution of such risk-diffusing institutions is a long, drawn-out process. What is proposed below, that the government should itself take over the task of risk diffusion, should be regarded as a shortcut to the slower and perhaps more logical development of risk markets. Of course, whether this assumption is correct for any particular country at any particular stage of development has to be verified on a case-by-case basis.

In discussing price variability, I have implicitly partitioned time into discrete blocks called production periods, or crop seasons. At the beginning of these periods resources are committed, and at the end of them the output is sold. Aiming for the elimination of price risk means fixing price expectations within each production period without any commitment of price movements from one period to another. In contrast, the price-stabilization literature concentrates on the elimination of price movements over time. In this sense, the concept of price risk is more specific and narrower than price variability. It is hoped that this greater specificity makes for a more practical policy.

The focus on producers may be criticized on the grounds that the consumers' interests are ignored. This again is a consequence of my definition of price risk. When consumers decide to make their purchases, they do not face the same risks that producers do, except for a small risk arising from the nonsynchronization of purchase and consumption.

There is another more serious risk that consumers may face as a result of unforeseeable movements of commodity prices. This can be used to justify government intervention, but to my knowledge it has not been treated in the price-stabilization literature. This risk occurs because many consumers negotiate wage contracts with their employers only in nominal terms. Commodity price movements during their contract periods may have serious consequences on their real incomes. Again, these risks if not diffused will impose a net excess burden on society. Important as this problem is, this chapter ignores it for three reasons. First, to get a firm grip on the problem would require a serious look at the labor market and the type and rationale of the contracts negotiated there. Second, to the extent that my proposals would lower commodity price fluctuations, the risks facing consumers are definitely reduced and thus it may be a partial solution to the problem. Finally, I conjecture that the risk problem that consumers face is essentially a labor market problem. As such, it is more amenable to a labor market solution, such as wage indexation. This last point is also of some policy relevance. For commodities such as food, which are major items in the workers' budget, any policies to allow nominal prices to move must be viewed in conjunction with policies on other nominal prices. Among these, money wages are by far the most important.

## Limitations to Policies that Reduce Price Risks

There are four limits on the scope of any government plan to reduce price risks for commodities. The first is that the plan becomes unwieldy if the production period is excessively long. The second is that the benefits of the plan are questionable if the country's share in world trade is significant. The third limit arises when the commodity for which government intervention reduces price risk is a major sector of the economy. Finally, the proposed scheme presupposes national borders relatively immune to smuggling. Each of these will now be examined in detail.

Recall that the notion of price risk defined in the previous section stresses the price movement between the time when resources are committed and the time that the crop is harvested. This notion sits most comfortably for crops whose annual variable costs form large fractions of the total costs of production. The set of such crops is mostly but not entirely coincidental with the set of annual crops. For those commodities (primarily tree crops and some annual crops) requiring large capital investments in crop-specific production or processing, the recovery of returns extends sometimes several decades (for example, natural rubber) after the commitment of resources. Reducing price risk for such commodities is almost identical to reducing price variability.

Why should the government be reluctant to reduce price risk (or price variability) for the latter set of commodities? If the only source of variability in commodities is random and the underlying probability distribution of price and other random factors remains stationary, then there can be no objection to an attempt to reduce the price risk (or price variability) for these commodities. Sadly, the major price risks that producers of these commodities face arise from nonstationary causes, for example from shifts in demand due to business cycles or, even worse, to technological changes, such as synthetics or to growth of production from alternative supply sources. A government commitment to guarantee returns to producers in such commodities implies a possibly costly commitment to a rigid economy in the face of changing world economic environments.

The second limitation requires that the random elements in the domestic production and the world price be statistically independent. For commodities for which the country is a relatively small buyer or seller in the world market, this condition will most probably hold.[3] For nontraded commodities, and for those commodities (usually export crops) in which the country has a substantial share of the world market, the present proposal is irrelevant. In such instances, the attempt to reduce price risk independently of any policies to tackle yield risk may well increase the total risks faced by producers.

The third limitation involves commodities, insured either singly or as a subset of those with high price intercorrelations, that form a very large part of the economy. Then government-provided price insurance for producers will reduce the private risks as perceived by them but will not reduce the social risks. For while producers' incomes will be stabilized, taxpayers' incomes will be significantly destabilized. There are then two possibilities:

3. It will not invariably hold. If the country is a small importer or exporter, but the deviation from its own normal production is highly correlated with the deviation from the world's normal production, then the world price and the domestic production deviation will not be independent.

The simplest possibility is when there exists a futures market at the world level (for example, in Chicago for maize, New York and London for sugar). Then the government may eliminate most of the social risk by hedging in such a market. That is, by selling futures for the commodity up to the level of the expected production of the crop. The risks that remain for the country are those arising from yield variability and the "basis" risk, but such risks are generally of a smaller order of magnitude than the price risk itself.[4] In periods when interest rates are highly variable, there is an additional risk of financing daily variable margin fluctuations on commodity exchanges during the holding period. This again is of a smaller order of magnitude and can in any case be hedged in financial-futures markets.

Where shifting of risk out of the economy is impossible, then the irreducible social risk has to be distributed between producers and nonproducers within the country—the second possibility. In the absence of any risk markets within the country, there is some ground for government intervention to force the risk to be shared between the producers and nonproducers. This can be shown to increase social welfare over the nonintervention case. To establish this point and to highlight critical issues, let me construct a highly artificial example.

Imagine a free trading country with half its population in an enclave producing a commodity with a highly risky world price and the other half producing goods and services with zero variation in prices and incomes. Assume the first group of population to be earning a high mean level of income but also with a high variance, while the second group is earning a low mean income with zero variance. Then, if individuals in both populations have identical and risk-averse utility functions, there is clearly some scope for the commodity producers to trade away part of their risks and higher income in favor of lower risks and a lower income. The nonproducers will want to do the opposite, thus giving rise to the possibility of welfare increasing trade either voluntarily through a risk market of some sort or involuntarily through the government.

This example highlights a few points. Government intervention to reduce risks when markets are incomplete can be justified, but the net improvement that can be brought about in actual cases depends on a number of factors. (1) The risks that commodity producers face must be evaluated relative to what the nonproducers face. In my model, the latter face zero risk. If they face even higher risks than the producers, then there is little

4. The government will lose money if production is lower than contracted for and the world price moves up during the contract period, or if production is larger than expected and the world price moves down during the contract period. Use of the futures market presupposes a high degree of correlation between prices in the central exchange and the market where the user actually trades in the real commodity (the cash market). The difference between the two is known as the basis. Since the correlation of prices in the two markets is not perfect, there is some risk involved (basis risk).

scope for any government intervention to stabilize the income of the commodity producers. (2) If individuals are allowed to work simultaneously in both sectors, or if they can own resources in both sectors (as when farmers diversify between export and food crops), then private decision making will automatically guide the economy toward a welfare-maximizing position, thereby undermining the case for government intervention. (3) If the number of sectors is increased, with an increased variety of risk characteristics, and if individuals also have different degrees of risk aversion, then one can expect the less risk-averse individuals to participate voluntarily in the riskier activities, and again the case for intervention is weakened.

The fourth limitation to policies that reduce price risks arises because the proposed scheme will operate through trade taxes and subsidies. Therefore, it is applicable to countries with relatively nonporous borders. Where smuggling is possible, the proposed scheme is irrelevant.

## The Proposed Scheme

On the assumption that market institutions in developing countries have not evolved to the point where risks can be effectively diffused, this chapter proposes that the government step in and take over some of the risks itself. In effect, the government should force or mediate the risk trading between the primary risk takers—in this case the farmers—and the taxpayers. The justification for such an action on the part of the government was first adumbrated by Arrow and Lind (1970) and is discussed at length in chapter 10.[5]

The proposed intervention is extremely simple. The government should cover the risks of price movements for each production period by announcing a guaranteed price for the crop at planting time. It should then ensure that farmers receive the announced price through a variable trade tax or subsidy to force the domestic price to stay at the announced level. Thus if the world price moves up between the announcement and the harvest, an export tax (or import subsidy) would be levied equal to the difference between the realized world price adjusted for transport (that is, for basis) and the announced one. In the opposite case, an export subsidy (or import tax) would be put into effect. These tax and subsidy rules should be preannounced to minimize uncertainty concerning government

5. Note that this justification is diametrically opposed to a few recent articles, notably Brainard and Cooper (1968) and Jabara and Thompson (1980). These writers express the fear that producers, if left to themselves, will not take sufficient account of the risks they face. The government should therefore introduce taxes and subsidies to guide production toward less risky crops. A government that is more risk-averse than the private agents is thus explicitly or implicitly posited.

behavior. If $E_s(p_h)$ is the harvest price that is expected at sowing time, $s$, then the announced price, $p^*$, would be this price. The export tax (or import subsidy) at harvest time would then be $p_h - p^*$, where $p_h$ is the realized world price at harvest time.

If the world price and the random factors that affect the export surplus (or import deficit) are independent, then it can be easily shown that the expected fiscal impact of the scheme would be zero, provided only that the announced price is an unbiased forecast (in the statistical sense) of the world price.[6] This requirement is essential.

There are two possible techniques that may be employed to ensure that the announced price is an unbiased forecast. Where there are active futures markets for the commodity at the world level (for example, wheat, maize, and sugar), it is now generally agreed that the futures prices are unbiased forecasts of the commodity prices at the date of contract maturity. An implementation problem is that these forecasts may not be statistically efficient. They are highly sensitive to all the information that enters the market and therefore may be excessively volatile. The price forecasting agency has to settle on a firm price at the time of the announcement. A second alternative is to use formal econometric models to do the forecasting work. There is then a choice problem among many econometric models. These are simply issues that would have to be resolved before implementation. The essential requirement is that every effort should be made to ensure that there is no bias in the forecast.

As the scheme is to be an insurance to stabilize producer's price, this implies a highly variable cash flow for the government. It is important that the financing of the scheme be separated from the central budget and that sufficient reserves be set aside to make the scheme credible.

The scheme in its simplest form will work for pure export commodities, where domestic consumption is negligible. In the case where there is substantial domestic consumption, the scheme has to be modified, as attention must then be paid to domestic storage. A scheme such as this will clearly influence the time path of the domestic prices of the commodity. Such an impact will in turn influence the incentives for private storage. In the extreme case, when prices are completely stabilized by this or any other scheme, the incentive for private storage will be reduced to zero. To maintain this incentive, the target prices used to calculate the tax or subsidy must be allowed to vary.

Two types of storage, seasonal storage and year-to-year storage, may be considered. For seasonal storage, the solution is straightforward. In-

6. Let $p$ be the random world price, $p^*$ the announced price, and $x$ be the random variable representing export surplus (or import deficit). Then the variable export levy would be $p - p^*$. The expected fiscal impact is then $E(p - p^*)x$. If $p$ and $x$ are independently distributed, then the expected fiscal impact is zero if $p^* = E(p)$.

stead of setting a unique price for the entire season, the government may announce a price path over the entire marketing season. The price path must increase over the season at a rate just adequate to cover the storage costs incurred by private traders.

The problem is vastly more complicated when it comes to year-to-year variation. The snag is this: between the announcement date and the harvest (when the price guarantee becomes operative), the world market does not stand still. Any movement in the world market generates expectations concerning the guaranteed price for the following harvest. Speculation based on these expectations naturally affects prices in the current year. To resolve this problem, let us consider two contrasting scenarios. Scenario I is when the world price moves downward relative to the announced price. Scenario II is when the world price moves sharply upward.

### *Scenario I*

Between the announcement and the harvest the world price moves downward. The futures price in the world market for the harvest month in the following year also drifts down, and local traders expect the government to announce a lower guaranteed price for the following year. There is a negative price for storage, and storers lose money. If the government had not guaranteed the storage cost through the entire marketing season, almost the entire crop would be sold in the first few months after the harvest. In the case of an export crop, this would endanger the domestic supply afterward. In the case of an import competing crop, the lack of any incentive to store might make the price guarantee untenable at harvest time.

The issue is best explicated by means of a diagram. Let us assume that the government is to set the price of a crop planted in July and harvested in December. Let us also assume that the situation in the world market is one of surplus, so that the world market futures price for different delivery dates are as shown by the line *AB* in figure 11.1. The government accepts the futures price *CB* as the unbiased price forecast of the crop price. Let us assume for analytical convenience that the basis is equal to *BD*, implying that the world price level, *CB*, converts to a domestic level, *DC*. The price path to be announced in July of year 0 for the postharvest period would then be *DE*. Now suppose that by the time December of year 0 rolls around, the futures market quotes prices for various contracts indicated by the path *FG*. At that point, traders will realize that a price path at the same level as *DE* would not be possible in year 2. In December of year 0 they will forecast a price level of *HJ* for December of year 1, and continuing along the path *JK*. If they hold on to a high level of stocks in December of year 1, when the price will drop from *HE* to *HJ*, they will suffer severe losses. Consequently, the level of stocks planned for that

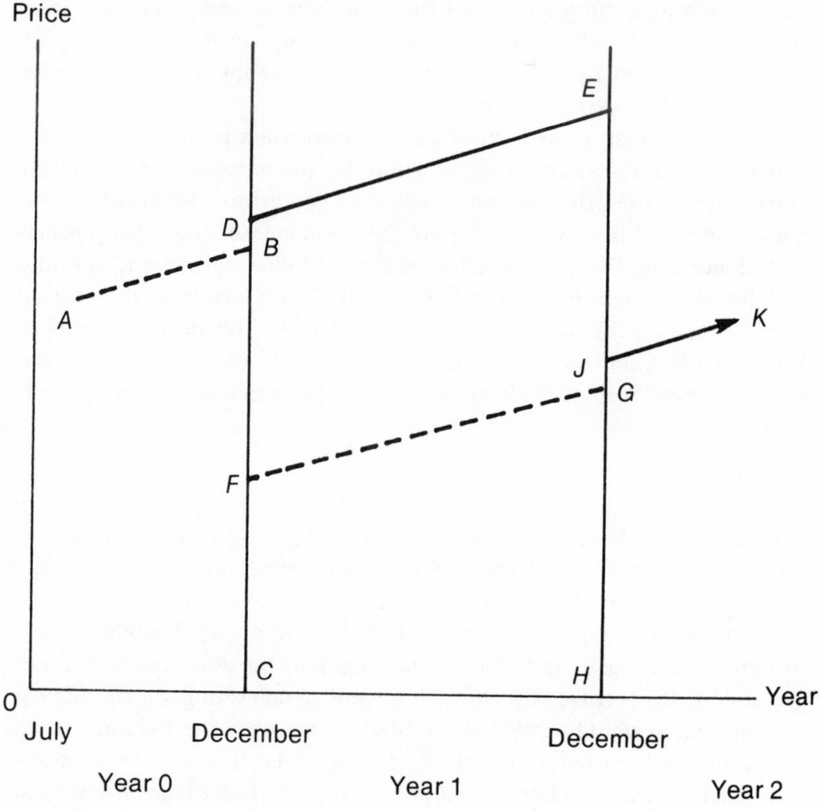


FIGURE 11.1 Illustrative price movements under scenario I

month will be pruned severely. This expected loss may soften prices somewhat in the few months before the harvest month in December of year 1 but will exert little impact on the feasibility of the price guarantee made for December of year 0.

However, one problem with this scenario is that the stocks planned for the end of year 1 may be excessively small, particularly if the expected drop in price *EJ* is very large. If during the year, the expected price, *HJ*, suddenly shoots up again on the basis of newer information, then the planned level of stock may be too small. There would then be an immediate upsurge of prices. To prevent such a whipsaw effect, it may be desirable for the government itself to hold stocks, which would not be released until the last three months of the marketing year.

*Scenario II*

It is less easy to deal with the reverse case. If there is a sharp upward move from *AB* to *FG* (figure 11.2) in the world price path between July and December of year 0, then the traders' expectations would be for the price path in year 2 to be *JK*. This price plan then would make the originally planned price path, *DE*, untenable, for along that price path it is unprofitable to release any stocks at all during year 1. It would be more desirable to hang on to the commodity and release it only when year 2 rolls around. Such attempts can only result in the equilibrium price path being shifted from *DE* to *D'J*.

Two policy stances are possible. The first, to be called rule A, is to consider *DE* not as an actual price path but as a price floor, so that the scheme in effect becomes an insurance only against downside risk. The variable trade tax or subsidy is in this case calculated as the difference between the realized world price (adjusted for transport costs or basis) and the realized domestic price. It is not calculated as the difference between the realized world price (adjusted for transport costs) and the preannounced price as originally stipulated. In fact, the change really implies that when the world prices move up, the trade tax and subsidy scheme will be in abeyance, as realized world price (adjusted for transport costs) and realized domestic price will be the same.

Combined with the conclusion of scenario I, this system implies that the government can and will cushion the economy from a downward movement in world prices. However, it will not do so when there is a sharp upward movement in prices. Such an asymmetric scheme can no longer be expected to have zero net fiscal impact. For an export crop, the change from a price guarantee to a price floor would cost the government money over the long term. For an import competing crop, it will earn money for the government. This policy stance obviously favors producers and works against consumers.

Another alternative, rule B, is for the government to adopt the policy rule that under no circumstances will the difference in the harvest-time prices of two succeeding years be allowed to exceed the annual storage cost. In terms of figure 11.2, this is equivalent to the government saying that if the world market situation moves sharply upward, the government will allow the price path to move up, but not until the following year and never to a level above the path *EK'*. In effect, this means that the variable trade tax remains the difference between the world price and the announced price. However, the price guarantee for year 2 is no longer an unbiased forecast of the expected world price. Because the price guarantee is a biased one, the fiscal impact is nonzero, and opposite to that of rule A. For export crops, adoption of such a policy rule would imply that in the

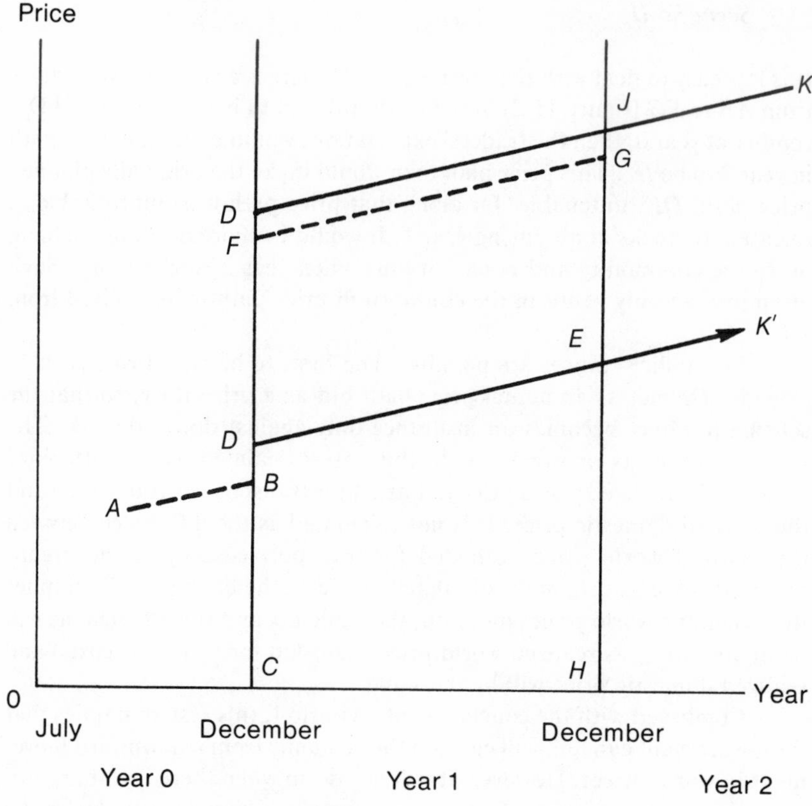


FIGURE 11.2 | Illustrative price movements under scenario II

long run the government will be a net recipient. For import competing crops, a net long-run subsidy is implied. The evaluation of the relative merits of these two rules will be postponed until the last section.

Thus the events described in scenario II—the sharp upward movement in the world prices between planting and harvesting times—has caused the abandonment, or at least modification, of the austere neutrality that was the original attraction of the scheme.

### *A Digression on State Trading and Quantitative Restrictions*

The proposed scheme assumes that import and export of the commodities concerned are in private hands, that domestic trade is in private hands and is competitive, and that foreign trade is not subject to any quantitative restriction. Of these, the assumption of private foreign trade is the least constricting.

If foreign trade in the commodities of interest is monopolized by the government, then to effectuate price insurance requires that the government agency stands ready to buy or sell the insured commodities at the preannounced price. This implies that the monopoly must import or export a sufficient amount of the commodity to maintain the domestic price at that announced level. Provided the government is as efficient as the private sector, the same amount would be needed as if the system was in private hands. In any given year, the foreign trade agency would make a profit or a loss equal to the amount that would have been taxed or subsidized. The issue of whether foreign trade is (or should be) in the private or public sector is thus not germane to the question of whether the price insurance scheme is feasible.

In principle, if imports and exports of the commodities are licensed, then, provided that the government issues the licenses in accordance with the exacting requirements of the scheme and continues to levy the variable tax or subsidy, the quantitative restrictions should not make any difference. In practice, however, the fact that two levels of decision are involved—one by the private firms and one by the licensing authority—leads to additional uncertainties. If foreign exchange scarcity makes licensing inevitable, then it is likely that direct state trading would be more efficient.

### *Comparison with Johnson's Proposal*

The proposal bears a close relationship to Johnson's (1947) proposal for U.S. agriculture. The main difference lies in the details. Johnson's proposal is for the U.S. government to make a forward price commitment to producers. However, that commitment should be fulfilled through a different procedure. Instead of intervening further in the market if the realized price falls short of the forecast price, Johnson proposes a deficiency payment directly to farmers equal to the price shortfall. This is an attractive technique, as the problem of risk to the farmers is tackled at the source. There are two problems with this approach, however.

First, this procedure requires a registration of eligible farmers, their planted acreage in various crops, and the expected yields. This has been achieved and is not a heavy burden for the United States, which is the target of Johnson's proposal, but appears to be too complex for most developing countries. This is particularly true if there are many small-scale farmers.

The more serious objection is that Johnson seems to envisage the government's forward price commitment as one-sided, setting a floor against price falls. There does not appear to be a symmetrical treatment of how to handle a situation in which the forecast price falls short of the realized price. This asymmetric treatment implies that the government will provide a net subsidy to agriculture over the long term and therefore draw resources into it over and above what is optimal.

Theoretically, it is possible for the government to levy a direct tax on producers should they receive a windfall gain from a rise in realized price over the forecast price. Practically, such an option is unlikely to be considered. For developing countries, this difficulty will prove fatal when taken in conjunction with the first objection.

### *Benefits and Costs*

The benefit of the proposal is conceptually straightforward—it is a reduction in the costs of producing various commodities by eliminating one component of the many risks that farmers face. The methodology to calculate this risk premium has been recently developed, so the premium can be estimated provided there is some estimate of the farmer's coefficient of risk aversion and his production function. Hazell (1982) surveyed the problems involved in estimating the risk premium when farmers face risks from unanticipated yield and price fluctuations.

There are four components of the costs of the scheme.

1. The most important cost arises because of the distortion on the consumption side. If the realized price at harvest time turns out to be different from the forecast price, there is nothing that can be done on the producer's side, because resources have already been committed. However, domestic consumption can and should be allowed to adjust to the new realized price. The use of a trade tax or subsidy in order to keep the domestic price fixed at the forecast level, even though the world price has shifted, will create a distortion on the consumption side (Corden 1974, pages 12–14). A better approach from the theoretical point of view is to provide a direct payment or impose a direct tax on the producers and allow market prices for the consumers to reflect fully the movements in world prices. Since this was ruled out as impractical (see the previous section), the unavoidable consumption distortion will thus have to be reckoned as part of the cost of the price insurance.

2. In the case where there are sudden price spurts in the world market (scenario II), I have suggested some modifications. It is not possible to determine beforehand the relative merits of rules A and B; there are two types of distortion involved. One is the distortion on the consumption side because the domestic price does not follow the world price, as explained above. The other is the distortion on the production side arising out of a net subsidy or tax for the commodity as a consequence of the nonneutral fiscal consequences. Because rule A allows domestic prices to respond immediately to a sharp jump in world prices, the consumption distortion is less than if rule B is followed.

Rule A does, however, draw resources permanently into agriculture, because of the bias in government policy inherent in converting the price forecast into a price floor. On the other hand, because rule B delays the passing on of the new knowledge regarding world prices, there are both consumption distortions and production distortions. The latter arise because resources are withheld from the sector until the domestic price has caught up with the world price. Unless there is a very strong continuous upward trend (which would delay the catching-up process), the production distortion is probably a temporary one.

3. Goods consumed domestically in significant amounts must be priced over the season in such a way as to induce sufficient storage. The losses arising from an insufficient private provision for storage can be substantial. This must be avoided by proper planning for storage and appropriate incentives for storage.

4. The final cost item is the tax collection cost, including the prevention of smuggling.

The most natural commodity for the proposed price insurance scheme is that which is almost entirely exported and for which foreign prices fluctuate a great deal. For importables and those exportables with large domestic consumption, the scheme is more likely to be beneficial the lower their price elasticities are, for then there will be less consumption distortion (see cost component 1). The question of how the degree of world price fluctuations affects the desirability of the scheme is more difficult to evaluate in advance. While greater fluctuations imply greater reductions in the risk premium and greater benefits from the insurance scheme, it also means that the domestic price movements are more constrained, thereby leading to larger consumption distortions.

## Concluding Remarks

This chapter has examined a few public policies that may be used to tackle large and frequent price movements in developing countries. It concentrates on the impact of these price movements on the risks that producers face when they commit resources to production, and on the possible loss in efficiency that results when these risks cannot be shared through existing market mechanisms. Such market failures justify some government intervention.

The proposal made to counteract this risk problem is restricted to commodities traded by the country concerned. It calls for the government to set a guaranteed price at planting time and to assure this price by using a trade tax or subsidy to bring the domestic price in line with the guaranteed price.

This is clearly a second-best policy for meeting the price risk problem. A first-best solution would be to make a supplementary payment or impose a direct supplementary tax to adjust producers' income to what it would be if they faced no price risk at all. Unfortunately, the difficulty of taxing farm incomes in developing countries precludes serious consideration of this approach.

An important drawback with the approach proposed in this chapter is that the scheme is in effect a compulsory insurance for all farmers. A voluntary scheme would depend on the existence of possibilities for forward-sales contracts by farmers with either private traders or the government. Also, private traders should then be able to diffuse their risks by reinsuring in a futures market. Where such contractual arrangements are possible and enforceable, voluntary arrangements are clearly better solutions to the risk problem. Where these are possible, the government should place priority on their development. The scheme proposed here should be considered only as a shortcut, or better still, as a stopgap measure before the development of these institutions has occurred.

The proposed scheme is not relevant for nontraded commodities, nor for those traded commodities in which the country has a substantial share of the world market.

# III

# Crop Insurance in Practice: Experience and Perspectives

# 12

# Experience with Crop Insurance Programs in the United States

Bruce L. Gardner
Randall A. Kramer

## History of Crop Insurance in the United States

Multiple-peril crop insurance was introduced in the United States by private companies in 1899, when the Realty Revenue Guaranty Company of Minneapolis agreed to purchase, at the insurer's request, his entire wheat crop at $5 per acre. Previously, the only insurance available for crop losses was the limited coverage afforded by hail and fire insurance. The fate of this early attempt at crop revenue insurance is not documented, but the company discontinued the program after one year (Hoffman 1925).

Crop insurance policies were written in 1917 in North Dakota, South Dakota, and Montana by three private companies (Valgren 1922). The companies suffered heavy losses because of a drought. Apparently their ventures covered an area too small to adequately distribute their risks. The Hartford Fire Insurance Company offered a policy in 1920 that insured both price and yield risk.The company's president later testified before Congress that, primarily because of sharp declines in crop prices, payments for insured losses exceeded premiums by $1.7 million (U.S. Congress 1923). Several other efforts by private companies to provide crop insurance were for the most part unsuccessful.

In 1922, the U.S. Senate passed a resolution calling for investigation of crop insurance. The resolution provided for the appointment of a select Senate committee to investigate crop insurance with particular reference to (1) the kinds and costs of insurance available; (2) the adequacy of the protection afforded by such insurance; (3) the desirability of any practical methods for extending the scope of such insurance; and (4) the availability and sufficiency of statistics necessary to properly and safely issue additional crop insurance (U.S. Congress 1923).

The select committee held hearings from April 24 through April 27, 1923. The hearings represented the first time that crop insurance was ap-

The following personnel of the U.S. Department of Agriculture were most helpful in providing advice and access to the data: Alan Walter, George Vohs, and Ralph Satterfield (Federal Crop Insurance Corporation); Ray Aldrich, Charles Riley, and Ed Matthews (Agricultural Stabilization and Conservation Service); and Tom Miller and Jim Johnson (Economic Research Service).

proached as a national problem. The 116 pages of testimony by experts from government, agriculture, and insurance interests suggested that a successful program would have to be national in scope and would require better data than currently available. The committee adjourned for the summer, and when it reconvened in the fall, economic conditions for agriculture had worsened to such an extent that agricultural interests in Congress turned their attention to more immediate measures of relief. By the time Congress adjourned in the summer of 1924, no additional crop insurance hearings had been held, and no action on crop insurance was undertaken.

In 1936, President Roosevelt appointed a committee to make recommendations for legislation providing for government-sponsored crop insurance. The committee's recommendations were largely adopted in the Federal Crop Insurance Act of 1938 (Title V of the Agricultural Adjustment Act of 1938).

To implement the crop insurance program, the legislation established the Federal Crop Insurance Corporation (FCIC), an agency within the U.S. Department of Agriculture. The management of the corporation was vested in a board of directors appointed by the secretary of agriculture. Insurance was authorized only for wheat. Growers could insure between 50 and 75 percent of their recorded or appraised average yields against losses because of "drought, flood, hail, wind, winterkill, lightning, tornado, insect infestation, plant disease, and such other unavoidable causes as may be determined by the Board" (52 *Stat.* 74). Premiums and losses could be paid in kind or cash equivalent.

Local committees of the Agricultural Adjustment Administration administered the crop insurance program. For those farms with annual yield data, the county committees determined premiums by calculating a loss experience based on the amount of indemnities a farm would have received if it had been insured in previous years. Using an average yield for the base period, the committees calculated the amount of indemnity or loss cost for each year had the farm been insured at the 75-percent (or 50-percent) level. The annual loss costs were used to obtain an average loss cost for the farm. This average loss cost was then averaged with the county loss experience to determine the premium rate (Rowe and Smith 1940).

The initial experience with federal crop insurance was less than encouraging. During the first year, nearly one-third of the insured farmers collected indemnities. Indemnities exceeded premiums by 2.6-million bushels; the loss ratio was 1.52. Part of the losses resulted from drought in several states, although national yields were slightly above average. In any actuarially based insurance program, one would not expect premiums to exactly equal indemnities in a given year, but there were some fundamental problems in the program's administration that contributed to the poor loss ratio in 1939. Adequate farm-level data were not available in many counties. Also, in many cases inexperienced estimators relied too heavily on county averages in setting premiums. This apparently led to an underestimate of yield variability of individual farms (Clendenin 1942).

Another factor contributing to the large underwriting losses in 1939 was the late completion of wheat contracts, which led to adverse selection. The calculation of premiums ran behind schedule, and many farmers did not receive premium notices until after their crops had been planted. Nearly half of the original applicants did not respond to premium notices and thus nullified their contracts. Presumably, those farmers cancelling their applications had crops in good condition (Clendenin 1942).

The poor performance of the 1939 program led to several changes in the methods used to calculate yields and premiums. Because inexperienced county committees were often appraising yields too high, especially on low-yielding farms, the FCIC established a key-farm system for future years. Under this system, a representative sample of between fifty and a hundred farms with good yield data was selected for each county. To appraise yields and loss costs for individual farms, committeemen were instructed to select a comparable farm from the key-farm list and use its data with appropriate modifications (FCIC *Annual Report* 1939). The FCIC also established county check yields. Farm yields and premium rates were then brought into alignment with estimated county averages by a factoring procedure. Individual farm figures were raised or lowered proportionally until their average was equal to the county check yield.

Participation in the program increased steadily. The number of insured farms was 165,775 in 1939, 360,596 in 1940, and 371,392 in 1941. Despite the growth in participation and the modifications in yield and premium calculations, the federal crop insurance program continued to pay indemnities in excess of premiums received (FCIC *Annual Report* 1943).

The disappointing results of the first three years of operation of the wheat insurance program led to a total subsidy from the Treasury for operating expenses and underwriting losses of about $28 million, or approximately $31 per farm per year. Although proponents of crop insurance had conceded at least a temporary need for a public subsidy of operating expenses, the annual subsidy of $4.4 million was larger than expected. Given the low level of participation, it became clear that the plan would not become self-supporting. For example, adding operating expenses to the premiums would cost the average insured wheat grower 13 percent of net income from wheat or 4 percent of gross income (Clendenin 1942). The annual underwriting losses of approximately $4 million were even more troublesome to policymakers, because these losses occurred during relatively good crop years when reserves should have been accumulated for paying indemnities in future bad years.

A similar crop insurance program for cotton began operation in 1942, and it encountered the same difficulties as the wheat program. Indemnities greatly exceeded premiums during 1942 and 1943. Administrative expenses totaled $3.5 million for the two years, and underwriting losses amounted to $11 million (Benedict 1953).

The crop insurance programs for wheat and cotton were severely criticized in 1943 congressional hearings. The Agricultural Appropriations Bill for 1943-44 prohibited the FCIC from writing any new crop insurance policies after July 31, 1943. The two major reasons for the congressional cancellation of the crop insurance program were (1) the large underwriting losses in each of the five years of the program's operations and (2) the low level of participation in the program. Although Congress had been willing to subsidize the program's administrative costs, it had expected premiums to cover indemnities in normal crop years (*Agricultural Finance Review* 1943).

The crop insurance program did not remain dead for long. In late 1944, an amendment to the Agricultural Adjustment Act of 1938 was passed, which revived and expanded the program. Insurance was authorized for wheat, cotton, and flax crops planted for harvest in 1945. However, because of drought, excessive rains, and boll weevil damage, there were large underwriting losses for cotton (FCIC *Annual Report* 1946).

Insurance was also offered on a trial basis in 1945 for corn in fifteen counties, and for tobacco in twelve counties (*Agricultural Finance Review* 1945). The program for corn had two options—a yield plan and an investment cost plan. The yield plan insured up to 75 percent of the farm average yield over a base period. The investment cost plan insured up to 75 percent of the investment a farmer had in his crop. Crop insurance for tobacco was also offered under two plans—an investment cost plan and a yield quality plan. Under the yield quality plan, a quality index was constructed for each farm based on the historical relationship between the price received by the grower and the seasonal price for the type or class of tobacco grown. The grower would then be insured for a return equal to three-fourths of his average yield, multiplied by his quality index, multiplied by the average market price for the year of the insurance. The dollar value of the coverage would not be known until the close of the marketing season; until then it would be carried in pounds weight. Under this plan, a grower was insured on the basis of his relative position in the market, but he still bore the risk of overall fluctuations in the market price (Wrather 1943).

The 1945 program also instituted increasing protection as crops progressed. If a crop was destroyed or substantially damaged early in the growing season, after it was too late to replant the same crop, and the FCIC released the acreage for another use, then protection was reduced to 40 or 50 percent of what it would have been for a harvested crop. After that time, the level of protection gradually increased. This provision was added to provide for a sounder insurance program, because it had been observed that in some cases it was more profitable to incur a crop loss than to have a successful harvest (FCIC *Annual Report* 1945).

Several new features were introduced in 1946. The FCIC had been experimenting for some time with a three-year contract for wheat. This was designed to reduce the adverse-selection problem and to reduce the cost of selling insurance. An important indicator of crop prospects is soil moisture at planting time. Many farmers purchased crop insurance only when soil moisture indicated a poor crop. The three-year contract eliminated this problem at least for the second and third year of the contract. A continuous contract for cotton was also introduced. This contract would remain in force year after year unless cancelled by the farmer or the FCIC.

It had become recognized that individual farm data might be adequate for determining expected yields but not for determining the variability of yields, because of the relatively few years of data available. There had been a trend toward using county data, and with the adoption of county premium rates in 1946, all crops were insured under countywide rates. This change was permitted by the 1944 amendments, which omitted a provision requiring premiums to be based on the recorded or appraised crop loss of the insured farm. Adjustments in premiums continued to be made for high-risk farms (*Agricultural Finance Review* 1946).

Partial coverage was offered for the first time in 1946. Farmers were allowed to purchase a percentage of the standard contract so as to receive a lower level of protection for a corresponding lower premium. This option did not prove to be popular with farmers.

In 1947, for the first time in history, the FCIC collected premiums in excess of indemnities on combined operations. Ironically, legislation passed that year severely curtailing the operations of the corporation. The 1947 amendments effectively reduced federal crop insurance to an experimental program. As a result of the legislation, the corporation reduced its operations from 2,500 to 375 counties in 1947. Although the scope of the program was reduced, the FCIC was given greater latitude in experimenting with alternative forms of insurance. Two new experimental programs were tried in 1948. One was a program for dry edible beans instituted in four widely separated counties with different types of farming. The other was a multiple-crop contract, with indemnities determined on the basis of combined coverage evaluated at predetermined prices (FCIC *Annual Report* 1948).

The drought of the 1930s provided impetus for the establishment of government-sponsored crop insurance; the drought of the early 1950s demonstrated the continued value of insurance to producers. In 1951 and 1952, indemnities totaled $42 million and enabled many farmers to avoid bankruptcy. Over the first five years of the experimental phase (1948–52), the surplus of premiums over indemnities was $2.25 million. The loss ratio was less than one in three of the five years, and the five-year loss ratio was 0.97. This suggests that the program was beginning to operate on a sound basis, although reserves were not building up as quickly as desirable. For example, the total reserves after five years were substantially less than the underwriting losses incurred in one year—1949 (FCIC *Annual Report* 1955).

During the 1950s, the crop insurance program began to stabilize. Although some new crops were added and minor experimentation continued, most changes involved fine tuning the program. The FCIC announced that, beginning in 1956, insurance would no longer be sold in fourteen counties in Colorado, New Mexico, and Texas. These were considered high-risk farming areas not suitable for insurance, because total indemnities had substantially exceeded total premiums. The board of directors was convinced that it would be impossible to develop a sound insurance program for these counties. If insurance had not been sold in these counties since 1948, the national program would have experienced a surplus of premiums over indemnities, rather than a deficit.

Beginning in 1957, there was a five-year period in which premiums exceeded indemnities every year. The loss ratio in 1958 of 0.26 was the lowest in nineteen years of operation. This was well below what was ever expected in the program. Premiums exceeded losses for every crop, and as a result, a total surplus of $2.5 million had collected since the experimental program began in 1948. In addition to good crop conditions, other factors contributing to the successes during this period were improved operating methods, including the withdrawal of the fourteen high-loss counties in 1956, and the advancement of closing dates for applications to reduce adverse selection.

The continued experimentation during the 1950s with methods and crops insured did not result in rapid increases in total coverage. In 1950, insured liabilities were $240 million. By 1959, this increased to $271 million, well below the $470-million worth of insurance written in 1947, before the beginning of the experimental phase. During the 1960s, the FCIC concentrated on increasing its coverage, which reached $920 million in 1969. This rapid increase did not come without cost. In the last three years of the decade, the corporation paid indemnities that were about 29 percent of the total indemnities paid during the entire 1948–69 period. Premiums did not keep pace with liabilities and indemnities. Premiums as a percent of liabilities declined from 6.9 in 1955–61 to 5.8 in 1963–69 (FCIC *Annual Report* 1969 and 1970).

Early in 1969, the secretary of agriculture appointed a new board of directors, manager, and deputy manager. The new management undertook a review of the program to indentify reasons for the poor financial position of the corporation. They concluded that it was due "in large measure to coverage increases and rate reductions which supporting statistics did not justify, and a concentration of sales results where comparatively high coverage and low premiums applied" (FCIC *Annual Report* 1969, p. 11). Adverse weather followed in some of the areas of increased coverage, particularly in cotton-growing areas. The corporation concluded that in many counties insurance structures had been weakened by the use of shorter time periods for determining coverages. The result was that coverages were based on recent trends rather than long-term averages. The cotton program was identified as one of the major sources of the corporation's problems. For the 1948–69 period, the cumulative loss ratio for cotton was 1.5. Without cotton, the cumulative loss ratio for all crops would have been 0.91 rather than 0.97.

The corporation's review revealed that in many cases premium rates had been reduced below what experience could justify. For some new crops, risks had been miscalculated and premiums set too low. Overall, it was concluded that "unfortunately, this process of increasing sales was geared too much to liberalized coverages for premium rates too low to result in sound operations" (FCIC *Annual Report* 1969, p. 12).

To offset these problems, the FCIC instituted several changes in the operation of its 1970 program. In most cotton counties, premiums were increased and coverage was decreased. The top cotton price election (used to calculate the value of insured losses) was reduced, to more adequately reflect market values. The experimental potato program, which had suffered large underwriting losses and had been utilized by few producers, was discontinued. Adjustments were made in the soybean and citrus programs to lower their loss ratios.

In 1970, the secretary of agriculture appointed a task force of nongovernmental insurance experts to study the FCIC. The task force criticized the practice of establishing premiums on a countywide basis. According to the task force, the most urgently needed change was to base the program on individual farm risks (FCIC Task Force 1970). The General Accounting Office concurred with the need for individualized protection (U.S. General Accounting Office 1977). The GAO concluded that low participation prevented FCIC from operating an effective disaster protection program. To increase farmers' participation in the federal crop insurance program, individualized protection was proposed.

### *Disaster Payments Program*

The Agriculture and Consumer Protection Act of 1973, and the Rice Production Act of 1975 established a disaster payments program, which, for some crops, overlapped with the protection provided by federal crop insurance. Payments for prevented planting and payments for abnormally-low yields were provided for producers of wheat, sorghum, corn, barley, upland cotton, and rice. Farmers participating in price- and income-support programs were eligible for payments. Payments for prevented planting were made to producers who were unable to plant or who underplanted because of drought, flood, or other natural conditions beyond their control. Low-yield payments were made when yields fell below two-thirds of normal. The Food and Agriculture Act of 1977 renewed this program, with low-yield payments activated when yields of wheat and feed grains fell below 60 percent of normal and when yields of rice and cotton fell below 75 percent of normal. The program ended in 1981. Disaster payments for 1974–80 totaled $3.392 billion.

The disaster payments program was popular with farmers, because it provided disaster protection with no premium costs and coverage in high-risk areas where crop insurance was not available. Critics charged that the program led to an inefficient use of the nation's resources, by encouraging production in high-risk areas. The program was also criticized for insuring against moral hazards, that is, avoidable losses caused by management decisions. A study by the GAO found that a substantial portion of 1974 payments went to Texas producers, whose cotton crops were damaged by drifting chemicals aerially applied to neighboring fields. Although the farmers may have had legal recourse against the damaging parties (who customarily carried insurance against such claims), they chose to collect disaster payments rather than pursue legal action (U.S. General Accounting Office 1976). Furthermore, the prevented plantings provision provided incentives for producers in arid regions to collect payments rather than plant under marginal conditions (Miller and Walter 1977).

The question arises whether the disaster payments program discouraged participation in the FCIC program. There does not appear to have been any large effect. In the three years before the implementation of the disaster payments program (1971–73), an average of 347-thousand producers insured their crops under FCIC. During the first six years of the disaster payments program (1974–79), the corresponding FCIC figure was 320 thousand.

### *The Federal Crop Insurance Act of 1980*

The Federal Crop Insurance Act of 1980 (94 *Stat.* 1312) expanded the crop insurance program to become the major form of disaster protection in the United States. The Act authorized the expansion of the program to all counties with significant agriculture. If sufficient actuarial data was available, the FCIC was permitted to insure any agricultural commodity (including aquacultural species) grown in the United States. The initial expansion of the program was targeted for those counties with substantial acreages of crops formerly covered by the disaster payments program. In order to provide a transition period, the Act extended the disaster payments program through 1981. To encourage greater participation, the Act authorized subsidies of 30 percent of premiums on the 50- and 65-percent yield levels and a somewhat smaller subsidy at the 75-percent yield level. Those producers with private hail and fire insurance were allowed to delete that coverage from the corporation's policy and pay premiums reduced by 15 to 30 percent.

The Act also permitted specific risk protection programs for prevented planting, wildlife depredation, tree damage and disease, and insect infestation, provided such protection was not available from private companies. It authorized research and pilot programs on rangeland, livestock poisoning and disease, destruction of bees due to pesticide use, and "other unique problems of special risk related to, but not limited to, fruits, nuts, vegetables, aquacultural species, forest industry needs (including appreciation), and other agricultural programs as determined by the Board." The Act required a pilot program of individual-risk underwriting in at least twenty-five counties from 1981 to 1985. The FCIC later announced that, beginning in 1982, farmers with at least three years of yield data may request individualized yield protection. Under this option, premiums and coverage would be calculated on an individual farm basis.

The GAO studied the effects of the new legislation on the 1981 program and found the insured acreage increased from about 26.3 million to 47.7 million. For the 1981 crop year, the FCIC extended its coverage to 1,340 additional county programs and 252 additional counties. (A county program is defined as all insurable acres of a crop in a county.) For the 1982 crop year, 8,278 county programs and 1,050 counties were added. Producers chose to exclude fire and hail coverage on only 3,125 of 497,336 policies (U.S. General Accounting Office 1981).

Of thirty private companies submitting applications for the 1981 reinsurance program, seventeen wrote policies resulting in premiums of $13 million, or 4 percent of the total premiums written. Another six companies entered into nonrisk-bearing sales and service agreements with the corporation. There were two major reasons that more private companies did not participate in reinsurance: (1) lack of sufficient time to implement the program, and (2) concern that reinsured companies might be considered federal contractors subject to equal opportunity regulations (U.S. General Accounting Office 1981).

### *Other Farm Programs*

The early development of U.S. crop insurance programs took place in conjunction with commodity price support policies. However, in the post-World War II period, commodity price support programs have developed independently of the FCIC programs. The most notable instance of this independence was the disaster payments program, which, as discussed earlier, was essentially a second crop insurance program superimposed on the FCIC. During the 1970s there were, in addition, programs such as those providing disaster loans at low interest, the emergency feed program, and special indemnity programs for dairy producers and beekeepers.

The economic impact of these other programs were often more important than FCIC insurance. In 1977, about two-thirds of U.S. counties were classified as disaster areas for purposes of disaster loan programs (even though the U.S. crop output index was at a record high).[1] In fiscal 1980, the Farmers' Home Administration made about $4.5 billion in emergency loans, at an interest rate of 5 percent, for the amount of losses claimed. An important purpose of the Federal Crop Insurance Act of 1980 was to create a better-coordinated overall system of federally subsidized crop insurance.

A general reason for coordinating price support programs and output insurance programs is that either one by itself may have only small risk-reducing effects in the absence of the other. This situation arises when price fluctuations are caused by random output variations that are correlated across farms, since in this situation low yields tend to be compensated by higher prices. When prices are stabilized by a government program, the risk-reducing features of crop insurance are enhanced. This is a possible reason that tobacco producers participate in FCIC programs more than producers of other crops.

Crop insurance and credit programs are also related. The two merge into the same policy in the case of disaster assistance, which takes the form of subsidized loans. The subsidy may involve interest rates below market rates, waiver of usual security terms, governmental guarantee of payoff to lenders in case of default, or even forgiveness of repayment of principal. In this case, credit policy and insurance are substitutes in risk management. However, the more usual case is that federal credit policy increases the demand for crop insurance. Federal farm credit policy consists essentially of programs to provide credit to farmers at terms more favorable than the terms available from nongovernmental lending institutions. This tends to increase farmers' use of credit, thus their leverage, and thus the value of insurance in reducing risks.

Unfortunately, we do not have the data necessary to test the importance of this effect and of the interactions of the various programs in influencing farmers' behavior by changing their risk-return alternatives. However, county-level data on the FCIC and disaster payments programs exists which may be useful in drawing lessons from the U.S. experience about

1. See the testimony of the secretary of agriculture before the Senate Agriculture Committee on May 2, 1978, as reported in Farm Credit Administration (1978).

farmers' demand for crop insurance and about the effects of insurance programs on farmers' risk taking.

## Previous Studies

Economic research on crop insurance has been conducted in the United States for the past sixty years. The research falls into four general categories. (1) Before 1938 several studies explored possible forms that a government-sponsored crop insurance program might take. (2) Given the low participation level and poor financial performance of the FCIC program in the early years of operation, researchers proposed alternative actuarial methods. (3) Several studies have been concerned with differences in the characteristics of program participants and nonparticipants. One purpose of this group of studies has been to shed light on factors influencing the demand for crop insurance. (4) The final set of studies examined the farm-level impacts of crop insurance. Most of the studies in this latter group were conducted in a simulation framework to analyze the stream of net returns of representative farms with and without insurance.

One of the earliest economic studies of crop insurance in the United States was a USDA bulletin by Valgren (1922). Reviewing the experience of private companies, Valgren identified principles fundamental to the development of a successful crop insurance plan. These principles were an elaboration of the basic requirements for crop insurance, which a German economist, Paul Mayet, had presented thirty years earlier to the Japanese government (see chapter 13):

> This insurance against failure of crops may be limited as follows, that a duty of indemnification exists only:
>
> I. When the failure is clearly due to natural causes and the farmer is not to blame, as when a whole province or county suffers loss.
>
> II. When the failure of the individual farmer of that province or county is a total or a considerable one, as for instance when the rice crop is less than 70% of an average crop, or that of other produce less than 60% or 50% or 40%, etc.
>
> III. When the indemnification is only partial and the farmer bears the other part of the burden.
>
> IV. When that indemnification is made, not according to market prices obtained during the year of failure, but according to an average price agreed upon when the insurance was first offered (Mayet 1893, pp. 60–61).

It is interesting to note that the danger of insuring against price risk was recognized before the turn of the century.

To Mayet's list, Valgren (1922, p. 26) added the requirement that "The premium, or cost of insurance, must bear a reasonable relationship to the value of the protection that it purchases." To accomplish this, Valgren suggested the use of farmers' organizations to keep the administrative costs as low as possible.

Department of Agriculture research on crop insurance was renewed in 1936. A substantial amount of data on wheat and cotton yields on individual farms had been collected by the Agricultural Adjustment Administration in the operation of its programs. Preliminary analysis of the wheat data indicated it could provide an actuarial basis for crop insurance (*Agricultural Finance Review* 1935; Green 1938).

After Congress temporarily suspended the FCIC in 1942, research began on alternative actuarial methods. This approach was designed to reduce adverse selection, which Sanderson (1943) blamed for the FCIC's problems. He proposed a program based on weather/yield relationships, using a regression equation to predict the effect of weather factors on yields. Under this plan, an equation would be estimated for each state. Farmers would receive indemnities if weather factors changed in a direction leading to below-average predicted yields. Increases in predicted yields would determine the per-acre premium paid by farmers in the state. Another version of this plan, also based on regression equations, would have resulted in fixed premiums and minimum-yield protection. Sanderson's plan did not receive a great deal of attention, possibly due to potential difficulties in selecting appropriate explanatory variables. Furthermore, a farmer with greater yield variability than the state as a whole would not likely obtain adequate risk protection from such a plan.

After analyzing the extreme yield fluctuations of the semiarid regions of the northern great plains, Pengra (1947, pp. 569–70) suggested a crop insurance plan that would discourage planting in dry years. He argued, "If a plan could be worked out to restrict or entirely eliminate the seeding of wheat during these low preseasonal precipitation years, the cost of the insurance would be greatly reduced as well as the losses that must still be borne by the farmer in spite of the benefits from his insurance protection." However, farmers often choose to plant in such seasons, even when they bear the full risk of crop losses. So there is a strong presumption that the encouragement of idling land in these years of likely scarcity would cause misallocation of resources from the social point of view.

An area-yield insurance plan was proposed by Halcrow (1948, 1949). Under this plan, premiums and indemnities would be based on the yield of an area with normally uniform crop conditions. If the mean area yield fell below a specified level, all insured farmers in the area would receive an indemnity. An obvious difficulty with such a plan is that it would not provide appropriate insurance for farms in the more risky environments within an area. This proposal was not adopted.

Lee (1953) proposed citrus temperature insurance as a substitute for citrus frost insurance in Southern California, due to the greater availability of temperature data. Growers would receive indemnities if temperatures fell below specified levels at nearby weather stations. This proposal also failed to gain acceptance.

U.S. crop insurance allows a reduction in premiums over time for those farmers without losses. Myrick (1970) examined this and other features of the program. Because there are credits to, but no debits against, base rates, the base rates must be weighted to balance the credits. Myrick argued that this discouraged participation, since premiums for new insureds are higher than average. He recommended a revised merit rating plan that would include debits as well as credits, which would tend to lower the premium rate for new insureds. He also suggested a provision for reducing rates for new insureds if their individual yield records indicated a favorable loss-cost history.

One of the first examples of research on characteristics of program participants and nonparticipants was a study published by the Stanford Food Research Institute in 1942. Based on surveys from individual farms in several states, Clendenin (1942) concluded that small farms were more likely to purchase insurance than large farms. Also, after classifying individual respondents' financial strength as best, medium, or weakest, he found that those in the weakest group were somewhat more willing to insure. This was less true in high-risk areas, where premium rates were an obstacle to participation. The investigation also revealed that tenants were slightly more likely to insure than owner/operators and nonfarming landlords. Surprisingly, farms heavily dependent on wheat income were less likely to insure than diversified farms. (It should be noted that Clendenin's conclusions on differences among groups were based on group averages; no statistical tests were conducted.) Examining data on county premium rates and level of participation, Clendenin observed an inverse relation between the two. Participation volume was substantially greater in the low-premium counties. He concluded that the demand for crop insurance was sensitive to price, as might be expected.

Several investigations of the characteristics of crop insurance participants and nonparticipants were conducted as a part of the Great Plains Regional Project GP-8. In an article summarizing the survey results from six states and more than 500 respondents, Loftsgard (1967, p. 34) noted that "a comparison of these characteristics, for farmers who participate versus those who aren't participating in the program, reveals little . . . for all the states studied, the only consistency observed was that participants are slightly older and rely more heavily on cash-grain income than nonparticipants." Most farmers who participated reported that they did so primarily to protect their investments in production expenses. The predominant reason given for nonparticipation was that the level of protection was too low. When farmers were asked their opinion of the programs, many expressed dissatisfaction with the length of time between inspection of loss and payment of indemnity. The majority of participants and nonparticipants were in favor of changing the program to allow contracts for separate fields or tracts. Farmers tended to oppose multiple-crop contracts, because these reduced their chances of collecting indemnities.

Shipley (1967) examined the relationship between FCIC participation, soil type, and groundwater availability in northwest Texas. The rate of participation was significantly higher among those farmers with a poor water supply and with difficult soils. Examining demographic and other characteristics of participants, prior participants, and nonparticipants, he found no significant difference in age, education, number of dependents, experience, or yields. For approximately half of the farmers surveyed, crop insurance substituted for diversification as a risk-management tool.

Bray (1963) and Starr (1963) surveyed FCIC participants in Nebraska. Bray found that most of those interviewed were strongly in favor of higher levels of coverage and said they would have been willing to pay higher premiums for increased protection. Crop insurance appeared to aid farmers in obtaining credit. Farmers in Starr's sample thought that constantly increasing yields were the cause of inadequate coverage levels.

In North Dakota, Delvo and Loftsgard (1967) surveyed farmers with FCIC insurance and farmers who had canceled it in the period 1960–62. In low- and medium-risk crop areas, participants operated the largest farms. In high-risk crop areas, nonparticipants operated the largest farms. Average crop yields and production costs were about the same for both groups. Nonparticipants believed that the probability of collecting an indemnity was too low to make crop insurance worthwhile.

A 1965 study based on survey data from Virginia and Montana found that insured farmers were in a somewhat riskier situation than their uninsured counterparts. They were less diversified, less likely to have irrigation, and had smaller incomes, fewer savings, and larger debts. Lenders reported better loan collections from those growers with crop insurance (Jones and Larson 1965).

Beeson (1971) conducted a personal interview survey of East Tennessee tobacco farmers in 1969. Total farm income and total assets were significantly higher among those who did not purchase FCIC insurance. Those with insurance obtained a higher percentage of income from tobacco, while those without insurance obtained a higher percentage of income from livestock. In contrast to the findings of Jones and Larson, those farmers without insurance had a significantly larger amount of debt. If FCIC insurance had not been available, 65 percent of those insured indicated they would not have made any changes in their operations; the rest would have substituted private hail insurance. Of those who had dropped FCIC insurance, only 9.4 percent did so because of the level of premiums. Most had dropped because of insufficient amounts of coverage or dislike of loss adjustment procedures. Only 2.5 percent of the nonpurchasers said that lower premiums would have induced them to purchase insurance; 73.8 percent said no changes in the program would cause them to purchase.

The first in a long series of simulation studies was conducted by Barber and Thair (1950). They constructed time series of net after-tax income with and without crop insurance for a Kansas grain farm and a North Dakota grain and livestock farm. Using constant input and output prices, and experiment station yields for 1915–48, they examined the effects of two types of crop insurance—wheat insurance only and a multiple-crop insurance plan. Crop insurance of either kind resulted in greater income stability for both farms, as indicated by higher average net after-tax income and by fewer years of negative income. (The authors did not report any variability measures.) However, there were as many years with insurance as without in which net income fell below estimated living costs. The authors suggested two program changes that would lead to greater income stability: (1) a higher yield coverage, and (2) premium payment only in years of above-average yields.

A similar study of a Montana wheat farm (Heisig 1946) demonstrated that crop insurance over the 1919–44 period would have resulted in sufficient income every year to cover cash operating expenses and family living expenses, except for minor deficits in a few years. In contrast, without insurance the farm would have experienced large deficits in five of the twenty-six years. However, Heisig pointed out that even with insurance, there would in many cases have been insufficient income or reserves to make debt payments and to replace machinery or equipment during an extended period of drought.

Another study of Montana wheat farms examined the effects of crop insurance on firm survival (Rodewald 1960). Once a charge was made for family living expenses, crop insurance alone was not adequate to guarantee survival. However, the use of insurance reduced the need for borrowing, while at the same time it enhanced the possibility of obtaining credit.

In another simulation study, Miller and Trock (1979) found that, with a 50-percent level of yield protection, crop insurance was more effective than the disaster payments program in stabilizing income from dryland winter wheat in Colorado. However, this analysis did not consider the relative cost of the two programs; that is, there was no adjustment made in the income calculations for crop insurance premiums.

Kramer and Pope (1982) analyzed the effectiveness of the 1981 crop insurance program in reducing risk for a representative Virginia corn farm. Using stochastic dominance analysis, a comparison was made of probability distributions of net returns for corn with and without crop insurance. The results suggested that crop insurance can be an attractive option for managing risk. Similar results were obtained in a study by King and Oamek (1981), which also used stochastic dominance analysis. For dryland wheat producers in Colorado, the investigators found that crop insurance would be attractive, particularly after the elimination of the disaster payments program.

In the remainder of this chapter, we consider two aspects of the U.S. experience in crop insurance. First, the demand for insurance—its response to the rate of indemnity payout, the premium charged, the variability of production, and various socioeconomic aspects of rural communities. This should help establish the conditions necessary for crop insurance to be accepted and indicate the responsiveness of demand to reductions in premiums relative to the average indemnity (for example, by subsidizing insurance). Second, we consider the results of the introduction of crop insurance, particularly its impact on alternative risk-reducing activities like crop diversification, fallowing, irrigation, pesticide use, and on farmers' willingness to expand farm size or to increase fertilizer use. We wish to know how much it may be possible to increase the "progressiveness," specialization, and so on, of farmers by introducing crop insurance in areas where it is unavailable.

## The Demand for Crop Insurance in the United States

### *A Competitive Insurance Market*

Crop insurance is a contingent contract, an agreement in which a farmer pays a price (the premium), after which his crop output (yield) determines a payout or indemnity. The contingency is that only certain (low) yields result in indemnities, and yield is a random variable whose value is unknown when the insurance contract is purchased. Sellers of insurance enter the business in pursuit of profit. Therefore, the expected indemnities must exceed the premium by the costs of writing insurance. The equilibrium condition is that in a competitive insurance industry there would be a tendency for expected indemnities to equal premiums plus these costs.[2]

A farmer's demand for a crop insurance contract depends on (1) the farmer's utility function for income, (2) his current income, (3) his subjective frequency distribution of future income, (4) the change in the frequency distribution of future income generated by the contract, and (5) the premium or price of the contract. Items (1) through (4) determine the re-

2. This would be true for the industry, and for each firm in the industry, and for each contract written. However, there may be no equilibrium in a competitive insurance market even if demand and cost conditions suggest at first glance that there should be. This situation, which depends on imperfect information about differences in individuals' risks, is explored in Rothschild and Stiglitz (1976). The competitive market equilibrium conditions are derived there for a simple two-state model.

turns from insurance and item (5) is its cost. With a viable competitive (or monopoly) insurance industry, the expected returns must fall short of the costs.

The preceding argument can be restated in terms of the demand for and supply of insurance as in figure 12.1. With risk-neutral producers, no insurance is sold. How much a producer will pay depends on his utility function, his income (unless the utility function exhibits constant risk aversion), and the nature of the insurance contract and how it fits in with his portfolio of other activities.

As risk aversion varies from producer to producer, this can generate a downward-sloping demand curve for insurance, as in figure 12.1 where the equilibrium amount of insurance written is $Q_1$, and the corresponding premium is $P_1$. Quantity of insurance refers to acreage or bushels covered and is limited by the crop acreage (although this is not a necessary constraint—one could have side bets on crop outputs as we do for prices in futures markets). In what follows we use as our quantity variable the percentage of the crop covered. Note that one should not imagine the terms of the contracts varying as $Q$ varies. Separate supply and demand curves are necessary for each type of contract written.

### *Government Involvement in Insurance*

Even if farmers are risk-neutral or not risk-averse enough to generate a viable insurance market, one can be created by having the government offer insurance at a premium that does not cover all costs. Thus in figure 12.1, the government could get the risk-neutral producers to buy quantity $Q_1$ by selling insurance at price $P_0$. Alternatively, in a market context, it could accomplish the same objective by paying a subsidy of $P_1 - P_0$ on privately issued insurance.

Why a government would wish to promote the use of insurance by farmers will be covered later. The point here is that the United States has provided crop insurance, and there has been sufficient experimentation to permit the estimation of some aspects of the U.S. demand for insurance. The relevant history was discussed earlier. The FCIC experiments are useful for present purposes, because crop insurance contracts for different crops in different counties vary considerably in their ratio of indemnity payments to premium payments over a long period. The loss ratio is indemnities divided by premiums. For the United States as a whole, in the 1948–79 period, total indemnities were \$1.21 billion and premiums were \$1.26 billion, for a loss ratio of $1.21/1.26 = 0.96$ (FCIC *Annual Report* 1980, p. 22). Thus if administrative costs were negligible, FCIC insurance would have been a profit-making business. FCIC estimates of these expenses add up to \$351 million for 1949–79 (FCIC *Annual Report* 1980, p.

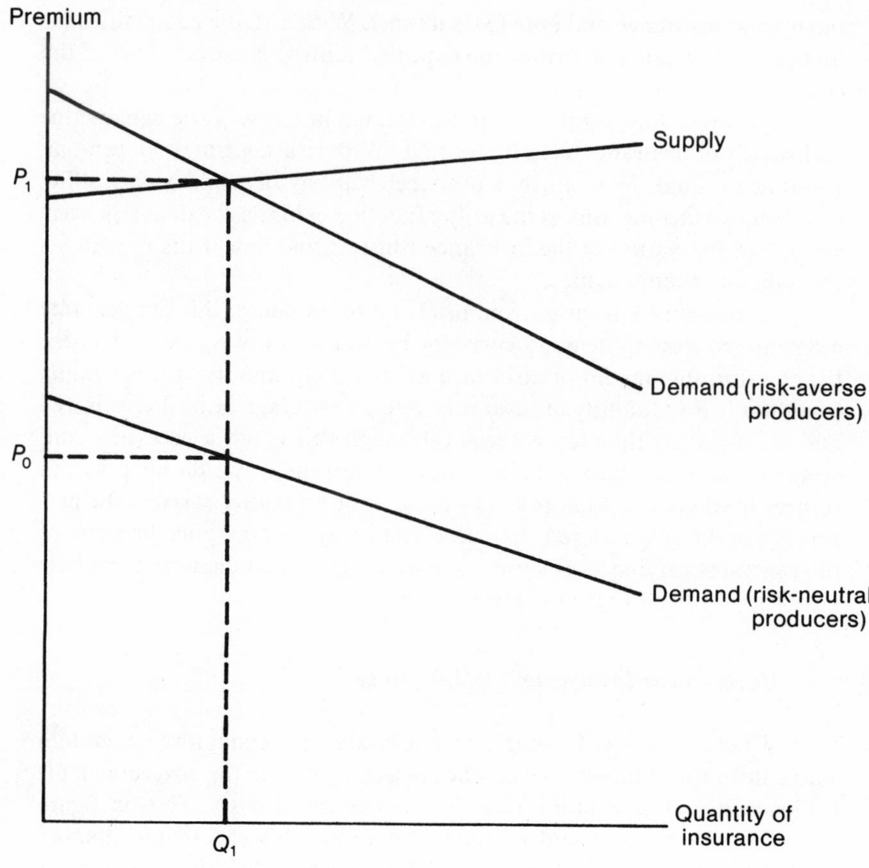


FIGURE 12.1 Demand and supply curves for insurance

17). Therefore the economically relevant loss ratio is $(1.21 + .35)/1.26 = 1.24$. This figure indicates that there has been roughly a 24 percent subsidy to FCIC crop insurance, in the sense that a break-even (and untaxed!) private insurance industry would have charged premiums 24 percent higher. Even so, overall participation has been low, as discussed earlier.

### *Empirical Estimation of U.S. Insurance Demand*

The relevant experimental data are variations in participation by crop and by county. They range from practically no participation for some Middle Western grains programs to more than 50 percent (more than half the eligible acreage) for tobacco in some Southeastern counties. The empirical question is what explains this variation. In the only empirical study of the price responsiveness of demand for U.S. crop insurance in the literature reviewed earlier, Clendenin (1942) explained farmers' participation rates as a function of the premium rate charged. The premium rate by itself does not determine the expected rate of return to investment in insurance, because the expected indemnity is not held constant. Of course, almost 40 years of further experience gives a better basis for estimating expected indemnities.

Our sample consists of fifty-seven observations in 1979. The counties and crops sampled, together with participation rate, premium rate, and past indemnity rate, are shown in table 12.1. The sample is not a random drawing of county programs. It was selected to obtain both high- and low-participation counties, and to obtain some counties located near counties with no FCIC program for purposes of the comparisons made later in this chapter. There is also some clustering in relatively few states in order to make data collection easier. However, the sample was not selected with reference to any independent variable to be used in the following regres-

TABLE 12.1 Statistics on FCIC insurance in a sample of 57 U.S. county programs, 1979

| State, county, and crop | Percentage of acreage insured | Premium as percent of liability | Expected return as percent of liability | Expected rate of return to insurance |
|---|---|---|---|---|
| *Arkansas* | | | | |
| Arkansas, soybeans | 2 | 5.2 | 1.50 | −71.2 |
| Jefferson, soybeans | 6 | 6.6 | 5.60 | −14.0 |
| *California* | | | | |
| Kern, cotton | 7 | 4.9 | 4.10 | −15.5 |
| *Colorado* | | | | |
| Cheyenne, wheat | 18 | 21.6 | 16.60 | −22.9 |
| Logan, wheat | 29 | 10.6 | 7.30 | −31.3 |
| *Georgia* | | | | |
| Bullock, tobacco | 11 | 6.3 | 6.70 | 5.8 |
| Bullock, peanuts | 8 | 4.7 | 1.80 | −61.3 |
| Coffee, tobacco | 36 | 2.8 | 4.70 | 69.3 |
| Coffee, peanuts | 22 | 4.8 | 1.60 | −66.1 |
| Worth, tobacco | 22 | 2.7 | 0.90 | −64.8 |
| Worth, peanuts | 9 | 3.5 | 0.80 | −76.7 |
| *Idaho* | | | | |
| Lewis, wheat | 48 | 3.3 | 3.70 | 11.6 |
| Power, wheat | 7 | 6.2 | 5.40 | −13.3 |
| *Indiana* | | | | |
| Benton, corn | 2 | 2.9 | 1.30 | −54.0 |
| Benton, soybeans | 2 | 3.1 | 0.02 | −99.5 |
| Morgan, corn | 2 | 3.6 | 2.80 | −22.9 |
| Morgan, soybeans | 3 | 4.5 | 3.80 | −15.2 |
| Tippecanoe, corn | 5 | 3.1 | 1.70 | −45.7 |

TABLE 12.1 *Continued*

| State, county, and crop | Percentage of acreage insured | Premium as percent of liability | Expected return as percent of liability | Expected rate of return to insurance |
|---|---|---|---|---|
| *Iowa* | | | | |
| Boone, corn | 22 | 4.2 | 5.50 | 31.3 |
| Boone, soybeans | 17 | 3.4 | 2.00 | −39.7 |
| Cass, corn | 21 | 4.5 | 4.90 | 9.1 |
| Cass, soybeans | 16 | 5.7 | 2.70 | −52.8 |
| Grundy, corn | 11 | 2.8 | 1.70 | −39.6 |
| Grundy, soybeans | 13 | 2.7 | 0.80 | −71.6 |
| Hancock, corn | 10 | 3.9 | 1.90 | −51.3 |
| Hancock, soybeans | 9 | 3.5 | 1.80 | −49.5 |
| Mills, corn | 28 | 5.4 | 8.00 | 48.0 |
| Mills, soybeans | 16 | 5.0 | 2.20 | −56.2 |
| Plymouth, corn | 32 | 6.3 | 6.80 | 8.2 |
| Plymouth, soybeans | 25 | 5.0 | 2.90 | −41.5 |
| Taylor, corn | 22 | 5.2 | 7.80 | 50.6 |
| Taylor, soybeans | 19 | 5.9 | 3.60 | −38.6 |
| *Kansas* | | | | |
| Harvey, wheat | 17 | 5.8 | 2.80 | −52.0 |
| Meade, wheat | 3 | 13.6 | 7.10 | −47.7 |
| Rush, wheat | 20 | 6.8 | 1.70 | −75.1 |
| *Maryland* | | | | |
| Caroline, wheat | 1 | 3.1 | 0.03 | −99.2 |
| Caroline, corn | 16 | 4.7 | 4.50 | −5.0 |
| Caroline, soybeans | 6 | 4.9 | 2.20 | −56.0 |
| Queen Anne's, corn | 11 | 3.9 | 3.40 | −13.7 |
| Queen Anne's, soybeans | 4 | 4.6 | 2.70 | −42.0 |
| Talbot, corn | 3 | 4.0 | 1.20 | −69.0 |
| Talbot, soybeans | 1 | 4.6 | 0.40 | −91.7 |
| *Mississippi* | | | | |
| Bolivar, cotton | 13 | 6.1 | 14.50 | 138.4 |
| Holmes, cotton | 29 | 3.3 | 5.80 | 74.7 |
| Leflore, cotton | 8 | 3.9 | 4.80 | 23.5 |
| *North Carolina* | | | | |
| Bladen, tobacco | 41 | 2.3 | 2.00 | −10.9 |
| Lenoir, tobacco | 75 | 1.8 | 1.90 | 7.9 |
| Granville, tobacco | 57 | 2.2 | 2.60 | 18.6 |
| Halifax, tobacco | 34 | 2.3 | 2.00 | −11.6 |
| Moore, tobacco | 22 | 2.0 | 0.80 | −58.3 |
| Wilkes, tobacco | 65 | 3.4 | 4.30 | 26.0 |
| *Tennessee* | | | | |
| Dyer, wheat | 14 | 4.9 | 12.70 | 158.8 |
| *Texas* | | | | |
| Briscoe, cotton | 12 | 12.3 | 15.30 | 24.7 |
| Dawson, cotton | 2 | 12.2 | 15.50 | 27.0 |
| Garza, cotton | 6 | 8.8 | 7.30 | −17.1 |
| Gray, wheat | 1 | 13.2 | 10.30 | −22.2 |
| Hockley, cotton | 15 | 9.5 | 14.60 | 53.7 |

sions, so we do not believe that sample selection bias is a problem.[3] The available data for each county program are as follows.

*Acreage insured and FCIC's estimate of potential acreage insurable.* The dependent variable, the quantity of insurance, is the percentage of potential acreage that is insured. In our sample, it varies from 1 percent for soybeans in Talbot County, Maryland, to 75 percent for tobacco in Lenoir County, North Carolina.

*The aggregate premiums paid for each crop in each county.* Premiums are sometimes adjusted for individual farms within counties, but we do not have individual farm data. In effect, we are treating each county as a single large farm. In order to obtain a common representation across crops and counties of different sizes, we express the premium as a percentage of the FCIC's liability, which is the value of indemnities if the county's crop is wiped out. This way of expressing the cost of insurance is analogous to expressing the cost of a lottery ticket as a percentage of the maximum prize. This could be misleading if the size structure of prizes in a multiprize lottery, which is the appropriate analogy for crop insurance, changes significantly. However, this does not seem to be the case in crop insurance.

*The ratio of aggregate indemnities to liability for the twelve years preceding 1979.* Also available is the FCIC's loss ratio (indemnities divided by premiums) for these twelve years. However, the loss ratio does not appropriately measure the expected returns to investment in insurance because the premiums are adjusted over time. Thus a county with a historically high loss ratio will tend not to be as attractive an investment as the loss ratio suggests, because the premium rate will have adjusted. Indeed, we were initially concerned whether the expected rate of return to buying insurance would vary enough across counties to permit a meaningful statistical analysis, because premiums are supposed to be set to equalize expected indemnities and premiums. For the United States as a whole, this is close to being the case, as the 0.96 aggregate loss ratio for 1948–79 indicates. However, there is substantial variation in the expected rate of return from county to county. The expected rate of return for 1979 is calculated as the twelve-year average ratio of indemnities to liability, divided by the 1979 ratio of premiums to liability, minus one. The rate of return so defined ranges from a low of −99.5 percent (for soybeans in Benton County, Indiana), to a high of 159 percent (for wheat in Dyer County, Tennessee). Benton County had a low premium rate but very little indemnity payments, while Dyer County had a premium rate almost as low but with much

3. There is unavoidable sample selection bias in the sense of Heckman (1974), since counties with no programs are excluded. This suggests a sample that may not be representative of U.S. farmers' utility functions, variability of output, or other relevant characteristics of insurance demand.

greater indemnities. Other counties such as Cheyenne and Logan in Colorado had even higher indemnities but premiums so much larger that the rate of return was lower than in Dyer County.

The results of a regression analysis to explain participation are shown in table 12.2. The coefficient of the expected rate of return indicates that participation does indeed respond to economic incentives. The coefficient of 18.5 in regression equation 1 implies that an increase in the rate of return of 0.10 percent would increase participation by 1.85 percentage points. Thus, to take an example pertinent to the Federal Crop Insurance Act of 1980, a subsidy of 30 percent on premiums would be expected to increase participation by 5.5 percentage points, or from 20-percent participation to 25.5-percent participation.

The proponents of an expanded U.S. crop insurance program are looking for larger effects than this. However, the GAO estimates cited earlier suggest that the 81-percent expansion of insured acreage in 1981 would increase participation from about 13 percent (26-million acres insured out of 200-million potential) to 24 percent, which is 11 percentage points, as the regression coefficient predicts, for a 30-percent subsidy. Nonetheless, the coefficient of the expected rate of return is likely to be understated in

TABLE 12.2 Regression coefficients explaining U.S. county data on FCIC participation, 1979

| Independent variables[a] | Regression equation 1 | 2 | 3 | 4 | 5[b] | 6 |
|---|---|---|---|---|---|---|
| Expected rate of return | 18.5 (3.9) | 19.6 (4.5) | 44.3 (0.8) | 20.4 (4.2) | 1.7 (4.9) | 15.4 (3.8) |
| Standard deviation of return | −.135 (2.7) | −.146 (4.5) | −.006[c] (1.5) | −.085[d] (3.3) | −.006 (2.9) | −.100 (2.2) |
| Return innovation | | 6.4 (4.6) | 4.7 (2.6) | 6.5 (4.5) | 0.4 (3.7) | 5.8 (3.6) |
| Education | | | | | | −.024 (1.5) |
| Tobacco | | | | | | 23.2 (5.2) |
| Part owners | | | | | | 25.1 (1.7) |
| Off-farm work | | | | | | −.956 (.04) |
| Intercept | 9.40 | 8.35 (4.9) | 17.5 (3.3) | 35.1 (9.1) | .70 (2.2) | 25.8 |
| $R^2$ | .219 | .432 | .338 | .431 | .393 | .630 |

*Note*: *t* statistics in parentheses.
[a]Dependent variable is percentage of acreage insured.
[b]Dependent variable is log $[x(1-x)]$, where $x$ is percentage of acreage insured.
[c]Standard deviation (farm) calculated using equation 7 (in text), with $\rho = 1$.
[d]Standard deviation (farm) calculated using equation 7 (in text), with $\rho = 0.3$.

the regressions because of a serious errors-in-variable problem. The twelve-year series is probably not long enough, yet the error structure of production would probably be changed in much older data. Moreover, the contract terms for indemnities have been changed over time when the loss experience suggested it. For example, the expected rate of return to the purchase of insurance in Dyer County is unlikely to be 159 percent. The big payoffs that generate the high returns occurred in four years out of the six-year period 1968–73, with none in 1974–79.

To test for the possibility of innovations in expected returns, owing either to changes in the FCIC contracts or to changes in the error structure of production, a return-innovation variable is added to equations 2 and 3. This is the difference between the rate of indemnity paid in the most recent two years and the twelve-year average. With a stable structure, this difference should be a random variable unrelated to the dependent variable. The fact that it is significantly positive indicates that farmers indeed place more weight on recent experience, which is consistent with a changing structure.

The standard deviation of returns from crop insurance is calculated from the same twelve years of data used to estimate mean returns for each county. It is used in the absence of county data on the variability of yields. Normally a greater variance in returns from an asset is expected to reduce the demand for the asset, which is what equation 2 shows. However, as a proxy for yield variance, this variable should have had a positive sign (the variance of returns from the portfolio of crops and insurance being reduced by the purchase of insurance).

There are difficulties in measuring this variable—for one reason, because our data are for counties while the relevant variance is that facing the individual producer. This becomes a problem, because the relationship between individual and county variance depends on the number of farms in the county, and this varies from county to county. Carter and Dean (1960) derived the relationship between individual and county variances as

$$\sigma^2(\text{county}) = \sigma^2(\text{farm})/[N(1 + (N - 1)\rho)]^{1/2}, \tag{7}$$

where $N$ is the number of farms, and $\rho$ is the (presumed equal) correlation coefficient between the yield deviations of each pair of farmers. If $\rho = 1$, the county variance equals the individual farm variance, and there is no problem with the regression equation as specified. If $\rho = 0$—that is, farmers' yields are independent—then the individual farm variance equals the county variance times $N$. In this case, we should multiply the county-variance variable by the square root of the number of farms in it for the regression equation. Unfortunately, we do not know what the value of $\rho$ really is.

In order to test for the importance of this problem, $\sigma^2$ (farm) was calculated for each county according to equation 7 with alternative values of $\rho$(0, 0.05, 0.10, 0.30, 0.50, and 1.00). Regression equation 2 has $\rho = 1$, so that $\sigma^2$(farm) = $\sigma^2$(county). Regression equation 3 has $\rho = 0$, and equation 4 has $\rho = 0.3$. Using $\rho = 0.3$ does result in a change in sign of the coefficient of the standard deviation of return, but overall, equation 3 performs worse than equation 2. Equation 4 fits almost as well as equation 2, but there is still a negative sign on the standard deviation of returns.

Equation 5 respecifies the dependent variable in logit form. This is done to rule out forecasts of negative participation. Equations 1 through 4 predict negative acreage insured in one or two counties. However, the logit specification does not appear to make any appreciable difference in the regression results.

Equation 6 adds other variables that may influence the demand for crop insurance. Education is not quite significant. If the negative sign held up, it would suggest that those with more education are less risk-averse, or that they have work options that diversify their income sources sufficiently to make crop insurance less valuable to them. However the off-farm work variable is insignificant. The fraction of part owners in a county is marginally significant and has a positive effect on insurance purchases. This perhaps reflects the more highly leveraged condition of part owners, as compared to full owners, with creditors encouraging or requiring crop insurance as part of the security for debts. (Both tenancy and full ownership have equally negative effects on participation rates, compared to part ownership.) Average farm size and age of farm operators were also included in a regression but had insignificant effects.

The most significant of the added variables is the tobacco variable, a dummy variable equal to one for tobacco crop insurance contracts. Other things being equal, participation is 23-percent higher for tobacco.

## The Effects of Crop Insurance in the United States

The U.S. crop insurance programs were introduced sporadically and in a variety of preprogram circumstances. However, it is still difficult to find experimental results that will permit inferences about the effects of crop insurance introduced on a permanent basis in an area where it previously did not exist. Many of the FCIC programs were not adopted widely enough by farmers to lead to any notable county-level effects, and the relevant data for individual farms are not available. For some of the massively adopted but short-lived insurance programs in the 1930s and 1940s, we do not have adequate before-and-after data.

The program that offers the best chance of observing the effects of policy intervention in the area of insurance is the disaster payments program, which covered major grains and cotton between 1974 and 1981. This program paid indemnities but charged no premiums. The indemnities were substantial, averaging about $400 million per year in 1974–79 (compared to $90 million for FCIC insurance over the same period).

There is good data for experimental observation since, in 1974, when the program should not yet have had much impact, there was a census of agriculture, which generated county-level data. (The census was taken at about the time the first indemnities were paid.) In 1978, another census of agriculture was undertaken, the county data from which was published in 1981. There should have been some reaction to the disaster payments program by the time of the 1978 census, so the basis for our tests is changes between the 1974 and 1978 census data at the county level. Of course, there is the problem of what changes would have occurred anyway as a consequence of other events. This problem can be evaded to some extent because of the variation in the pre-1974 insurance regime.

There are a number of counties in the Great Plains states and the Southeast that have significant crop production but no FCIC program. Some of these are the fourteen counties mentioned earlier, whose FCIC programs were eliminated in 1956. Thus they are counties in which production is especially risky. If the disaster payments program has significant effects, they should show up in these counties.

Table 12.3 shows some data for a small sample of non-FCIC counties. The average payments per acre under the disaster program have been greater for the non-FCIC counties, confirming that they are indeed riskier production areas. However, this is observed because the non-FCIC counties are concentrated in the Southwest. In order to obtain a geographically comparable comparison, a subsample of eighteen Texas and Colorado counties was compared, with nine counties having FCIC programs and nine counties having no programs. In this subsample, the non-FCIC counties received less disaster payments per acre in the four years for which county data were available (1976–79).[4] Note however that the non-FCIC counties received well above the U.S. average disaster payment of ninety cents per cropland acre (last column of table 12.3).

The data of table 12.3 indicate that cropland was expanded more in the non-FCIC counties. This can be attributed to either higher expected returns or reduced risk in non-FCIC counties due to the disaster payments program. The difference in gain in expected returns between non-FCIC and average U.S. counties is $4.4 - 0.9 = \$3.50$ per acre. With average rental value of cropland at $540 per acre, the disaster program increased the expected rate of return to land by about 8 percent in the non-FCIC counties, compared to all U.S. counties. The difference in rate of growth of

4. The 1974–75 data exist but not in a form that could be made available in time for this study. At the national level, 1976–79 is representative of the whole 1974–79 period. U.S. aggregate payments averaged $404 million annually in 1976–79 and $420 million in 1974–75.

TABLE 12.3 Agricultural data for U.S. counties, 1974–78

| Item | Sample counties: Non FCIC[a] | Sample counties: FCIC | Texas and Colorado: Non FCIC | Texas and Colorado: FCIC | All counties |
|---|---|---|---|---|---|
| Disaster payments per year (dollars/cropland acre) | 4.4 | 3.0 | 4.7 | 6.4 | 0.9 |
| Acres per farm | 2,404 | 721 | 3,068 | 1,601 | 497 |
| Cropland harvested | | | | | |
| Thousand acres, 1978 | 68 | 193 | 68 | 231 | 440,000 |
| Percent change, 1974–78 | 20.3 | 6.8 | 30.1 | 20.4 | 6.5 |
| Crop failure | | | | | |
| Thousand acres, 1978 | 13 | 7 | 16 | 30 | 5,700 |
| Percent change, 1974–78 | 3.9 | −2.0 | 4.0 | −9.5 | −0.4 |
| Summer fallow | | | | | |
| Thousand acres, 1978 | 20 | 18 | 27 | 52 | 33,000 |
| Percent change, 1974–78 | 1.4 | −0.4 | 1.8 | −1.5 | 0.0 |
| Diversification | | | | | |
| Herfindahl index, 1978 | .634 | .534 | .701 | .652 | |
| Change, 1974–78 | .095 | .044 | .134 | .126 | |
| Cover crops | | | | | |
| Thousand acres, 1978 | 21 | 26 | 27 | 52 | 6,600 |
| Percent change, 1974–78 | −0.5 | 0.1 | −0.3 | −0.4 | −0.5 |
| Number of counties | 12 | 44 | 9 | 9 | |

*Note*: Data is average per county.
[a]These counties are in Texas (Armstrong, Andrews, Borden, Donley, Kent, Motley, Scurry, and Wheeler); Colorado (Kiowa); and Georgia (Screven, Telfair, and Washington).

cropland is 13.8 percent. Therefore, the elasticity of supply of cropland in the non-FCIC counties would have to be 1.5 or more if the difference in expected return due to the disaster program were to explain the acreage expansion in the non-FCIC counties. Unfortunately, without information on the elasticity of cropland supply, we cannot tell how much if any of the observed acreage expansion is due to response by risk-averse producers to reduction in risk under the program.

The other items in table 12.3 are intended to detect behavioral changes that might be attributable to the introduction of the disaster program. The Herfindahl index, the sum of squared shares of crops in a county's crops, is an indicator of specialization. If only one crop is grown in a county, then the index is 1.0. If two crops are grown, each occupying one-half the county's land, then the index is $0.5^2 + 0.5^2 = 0.50$. If there are five crops, each using one-fifth of the land, the index is $5(0.2)^2 = 0.20$. This index is widely used in the study of industrial concentration. Its use as a measure of specialization is discussed in Pope and Prescott (1980). The table 12.3 data suggest that specialization has increased everywhere, but slightly faster in the non-FCIC counties. This is consistent with the idea that the introduction of crop insurance induces farmers to undertake riskier farming practices. Crop failure increased in the non-FCIC counties, while it decreased elsewhere. In addition, the use of cover crops decreased in the non-FCIC counties, while it increased slightly in the United States as a whole. However, summer fallow increased as a fraction of cropland in the non-FCIC counties, while it decreased elsewhere. Generally, it appears that the disaster payments program encouraged crop production, specialization, and perhaps other elements of risk taking in the risky production areas (Texas and Colorado, in our sample), as compared to the United States as a whole. The program especially encouraged expansion in the areas that previously had no crop insurance available.

There is also evidence that the introduction of the program had effects in the land market. The nine non-FCIC counties in Texas and Colorado experienced annual rates of land price increase that averaged 15.5 percent between the 1974 and the 1978 censuses. The nine sample FCIC counties in these states had a rate of land price increase of 10.5 percent, while the U.S. average farm real-estate price index also increased at a 10.6-percent annual rate between November 1974 and November 1978.

At the same time, however, the average size of farms in the Texas-Colorado sample increased more for FCIC counties (3.6 percent) than for the non-FCIC counties (−0.7 percent). The number of farms increased at practically the same rate in FCIC and non-FCIC counties (2.8 and 2.5 percent, respectively). Thus the disaster program seems to have encouraged cropping of previously uncropped acreage but not farm enlargement or new farming enterprises.

No test statistics have been presented on the statistical significance of these differences. Under the assumptions of (1) a common underlying variance (not of yields but of land price changes, acreage changes, and so forth) and (2) counties as independent observations, the standard $F$ statistic cannot reject the null hypotheses of the same changes in the non-FCIC counties and the FCIC counties at the 10-percent level. However, some of the differences between the Texas and Colorado counties and the U.S. average are significant. It may be said, though, that taking counties as observations greatly understates the degrees of freedom, since each county figure is an average of hundreds of individual farms. In this case, if assumption 1 holds, there should be a quite small between-county variance within the nine non-FCIC counties in Texas and Colorado. In fact, there is substantial variation from county to county in most of the 1974–78 changes calculated. The standard analysis-of-variance test takes this into account; thus the marginal-at-best significance of the table 12.3 differences must be taken seriously. It will require a larger sample of counties to nail down the effects of the disaster payments program. Nonetheless, the table-12.3 data suggest some effects of the kind hoped for when a crop insurance program is introduced. (At least they are hoped for in the context of developing countries; the disaster program in the United States was not intended to promote risk taking and output expansion in marginal production areas). The likelihood of such effects was seen, for example, by Miller and Walter (1977) as a drawback of the program. The present results can be taken as a confirmation of the potential problems they saw as a result of their study of Kiowa County, Colorado.[5]

## Summary and Conclusions

The U.S. government became involved in crop insurance only after several attempts in the private sector to provide multiple-peril crop insurance failed. These private efforts failed for a number of reasons: (1) coverage of price as well as yield risk, (2) inadequate geographical dispersion of risks, (3) insufficient data for a sound actuarial program, and (4) improper timing of sales and wide zoning of rates, leading to adverse selection. The public program begun in 1938 encountered some of these same difficulties, particularly inadequate data and adverse selection. High loss ratios resulted, and the program was subsequently reduced to an experimental basis in 1948. During the next several decades, the program gradually expanded and operated on a limited but successful basis.

Because of the high cost of the disaster payment programs during the 1970s, the crop insurance program was expanded by 1980 legislation to become the nation's primary means of disaster protection for farmers. Subsidies were greatly increased, and the private insurance industry was encouraged to assume much of the marketing role for FCIC.

While the small sample size makes the empirical analysis of this chapter more a pilot study than a definitive research project, the U.S. experience with crop insurance seems to show the following. (1) An insurance program against low yields, with expected indemnities roughly equal to premiums paid, induces participation of 10 to 20 percent of farmers. (2) U.S. farmers respond to both the premiums charged and the expected level of indemnities. Each percentage point increase in the rate of return to investment in insurance increases the participation rate of farmers by about one-third of a percentage point. Thus it would take a quite large subsidy, probably more than 50 percent of premiums charged, to get a majority of U.S. farmers enrolled. (3) The introduction of a widely adopted crop insurance program, as exemplified in the disaster payments program, appears to encourage crop production in marginal areas and other risk taking in farming. However, the effects detectable as of 1978 from the program introduced in 1974 do not appear dramatic, even in areas that had no FCIC coverage before the disaster payments program.

5. Miller and Walter, based on thirty-one years of data (1945–76), forecast average annual disaster payments of $4.02 per acre in Kiowa County. This is very close to the $4.13 per acre actually paid out on average in 1976–79 in this county—a little less than the $4.70 average for the nine Texas and Colorado counties shown in table 12.3.

# 13

# Evolution of the Crop Insurance Program in Japan

Toyoji Yamauchi

Japan's geographical position and climatic conditions conspire to produce frequent agricultural calamities. These include crop damage due to wind, drought, insects, diseases, and cold summers. Losses can be severe, and they occur almost every year in at least some part of Japan.

Most Japanese farms are small; the average size in 1975 was only 1.1 hectares. Farms of this size cannot cope with major and frequent calamities. Japan has a long history of public intervention to prevent the decapitalization and impoverishment of its farmers. Grain-storage schemes were introduced from China during the eighth century, and these became the major means of public relief throughout the Edo Period (1603 to 1867). After the Meiji Restoration and the accompanying land reform, which created many small, owner-operated farms, interest in formal crop insurance began to grow. Many small-scale farmers were having difficulty retaining their new ownership status, having to mortgage their land to moneylenders in times of natural calamity. Their ability to avoid or repay these loans was also handicapped by the burden of land taxes, which had to be paid to the government even during times of crop failure.

As early as 1888, Paul Mayet, a German consultant to the Japanese government, advised that an agricultural insurance scheme be established. However, it was not until the 1920s that crop insurance proposals were first debated in the Diet.[1] In 1928, the Ministry of Agriculture started to conduct surveys and collect statistical data necessary for implementation of a crop insurance scheme. After prolonged debate, the Agricultural Insurance Law (Law No. 68) was enacted by the Diet in April 1938. The scheme began operations in April 1939 and provided nationwide coverage for paddy rice, wheat, barley, and mulberries. The government subsidized the scheme at a rate of 15 percent of the premiums.

After the Second World War and the enforcement of agricultural land reform, Japanese crop insurance was reorganized under the Agricul-

1. A proposal to insure crop losses for tenant farmers to assist them in paying their rents was submitted by four members of the Diet in 1922. A more general crop insurance program was proposed in 1924 with the backing of the Landowner Association and the Farmers' Union. A livestock insurance scheme was also proposed and enacted in 1929.

tural Loss Compensation Law, enacted in December 1947. This Act combined the former Agricultural Insurance Law with the Livestock Insurance Law, which had been enacted in 1929. The reorganization helped newly created owner/farmers to withstand yield losses arising from natural calamities and thus to avoid reverting back to tenant status.

This reorganization changed the previous crop insurance program in several ways. It expanded the insurable crops to include upland rice, and it extended the coverage to include yield damage due to cold summer weather or unavoidable plant diseases. It also stipulated that the amount of coverage should be adjusted each year to reflect changes in government fixed prices. Finally, the government increased its subsidy from 15 percent of the premium to about one-half.

## The Crop Insurance Program Enacted in 1947

### *Organization of the Scheme*

The Japanese crop insurance scheme under the Agricultural Loss Compensation Law has been amended several times since its enforcement in 1947. Therefore, it is helpful to first explain how the original scheme was organized at the time of its enforcement, and then how the scheme has been improved in the course of its operation.

The scheme consists of three tiers: the Agricultural Mutual Relief Associations, federations of Agricultural Mutual Relief Associations, and the Agricultural Mutual Relief Reinsurance Special Account. In addition to these three tiers, the Agricultural Mutual Relief Fund has been established as a credit facility for the federations (see figure 13.1).

*Agricultural Mutual Relief Association (AMRA).* An AMRA is an organization established in each village, town, and city, with the surrounding farmers as its members. When an association is established, all farmers in the district whose planted acreage of an insurable crop is above a certain minimum automatically become association members. Thus, in effect, Japanese crop insurance is compulsory.

An AMRA is responsible for the local operation of the insurance program. It writes the insurance contracts between the association and its members, covering rice, wheat, barley, silkworm cocoons, and livestock. It collects the insurance premiums, makes loss adjustments on insured crops, and pays indemnities to the insured. Each AMRA originally had to insure from its own resources at least 10 percent of the total coverage written. This meant that a similar proportion of the total premiums collected were retained by the association. Each AMRA also provides its members with facilities for the prevention and control of plant diseases and insect pests and dispensary facilities for insured livestock.

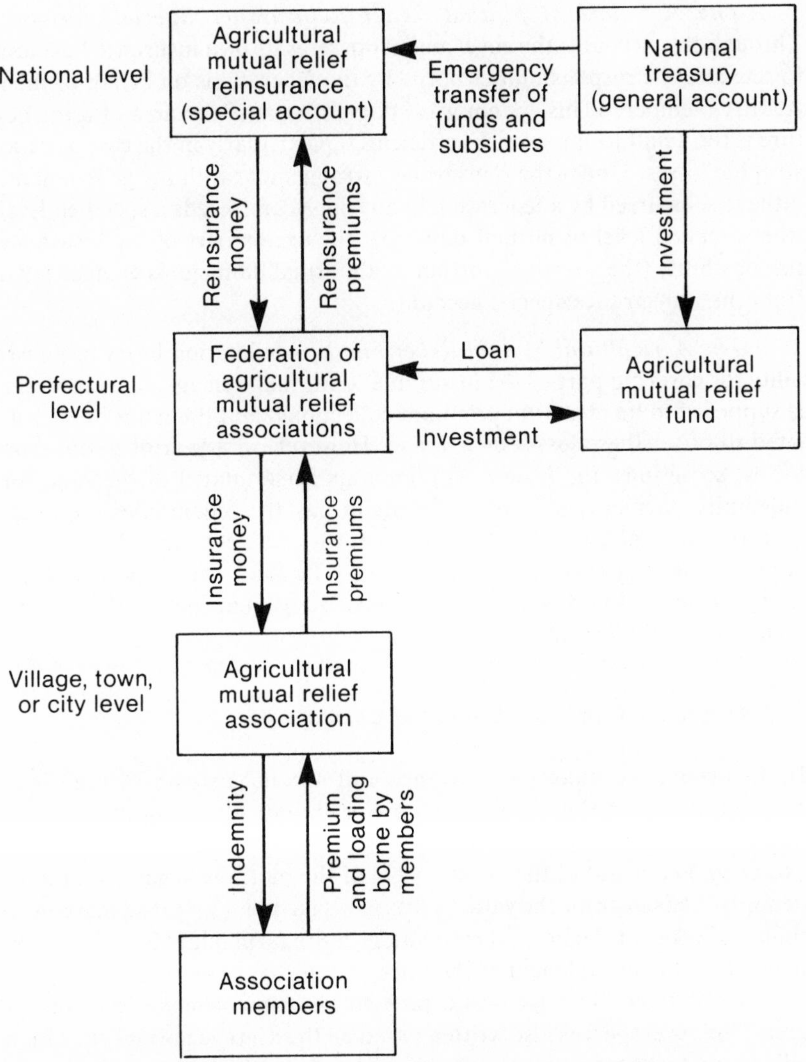


FIGURE 13.1 Organization of the Japanese crop insurance scheme

*Federation of Agricultural Mutual Relief Associations.* A federation of AMRAS operates in each prefecture (county) and has all the AMRAs within the prefecture as its members. As individual AMRAs are too small to fully cover the risks insured for their members, they reinsure some part of their coverage with the local federation. The federations also give guidance to members on the control of injurious insects and diseases.

*The Agricultural Mutual Relief Reinsurance Special Account.* Through this account, the government operates its own insurance business to reinsure the responsibilities borne by the federations on behalf of their AMRA members. This system was adopted because the area of a prefecture is too small to spread risks efficiently, particularly in the case of catastrophic losses. Under the reinsurance arrangement with the government, if the loss incurred by a federation in any one year exceeds a specified level (the so-called level of normal damage), the excess part of the insurance responsibility (the so-called portion of abnormal damage) is compensated from the reinsurance special account.

*The Agricultural Mutual Relief Fund.* A federation bears responsibility for covering part of the losses due to normal damage. This coverage is supposed to be met from premium collections, and the latter are calculated to offset these losses on average. However, in a year of severe crop losses, sometimes the insurance premiums accumulated in the fund for indemnity payments are not sufficient to pay the indemnities required. The Agricultural Mutual Relief Fund was therefore established to provide credit to the federations in disaster years. The fund was invested with an initial capital of three billion *yen*, provided 50 percent each by the government and all the federations in Japan.

### *Insurance Units and Amount of Coverage*

In the original scheme, the insurance unit was not necessarily the whole farm cultivated by the insured farmer but an individual plot of land that was a part of the farm unit. If the loss of the insured crop on one plot exceeded 30 percent of the normal yield of the plot, the scheme would indemnify the farmer for the value of loss. This payment would be made even though the loss of the insured crop on the entire farm might be less than 30 percent of the normal yield of the farm.

Until 1959, coverage was expressed in terms of money per unit of area. The coverage was also written based on the average normal yield for a village, and villages were classified by risk category. The coverage was expected to indemnify, at the most, 50 percent of the value of normal yield, at current price, of the insured crops. This was expected to cover the variable costs of production as well as part of the cost of family labor. Since the coverage was determined on the basis of the average normal yield for each village, the coverage per unit area was the same for all fields in a village. The amount of indemnity was determined by the extent of crop damage to the insured plot. The maximum indemnity payable per unit area in the case of a total crop loss is shown in table 13.1. In the event of a partial crop loss, only part of the maximum indemnity was paid. This share was 10

TABLE 13.1 Insurance coverage for one *tan* of paddy rice, Japan, 1947–52 (*yen*)

| Year | Average yield for village | | |
| --- | --- | --- | --- |
| | Over 2.0 *koku* per *tan* | 1.5–2.0 *koku* per *tan* | Below 1.5 *koku* per *tan* |
| 1947 | 1,200 | 900 | 600 |
| 1948 | 1,600 | 1,200 | 800 |
| 1949 | 3,900 | 3,000 | 2,000 |
| 1950 | 4,400 | 3,200 | 2,000 |
| 1951 | 6,000 | 4,800 | 3,200 |
| 1952 | | | |
| Village risk 1 | 6,800 | 5,200 | 3,600 |
| Village risk 2 | 6,400 | 4,800 | 3,200 |
| Village risk 3 | 6,000 | 4,400 | 2,800 |

*Note*: 1 *tan* equals 0.1 hectare; 1 *koku* equals 150 kilograms.

percent for a 30- to 40-percent crop loss and increased in steps of 15 percent for each additional 10-percent increase in the crop loss ratio.

However, the productivity of any individual farm is often different from that of its neighbors, owing to differences in natural conditions and the technical abilities of farmers. In the case of a farmer who had lower than average productivity, the coverage was higher than 50 percent of the value of the normal yield of his farm. On the other hand, in the case of a farmer who had higher than average productivity, the coverage was lower than 50 percent of the value of the normal yield of his farm. Consequently, many farmers who were obtaining high yields complained that they were underinsured.

### *Premium Rates and the Schedule for Premium Subsidies*

The premium rate was based upon the damage rate experienced in each prefecture during the previous twenty years. The damage rate was calculated each year by the following formula:

$$\frac{\text{Amount of indemnity paid}}{\text{Maximum indemnity payable}} \times 100.$$

A standard premium rate was determined for each prefecture by the Ministry of Agriculture, using damage rate data for the preceding twenty years. Each prefectural government classified its villages into risk grades on the basis of the incidence of crop failure. The standard premium rate initially calculated for the prefecture was then distributed among villages, towns, and cities according to their respective risk grades.

In order to determine the amount of premium subsidy, and the extent of government reinsurance required, the standard premium rate calculated for each prefecture was divided into three parts: (1) the normal premium rate, (2) the abnormal premium rate, and (3) the superabnormal premium rate. The terms *normal standard-damage rate* and *abnormal standard-damage rate* defined the boundaries between these three components of the premium rate. These rates were determined by means of a specific statistical procedure (using the Poisson distribution) applied to historical data on crop losses.[2]

The calculation of the premium rate is given below for paddy rice in Hokkaido (see table 13.2 for Hokkaido's damage rates). First, the normal damage rate (3.496 percent), and the abnormal damage rate (10 percent) have been determined by the Ministry of Agriculture as the relevant rates applicable to Hokkaido. The damage rates in Hokkaido for each of the years 1931-50 are classified into normal rates of damage, abnormal rates

TABLE 13.2 Damage rate, paddy rice, Hokkaido, Japan, 1931-50 (percent)

| Year | Actual damage rate | Standard damage rates | | |
|---|---|---|---|---|
| | | Normal | Abnormal | Superabnormal |
| 1931 | 57.306 | 3.496 | 6.504 | 47.306 |
| 1932 | 60.045 | 3.496 | 6.504 | 50.045 |
| 1933 | 6.248 | 3.496 | 2.752 | 0.000 |
| 1934 | 30.301 | 3.496 | 6.504 | 20.301 |
| 1935 | 33.338 | 3.496 | 6.504 | 23.338 |
| 1936 | 0.740 | 0.740 | 0.000 | 0.000 |
| 1937 | 0.304 | 0.304 | 0.000 | 0.000 |
| 1938 | 0.483 | 0.483 | 0.000 | 0.000 |
| 1939 | 0.605 | 0.605 | 0.000 | 0.000 |
| 1940 | 21.330 | 3.496 | 6.504 | 11.330 |
| 1941 | 43.611 | 3.496 | 6.504 | 33.610 |
| 1942 | 1.655 | 1.655 | 0.000 | 0.000 |
| 1943 | 1.635 | 1.635 | 0.000 | 0.000 |
| 1944 | 1.265 | 1.265 | 0.000 | 0.000 |
| 1945 | 64.158 | 3.496 | 6.504 | 54.158 |
| 1946 | 2.458 | 2.458 | 0.000 | 0.000 |
| 1947 | 16.116 | 3.496 | 6.504 | 6.116 |
| 1948 | 2.612 | 2.612 | 0.000 | 0.000 |
| 1949 | 10.167 | 3.496 | 6.504 | 0.167 |
| 1950 | 1.954 | 1.954 | 0.000 | 0.000 |
| Weighted mean[a] | 14.640 | 2.536 | 2.996 | 9.108 |

[a]Calculated using the following weights for each time period: 1931-38, 1/40; 1939-46, 1/20; 1947-50, 1/10.

2. For further details on the method of calculating the premium rate, see Yamauchi (1973).

of damage, and superabnormal rates of damage. Finally, a weighted mean of the three damage rate classes is calculated using different weights for the years preceding the enforcement of the Agricultural Insurance Law (1931–38), for the years of enforcement of the law (1939–46), and for the years when the Agricultural Loss Compensation Law was enforced (1947–50). The weighted average of the normal rate of damage (2.536 percent), plus that of abnormal rate of damage (2.996 percent), plus that of superabnormal rate of damage (9.108 percent) gives the standard premium rate for Hokkaido (15.024 percent).

The premium rates for each prefecture vary with the extent of historical crop losses. For example, the premium rate of Hokkaido (15.024 percent) is 2.5 times that of the national average (5.998 percent). In contrast, the premium rate of Niigata Prefecture (2.419 percent) is 40 percent of that of the national average, as shown in table 13.3.

To reduce the cost of insurance to farmers, the government subsidizes the premium rate. The entire portion represented by the superabnormal premium rate is paid by the government, together with one-half of the portion represented by the abnormal premium rate. In addition, a part of the normal premium rate is also subsidized. The proportion of the premium rate that the government bears on behalf of farmers is greater in areas subject to frequent damage, like Hokkaido. However, in spite of this arrangement, the amount of the premium per unit borne by farmers in high-risk areas is still greater than that in low-risk areas. (Table 13.3 gives the proportion of the premium rate shared by farmers and the national treasury in selected areas.)

## Evolution of the Program since 1947

The crop insurance program enacted in 1947 proved to be expensive for the Japanese government. In 1950 for example, the program cost the government 9.4-billion *yen* (see chapter 9). Catastrophic losses in 1953 increased the cost to the government to 36.4-billion *yen* that year. Despite these large

TABLE 13.3 Premium rates for paddy rice, high-risk and low-risk areas, Japan (percent)

| Area | Premium rate | Farmers' share | National treasury's share |
|---|---|---|---|
| Hokkaido: | | | |
| subject to frequent damage | 15.024 | 3.149 | 11.875 |
| Niigata Prefecture: | | | |
| subject to infrequent damage | 2.419 | 1.401 | 1.018 |
| National average | 5.998 | 2.430 | 3.568 |

net outflows from government, farmers complained bitterly about the insurance program. Many of the complaints were inevitable for a compulsory scheme—the premiums were too high, farmers in the riskier areas received all the benefits, and so forth. Problems arose in collecting the premiums, and in some cases AMRAs had to cease operations because of farmers' hostility. In response to these problems, the insurance program was modified and improved on a number of occasions.

### *Improvement of the Indemnity Schedule*

Since the coverage per unit area was originally the same for all farmers in a village, and it only covered up to 50 percent of the value of the average normal yield, farmers who achieved higher than average yields were underinsured. Therefore, the calculation of coverage per unit of area was revised in 1957 so as to tie the coverage to the productivity of individual plots.

The amount of coverage was determined in terms of the normal yield of each plot of the insured crop. For example, the maximum coverage for rice per *koku* (150 kilograms) was 4,900 *yen* in 1957. This was determined as 70 percent of the insurance value of the crop, where the insurance value was calculated as 70 percent of the government's fixed price for 1957 of 10,000 *yen* per *koku* of rice. In this case, if one plot of an insured farmer had an average productivity of three *koku* and was completely damaged, the maximum indemnity was 14,700 *yen* (4,900 *yen* × 3 *koku*). An indemnity was only paid to the farmer in case of a crop loss greater than 30 percent of the normal yield on his plot.

In order to introduce greater flexibility into the scheme so that farmers could better match the coverage with their insurance needs, a flexible system of determining the insurance value of each plot was introduced. In 1957, a farmer could choose among insurance values of 2-, 3-, 4-, 5-, and 7-thousand *yen* per *koku* of rice. However, to simplify office work, selection of insurance values is done by the AMRA, which reflects the opinion of the member farmers. Given a chosen insurance value, the amount of indemnity paid a farmer is calculated as follows. Indemnity to be paid equals (insurance value per *koku*) times (70 percent of the normal yield of the plot minus actual yield of the plot).

In 1963 the maximum insurance value of insured crops per *koku* was increased to 90 percent of the fixed price. The maximum indemnity payable with a complete crop loss was increased to 63 percent of the loss.

In 1971 a farm unit insurance scheme was also introduced, which indemnifies crop losses on the basis of the normal yield for the whole farm. The member farmers of the AMRAs participate in the scheme on an optional basis, though this has to be a group choice made at a general meeting of the AMRA. In this scheme, the maximum amount of coverage of the insured crop has been determined at 72 percent of the normal yield of the whole farm. This is equivalent to 80 percent of the insured value of the crop for the whole farm, where the insurance value itself is determined as the normal yield times 90 percent of the government fixed price per *koku*.

In this scheme, indemnities are computed from the following formula. Indemnity to be paid equals (90 percent of the fixed price per *koku*) times (80 percent of the normal yield on the whole farm minus actual yield of the farm).

In the event of a complete crop loss, the maximum indemnity rate of the farm unit insurance is much higher than that of the plot unit insurance scheme. Any crop loss exceeding 20 percent of the normal yield of the insured farm is indemnified. Farm unit insurance should therefore be more effective in protecting farmers from natural hazards than plot unit insurance. However, it can be shown that indemnities will usually be lower for farmers who participate in the farm unit insurance than for those who participate in the plot unit insurance. This follows because, even though there may be a crop loss on one plot of several cultivated by a farmer, there may be little or no loss for the farm as a whole if plot yields are not highly and positively correlated. As a result, the majority of AMRAs chose to continue to participate in the plot unit insurance scheme.

### *Individualization of the Premium for Insured Farmers*

Another modification to mitigate farmers' complaints against compulsory crop insurance was to provide greater individualization of the premium rates to better reflect differences in risk levels. This could not be done at the individual farm level, but areas within each village that differed significantly in their risk levels were delineated on the basis of past crop loss. This modification was taken up at the revision of the Agricultural Loss Compensation Law in 1957.

### *Change in Eligibility for Crop Insurance*

Yet another modification to lessen farmers' complaints increased the minimum acreage of crops that could be grown before insurance became compulsory. Before 1957, a farmer had to purchase insurance if he planted more than 0.1 hectares of an insurable crop. After the revisions of 1957, insurance was only compulsory if the farmer grew more than 0.3 hectares of an insurable crop. This change allowed many part-time farmers to avoid insurance.

### *Reorganization of the Crop Insurance Scheme*

In spite of the above improvements, farmers' complaints about crop insurance continued. There were also changes in the economic and institutional environment over the years, which led to some questioning of the continued relevance of the original organization of the insurance scheme. Rice yields were not only increasing rapidly but were also becoming less risky. At the same time, increased integration of villages, towns, and cities was increasing the size of the AMRAs.

Within this setting, it became appropriate for each AMRA to take more responsibility for its members. Previously, the AMRAs were only responsible for 10 percent of the coverage they wrote, but in 1963 their liability was increased by law to between 50 and 80 percent of the normal damage component of crop losses. The federations of Agricultural Mutual Relief Associations continued to reinsure losses. This change increased the reserves carried by the AMRAs and improved their ability to finance preventive work against pest and disease damage. It also provided the AMRAs with the flexibility to return part of the premiums paid by farmers if they did not collect indemnities for several years. This became increasingly important in placating farmers as changes in rice technology reduced yield risks.

The method of calculating premium rates was also changed in 1967. The new rates were determined by the AMRAs on the basis of statistical data collected in the course of the insurance operation at the local level. This localization of the premium rate calculations permitted more accurate determination of damage rates and of their changes over time.

### *Changes in the Crops Insured*

Some of the insured crops in the 1947 crop insurance scheme were becoming less important (wheat, barley, rye, and upland rice) in the farm economy. Others, particularly fruits and intensive horticultural crops, were becoming more important. Both fruit cultivation and horticulture sometimes suffered extensive damage because of typhoons, hail, and other meteorological risks, and growers expressed a need for insurance.

A fruit insurance scheme was launched on a voluntary basis in 1972 after a five-year pilot scheme. Also, an insurance scheme for horticultural growers was launched on a voluntary basis in 1979. This scheme insured plants cultivated under plastic or in greenhouses. It also insured the protective structures themselves, together with such equipment as heaters. Again, the launching of the insurance scheme was preceded by a five-year pilot project.

It is noteworthy that these new crop insurance schemes are being operated on a voluntary basis. It has always been assumed that crop insurance would be impossible to implement in a small-scale farmers' society like Japan without compulsory participation. The production costs per acre of fruits are two or three times that of rice cultivation, and that of intensive vegetables is ten times larger. This indicates why such insurance could be operated under a voluntary scheme. However, it should be noted that a considerable part of the premium rates established for these new crop insurances is still subsidized by the government.

## The Benefits from Crop Insurance

The crop insurance program continues to be expensive for the Japanese government. If total government contributions to premiums, administration costs, and reinsurance are added together, they amount to about 150-billion *yen* per year during the latter part of the 1970s. These subsidies are examined in some detail in chapter 9, together with a cost/benefit analysis of their returns to society. Here we limit our analysis to the effects of the insurance program on farmers' welfare and the production of rice.

### *Benefits to Farmers*

In 1980, about 3.6-million farmers took out rice insurance policies, while 400 thousand insured their crops of wheat and barley. This number is less than it was at the start of the scheme (table 13.4), because the number of operating farms in Japan has declined. At the same time, planted acreage of barley and wheat as winter crops has been considerably reduced because of the increase in employment opportunities during the winter in urban districts. During recent years (1970–80), the average proportion of insured farmers who receive indemnities for rice has remained at about 32 percent, for wheat and barley, 46 percent.

The following case studies show how Japanese crop insurance has contributed to the stabilization of farm and regional incomes in disaster years. Table 13.5 gives insurance data of rice farmers in Hokuriku during 1953, a year of disastrous yields. To show the magnitude of the crop loss, yields and gross incomes from paddy farming are also given for 1952, a more normal crop year. Without the insurance program, farmers in all four farm-size groups would have suffered severely. The impact of the insurance is shown by the calculated ratios of indemnities paid to the value of the crop loss for each size group. These ratios vary between 17 and 26 percent, and they were sufficient to raise the compensated farm income in

TABLE 13.4 Statistics on crop insurance for paddy rice, upland rice, wheat, and barley, Japan, selected years, 1947–80

| Crop and year | Insured farmers (thousands) | Insured area (1,000 hectares) | Total premium (million *yen*) | Total indemnity (million *yen*) |
|---|---|---|---|---|
| *Paddy rice* | | | | |
| 1947 | 5,058 | 2,675 | 1,256 | 1,849 |
| 1950 | 5,107 | 2,698 | 4,635 | 6,318 |
| 1955 | 5,094 | 2,733 | 10,866 | 1,373 |
| 1960 | 4,894 | 2,740 | 10,816 | 4,562 |
| 1965 | 4,629 | 2,710 | 19,555 | 22,269 |
| 1970 | 4,279 | 2,517 | 29,905 | 12,570 |
| 1975 | 3,896 | 2,416 | 55,010 | 18,722 |
| 1980 | 3,593 | 2,122 | 73,500 | 248,343 |
| *Upland rice* | | | | |
| 1948 | 586 | 54 | 52 | 12 |
| 1950 | 769 | 73 | 193 | 49 |
| 1955 | 703 | 86 | 497 | 307 |
| 1960 | 629 | 56 | 444 | 528 |
| 1965 | 359 | 30 | 548 | 865 |
| 1970 | 192 | 16 | 603 | 832 |
| 1975 | 91 | 1 | 766 | 1,308 |
| 1980 | 55 | 0 | 811 | 452 |
| *Wheat and barley* | | | | |
| 1948 | 4,975 | 1,377 | 102 | 668 |
| 1950 | 5,241 | 1,461 | 461 | 2,579 |
| 1955 | 4,504 | 1,225 | 1,698 | 1,585 |
| 1960 | 3,403 | 970 | 1,592 | 1,419 |
| 1965 | 2,151 | 597 | 2,434 | 2,183 |
| 1970 | 934 | 256 | 2,694 | 6,357 |
| 1975 | 271 | 102 | 1,849 | 1,720 |
| 1980 | 409 | 210 | 12,972 | 5,782 |

*Source*: *1972 Annual Report on the Agricultural Loss Compensation System*, and *1981 Crop Insurance Statistical Year Book* (Tokyo: Ministry of Agriculture, Forestry, and Fisheries).

1953 to at least 70 percent of the normal gross income for all farm-size groups.

Another example of the benefits of crop insurance is taken from a case study conducted in Aomori Prefecture in the northern part of mainland Japan. Data were obtained from a sample of fifteen farmers living in a village that suffered complete loss of its paddy crop in 1980 as a result of a severely cool summer. Table 13.6 shows the survey results for the disaster year and a year with normal crop conditions (1979). Rice insurance indemnified 64 percent of the expected normal gross income from paddy farming. The coverage was therefore adequate not only to cover the operating cost of paddy farming but also to cover a considerable part of the net income lost.

TABLE 13.5 Paddy rice insurance data, 1953 crop failure, Hokuriku, Japan[a]

| Item | Farm size (hectares) | | | | | |
|---|---|---|---|---|---|---|
| | Under 0.5 | 0.5–1.0 | 1.0–1.5 | 1.5–2.0 | Over 2.0 | Average[b] |
| *Average size of paddy field (hectares)* | 0.28 | 0.63 | 1.04 | 1.52 | 1.88 | 0.88 |
| *Yield of paddy field* | | | | | | |
| 1952 (*koku*/hectare) | 6.26 | 14.69 | 23.69 | 36.29 | 43.91 | 20.59 |
| 1953 (*koku*/hectare) | 4.76 | 10.28 | 16.77 | 27.22 | 29.42 | 14.62 |
| 1953/52 (percent) | 71.00 | 70.00 | 71.00 | 75.00 | 67.00 | 61.00 |
| *Income from paddy farming* | | | | | | |
| 1952[c] (*yen*/hectare) | 59,669 | 142,922 | 242,827 | 397,610 | 430,618 | 213,854 |
| 1953 (*yen*/hectare) | 38,919 | 90,828 | 153,581 | 254,645 | 279,500 | 131,513 |
| 1953/52 (percent) | 65 | 64 | 63 | 64 | 65 | 62 |
| *Crop loss (yen/hectare)* | 20,780 | 52,094 | 89,246 | 142,965 | 151,118 | 82,341 |
| *Insurance Indemnity (yen/hectare)* | | | | | | |
| Per paddy field | 5,436 | 10,174 | 20,444 | 24,010 | 27,626 | 15,148 |
| Per 0.1 hectare | 1,941 | 1,615 | 1,966 | 1,586 | 1,470 | 1,821 |
| *Indemnity/crop loss (percent)* | 26 | 20 | 23 | 17 | 18 | 18 |
| *1953 income + indemnity/1952 income (percent)* | 74 | 71 | 72 | 70 | 71 | 69 |

*Source*: *History of Agricultural Loss Compensation System*, vol. 2 (Tokyo: Ministry of Agriculture and Forestry, 1963), table 83.

[a]Hokuriku comprises Niigata, Toyama, Ishikowa, and Fukui prefectures.

[b]Number of farmers in samples: under 0.5 hectare, 21; 0.5–1.0, 58; 1.0–1.5, 40; 1.5–2.0, 19; over 2.0, 9.

[c]Adjusted to 1953 rice price.

Because of the government subsidy to the insurance program, many farmers have effectively received net income transfers from insurance, in addition to its stabilizing benefits. Table 13.7 shows, for three villages, the ratio of the total indemnities received between 1949 and 1958 to the total premiums paid during this period.[3] In Shiratori village, which has very unstable rice yields, 91 percent of the farmers received a net income transfer from the insurance scheme. In fact, for about half the farmers in the village, the amount of indemnities received between 1949 and 1958 was equal to or greater than twice the total amount of premiums paid.

On the other hand, farmers in less risky villages benefited less significantly from the insurance subsidies. In Fujishima village, which has quite stable yields, only 24 percent of the farmers received sufficient indemnities to offset their premiums over the period 1949–58. The crop insurance pro-

3. See Yamauchi (1964).

TABLE 13.6 Paddy rice insurance data, 1980 crop failure, Aomori Prefecture, Japan

| Item | 1979 (normal year) | 1980 (loss year) |
|---|---|---|
| Average area of paddy grown (hectares) | 1.355 | 1.353 |
| Average yield (kilograms/hectare) | 5.570 | 0.000 |
| First- and second-grade rice (percent of crop) | 94.300 | 0.000 |
| Third-grade rice (percent of crop) | 5.700 | 0.000 |
| Income from paddy rice (*yen*/hectare) | 1,491,560 | 0 |
| Insurance indemnity (*yen*/hectare) | 0 | 965,320 |
| Operating costs (*yen*/hectare)[a] | 658,090 | 633,400 |
| Net income (*yen*/hectare) | 833,470 | 331,920 |
| Net income per farm (*yen*) | 1,129,627 | 449,088 |

[a]Operating costs comprise the following: seed, fertilizers and manures, pesticides and herbicides, hired labor costs, depreciation costs on farm buildings and farm machinery, electricity and fuel, irrigation charges, insurance premiums, rent on leased paddy land, and interest on borrowed money.

TABLE 13.7 Crop insurance indemnities received, as percent of premiums paid, by farmers in three villages, Japan, 1949-58

| Indemnity as percent of premium | Number of farmers: Stable village[a] | Slightly unstable village[b] | Very unstable village[c] |
|---|---|---|---|
| 0-50 | 74 | 5 | 17 |
| 51-100 | 77 | 11 | 37 |
| 101-150 | 27 | 20 | 109 |
| 151-200 | 10 | 19 | 146 |
| 201-250 | 5 | 11 | 101 |
| 251-300 | 1 | 5 | 78 |
| 301-350 | 6 | 3 | 34 |
| 351-400 | 0 | 0 | 22 |
| 401-450 | 0 | 1 | 13 |
| 451-500 | 0 | 0 | 6 |
| 501-550 | 0 | 0 | 3 |
| 551-600 | 0 | 0 | 1 |
| Over 600 | 0 | 0 | 6 |
| Total | 200 | 75 | 573 |

[a]Fujishima village in Yamagata Prefecture: two communities surveyed.
[b]Hobara village in Fukushima Prefecture: one community surveyed.
[c]Shiratori village in Kagawa Prefecture: six communities surveyed.

gram therefore tends to encourage increased rice production in riskier areas and to discourage production in more stable areas.

Let us examine how crop insurance has mitigated the impact of economic loss due to a large-scale crop failure on a regional economy. Table 13.8 shows the compensation provided by various measures for crop losses in Aomori Prefecture. Crop insurance indemnified 41 percent of the total

TABLE 13.8 Compensation for crop failure, Aomori Prefecture, Japan, 1981

| Item | Billions of *yen* |
|---|---|
| Crop loss | 68.3 |
| Compensation | 50.0 |
| Source of compensation | |
| Rice crop insurance | 23.0 |
| Fruit crop insurance | 5.3 |
| Emergency credit | 13.6 |
| Emergency relief | 1.3 |
| Outside wages | 6.4 |
| Tax reduction | 0.2 |
| Other | 0.2 |

loss. It therefore played a major role in compensating for the crop loss in Aomori Prefecture and helped prevent a severe contraction of the regional economy.

Another major benefit of the crop insurance scheme to farmers was that it enabled them to secure credit. The Japanese land reform of 1947 prohibited farmers from using their land as security for loans. The rural money market was very stringent at the time of the land reform due to the devastated national economy following the Second World War. However, self-sufficiency in food was then an essential requirement to the reconstruction of the national economy. To facilitate this objective, the government created a short-term credit system in 1948. It offered credit to insured farmers to buy necessary amounts of fertilizer, seed, herbicides, and farming implements. Loans under the credit system were given on the sole security of the maximum amount of indemnity payable in the case of calamity under the crop insurance scheme. According to statistics for the year 1954, 27,225-million *yen* were loaned to insured farmers through the agricultural cooperatives under this credit program. (This sum was equal to 13 percent of the total amount of insurance carried by farmers under the crop insurance scheme that year.)

However, the link between the credit system and crop insurance was abolished in 1958. This occurred because the demand for credit declined sharply with the introduction of a prepayment system for rice cultivators in 1955. Under this system, a portion of the expected income from selling rice at harvest time was advanced to each farmer by the government food agency.

### *Contribution to Increased Food Production*

Japan's crop insurance scheme was formulated during the food shortages following the Second World War as part of a program to increase national rice production. It has played an effective role in encouraging the expansion of rice production into riskier areas. This has been especially true in the northern part of Japan, which is frequently hit by cold temperatures during the growing season. Both the income-stabilizing role of insurance and the associated subsidy have been useful in attaining these ends. In Hokkaido, which is one of the riskier rice regions in Japan, the annual rice acreage increased from 131-thousand hectares in 1950 to 203-thousand hectares in 1965. At the national level, rice production increased from 9.4-million tons per year during 1948–50 to 14.1-million tons during the period 1967–69. Of course, improved technologies and rice price policies have also played an important role in increasing rice production.

The productivity contributions of the pest- and disease-prevention programs of the crop insurance scheme should also be stressed. Each AMRA provides the equipment and material for prevention of plant damage due to insects and disease. Association technicians also assist the insured farmers in their preventive work, and the AMRAs provide an information system to warn farmers about impending calamities. These activities not only help increase rice yields but also act to reduce the cost of insurance.

## Conclusions

Looking back at the way Japanese crop insurance has developed, we see a number of problems. The most difficult problem was how to solve farmers' complaints against a compulsory scheme of crop insurance. These complaints arose mainly from the disparity between the insurance benefits received by farmers in unstable areas and those received by the farmers in stable areas.

All-risk crop insurance is one of the few agricultural policies available to promote farmers' welfare through income stabilization. However, crop insurance programs cannot be set up without the participation of a sufficiently large number of farmers. Therefore, a compulsory crop insurance scheme was thought necessary to introduce crop insurance into a country of small farms, like Japan. In this connection, Japanese crop insurance programs have been designed to mitigate the friction between farmers' conservative attitudes and their compulsory participation in a crop insurance scheme. This was done through rationalization of the premium schedules, expansion of benefits, and reorganization of the program. Japan's experience in overcoming these problems may be helpful in understanding how small-scale farmers' reactions toward compulsory crop insurance can be accommodated in other countries, and how compulsory crop insurance can be made attractive to small-scale farmers in relatively stable areas.

The Japanese crop insurance program has contributed to the national attainment of self-sufficiency in stable foods in the following ways:

1. It has enabled farmers to increase cultivation in unstable areas, both because of its indemnity function in bad years and because of its subsidy component, which acts as an income transfer to increase the profitability of crop production in these areas.
2. The prevention activities against insects and diseases adopted by the crop insurance organization have not only helped reduce the cost of insurance but they have also contributed to increases in average yields.
3. A short-term credit system linked to crop insurance contributed importantly to increases in the production of staple food in the early postwar years.
4. Finally, the regional economic impacts of catastrophic losses in agriculture have been successfully contained.

# 14

# The Brazilian Experience with Crop Insurance Programs

Mauro de Rezende Lopes
Guilherme Leite da Silva Dias

The first national experience with crop insurance in Brazil occurred when Decree Law 2168 created the National Crop Insurance Company in 1954. This was essentially an experimental operation, and it was terminated in 1966 by Decree Law 73. Several reasons contributed to the failure of this preliminary experience with crop insurance. These included premium underrating, inadequacy of the insurance contracts, insufficient funding to back the losses in the beginning years, a lack of trained personnel, and the concentration of risks in a small number of operations.

Decree Law 73 also reorganized private insurance in Brazil and created the National Council of Private Insurance. Furthermore, it created the Crop Insurance Stabilization Fund within the administrative supervision of the Institute of Reinsurance of Brazil. This decree established the legal foundations for crop insurance in Brazil.

Through Resolution 5/70, the National Council of Private Insurance approved in 1970 regulations for an experimental crop insurance program in the state of Sao Paulo. The insurance was to be managed by the Insurance Company of Sao Paulo (COSESP), a state-owned insurance company. Two years later, Resolution 2/72 extended the same set of regulations to the state of Minas Gerais through the Insurance Company of Minas Gerais (COSEMIG), another state-owned insurance company.

Through Law 5969 in 1973, the federal government created the Program of Guarantee of Agricultural Activities (or PROAGRO). The program was not experimental and was intended to cover all crops in all states financed under the National System of Agricultural Credit. In terms of the resources used, this program is now by far the most important crop insurance system in Brazil. Nevertheless, the two state-level programs provide extremely interesting experiences of crop insurance. Both are reviewed in this chapter along with PROAGRO.

The authors would like to recognize the special contributions of several people in Banco Central do Brasil, Companhia de Seguros do Estado de Sao Paulo, and Companhia de Seguros de Minas Gerais, who provided data, references, and discussions of operational details of the insurance programs. Views and opinions expressed herein do not necessarily represent those of the Commission for Production Financing.

It is worth pointing out that before 1973, the year when PROAGRO was created, the federal government acted as the sole guarantor of crop and livestock losses in calamitous years. In disaster years, indiscriminate cancellation of debt was the only solution to avoid widespread bankruptcy among farmers. In cases of localized losses, postponement of debt repayment was adopted as a partial solution. These policies contributed to the decapitalization of lending institutions and hindered credit expansion and monetary policy.[1]

## PROAGRO

Together with the minimum price program and a policy of subsidized farm credit, PROAGRO is one of the most important short-run instruments of agricultural policy in Brazil. After the severe droughts that struck the country in 1978 and 1979, the government decided to place agriculture among its top economic priorities. In order to stimulate output expansion and reduce food imports, policies were selected that had a high potential impact on reducing uncertainty, such as an aggressive minimum price policy and PROAGRO. A policy of increasing liquidity in farming through a broad credit program was also implemented.

Considering not only the policy drive behind the program but also its results in terms of loss ratios and implicit subsidies, PROAGRO is more a government support program than a crop insurance system. It was viewed by farmers and policymakers as an integrated part of a comprehensive program of new government incentives to foster output expansion.

In principle, PROAGRO is intended to be a short-term credit insurance scheme. It is a way of insulating farmers from financial disaster and is intended to increase their confidence in taking borrowing risks. PROAGRO is also supposed to strengthen the financial position of credit institutions with agricultural portfolios and to alleviate internal and external rationing of agricultural credit. It was expected that this would improve the position of farmers with credit institutions, which, in the absence of such a program, could grant credit only to low-risk farmers.

The program started in 1973 under Law 5969, which established that the program should be supervised by the National Monetary Council and administered by the Central Bank. It also stipulated that the basic premium rate should not exceed 1 percent on any credit operation, either for production or investment. The limit of coverage was restricted to a maximum of 80 percent of the credit granted. There was no minimum require-

1. Agricultural lending institutions were already being decapitalized by stringent interest rate regulations. With inflation running between 40 and 80 percent, interest rates for agricultural lending were variously restricted between 18 and 45 percent.

ment, because the scheme was initially voluntary. Besides the revenue from the premium rates, the program is funded through resources allocated by the federal budget, under the control of the National Monetary Council.

The stated objectives of the program are (1) to relieve farmers from their obligations to repay credit borrowed for production, investment, or farm assets in the event of natural disasters; and (2) to stimulate the adoption of modern technology under the supervision of the extension service. To achieve the second objective, insured farmers are obliged to use the best available technology capable of achieving the proposed yields.

Due to the relatively poor performance of the program in terms of high loss ratios, some changes gradually took place. In 1980 PROAGRO became compulsory for all credit for crop and livestock production. It remained voluntary for investment credit. Concurrently, the premium rate was raised to 3 percent on production credit granted without any restrictions on the choice of technology.[2] The program was also changed to automatically exclude any crop within a region that has been indemnified in the previous two years due to the same cause, except when the repetition of the cause is considered by the extension service as an entirely random event.

Insurance is written mainly against excess rainfall, lightning, frost, hail, drought, rainstorm, freeze, windstorm, and extreme temperature variations. Coverage also includes any natural phenomena that affects production and any plague or disease without a known method of control. It does not cover fire, except if caused by lightning. Therefore it is an all-risk insurance, in which any unavoidable loss is eligible for compensation.

PROAGRO covers the balance due of the loan up to the limit of the credit upon which the premium is charged. It also covers that portion of farmers' own capital listed in the credit arrangement unless they exclude it from the insurance contract. All the financial charges (interest rates and taxes) that are due on the loan are also covered.

An important feature of PROAGRO is that coverage is due for indemnity only if the revenue resulting from the sale of production is not enough to pay for the loan. In other words, in case of partial loss, the revenue from sales of the remaining production must be deducted from the value of the indemnity. Farmers are obliged to make a deposit from any sale of the product into their credit accounts and also to present all documents on the sales made. When the quantity harvested and sold at market prices is just enough to cover the balance due, no indemnity is paid, even if yields have been below normal.

The amount of indemnity is reduced if the crop is not harvested, and substantially so if the crop is destroyed at early stages of cultivation. The

2. Farmers are eligible for the lower rate of 1 percent if they spend at least 15 percent of production costs on modern inputs such as fertilizer and improved seeds.

indemnity is virtually zero if an area seeded with a crop (for example rice) is also seeded with pasture. This prohibition prevents farmers from using PROAGRO indemnities to partially finance the costs of seeding pasture, a reasonably large cause of heavy indemnities in the past. All these procedures serve to restrict the amount of indemnities to approximately the value of the investments insured farmers have made in their crops.

### *Premium Rates*

When PROAGRO was started, farmers could insure (voluntarily) up to 80 percent of the credit granted, and they were charged a flat premium rate of 1 percent of the coverage.

New policy directions in 1980 raised interest rates and reduced the share of basic production costs financed under subsidized interest rates from 100 percent to 60 percent for large-scale farmers, and from 100 percent to 80 percent for medium-scale farmers. Farmers were compelled to insure at least 70 percent of their basic production costs, but the regulations were again changed in 1981 so that they could insure the remaining 30 percent of their costs on a voluntary basis. Under the new credit rules, most of this 30 percent had to be financed with unsubsidized credit, or from farmers' own resources.

Also in 1980 a system of increasing premiums was adopted to relate premiums more realistically to indemnities. The premium now increases with the coverage of production costs, with the number of indemnities paid the farmer in the last three years, and with the choice of technology (see table 14.1).

### *Performance*

During its early years, PROAGRO experienced high loss ratios (table 14.2). In 1975 severe losses in wheat and rice contributed to these ratios. It is worth noting that the losses of the first two years were substantially higher than the losses in 1978 and 1979, the years of the severe drought. One possible reason for the extremely high loss ratios in 1975 and 1976 is the fact that premium rates did not correspond to the risk. A simple comparison with the rates charged by the Insurance Company of Sao Paulo indicates that, under the system of voluntary participation, in order to equate premiums to indemnities in crops such as rice and corn, the premium rates should not have been lower than 6 percent. The flat premium rate of 1 percent was therefore heavily subsidized. Another reason for the early losses was that farmers very often seeded pasture together with rice, and if the rice crop was destroyed they claimed indemnities on rice. As a result of the changes effected in 1980, the loss ratio dropped. When PRO-

TABLE 14.1 PROAGRO premium rates, by type of production credit and number of indemnities received in preceding three years, Brazil (percent)

| Indemnities received in previous three years | Percent of production credit covered by insurance | | | |
|---|---|---|---|---|
| | 70 | 80 | 90 | 100 |
| | *Premium rate for farmers following recommended technique* | | | |
| 0 | 1.0 | 2.5 | 3.5 | 5.5 |
| 1 | 3.0 | 4.5 | 6.0 | 8.0 |
| 2 | 5.0 | 7.5 | 10.0 | 12.5 |
| 3 | 7.0 | 11.0 | 15.0 | 18.5 |
| | *Premium rate for farmers following other technique* | | | |
| 0 | 3.0 | 4.5 | 6.0 | 8.0 |
| 1 | 5.0 | 7.5 | 10.0 | 12.5 |
| 2 | 7.0 | 11.0 | 15.0 | 18.5 |
| 3 | 7.0 | 11.0 | 15.0 | 18.5 |

*Source*: Banco Central do Brasil.

TABLE 14.2 PROAGRO loss ratios, Brazil, 1975–81

| Year | Million *cruzeiros* | | Loss ratio[a] | Million 1981 *cruzeiros* | |
|---|---|---|---|---|---|
| | Premium | Indemnity | | Premium | Indemnity |
| 1975[b] | 0.7 | 28.1 | 40.14 | 12.6 | 508.0 |
| 1976 | 9.2 | 386.9 | 42.05 | 117.7 | 4,952.4 |
| 1977 | 76.1 | 693.8 | 9.12 | 682.8 | 6,225.4 |
| 1978 | 215.4 | 2,397.6 | 11.13 | 1,393.1 | 15,506.2 |
| 1979 | 128.5 | 3,056.3 | 23.78 | 540.0 | 12,843.0 |
| 1980 | 5,689.9 | 15,601.7 | 2.74 | 11,943.1 | 32,747.9 |
| 1981[c] | 11,089.3 | 27,076.9 | 2.44 | 11,089.3 | 27,076.9 |

*Source*: Banco Central do Brasil.
[a]Indemnity ÷ premium.
[b]Program started in 1975.
[c]Preliminary data.

AGRO became compulsory, this considerably broadened the base of contribution. The loss ratio dropped to 2.74 in 1980 and 2.44 in 1981.

While the program was voluntary, only a relatively small number of participants adhered to the program. The losses at the beginning were concentrated in wheat and upland rice. Although reliable statistics are not available, it is clear that only high-risk farmers and regions participated in the program.

Table 14.3 shows each crop's share of total indemnities paid from 1979 through September 1981. Wheat accounts for by far the largest share, ranging from 29 percent in 1981 to 52 percent in 1979. Indemnities

TABLE 14.3 PROAGRO indemnity payments by crop, Brazil, 1979–81

| Crop | 1979 | | 1980 | | 1981[a] | |
|---|---|---|---|---|---|---|
| | Value (thousand *cruzeiros*) | Participation (percent) | Value (thousand *cruzeiros*) | Participation (percent) | Value (thousand *cruzeiros*) | Participation (percent) |
| Cotton | 67,679 | 2.22 | 1,161,259 | 7.44 | 180,193 | 1.18 |
| Rice | 539,920 | 17.66 | 739,429 | 4.74 | 3,268,456 | 21.35 |
| Coffee | 142,231 | 4.65 | 130,178 | 0.83 | 38,021 | 0.25 |
| Edible beans | 61,687 | 2.02 | 1,171,552 | 7.51 | 1,949,530 | 12.74 |
| Corn | 87,771 | 2.87 | 176,539 | 1.13 | 324,771 | 2.12 |
| Soybeans | 430,713 | 14.09 | 377,783 | 2.42 | 236,797 | 1.55 |
| Wheat | 1,599,539 | 52.34 | 7,141,207 | 45.78 | 4,447,533 | 29.06 |
| Other | 126,746 | 4.15 | 4,703,788 | 30.15 | 4,859,119 | 31.75 |
| Total | 3,056,286 | 100.00 | 15,601,735 | 100.00 | 15,304,430 | 100.00 |

*Source*: Banco Central do Brasil.
[a]January through September 30.

for wheat were initially 3.7 percent of the total value of production and reached 22.4 percent in 1980 (table 14.4). This crop will be particularly affected by the recently adopted system of progressive premium rates. In fact, the adoption of the progressive premium rates for repetitive events was largely a result of PROAGRO's wheat experience.

Table 14.5 shows the source of funds and the expenditures of the program from 1975 through 1980. These data show not only how much PROAGRO depends on external sources for funds but also how vulnerable the whole program is. Even in 1980, when compulsory insurance premiums had become quite important as a source of funds, the federal budget still had to cover over 50 percent of the costs of the program (113-million *cruzeiros* in 1979 to a whopping 7,801-million *cruzeiros* in 1980). In order for PROAGRO to survive, it is desirable to reduce its dependence on the federal budget.

### *Concluding Remarks*

When it started, PROAGRO was a temerity. It did not start on an experimental basis, but it had to learn from its own experience. This led to relatively high losses at the beginning. Some corrections were soon adopted, such as compulsory participation, increases in premium rates, and voluntary coverage of the 30 percent of basic production costs not otherwise insured.

PROAGRO still concentrates on relatively few Brazilian farmers, but so does agricultural credit. Since we cannot separate one from the other, the program further aggravates the problem of inequitable distribution of subsidized agricultural credit in Brazil. However, PROAGRO immensely increased the attractiveness of borrowing, far beyond the attractiveness of subsidized interest rates by themselves.

There are a few positive features of PROAGRO which deserve mention. First, financial institutions only started to lend to small-scale farmers in significant volume when credit was insured under the system. PRO-

TABLE 14.4 PROAGRO indemnity payments for wheat, Brazil, 1976–80

| Year | Million *cruzeiros* | | Indemnity/output ratio (percent) |
|---|---|---|---|
| | Output | Indemnity | |
| 1976 | 6,710 | 245 | 3.7 |
| 1977 | 6,550 | 405 | 6.2 |
| 1978 | 11,126 | 607 | 5.5 |
| 1979 | 15,541 | 1,600 | 10.3 |
| 1980 | 31,860 | 7,141 | 22.4 |

*Source*: Banco Central do Brasil.

TABLE 14.5 PROAGRO fund, outgo and income, Brazil, 1975–80

| Item | 1975 | 1976 | 1977 | 1978 | 1979 | 1980 |
|---|---|---|---|---|---|---|
| *Outgo* | | | | | | |
| Indemnities | | | | | | |
| Million *cruzeiros* | 28.10 | 386.90 | 693.80 | 2,397.60 | 3,056.30 | 15,601.70 |
| Percent | 58.91 | 85.43 | 90.97 | 93.19 | 89.58 | 95.46 |
| Extension service | | | | | | |
| Million *cruzeiros* | 19.60 | 66.00 | 68.90 | 175.10 | 355.70 | 692.50 |
| Percent | 41.09 | 14.57 | 9.03 | 6.81 | 10.42 | 4.25 |
| Financial institutions | | | | | | |
| Million *cruzeiros* | 0.00 | 0.00 | 0.00 | 0.00 | 0.00 | 39.90 |
| Percent | 0.00 | 0.00 | 0.00 | 0.00 | 0.00 | 0.24 |
| Topographical services | | | | | | |
| Million *cruzeiros* | 0.00 | 0.00 | 0.00 | 0.00 | 0.00 | 9.10 |
| Percent | 0.00 | 0.00 | 0.00 | 0.00 | 0.00 | 0.05 |
| Total (million *cruzeiros*) | 47.70 | 452.90 | 762.70 | 2,572.70 | 3,412.00 | 16,343.20 |
| *Income* | | | | | | |
| Premiums | | | | | | |
| Million *cruzeiros* | 0.70 | 9.20 | 76.10 | 215.40 | 128.50 | 5,689.90 |
| Percent | 100.00 | 8.42 | 43.21 | 6.07 | 4.82 | 42.15 |
| Federal budget | | | | | | |
| Million *cruzeiros* | 0.00 | 100.00 | 100.00 | 106.20 | 112.60 | 7,800.60 |
| Percent | 0.00 | 91.58 | 56.79 | 2.99 | 4.23 | 57.79 |
| Monetary budget | | | | | | |
| Million *cruzeiros* | 0.00 | 0.00 | 0.00 | 3,228.40 | 2,422.30 | 0.00 |
| Percent | 0.00 | 0.00 | 0.00 | 90.94 | 90.94 | 0.00 |
| Fund for the development of agriculture | | | | | | |
| Million *cruzeiros* | 0.00 | 0.00 | 0.00 | 0.00 | 0.00 | 1.80 |
| Percent | 0.00 | 0.00 | 0.00 | 0.00 | 0.00 | 0.01 |
| Fines | | | | | | |
| Million *cruzeiros* | 0.00 | 0.00 | 0.00 | 0.00 | 0.30 | 6.70 |
| Percent | 0.00 | 0.00 | 0.00 | 0.00 | 0.01 | 0.05 |
| Total (million *cruzeiros*) | 0.70 | 109.20 | 176.10 | 3,550.00 | 2,663.70 | 13,499.00 |

*Source*: Banco Central do Brasil.
*Note*: The difference between total payments and total funds represents a deficit covered by advances from the Central Bank.

AGRO extended both supervised and unsupervised credit operations to medium-sized and small-sized farms. Second, in reducing farmers borrowing risks, PROAGRO has contributed to the adoption of modern technologies and helped increase agricultural production. Third, because credit insurance acts as a substitute for collateral (see chapter 4), PROAGRO has enabled financial institutions to lend to landless farmers (tenants and sharecroppers). This is a very important consideration in Brazil, given the size of this group of farmers.

A key question is whether the losses experienced with the program are justifiable in terms of the broad range of benefits achieved. Although there is a full recognition of the benefits of the program, there is a consensus among government policymakers that the losses must be brought under control if the program is to be continued. It is hoped that the recent changes will bring about a considerable improvement in the performance of the program. The program is now in a second probation period.

In the coming years, with the gradual elimination of subsidized interest rates in agriculture, the role of PROAGRO will become extremely important for borrowers and lenders alike. Interest rates have already been increased from 20 to 45 percent, and the portion of credit granted at subsidized rates is being reduced. The government wants to gradually push medium-scale and large-scale farmers to market rates. Within this setting, borrowing risks will become increasingly important in determining the allocation of credit, and PROAGRO's role in reducing these risks will be enhanced.

## Crop Insurance in Sao Paulo

Crop insurance first began in the state of Sao Paulo in 1939, when an experimental program was set up to write hail insurance for cotton growers. In 1952 hail coverage was extended to grapes. Then in 1954 frost insurance was extended to garden crops and fruits. All of this insurance was fully supported by the state secretary of agriculture.

What is now the crop insurance system of Sao Paulo started from that previous experience and was further developed following (1) Degree Law 73 of 1966, which created the national insurance regulations in Brazil, (2) the foundation of COSESP in 1967, and (3) Resolution 5/70, which authorized COSESP to operate crop insurance on an experimental basis in the state.

All-risk insurance appeared in 1974, initially only for cotton but later extended to other crops. Currently, coverage is written on cotton, grapes, peanuts, corn, soybeans, bananas, wheat, garden crops, forests, and livestock. Coverage of potatoes and tomatoes was also tried but was discontinued in 1981 due to poor performance and lack of interest on the part of farmers. Although Resolution 5/70 authorized insurance on farm assets, COSESP does not offer this coverage.

Except for insurance on cotton, which is strictly compulsory, all other COSESP insurance is voluntary. Since 1980 though, when crop credit insurance became compulsory at the national level, farmers in Sao Paulo have had to choose between COSESP or PROAGRO insurance when borrowing official credit. COSESP insurance is written against hail, frost, drought, excessive rainfall, rainstorm, windstorm, forest fire, and uncontrolled plagues and diseases.

Coverage is based on an estimated value of out-of-pocket costs—the maximum conventional value, which is established according to the technology used. For permanent crops, coverage is established on the basis of yearly expenditure on plant care. Three levels of maximum value are calculated according to technical cost coefficients recommended by experimental stations and extension services. Level A is based on the best technology available, level B roughly corresponds to the state average, and level C corresponds to farm practices using a minimum amount of modern inputs.

In determining indemnities, if the area insured had a 100-percent loss, a technician will calculate all expenses incurred by the farmer until the date of the loss. If the farmer replants the area, the technician will also calculate the costs of replanting the area, and the indemnity fully covers the initial losses. In case of partial losses, indemnities are based on the following formula:

$$IV = MIV - (RP \times MP),$$

in which $IV$ is the amount of the indemnity paid, $MIV$ is the maximum amount of insured out-of-pocket costs of production, $RP$ is the production harvested after the loss, and $MP$ is the guaranteed official minimum price.

The operations are fully backed by the Crop Insurance Stabilization Fund, under the supervision of the Institute of Reinsurance of Brazil. The institute reinsures all operations on a quota share basis and in fact underwrites 80 percent of the coverage written by COSESP.

The state government developed this system in part as a response to repeated losses for grapes, cotton, and grains. These losses were caused predominantly by rain damage (50 percent of the total value of indemnities paid), hail (15 percent), windstorm (15 percent), and drought. It was hoped that a broad insurance system could avoid large disbursements of relief funds by the state government and end the postponement of crop credit debt at repayment to state-owned financial institutions.

### *Premium Rates*

Premium rates expressed in terms of the percent of coverage are directly applied to the out-of-pocket costs calculated by COSESP. These rates changed between 1970 and 1981 (table 14.6).

Raising premium rates to offset losses can be a self-defeating policy. If participation is already low, raising premium rates will result in even lower program participation on the part of farmers. The elasticity of program participation with respect to premium rates is quite high in absolute

TABLE 14.6 COSESP premium rates, Brazil, 1970 and 1981 (percent)

| Item covered | Premium rate | |
|---|---|---|
| | 1970[a] | 1981 |
| Cotton | 2.50 | 2.50 |
| Grapes | 2.50 | 5.00 |
| Corn, soybeans, peanuts | 2.50 | 6.50 |
| Wheat | 2.50 | 7.00 |
| Potatoes[b] | 2.50 | 8.00 |
| Tomatoes[b] | 2.50 | 8.00 |
| Bananas | 2.50 | 5.00 |
| Irrigated edible beans | 2.50 | 3.50 |
| Zucchini, carrots, cucumbers, green peppers, lettuce | 2.50 | 4.50 |
| Cattle | 3.55–4.50 | 2.50–3.50 |
| Horses | 3.55–4.50 | 4.00–4.50 |
| Forests | 3.55–4.50 | 0.95–2.80 |

*Source*: COSESP (Insurance Company of Sao Paulo).

[a] Resolution 5/70 fixed the minimum premium rate at 2.5 percent for compulsory crop insurance. This rate has been maintained for cotton, because low loss ratios made this particular insurance quite successful. However, the premium rate for all other crops has since been increased, and in 1981 these rates were as high as 8 percent. In contrast, livestock coverage turned out to be less risky than anticipated in Resolution 5/70, and the premium rates had been reduced by 1981.

[b] Insurance canceled in 1981.

value, particularly at premium rates as high as 6 and 7 percent. High premium rates also tend to concentrate the participants in high-risk groups, and this leads to increased operational costs. Increases in premium rates can therefore create the need for further increases, and if this process continues, the entire program could be jeopardized. In order to cut deep losses with potatoes and tomatoes, COSESP decided to cancel these two insurances when premium rates reached 8 percent.

### *A Review of the Experience*

Our analyses focuses primarily on cotton and grape insurance, both of which operated throughout the seventeen-year period, 1965–81, for which data are available. Data for these two crops are presented in tables 14.7 and 14.8.

*Cotton.* Cotton insurance has operated for forty-one years in the state of Sao Paulo. The scheme covers all cotton growers in the state, even small-scale farmers who do not have access to credit. It is a compulsory insurance scheme.

TABLE 14.7 COSESP loss ratios and insured area for cotton, Brazil, 1964–80

| Year | Thousand *cruzeiros* | | Loss ratio[a] | Area insured (hectares) | Area damaged | |
|---|---|---|---|---|---|---|
| | Premium | Indemnity | | | Hectares | As percent of area insured |
| 1964 | 644.6 | 308.8 | 0.48 | 653,400 | 11,788 | 1.80 |
| 1965 | 833.2 | 370.3 | 0.44 | 474,320 | 10,902 | 2.30 |
| 1966 | 468.4 | 327.9 | 0.70 | 287,980 | 8,244 | 2.86 |
| 1967 | 812.7 | 787.5 | 0.97 | 338,800 | 17,378 | 5.13 |
| 1968 | 1,209.1 | 1,021.6 | 0.85 | 447,700 | 25,843 | 5.77 |
| 1969 | 3,689.2 | 1,753.1 | 0.48 | 641,300 | 20,366 | 3.18 |
| 1970 | 3,194.6 | 3,328.6 | 1.04 | 605,000 | 31,123 | 5.14 |
| 1971 | 3,123.5 | 2,385.6 | 0.76 | 594,954 | 23,805 | 4.00 |
| 1972 | 3,264.1 | 1,764.8 | 0.54 | 615,863 | 13,178 | 2.14 |
| 1973 | 3,016.2 | 2,041.2 | 0.68 | 379,401 | 15,604 | 4.11 |
| 1974 | 7,006.8 | 7,249.9 | 1.04 | 333,655 | 19,961 | 5.98 |
| 1975 | 12,654.5 | 25,708.8 | 2.03 | 220,517 | 30,200 | 13.69 |
| 1976 | 30,871.5 | 25,141.1 | 0.81 | 358,039 | 39,625 | 11.07 |
| 1977 | 33,674.6 | 72,455.6 | 2.15 | 339,029 | 47,698 | 14.07 |
| 1978 | 36,291.8 | 31,651.9 | 0.87 | 248,982 | 18,166 | 7.03 |
| 1979 | 63,217.5 | 111,659.7 | 1.77 | 276,117 | 30,962 | 11.21 |
| 1980 | 126,154.6 | 98,088.9 | 0.78 | 284,301 | ... | ... |

*Source*: COSESP.
[a]Indemnity ÷ premium.

During 1964–80, the cotton program had a loss ratio below 1.0 in twelve of the seventeen years. Since a company such as COSESP is highly sensitive to high-loss years, particularly at the beginning, these loss ratios made the program quite successful: high-loss years only occurred after a premium surplus had been accumulated. The annual loss ratios ranged from 0.44 to 2.03, and averaged 0.96 in the seventeen-year period. The area damaged represents a small proportion of the total insured area; in the eleven-year period from 1964 to 1974, the area damaged did not exceed 6 percent of the total insured area, and in three years the proportion was as low as 2 percent.

In the state of Sao Paulo, soybeans replaced cotton in many important producing counties. The average insured area dropped from 517,720 hectares per year in the period 1964 to 1972 to 305,005 hectares in the period 1972 to 1980. This partially explains the relatively poor performance of cotton insurance in Sao Paulo during the last few years.

*Grapes.* The results for grapes are not as good as those for cotton. During the seventeen-year period reported in table 14.8, the annual loss ratios ranged from 0.34 to 2.88, and averaged 1.22. At the beginning of the period, the loss ratios were below 1.0 for three consecutive years. Unfortu-

TABLE 14.8 COSESP loss ratios and insured grapevines, Brazil, 1964–80

| Year | Thousand *cruzeiros* | | Loss ratio[a] | Vines insured | Vines damaged | |
|---|---|---|---|---|---|---|
| | Premium | Indemnity | | | Number | As percent of vines insured |
| 1964 | 33.2 | 11.3 | 0.34 | 5,568 | 1,156 | 20.76 |
| 1965 | 44.7 | 32.7 | 0.73 | 6,400 | 1,430 | 22.34 |
| 1966 | 31.7 | 23.9 | 0.75 | 3,511 | 965 | 27.49 |
| 1967 | 92.8 | 150.7 | 1.62 | 5,642 | 2,607 | 46.21 |
| 1968 | 158.9 | 237.7 | 1.49 | 5,728 | 2,945 | 51.41 |
| 1969 | 268.6 | 292.6 | 1.09 | 6,592 | 3,236 | 49.09 |
| 1970 | 373.7 | 552.3 | 1.48 | 7,217 | 5,098 | 70.64 |
| 1971 | 557.7 | 1,608.5 | 2.88 | 8,525 | 7,874 | 92.36 |
| 1972 | 755.5 | 579.4 | 0.77 | 8,495 | 2,779 | 32.71 |
| 1973 | 901.1 | 1,077.7 | 1.20 | 9,723 | 5,156 | 53.03 |
| 1974 | 1,383.8 | 685.9 | 0.49 | 9,818 | 2,322 | 23.65 |
| 1975 | 1,393.3 | 818.7 | 0.59 | 7,654 | 1,564 | 20.43 |
| 1976 | 1,275.9 | 2,170.2 | 1.70 | 3,901 | 1,405 | 36.02 |
| 1977 | 1,238.1 | 740.5 | 0.60 | 2,931 | 523 | 17.84 |
| 1978 | 1,475.6 | 1,070.4 | 0.72 | 2,631 | 495 | 18.81 |
| 1979 | 1,608.5 | 3,074.9 | 1.91 | 2,503 | 688 | 27.49 |
| 1980 | 1,960.5 | 4,892.1 | 2.49 | 2,078 | 853 | 41.05 |

*Source*: COSESP.
[a]Indemnity ÷ premium.

nately, this period was followed by a five-year period of ratios above 1.00. The proportion of damaged to insured vines ranged from 18 to 92 percent over the reported period. Considering that almost all vines are insured, the extent of the crop damaged is quite high. In seven of the seventeen years, damage exceeded 40 percent of the insured vines.

*Potatoes, tomatoes, and bananas.* Low levels of participation (the insurance is voluntary) and a concentration in high-risk operations has led to high loss ratios for these crops (table 14.9). Coverage written on potatoes and tomatoes started in 1975. After experiencing large loss ratios in 1978, 1979, and 1980, and poor participation (only twenty-three farmers insured potatoes in 1980 and only five farmers insured tomatoes in 1981) the program was canceled. Coverage written on bananas started in 1979, and also experienced high loss ratios: 5.82 in 1979 and 5.00 in 1980. It may also be canceled in the near future.

*Grains and livestock*. The results for this group of products are presented in tables 14.10 and 14.11. Although the results in terms of loss ratios are still poor for peanuts, corn, soybeans, and wheat, the results for livestock are rather encouraging. In fact the low loss ratios for livestock led to a reduction in the premium rates from 3.55 percent (established in Resolution 5/70) to 2.5 percent (the present rate for cattle). The number of

TABLE 14.9 COSESP loss ratios for potatoes, tomatoes, and bananas, Brazil, 1975–80

| | Potatoes | | | Tomatoes | | | Bananas | | |
|---|---|---|---|---|---|---|---|---|---|
| Year | Premium[a] | Indemnity[a] | Loss ratio[b] | Premium[a] | Indemnity[a] | Loss ratio[b] | Premium[a] | Indemnity[a] | Loss ratio[b] |
| 1975 | 595.2 | 5,010.8 | 8.42 | 163.4 | 1,715.4 | 10.50 | | | |
| 1976 | 769.4 | 18.9 | 0.02 | 279.9 | 0.0 | 0.00 | | | |
| 1977 | 387.7 | 178.5 | 0.46 | 20.2 | 0.0 | 0.00 | | | |
| 1978 | 606.6 | 3,610.6 | 5.95 | 174.2 | 71.4 | 0.41 | | | |
| 1979 | 2,030.9 | 13,006.5 | 6.40 | 218.5 | 1,151.2 | 5.27 | 709.3 | 4,131.2 | 5.82 |
| 1980 | 1,184.9 | 3,600.7 | 3.04 | 232.6 | 217.1 | 0.93 | 2,019.1 | 10,103.7 | 5.00 |

*Source*: COSESP.
*Note*: Insurance for bananas started in 1979. Insurance for potatoes and tomatoes was canceled in 1981.
[a]Thousand *cruzeiros*.
[b]Indemnity ÷ premium.

TABLE 14.10 COSESP loss ratios for peanuts, corn, and soybeans, Brazil, 1976–80

| | Peanuts | | | Corn | | | Soybeans | | |
|---|---|---|---|---|---|---|---|---|---|
| Year | Premium[a] | Indemnity[a] | Loss ratio[b] | Premium[a] | Indemnity[a] | Loss ratio[b] | Premium[a] | Indemnity[a] | Loss ratio[b] |
| 1976 | 328.9 | 0.0 | 0.00 | 294.1 | 0.0 | 0.00 | 1,154.4 | 0.0 | 0.00 |
| 1977 | 260.3 | 979.9 | 3.76 | 100.1 | 337.5 | 3.37 | 1,161.4 | 4,103.7 | 3.53 |
| 1978 | 229.8 | 634.7 | 2.76 | 456.3 | 634.8 | 1.39 | 1,485.3 | 7,832.9 | 5.27 |
| 1979 | 65.8 | 68.5 | 1.04 | 59.1 | 957.1 | 16.19 | 1,845.2 | 15,708.2 | 8.51 |
| 1980 | | | | 117.9 | 0.0 | 0.00 | 398.8 | 3,382.5 | 8.48 |

*Source*: COSESP.
[a]Thousand *cruzeiros*.
[b]Indemnity ÷ premium.

TABLE 14.11 COSESP loss ratios for wheat and livestock, Brazil, 1975–80

| | Wheat | | | Livestock | | |
|---|---|---|---|---|---|---|
| Year | Premium[a] | Indemnity[a] | Loss ratio[b] | Premium[a] | Indemnity[a] | Loss ratio[b] |
| 1975 | | | | 41.4 | 0.0 | 0.00 |
| 1976 | 2,223.0 | 2,824.3 | 1.27 | 71.2 | 0.0 | 0.00 |
| 1977 | 6,276.7 | 33,406.5 | 5.32 | 878.8 | 497.4 | 0.57 |
| 1978 | 3,428.0 | 43,786.1 | 12.77 | 1,156.3 | 865.1 | 0.75 |
| 1979 | 3,855.0 | 17,388.0 | 4.51 | 3,823.9 | 4,896.0 | 1.28 |
| 1980 | | | | 9,399.9 | 4,533.0 | 0.48 |

*Source*: COSESP.
[a]Thousand *cruzeiros*.
[b]Indemnity ÷ premium.

participants has continued to grow for livestock insurance, but the number purchasing peanuts, soybeans, and corn insurance has declined.

### *Overall Performance*

Given COSESP's relatively poor performance in recent years, the state government may feel inclined to drastically reduce its operations. Beginning with the 1977 crop year, the system accumulated heavy losses, as shown in table 14.12. The 120-million *cruzeiros* lost in the last five years will never be recovered from operations, despite the fact that at least part

TABLE 14.12 COSESP loss ratios, all crops, Brazil, 1971–80

| | Thousand *cruzeiros* | | | Thousand *cruzeiros* | |
|---|---|---|---|---|---|
| Year | Premium | Indemnity | Loss ratio[a] | Balance | Cumulative premium fund[b] |
| 1971 | 3,568.9 | 174.8 | 0.05 | 3,394.0 | 3,394.0 |
| 1972 | 4,224.2 | 4,823.8 | 1.14 | −559.6 | 3,343.5 |
| 1973 | 4,292.8 | 2,295.5 | 0.53 | 1,997.3 | 5,775.5 |
| 1974 | 11,005.5 | 3,604.6 | 0.33 | 7,400.9 | 15,082.3 |
| 1975 | 16,130.7 | 30,106.9 | 1.87 | −13,976.3 | 4,725.7 |
| 1976 | 37,091.1 | 29,254.1 | 0.79 | 7,836.9 | 14,311.1 |
| 1977 | 44,139.6 | 66,789.4 | 1.51 | −22,649.8 | −4,045.4 |
| 1978 | 45,377.8 | 131,290.9 | 2.89 | −85,913.2 | −91,414.8 |
| 1979 | 73,142.4 | 92,437.4 | 1.26 | −19,294.9 | −153,674.7 |
| 1980 | 142,201.9 | 145,344.3 | 1.02 | −3,142.3 | −235,191.0 |

*Source*: COSESP.
[a]Indemnity ÷ premium.
[b]Fund capitalized at government borrowing rate.

of the losses are spread over a large number of insurance companies through the Institute of Reinsurance of Brazil.

In any insurance system, it is to be hoped that, within certain limits, the premium fund will keep ahead of the claims against it. This is not the case with COSESP's operations, as shown in the last column of table 14.12. In some years, indemnity claims far exceeded premium revenues, and there have been successive years of severe losses that have threatened the entire program.

On balance, if it were possible to drop several drought years, such as 1978, COSESP's record on most insurances would be much more acceptable. Unfortunately, the single year 1978 added a net deficit to the premium fund of 86-million *cruzeiros*.

### *Concluding Remarks*

Most of COSESP's indemnity claims have been for damages caused by rain (over 60 percent); hail and windstorm together account for only about 25 percent. Also, claims have been concentrated in a few areas. These results indicate the need for an actuarial study to check whether concentration of high-risk operations are burdening the whole program.

Between 1976 and 1980, the government injected 125.1-million *cruzeiros* into COSESP to cover the excess of indemnities over premium revenues. An additional 79.9-million *cruzeiros* were provided by the state itself and by the state bank through its uncharged administration services.

Administration costs are still high when compared to premium revenue (table 14.13). Administration costs ranged from 14 to 33 percent of premium revenue in the 1976–80 period. If it were not for the subsidy provided to the program by state agencies, the entire program would have folded.

Although the premium rates for COSESP's crop insurance are substantially higher than PROAGRO's, farmers nevertheless prefer COSESP's system. Damages at the beginning of the crop season are fully

TABLE 14.13 COSESP premium revenue and administration costs, Brazil, 1976–80

| Year | Million *cruzeiros* | | Ratio of cost to revenue (percent) |
|---|---|---|---|
| | Premium revenue | Administration cost | |
| 1976 | 37.1 | 5.2 | 14.0 |
| 1977 | 44.1 | 7.2 | 16.3 |
| 1978 | 45.4 | 14.9 | 32.8 |
| 1979 | 77.5 | 18.6 | 24.0 |
| 1980 | 142.2 | 34.0 | 23.9 |

*Source*: COSESP.

indemnified under COSESP, and farmers can replant the area destroyed. Under PROAGRO, farmers have to wait until the crop is harvested, and then they receive indemnities only if the revenue from the sale of the product is not enough to cover the balance of the credit due.

Since crop insurance is only a branch of COSESP's operations, the insurance draws from COSESP's capital reserves. At the prevailing loss ratios, crop insurance is reducing the financial stability of the company. It is also reducing the capacity of the company to finance the full risk burden. Continued losses could threaten the solvency of the program and eventually bankrupt the entire company. Although the results have been poor so far, crop insurance is quite important for the agricultural sector of the state. The low level of participation for some crops can be explained both by high premium rates and by the fact that the scheme is voluntary.

## Crop Insurance in Minas Gerais

The system of crop insurance in the state of Minas Gerais was developed along the same lines as the one in Sao Paulo. Resolution 2/72 of the National Council of Private Insurance extended authorization to write coverage on several crops and farm assets to COSEMIG. The program began on an experimental basis in the 1973–74 crop year.

The insurance was linked to a planned agricultural credit program developed by the state government in the *cerrados* areas of the southwestern part of the state, (the Triangulo Mineiro). Thus the program does not cover all of the state. At the beginning, the basic credit source was the Bank of Development of Minas Gerais, supported by the state extension service. Later on, with the implementation of a federal government program for the *cerrados*—the so-called POLOCENTRO—federal credit was added to the existing system, which further enhanced the entire project.

The experience in Minas Gerais is rather interesting in several aspects. (1) At the beginning, the program was concentrated in a relatively small area of poor soils, which were being newly claimed for farming. Crop yields were initially low but were increased over three to four years after heavy lime treatments of the soil. (2) The program integrated credit and insurance, since it covered all production and investment credit requirements. (3) The program was specifically designed as part of an integrated plan of regional development and was subsidized as part of the whole plan.

COSEMIG has been cautious in extending crop insurance to other areas of the state, although the need to do so is recognized. Additional areas will not be added until the company is sure that a satisfactory program can be developed for the newly insured crops and counties.

COSEMIG writes coverage on all the important crops grown in the state, such as cotton, peanuts, rice, edible beans, corn, soybeans, wheat, and sorghum. Besides crops, it covers all farm assets such as buildings, machinery, vehicles, and stored products. It is also an all-risk insurance scheme.

COSEMIG insurance has almost all the characteristics of the system prevailing in Sao Paulo. The most important difference is related to the calculation of the indemnity. An indemnity is payable only if the yield from the insured crop is less than the average yield of the region, and farmers are paid up to the maximum of the expenses they incurred.

### *Premium Rates*

The premium rates are reported in table 14.14. The 1981 rates for crops (3.5 percent) are higher than the ones stipulated by Resolution 5/70 (2.5 percent) but lower than the ones for insurance in Sao Paulo (6 percent). The rate for buildings is expected to drop to 0.35 percent, and to rise to 6 percent on vehicles. The true actuarial rate for regular insurance on vehicles is between 6 and 8 percent. Insufficient time-series data on crop yields and losses make the determination of the premium rates difficult. Therefore, the current premium rates are tentative and are based on the farmer's capacity to pay.

TABLE 14.14 COSEMIG premium rates, Brazil, 1970 and 1981 (percent)

| Item covered | Premium rate | |
|---|---|---|
| | 1970[a] | 1981 |
| Crops[b] | 2.5 | 3.5 |
| Buildings | 0.4 | 0.4 |
| Machinery and equipment | | |
| Owned | 0.8 | 0.8 |
| Rented | 0.8 | 1.5 |
| Vehicles | | |
| Owned | 2.0 | 2.0 |
| Rented | 2.0 | 4.0 |
| Forests | | 0.95–2.8 |
| Horses and cattle | 3.5–4.5 | 2.5–3.5 |
| Temporary life insurance | 0.5 | |
| Stored products | 0.4 | |
| Marketing loans | 0.3 | |

*Source*: COSEMIG (Insurance Company of Minas Gerais).
[a]See table 14.6, note a, for description of Resolution 5/70.
[b]Includes cotton, peanuts, rice, edible beans, corn, soybeans, and wheat.

### *Overall Performance*

The financial performance of the scheme is reported in tables 14.15 through 14.22. The program started to operate in the 1973–74 crop year, which permits a reasonable evaluation of its performance.

The results for all crops have been extremely poor in terms of loss ratios. The average loss ratios ranged from 2.77 for corn to 7.62 for rice. The average loss ratio in the seven-year period for all the crops combined was 3.64, and it fluctuated widely from year to year. During this period, the Crop Insurance Stabilization Fund had to cover the deficit between the premium revenues and the indemnities paid.

Except for soybeans, the insured proportion of the total cultivated acreage of each crop is very low—less than 10 percent. For edible beans and corn, the insured area does not even reach 1 percent of the total area grown. On the other hand, the results of farm asset insurance are ex-

TABLE 14.15 COSEMIG loss ratios and insured area for cotton, Brazil, 1973–79

| Year | Thousand *cruzeiros* | | Loss | Area (hectares) | | Percent of cultivated |
|---|---|---|---|---|---|---|
| | Premium | Indemnity | ratio[a] | Insured | Cultivated | area insured |
| 1973 | 124.6 | 1,005.3 | 8.06 | 2,311 | 98,000 | 2.4 |
| 1974 | 419.7 | 1,005.6 | 2.40 | 5,695 | 108,202 | 5.3 |
| 1975 | 275.9 | 50.9 | 0.18 | 3,055 | 93,623 | 3.3 |
| 1976 | 551.3 | 1,772.7 | 3.22 | 4,146 | 116,144 | 3.5 |
| 1977 | 761.0 | 3,997.4 | 5.25 | 3,185 | 120,419 | 2.6 |
| 1978 | 386.2 | 0.0 | 0.00 | 1,018 | 100,043 | 1.0 |
| 1979 | 584.6 | 0.0 | 0.00 | 953 | 103,195 | 0.9 |

*Source*: COSEMIG.
[a]Indemnity ÷ premium.

TABLE 14.16 COSEMIG loss ratios and insured area for peanuts, Brazil, 1973–78

| Year | Thousand *cruzeiros* | | Loss | Area (hectares) | | Percent of cultivated |
|---|---|---|---|---|---|---|
| | Premium | Indemnity | ratio[a] | Insured | Cultivated | area insured |
| 1973 | 5.9 | 0.0 | 0.00 | 177 | 8,256 | 2.1 |
| 1974 | 2.9 | 0.0 | 0.00 | 77 | 6,305 | 1.2 |
| 1975 | 13.2 | 70.6 | 5.35 | 230 | 3,807 | 6.0 |
| 1976 | 11.9 | 0.0 | 0.00 | 152 | 2,972 | 5.1 |
| 1977 | 23.9 | 55.4 | 2.32 | 158 | 3,247 | 4.9 |
| 1978 | 46.4 | 118.6 | 2.55 | 175 | 4,542 | 3.8 |

*Source*: COSEMIG.
[a]Indemnity ÷ premium.

TABLE 14.17 COSEMIG loss ratios and insured area for rice, Brazil, 1973–79

| Year | Thousand *cruzeiros* | | Loss | Area (hectares) | | Percent of cultivated |
|---|---|---|---|---|---|---|
| | Premium | Indemnity | ratio[a] | Insured | Cultivated | area insured |
| 1973 | 34.0 | 312.6 | 9.19 | 2,420 | 713,908 | 0.3 |
| 1974 | 439.8 | 5,779.6 | 13.14 | 17,407 | 814,100 | 2.1 |
| 1975 | 419.0 | 1,355.2 | 3.23 | 12,829 | 852,656 | 1.5 |
| 1976 | 220.9 | 2,421.2 | 10.96 | 5,719 | 708,883 | 0.8 |
| 1977 | 212.9 | 1,334.9 | 6.27 | 2,636 | 631,943 | 0.4 |
| 1978 | 139.8 | 408.7 | 2.92 | 1,585 | 509,364 | 0.3 |
| 1979 | 73.4 | 0.0 | 0.0 | ... | ... | ... |

*Source*: COSEMIG.
[a]Indemnity ÷ premium.

TABLE 14.18 COSEMIG loss ratios and insured area for edible beans, Brazil, 1973–78

| Year | Thousand *cruzeiros* | | Loss | Area (hectares) | | Percent of cultivated |
|---|---|---|---|---|---|---|
| | Premium | Indemnity | ratio[a] | Insured | Cultivated | area insured |
| 1973 | 7.9 | 26.6 | 3.37 | 399 | 849,330 | 0.04 |
| 1974 | 69.5 | 783.9 | 11.28 | 1,921 | 566,997 | 0.30 |
| 1975 | 77.8 | 110.5 | 1.42 | 1,795 | 555,534 | 0.30 |
| 1976 | 87.9 | 1,146.9 | 13.05 | 1,936 | 598,460 | 0.30 |
| 1977 | 99.8 | 420.4 | 4.21 | 724 | 559,384 | 0.10 |
| 1978 | 56.8 | 24.6 | 0.43 | 608 | 449,943 | 0.10 |

*Source*: COSEMIG.
[a]Indemnity ÷ premium.

TABLE 14.19 COSEMIG loss ratios and insured area for corn, Brazil, 1973–79

| Year | Thousand *cruzeiros* | | Loss | Area (hectares) | | Percent of cultivated |
|---|---|---|---|---|---|---|
| | Premium | Indemnity | ratio[a] | Insured | Cultivated | area insured |
| 1973 | 25.4 | 0.5 | 0.02 | 1,201 | 1,281,000 | 0.1 |
| 1974 | 298.0 | 1,837.7 | 6.17 | 8,832 | 1,622,706 | 0.5 |
| 1975 | 590.9 | 1,055.6 | 1.79 | 14,062 | 1,682,588 | 0.8 |
| 1976 | 514.2 | 1,127.5 | 2.19 | 9,700 | 1,795,197 | 0.5 |
| 1977 | 802.3 | 4,159.5 | 5.18 | 7,916 | 1,691,222 | 0.4 |
| 1978 | 608.5 | 647.3 | 1.06 | 4,547 | 1,595,629 | 0.3 |
| 1979 | 234.8 | 55.0 | 0.23 | 1,235 | 1,740,046 | 0.1 |

*Source*: COSEMIG.
[a]Indemnity ÷ premium.

TABLE 14.20 COSEMIG loss ratios and insured area for soybeans, Brazil, 1973–79

| Year | Thousand *cruzeiros* | | Loss ratio[a] | Area (hectares) | | Percent of cultivated area insured |
|---|---|---|---|---|---|---|
| | Premium | Indemnity | | Insured | Cultivated | |
| 1973 | 291.2 | 1,839.1 | 6.31 | 11,186 | 48,000 | 23.3 |
| 1974 | 1,021.9 | 4,462.8 | 4.37 | 34,107 | 75,781 | 45.0 |
| 1975 | 1,484.2 | 1,398.7 | 0.94 | 38,222 | 79,664 | 47.9 |
| 1976 | 1,984.9 | 14,757.5 | 7.34 | 41,843 | 99,820 | 41.9 |
| 1977 | 3,471.5 | 8,919.8 | 2.57 | 39,209 | 112,094 | 34.9 |
| 1978 | 3,201.7 | 200.1 | 0.06 | 22,996 | 117,149 | 19.6 |
| 1979 | 1,115.6 | 1,199.5 | 1.07 | 4,613 | 162,799 | 2.8 |

*Source*: COSEMIG.
[a]Indemnity ÷ premium.

TABLE 14.21 COSEMIG loss ratios for wheat, Brazil, 1975–79

| Year | Thousand *cruzeiros* | | Loss ratio[a] |
|---|---|---|---|
| | Premium | Indemnity | |
| 1975 | 72.9 | 366.4 | 5.03 |
| 1976 | 216.7 | 1,205.5 | 5.56 |
| 1977 | 581.6 | 458.0 | 0.79 |
| 1978 | 946.6 | 2,073.7 | 2.19 |
| 1979 | 15.2 | 819.8 | 53.93 |

*Source*: COSEMIG.
[a]Indemnity ÷ premium.

tremely good. The overall loss ratio for the entire insurance portfolio in Minas Gerais ranged from 0.24 to 5.07, with an average of 2.53.

## Concluding Comments

Brazil is learning how to manage crop insurance from its own experience. Like the United States in the 1940s, loss ratios are particularly high, averaging 18.8 for PROAGRO, 1.2 for Sao Paulo, and 2.53 for Minas Gerais. For individual crops such as wheat, corn, and soybeans, the average loss ratios over the experimental period were extremely high.

After reviewing the heavy losses in the beginning years, the state insurance companies decided to raise premium rates, hoping to build up reserves after matching premiums to indemnities. In some cases, raising rates up to 6 and 7 percent caused such a drop in participation that programs had to be discontinued. In the case of COSEMIG, premium rates

TABLE 14.22 COSEMIG loss ratios for crops, buildings, machinery, and vehicles, Brazil, 1973–79

| Year | Crops | Buildings | Machinery | Vehicles |
|---|---|---|---|---|
| 1973 | | | | |
| Premiums (thousand *cruzeiros*) | 489.3 | 16.8 | 125.8 | 12.2 |
| Indemnities (thousand *cruzeiros*) | 3,184.1 | 39.9 | 5.5 | 12.3 |
| Loss ratio[a] | 6.51 | 2.38 | 0.04 | 1.01 |
| 1974 | | | | |
| Premiums (thousand *cruzeiros*) | 2,256.9 | 119.9 | 677.6 | 179.4 |
| Indemnities (thousand *cruzeiros*) | 13,956.7 | 306.9 | 94.3 | 94.8 |
| Loss ratio[a] | 6.18 | 2.56 | 0.14 | 0.53 |
| 1975 | | | | |
| Premiums (thousand *cruzeiros*) | 2,933.9 | 291.7 | 1,250.6 | 355.7 |
| Indemnities (thousand *cruzeiros*) | 4,408.4 | 589.6 | 253.6 | 379.1 |
| Loss ratio[a] | 1.50 | 2.02 | 0.20 | 1.07 |
| 1976 | | | | |
| Premiums (thousand *cruzeiros*) | 3,587.8 | 355.9 | 1,450.0 | 407.8 |
| Indemnities (thousand *cruzeiros*) | 22,431.3 | 647.0 | 385.9 | 222.2 |
| Loss ratio[a] | 6.25 | 1.82 | 0.27 | 0.55 |
| 1977 | | | | |
| Premiums (thousand *cruzeiros*) | 5,952.9 | 664.2 | 1,729.4 | 506.0 |
| Indemnities (thousand *cruzeiros*) | 19,345.3 | 911.9 | 145.3 | 267.7 |
| Loss ratio[a] | 3.25 | 1.37 | 0.08 | 0.53 |
| 1978 | | | | |
| Premiums (thousand *cruzeiros*) | 5,386.2 | 2,315.5 | 3,954.2 | 769.7 |
| Indemnities (thousand *cruzeiros*) | 3,473.2 | 606.4 | 513.7 | 175.2 |
| Loss ratio[a] | 0.65 | 0.26 | 0.13 | 0.23 |
| 1979 | | | | |
| Premiums (thousand *cruzeiros*) | 2,023.6 | 4,822.4 | 6,450.5 | 1,837.8 |
| Indemnities (thousand *cruzeiros*) | 2,301.5 | 343.6 | 709.8 | 352.6 |
| Loss ratio[a] | 1.14 | 0.07 | 0.11 | 0.19 |

*Source*: COSEMIG.
[a]Indemnity ÷ premium.

were increased only moderately (to 3.5 percent), and this did not reduce the deficit between the indemnities and premium revenue.

In 1981, PROAGRO was entirely reshaped, with the introduction of progressive premium rates and full coverage of credit granted. However, before these changes, the results were quite unsatisfactory. The program drew heavily upon the federal budget, which made the program particularly vulnerable. Although there is some argument for government to subsidize insurance in the initial years (see chapter 7), when huge losses are accumulated over time it is hard to justify grants from the federal budget in increasing amounts.

Although Brazil's experience with crop insurance is not positive, the prevailing systems have several advantages over the previous system, in which the government was the sole guarantor for the farmer in years of severe floods or droughts. Under the present system, premium revenue is important, although it is not enough to cover the indemnities paid. There is more control in the present system, since extension-service agents and staff from financial institutions are responsible for checking damages. There is probably a stronger inducement to adopting new technologies, a better distribution of credit, and a greater acceptability of farmers as credit risks by the banks.

The basic virtue of the state systems in Sao Paulo and Minas Gerais is that they are a possible bridgehead for the future transfer of the responsibility of crop insurance from the government to other agents. Both state programs are now accomplished in providing agricultural insurance. Capable and sufficient staffs provided by state governments, state banks, state extension services, and state insurance companies, have played a critical role in the relative success of the programs. Both state programs were attached to the Institute of Reinsurance of Brazil, which has provided adequate support and financing.

However, the common failure in the two state programs has been the heavy loss ratios, which necessitated continuing subsidies. These losses bring the financial viability of both programs into question. Furthermore, the size of the economic benefits are questionable. Since the state insurance programs are voluntary, participation has remained low, with only a small share of the total number of farmers insuring. The effect of insurance on the adoption of new technology is also questionable. The programs appear to have benefited only high-risk farmers, because of the relatively larger subsidy they receive.

The performance of both state programs might be improved by making the insurance compulsory, rather than letting farmers choose the PROAGRO alternative. This might also enable the premium rates to be reduced, except for certain high-risk farmers and activities, for whom rates as high as 6 to 7 percent are not high enough to prevent excess losses. Changing the state insurance schemes from voluntary to obligatory should also protect both programs against adverse-selection problems. If these changes were made, state companies might take over all insurance in Sao Paulo and Minas Gerais, replacing PROAGRO's credit insurance operations.

# 15

# Planning for the Efficient Operation of Crop Credit Insurance Schemes

William M. Gudger
Luis Avalos

The starting point for this chapter is an expressed desire of a government (or more properly someone within that government) to establish an agricultural insurer. What are the processes required to build an institution capable of assuming the new and specific function of agricultural insurance?

Our mode of analysis is that of the rational conscious action. We do not believe that viable institutions such as insurers have much possibility of developing without a guiding hand capable of shaping their structure and function. This chapter takes the view of a practitioner called upon to assist in planning an insurer and at the same time working jointly with national staff to preside over its establishment and initial operation. In presenting our views on the structure and function of agricultural insurers, we use the Costa Rican experience to illustrate what can and frequently does go wrong in the design and operation of an agricultural insurer.

## Institutional Structure

It is likely that no single planning decision is as important as the institutional structure of the new insurer. To a very significant extent, this structure influences the method of operation and opens or closes opportunities for growth. Structure is an important variable in managerial control and even in the content of managerial decisions. It affects the ability of the insurer to sustain the "worst possible loss" or the "drought (or flood) of the century." Administrative structure may in certain cases open the insurer to exogenous decision making based upon other than technical grounds. Likewise, the administrative structure very strongly affects the ability of the insurer to have its product made obligatory. Thus it affects operational costs and diversification of its portfolio. Finally, the administrative structure and the autonomy of managerial decision making bears upon the ability of the insurer to purchase reinsurance under favorable terms.

### A Public Institution

Historically, most agricultural insurers have been the product of legislative enactments. Almost without exception, these insurers have been public sector entities provided with finance from the treasury and with direction, guidance, or control from other public sector entities. In many cases, the insurer forms part of the agricultural bureaucracy under the control of a ministry of agriculture. Thus the insurer serves as part of the overall agricultural policy apparatus.

There are very distinct advantages to utilizing the legislative process. The insurer, once established, is almost certainly a permanent bureaucracy. As a government agency, it has priority access to the budget. Likewise, it can more easily work with other government institutions such as banks and ministries. Finally, the government is usually willing to guarantee its financial solvency from its own resources, or from loans, grants, and guarantees obtained abroad.

This would seem to be a very strong case indeed for a public sector insurer created by legislative fiat. However, in practice, the creation process is lengthy and beset with problems. Many agricultural insurers around the world have failed because of poorly drafted legislation or because of the impact of special interest groups upon the final legislation. The legislative process can risk the dilution or loss of technical control of structure.

It is also usual that insurers created by legislative action operate under the personnel rules of the public sector. As a result, the insurer is frequently staffed with the discards of other ministries, or with inexperienced but politically well-connected management. Frequently, neither staff nor management are held to more than financial accountability criteria (and sometimes not too strictly to those).

Public sector institutions confront a very serious problem of innovation. Legislatures usually write restrictive legislation and require legislative approval for modifications. Likewise, management seldom has the ability to innovate and initiate new and experimental programs. As agricultural insurance is a new and experimental field that requires constant innovation, situating the insurer in the public sector can pose substantial problems. Finally, in a public sector insurer, decisions on premium rates, coverages, underwriting, and loss-adjusting criteria frequently have a political dimension.

The problem of a public sector insurer can further be complicated in developing countries reluctant to accept all the risk inherent in a large-scale program. Indeed, many do not have the liquid assets at any given time to pay the maximum possible loss. The solution is to utilize the international reinsurance market to arrange intertemporal resource transfers.

At present, the international reinsurance markets have shown willingness to reinsure viable, well-managed programs. The condition upon which reinsurances will be accepted is that the decision-making process be based upon technical considerations and that the moral hazard of politically expedient decision making be contained and minimized. Under these conditions, Panama, Bolivia, Puerto Rico, and Chile have obtained reinsurance in international markets.

For precisely the same reason, Costa Rica lost its reinsurance coverage. The Costa Rican case illustrates a design failure, which has had severe financial consequences. Both premium rates and decision making on indemnities have been politically influenced, with a major indemnity in one case ordered by the government. Likewise, inadequate premium rates have been offset by permitting the insurer to place bonds in the state banking system. The result has been a financially nonviable structure, because the sociopolitical risks have not been minimized. Thus, the program is not reinsured and is probably not reinsurable.

There are means of reducing the sociopolitical risks in the process of preparing the basic law and, far more importantly, in writing the insurers' bylaws. However, this risk will to some degree be present in any insurer in the public sector.[1]

There is then a trade-off. Entry into the government club requires payment of a high membership fee and fairly large maintenance fees. Once a member, many financial problems are reduced, but administration can be complicated by the internal rules. Government-owned insurers have severe moral hazards incorporated into their very structure, unless very careful thought is given to designing a law that will give management considerable autonomy over what is insured, at what premium, and when indemnities are to be paid. Even careful design can only reduce, not eliminate, the moral hazard presented by politically motivated decision making.

### *Mixed-Capital Ventures*

Mixed-capital ventures may meliorate the problem of politically motivated decision making and provide more flexibility than offered by public administration. Such an approach is being tried in Ecuador, with assistance from the Inter-American Institute for Cooperation in Agriculture (IICA).

The Ecuadorian insurer, Compania Nacional de Seguros Agrope-

1. One obvious solution is for the reinsurers to develop a loss verification capacity, which would provide an independent determination of the frequency and severity of losses. The market, however, is still far too small for this to be financially practical.

cuarios, was established as a regular stock company would be. Enabling legislation of only one paragraph was required. The establishment of the company followed the procedures established by the commercial code and the insurance regulatory agency. The stock was purchased by both public and private entities. At the outset, the public sector holds an overwhelming capital position. In addition, the central bank supplied the reserve. However, the bylaws are open to (and management openly seeks) new investors from the private sector. Cooperatives, mutual aid associations, organized producers, and other service or financial institutions can supply capital and participate as members of the board of directors.[2] The insurer is in the private, nonprofit sector, and as such operates as an independent entity controlled by its board of directors and regulated by the insurance laws of the country. The insurer is thus outside the government hierarchy and operates under its own rules and bylaws.

The mixed-capital enterprise is more than an alternative way of structuring capital. It profoundly alters the decision-making environment and the scope of managerial autonomy and entrepreneurship. To the extent that the board of directors functions effectively, important decisions are made collegially at open meetings instead of hierarchically within government bureaucracies. Likewise, a wider variety of interests are represented. The manager has relative autonomy over the technical decisions and considerable independence in personnel policy and investment strategies. The institution thus escapes the rigidity of public sector bureaucracy, and to a substantial extent avoids the risk of politically motivated decision making.

This autonomy has its price, however. The insurer has no priority access to public funds and may not be tax-exempt. It likewise must negotiate a government full-faith-and-credit guarantee, as well as exhibit considerable entrepreneurship in obtaining additional reserve capital and an operational subsidy. Most of these problems are medium-term ones. To the extent that a mixed-capital insurer can overcome the initial capitalization problem through government grants, soft loans, guarantees, and other financial instruments, and to the extent it can arrange adequate reinsurance, it has a very good chance of becoming a viable insurer.

### *The Private Sector Alternative*

A private sector agricultural insurer does not seem to be a viable choice under conditions of development. Private sectors are not likely to put at

2. Unfortunately, Ecuadorian law prohibits the participation of banks in the capital structure.

risk very large volumes of capital on an unproven and probably unprofitable enterprise without any substantial guarantees from the government.

There are a number of private sector agricultural insurance schemes around the world. In Spain, the private sector carries out a limited-risk program with a very heavy concessional government reinsurance and an administrative subsidy. The United States has numerous insurers against hail risk. In 1981 a private Chilean company began an insurance program for fruits and grains, which bears careful observation to see if it can reach a mass market or if it will be confined to relatively few large-scale farmers. The Swiss have had a private sector insurer for many years. Almost all these institutions are characterized by their small size, limited clientele, and inability to sustain catastrophic losses. While the Spanish system can survive catastrophic losses due to heavy concessional reinsurance from the government, most other programs run by private companies probably could not. Likewise, there is always the risk that management and investors will seek more profitable, less risky investment alternatives. Indeed, this has happened many times. One would certainly wonder at the rationality or perhaps even sanity of an investor who would reinvest in an agricultural insurer that had been hit by very adverse experience.

There is, however, a form of private sector insurer that may be viable under certain circumstances. In Bolivia, a slightly different approach to the mixed-capital venture is being tried—a private sector, nonprofit, mutual insurer. Aseguradora Boliviana Agropecuaria began as a government institution but is evolving toward a mutual institution in which the insureds themselves are the owners of the company. However, a professional management is retained to function as an intermediary and to protect the company's assets.

Must it be concluded that a private sector insurer cannot be viable? The historical experience to date is discouraging. The basic problem is that a new insurer must bear the risk of catastrophic losses while it capitalizes its reserve. Commercial coinsurance is useful in expanding underwriting capacity and in providing coverage against infrequent but severe aggregate losses. However, a new insurer can expect many years to pass before it can purchase reinsurance to protect itself against truly catastrophic losses.

Here government can make a most useful contribution. By supporting an infant industry until it reaches a critical size, and by protecting the insurer against catastrophic losses that cannot be placed in the international reinsurance market, the government can make a private sector initiative viable though not necessarily profitable. However, this support must be impartial in the sense that the insurer is not asked to trade its decision-making autonomy for financial support. On this point, historical experience is not encouraging. Thus far, no government that we know of has shown such disinterested support.

## Financial Planning

The cost of crop credit insurance consists of two parts, the administrative costs and the contingent costs. The former are composed of the central office staff, the field staff, and the operating costs. The latter are composed of indemnity costs, the cost of establishing, and in the case of adverse experience, replenishing a reserve for the insurer.

### *Central Office Staff*

Administrative costs are relatively easy to estimate once a program size is decided upon and a medium-term growth plan is laid out in its broadest parameters. The central office staff should as a very general rule not exceed five or six persons at the outset. It may be expected to grow to ten or fifteen during the next five to eight years. The staff is responsible for planning, product development, interinstitutional relations, budgeting, accounting, policy emission, claims processing, and payment and control of the field staff. There has been a tendency to contract a large and highly specialized staff of lawyers, certified accountants, and actuaries, but these professionals are not fully utilized by a new insurer. Instead, all that is required at the outset is a core staff of managers capable of designing and implementing the administrative, accounting, and auditing functions. At current prices in Latin America for pilot projects, our experience has been that this cost is about $120 thousand per year, plus a one-time $100 thousand start-up expense. The growth of the central office should be relatively slow, perhaps reaching $150 thousand per year in the fourth or fifth year.

At the outset, it is critically important to develop and enforce a personnel plan that carefully lays out what specialists will be contracted and when, so as to avoid overstaffing. The central office functions can be routinized with only two exceptions, the managerial and research and product development. The latter specialist would test the acceptance of the product among the insureds and develop new lines of insurance and new ways of insuring to meet the demands.

Very considerable savings can be made by quickly moving from a manual to a computerized information system—for personnel, for each insured's records, and for budgeting and accounting. Again, the tendency to overbuy must be avoided. Small computers that can be integrated into larger systems are quite adequate for the first ten years of the insurer's life.

Finally, the central office should resist a tendency to permit the staff to grow as the program grows. Additional insurance can be undertaken without necessarily increasing staff. At the outset, the insurer will probbly have relatively few policies to service, and thus the number of policies per employee will be very small. Most insurance policies do not require other than routine processing and can be handled quickly. It is when indemnities are to be paid that the amount of time per policy increases. The initial staff of five to six persons should handle three-thousand policies per year without difficulty with a small computer system. Again as a general rule, an additional staff member will be required for each two-thousand policies per year up to about ten thousand. After that, new staff should not be required until the insurer is quite large.

At the outset, a monitoring system should be established to insure that the administrative costs per hectare or per unit of coverage are steadily declining. The impact of new hiring on this ratio should be carefully watched. Likewise, management should, for internal purposes, segregate the central office costs and verify that these costs decline—rapidly at first and steadily thereafter—as a percentage of total costs. At some point (rather distant we think), an equilibrium will be reached. New personnel and administrative costs should be measured against this ratio to ensure that the administration remains efficient.

### *Field Staff and Operating Costs*

The second element of administrative costs are the field operations costs. These costs are much more problematic, as they vary according to the method of operation selected, the human and physical infrastructure, and the loss experience. If the insurer must undertake functions related to insurance but usually performed by other agencies, such as credit supervision or extension work, field costs will rise considerably. Likewise if field agents are assigned to zones with small scattered holdings or with little physical infrastructure, operational costs will rise. Our experience demonstrates that the major cost of field work is to put an inspector on a farm. Once he is there, the marginal cost of additional inspections on adjoining farms is slight. More-educated farmers and larger farms are less costly to service than are their counterparts. Likewise, monocultures are less expensive to service than highly diversified farming systems.

Although an exact quantification is elusive, field operations costs are quite high in absolute terms. A very substantial cost occurs because other institutions, such as extension services, do not exist or do not function well, as is the case with credit supervision. To protect its financial interests, the insurer must assume many of these functions.

To lower these operational costs, the insurer must work with other institutions to obtain the required extension and supervision among the insureds. As a condition for protecting itself against lack of recovery, the bank should provide effective credit supervision. Working with rural, integrated development projects offers another cost-reduction strategy. By offering reduced premiums or increased coverages to groups, operating costs can also be lowered.

Internally, the insurer must plan carefully to reduce field operations costs. The cyclical nature of agriculture offers the single largest opportunity. In most countries of Latin America, a second production cycle is possible with irrigation or occasionally drainage. Likewise, the mountainous topography creates microclimates suited to distinct production cycles. Permanent crops also offer opportunities. An insurer must carefully plan to utilize the field staff year-round to the extent permitted by the environment. Since dry-cycle agriculture is irrigated and quite capital-intense, it may be possible to triple or even quadruple the total amount of coverage (the basis upon which premium is calculated) under the control of a single agent. Cross-training in other insurance, such as livestock and fish pond, will further increase the efficiency of the field agents. However, moving inspectors from zone to zone is seldom advisable, except for short periods of intense activities, such as occur at seeding and harvest times or following disasters; subsistence and travel costs usually offset any gains. Thus a careful selection of the distinct elements that compose the portfolio will affect the cost and relative efficiency of the insurer's field staff.

Other recommended strategies of cost containment are the training and employment of part-time agents and the use of self-reporting systems for certain clients. Training of village personnel to carry out some of the more routine tasks will significantly lower costs. Many of the inspections do not require the presence of an insurer's agent or can be spot-checked at a later date. For example, there is little need for an inspector to verify the amount of land insured and then return to verify an adequate germination. Likewise, limited damage by many phenomena, such as hail, can be reported by a paraprofessional.

Insurers can also grade their clients by their past records and gradually reduce inspections for clients who have few problems, while concentrating on those who have losses year after year. Although hard-pressed inspectors do this almost subconsciously, this practice should be formalized with clear criteria and with a financial incentive, such as reduced premiums for the better insureds. Spot checks and random-sampling techniques can determine if the fraud losses exceed the savings. Those who cheat on self-reporting and limited inspection systems can be denied insurance.

Finally, the efficiency of the agents themselves should be carefully monitored and spot checked for veracity and accuracy. The number of field checks performed and the accuracy of the adjustments made should be monitored to ensure that the field staff is performing effectively.

### *Financing the Administration*

Few developing countries are in a position to assume additional financial obligation. Yet quite frequently, for social and political reasons, they are unwilling to charge the whole cost of administration to the insureds. This situation requires considerable entrepreneurship on the part of planners to create a viable financial system. The options for financing agricultural insurance that follow are by no means inclusive but are those we have found to be feasible.

At the outset, a planner must have a clear understanding of how public and private financial institutions operate in the agricultural sector. There is a tendency to view an insurer as yet another expensive bureaucracy. Indeed it may be, without careful planning. However, since under a crop credit insurance scheme the insurer reimburses the bank for natural losses, the total amount of money flowing in the credit system should remain roughly the same. Lenders should require less frequent recapitalizations and should have lower loss ratios with insurance. If extension, marketing, and other services are available and the insurer can confine itself to relatively low-cost pure-insurance functions, the administration costs of insurance simply replace the carrying costs of unpaid bank loans. The latter costs have been estimated at about fifty dollars per year per loan. For considerably less, a well-designed insurer should be able to provide a cheaper alternative.

Thus two options for finance can be explored, which add little to total government expenditure. To lower the frequency of recapitalizing agricultural banks, governments might cover part of the administrative costs of an insurer from general revenues or from a special fund that would otherwise be destined to recapitalization. If the central bank has a rediscount operation, a percentage point or two of the interest rate differential for funds flowing to agriculture could finance part of the administrative cost of insurance.

Banks are the direct beneficiaries of credit insurance. They should show higher recovery rates, and since their risk is substantially lower with insured clients, their operating costs should likewise decline. Thus banks could allocate a percent or two of the interest charged to the borrower to help cover the administrative costs of insurance. Alternatively, banks could establish a revolving fund capitalized by the increase in recovery rate to help finance the insurer. This fund would be divided between the bank and the insurer according to preestablished rules.

These two sources of finance pose few policy questions. The money is roughly the same; it merely flows in a different manner. The most salient policy problem of administrative-cost structuring is what, if any, portion of administrative costs should be charged to the farmer. The arguments for and against charging administrative costs are considered in chapter 7. Our view is that agricultural production is characterized by many disarticulated direct and indirect subsidies, cross subsidies, incentives, disincentives, and penalties at all steps of the production process. It is therefore very difficult indeed to generalize about the desirability or the financial ability of the insureds to bear the administrative costs.

Nevertheless, where subsidies are to be used, we recommend that the subsidy arrangements be made explicit. Instead of absorbing a specified percentage of total costs, we recommend that the decision be taken by the government on a crop-by-crop basis. It would therefore be possible to target subsidies to socially or economically desirable ends. If an administrative subsidy is offered, we strongly urge it be offered selectively. Each year, the insurer can estimate the cost of insuring a given clientele and negotiate with the government what portion it will bear. In all cases, it is highly advisable that the entire premium paid by farmers be financed to ease their cash-flow problem, irrespective of whether the premium is pure risk premium, or risk premium plus administrative costs.

In addition to domestic sources of finance for administrative costs, external grants or loan funds may be available from international institutions. These funds should be considered only as short- or medium-term sources of capital. It is unrealistic to believe an external subsidy is likely to do more than help offset the initial costs. From the beginning, financial planning should anticipate replacing these funds with domestically generated ones. The most useful role of these funds is to help cover the extremely high per-unit costs during the experimental period—the first five to ten years. Any such grants and concessional loans should identify sources of replacement and contain a fade-out schedule.

### *Capitalizing and Maintaining a Reserve*

Administrative costs are certain costs, whose magnitude can be estimated with reasonable precision. On the other hand, the reserve is a contingent cost. Structuring a reserve poses a peculiar problem: the charges to be made against it are the product of stochastic variables such as wind, drought, and freezes. At the outset, neither the frequency nor the severity can be estimated in other than a rough manner. As if these problems did not present a sufficient challenge to planners, agricultural insurance has a catastrophic-loss potential, and the events producing losses cannot be assumed to be independent of each other. A widespread drought can easily destroy the agriculture of a region or nation.

The sources for capitalizing a reserve are much the same as those for covering administrative expenses and thus need not be repeated. However, the accumulation of the reserve may be gradual, with increased amounts destined to the reserve as the insurer's coverage increases. The fact that the reserve cost is a contingent cost means that an insurer need not hold a reserve equal to the maximum probable loss; it need only have the means to cover this loss should it occur.

To establish this reserve, guarantee mechanisms, contingent loans, and concessional as well as commercial reinsurance could be mixed into a reserve "cocktail." In addition, public sector agencies such as ministries, central banks, development banks, international lenders, and development agencies could extend a guarantee to cover excess losses.

A government guarantee is perhaps the easiest to obtain but probably the most difficult in terms of operations. When insurers are hit by excess losses, they require an immediate flow of cash. The process of cashing a government guarantee can be lengthy.

A contingent loan is a much better mechanism to insure the solidity of the insurer. This prearranged loan could be drawn when losses reached a specified magnitude. As an acquired obligation, the bank would increase its reserves to ensure it could make the loan when required. The insurer would in turn have a contractual right to draw on the loan under specified circumstances.

At present, commercial reinsurance is available to those insurers who either have several years of favorable experience or appear to have overcome organizational problems. It is likewise available to programs that have been designed to be reinsurable by collaboration between the insurer and the reinsurer. While commercial reinsurers may be willing to offer one of several risk-spreading schemes to cover higher-than-expected losses, it is unlikely that they would be willing to bear the catastrophic-loss risk.

Reinsurance is rather complex, and each contract is individually negotiated. A usual package of reinsurance consists of a quota-share agreement, under which the reinsurer accepts a specified part of the risk of the company and receives a specified part of the premium income. This expands the insurer's capacity—it can write more insurance against a given reserve. Coupled with this quota-share agreement is usually an excess-of-loss (stop-loss) agreement, whereby, for an additional part of the premium, the reinsurer agrees to pay losses in excess of a given amount up to a maximum figure, usually 200 to 300 percent of premium income.

Reinsurance from commercial insurers is a commercial product, and the market may not be willing to take the risk, or the premium quoted may be too high. Likewise, the level of coverage may be inadequate for major disasters. Many governments operate reinsurance funds, either as a substitute for commercial reinsurance or in a pool arrangement with commercial reinsurers.

## Operational Planning

### *Developing the Pilot Project*

Once the planning staff has developed the institutional, legal, and financial structures of the insurer, it can move on to design the operations of the insurer. There are two theories as to how to proceed. The theory used in parts of Asia—and perhaps influenced by Ray's (1967) work—holds that agricultural insurance is not distinct from other classes of administrative activities, and there is no reason not to proceed to a large-scale multicrop program. The theory current in Latin America, probably arising from some chastising failures and the conversion of insurers into expensive subsidy channels with little noticeable policy impact, holds that agricultural insurance is a special class of business. Catastrophic risk, coupled with the sociopolitical risk of putting perpetually cash-short governments into the insurance business, requires detailed studies, careful negotiations, and embodiment in law of all operational aspects.

Both theories overlook the key element of operational learning. Agricultural insurance is similar to other classes of business and can be administered as most other enterprises. However, some aspects of agricultural insurance can be learned only from actually operating as an insurer. Errors are to be expected; planners must design mechanisms to convert these errors into learning experiences for the bureaucracy. The unity of theory and action, with the latter continually enriching and modifying the former, is the way to develop an efficient, effective insurer.

To that end, we strongly urge that countries develop experimental programs that begin quite small and grow as they learn. Admittedly, this approach must steer a course between two equally hazardous alternatives. It risks either the creation of a small, complacent insurer and a loss of dynamism, or a too-rapid expansion driven by the urge to get the job done. In the pilot stage of five to ten years, bureaucratic routines must be developed to handle the bulk of the work flow in a smooth and orderly manner, and several problems must be confronted and resolved.

*Interinstitutional relations.* One problem is interinstitutional relations. As the new insurer covers the credit extended by other institutions, it must carefully work out detailed formal agreements specifying the obligations and rights of each party—who does what, when, where, and how. The critical points in an insurer/lender agreement are how much credit will be extended for each crop, zone, and technology; how much insurance will be offered; and who will do what in the countryside. Communication must receive special attention—banks must advise insurers when credits are approved, insurers must report to banks when coverage is approved, and information about the crop cycle must move quickly between institutions.

The partially conflictive, partially cooperative nature of agricultural credit insurance requires both lender and insurer to accept and live with a negotiated, less than optimal situation. Otherwise, destructive tensions arise, the bank claiming that the insurer only wants to insure loans it knows the bank will recover, and the insurer claiming that the bank wants it to insure only its sure-loser loans. We suggest two ways to foster cooperation, one technical, the other administrative. Technically, the creation of a joint portfolio-management model, in which the insurer and the bank engage in a bargaining process, moves the discussion from generalities to concrete solutions. Administratively, each institution could be represented on the other's board. Capital participation is also highly recommended.

At the field level, several problems arise. Banks frequently loosen loan-eligibility requirements and suspend costly credit supervision when the loans are insured. Loss adjustments have a judgmental element, so that banks and insurers frequently disagree over the cause or magnitude of losses. Indemnity arbitration committees should have representation from the bank, the insurer, the farmers, and from a disinterested expert and operate under rules that structure decisions on purely technical grounds.

*Insurance plan.* Another problem to be resolved in the pilot stage is the insurer's internal operational plan. What will be insured, where, and at what price? How will the business be serviced and by whom? Developing the policies, forms, notices, and other information and documentation is a gradual process. An understanding of what to insure, at what premium rate, and with what level of coverage also improves with experience. Continual review and revision must be built into the system, so that experience informs the premium determination process. Special care is required so that one group or crop does not inadvertently subsidize another.

Developing countries are usually as short of skilled professionals as they are of financial capital. To implement the plan of insurance, a field staff capable of the demanding task of risk management and loss adjustment must be recruited, trained, and administered. Agricultural professionals have to be cross trained in insurance techniques, which requires formal training and extensive field experience. Management needs to determine how many insureds can be assigned to an inspector and to develop a system for utilizing them year-round, moving them from zone to zone for critical periods like seeding and harvesting. Finally, management needs to develop supervision and management routines to ensure that inspectors are inspecting and that adjustments are timely and accurate.

*Financial plan.* During the pilot phase, management needs to develop an investment strategy that provides security, liquidity, and acceptable yields on investment. In unstable financial markets, such as those that characterize Latin America, management needs to carefully consider the exchange requirements of the insurer for payment of reinsurance premiums and the periodic devaluations that will make reinsurance progressively more expensive. One solution is a wholly owned reserve in a hard currency held by a reinsurer, if this is permitted by law. Through its pilot years, the insurer must develop an accurate cash budget, so that it will have adequate liquid funds available when indemnity and other payments fall due without being forced to sell off productive investments to meet cash-flow requirements.

*Client relations.* During the pilot phase, the insurer must develop an insurance product that meets the requirements of the insureds. Satisfaction with product and service is crucial to the farmers' acceptance. A given of insurance is that, to the insured, the premium is too high, and the indemnity too low and too infrequent; deductibles and salvage values tend to be viewed as tricks to avoid payment. Communication and education can help farmers understand what their premium buys and exactly what their policies cover. However, it is important, and especially so in voluntary systems, that insurers have accurate information about their clients' needs and their potential market.

*Research and development.* To carry out operational planning, insurers should develop a research and development capacity from the very outset, staffed initially by a single professional. This department would report directly to top management. It would develop new products, survey insureds needs and desires, produce educational materials, and work with management to monitor the performance of the administrative systems.

### *Expansion to the National Scale*

Bureaucracy is to a large degree a function of size—change becomes increasingly difficult and slow as the organization grows. Therefore it is crucial that the insurer's operation begin with a pilot program to develop effective, efficient operational strategies. At the end of the pilot phase, a detailed study should be done before the insurer attempts to reach a national market. This gradual process will seem overly conservative to many. However, we are convinced that only through careful monitoring of the results and through planned evaluations can institutions be built that can coordinate all the components of a successful agricultural insurance program.

The study of the results of the pilot phase should address three sets of considerations. First, a careful evaluation should be carried out to determine if the new insurer has had a positive impact on farmers. Has insurance affected farmers' production or productivity? Has insurance affected farmers' financial position? These effects are a matter of degree and should be measured against the costs of operating the system. It is highly likely that some socioeconomic strata will be more affected than others.

Second, another evaluation should be carried out to determine the effect of the insurance on the credit system. One rough measure is recovery rates measured against operational costs. Another measure is the demand for credit. One would expect insurance to increase demand. However, the premium rate almost certainly affects the marginal increase in demand. One would also expect that at some premium rate, insurance would stimulate demands for agricultural credit that could not be met, resulting in frustrated and perhaps angry farmers. Insurance is also a credit-rationing device, which may have positive or negative effects on the allocation of credit among the various groups and production options.

The third set of considerations that merits careful study is the effectiveness of the insurer's operation and the utility of its product. Has management developed adequate administrative and financial systems? Do farmers find the product useful? Are there better ways of providing insurance or other equally useful products? Finally, the insurer must carefully measure its own ability to plan, program, administer, and supervise a nationwide program.

### *A Case Study*

At the time of writing this chapter, the Costa Rican crop insurance program was in dire trouble.[3] A drought in Costa Rica's rice-producing areas of the Pacific produced losses estimated at over $7.3 million for the 1981–82 cycle. The reserve held by the National Insurance Institute (INS) totaled only $1.9 million, of which the government had already taken $872 thousand for other purposes, leaving a reserve of $1 million to meet indemnity obligations (*La Nacion*, September 6, 1982). Thus, during the worst economic crisis since the Great Depression, the government needed to find $6.3 million to meet its obligations to the insureds. The magnitude of these losses take on added significance in light of the fact that the program insured only about 1.5 percent of Costa Rica's farmers (817 in 1981 and 1,089 in 1982). Taking the latter figure, this implies an indemnity of $6,700 per farmer. However, the size of these indemnities is consistent with historical losses. The lessons that can be learned from Costa Rica's mistakes are institutional, financial, operational, legal and political.

*Institutional aspects.* Costa Rica's agricultural insurance program was placed logically enough within the state insurance monopoly. How-

3. The opinions expressed in this section are exclusively those of William Gudger.

ever, while the National Insurance Institute is reasonably good as an insurer, it had no agricultural expertise. It was generally unable (or unwilling, for reasons we will see later) to develop adequate underwriting standards to reflect the different technology levels and degrees of riskiness, despite the availability of good time-series data. This alone would make failure reasonably certain. However, this situation was aggravated by other factors.

*Financial aspects.* The crop insurance program was financed in a way that created a very severe moral hazard. The program was entitled to a large part of the profit earned by INS. When this was inadequate, INS could place bonds in the state banking monopoly to cover the shortfall in reserves. Predictably, when the losses that would trigger the emergency financing occurred, INS first collected from its reinsurer (who paid off and pulled out), then placed essentially worthless bonds in the state banking monopoly.

*Operational aspects.* The major shortfalls in program administration were a lack of strict underwriting and a lack of adequate field staff. As a result, inspections were lax and infrequent, and, worse still, frequently inaccurate on measurement of areas sown and plant densities and varieties. The program also failed to diversify its spread of risk. The heavy losses for 1982 are explicable by the fact that over 85 percent of both the area insured and the total coverage is in rice, most of which was concentrated in the dry Pacific provinces.[4]

*Legal aspects.* The law that established the program required that INS charge actuarially adequate premiums. It never did. Only about a quarter of the historic loss costs were covered by premiums.

*Political aspects.* All the preceding aspects came together with the introduction of pressure-group politics. For many years before the crop insurance law took effect in 1976, Costa Rica imported rice. Logically enough, local producers argued that they could produce rice for national consumption and even for export. The missing element was an adequate incentive. Insurance was part of a larger subsidy package extended to rice producers. At the same time, the local currency was overvalued to keep down the costs of the heavy imports required to produce the rice (for example, chemicals, machinery, vehicles, and fuel). Costa Rica quickly reached self-sufficiency and even produced a small exportable surplus. However, subsidy and exchange policies made self-sufficiency costly.

The beneficiary of state largess was primarily large commercial farmers, many of whom were also rice processors and wholesalers. (Only

4. Figure is from INS preliminary data for 1981.

10 percent of the insureds had less than 20 hectares.) It was this beneficiary group, frequently aided by urban consumers who benefited from the low prices, that prevented several attempts to reform the crop insurance law. The program thus became one of state policy protecting a privileged elite of large-scale farmers. The clearest evidence of this is that, in one election year, the government declared a disaster and ordered INS to pay off, despite late-season rains that saved a large part of the crop. Thus politics was coupled with economics to produce rice on large holdings and to sell it at low prices, underwritten by overt and covert (crop insurance) subsidies.

## Conclusions

The obvious mistakes of Costa Rica do not need to be repeated. Agricultural insurers must follow professional insurance practices, developing a highly diversified portfolio of agricultural and livestock risks, spread both geographically and temporally. No single crop can be allowed to dominate the portfolio. Particular attention should be paid to the correlations among the various elements of the portfolio to minimize the impact of strong positive correlations upon the aggregate reserves. Livestock, machinery, and structural risks should be included to offset the great variability of crop risks. The premiums must have a solid actuarial base, together with an effective and enforced system of underwriting and loss adjusting. Management must have some interest in protecting the reserves, not merely serving as the pay agents for public resources. The insurer must have both agricultural and insurance expertise. To this end, it is probably easier to teach insurance principles to agricultural professionals than vice versa.

Finally, and most importantly, agricultural insurers must be isolated from the political hazard implicit in a public sector program. If it is impossible to develop insurance in the private nonprofit sector (for example, a farmer's cooperative) or in the private for-profit sector (a mixed-capital venture), careful thought must be given to designing a public structure in which the farmer's overwhelming interest in collecting an indemnity is counterbalanced by other interested parties. A strong commercial reinsurance program is perhaps the best protection against agricultural insurance programs making unethical payoffs to important groups. When the reinsurance relationship disappears, one should expect the political hazard to appear. Likewise, programs that are given a blank check upon the treasury can be expected to use it; agricultural insurance must be conscious of the bottom line. This does not mean that governments should not subsidize insurers but that these subsidies be explicit within the framework of adequate premium rates, adequate underwriting and loss-adjusting criteria, and adequate reinsurance (which in itself is a vote of confidence by professional reinsurers in the soundness and integrity of the program).

Agricultural insurance in practice is not markedly different than other lines of insurance, although it is more difficult to implement. Before embarking upon an agricultural insurance project, decision makers need to give very careful thought to structuring the institution according to established insurance principles. It is equally important to carefully consider who benefits from, and who pays for, the insurance and to achieve a satisfactory resolution of any discrepancies between these two groups. Politics is always just below the surface of the technical design. It is therefore advisable to consider it explicitly at the outset, rather than to confront costly surprises in the future.

# 16

# The Financial Viability of Agricultural Insurance

Carlos Pomareda

This chapter discusses problems and approaches to the provision of low-cost agricultural insurance, beginning with an analysis (to the extent that data permit) of cost and finance considerations for several existing agricultural insurance programs.

The cost of insurance has two components: the cost of risk (the indemnities) and the administration cost. While the administration cost can be assumed to be relatively constant over time (in real terms) after the insurer has passed its pilot stage, indemnity costs can vary significantly over time. The risk, or indemnity component, of an agricultural insurance premium should be calculated from historical data. When such data are not available, yield data can be used to calculate the premiums. Alternative definitions, actuarial methods, and problems related to setting premium rates are discussed in this chapter.

Although actuarial principles and practices are a key element in agricultural insurance, the overall performance of the insurer can be strongly influenced by a comprehensive financial-management strategy. The structure of the insurance and investment portfolios and the management of reserves are important factors. The long-term financial viability of the insurer can also be determined by its access to reinsurance or to emergency government funds.

## The Cost of Agricultural Insurance

Experience throughout the world reveals that, on average, indemnities have been around 15 percent of coverage (table 16.1). This suggests that the pure risk part of the premium should have been at least that high. However, this aggregate figure varies widely between countries and crops. For some annual crops and livestock it is as low as 2 percent, and for other crops it is as high as 26 percent. The ratio is particularly low for citrus trees in Israel. In contrast, peaches and apples in the United States have some of the largest indemnity-to-coverage ratios.

An examination of the data in table 16.2 shows that indemnities account for about 93 percent of the total cost of the national programs in

TABLE 16.1 Ratio of indemnities to coverage, five national agricultural insurance programs

| Country, program, crop, and years | Indemnities as percent of coverage |
|---|---|
| *Mexico, ANAGSA* | |
| All crops, 1963–79 | 10.84 |
| *Costa Rica, INS* | |
| All crops, 1970–81 | 16.54 |
| Rice, 1970–81 | 16.24 |
| Corn, 1970–81 | 26.20 |
| *Panama, ISA* | |
| All coverage, 1977–82 | 7.18 |
| Crops, 1977–82 | 8.46 |
| Livestock, 1977–82 | 4.67 |
| *United States, FCIC* | |
| All crops, 1948–78 | 5.28 |
| Peaches, 1963–78 | 18.85 |
| Apples, 1963–78 | 13.17 |
| Potatoes, 1962–78 | 12.92 |
| Rice, 1960–78 | 1.52 |
| Wheat, 1948–78 | 6.15 |
| *Israel, IFNRA* | |
| All crops, 1967–77 | 1.77 |
| Citrus, 1967–77 | 2.47 |
| Flowers, 1961–77 | 19.20 |

*Source*: ANAGSA 1980; Arauz 1983; Arcia 1983; Velasquez 1983; FCIC 1980; IFNRA 1978.

Brazil and Costa Rica, and for 86 percent in Mexico. In the case of the United States, indemnities have been a much smaller proportion of the total cost of the program.

The administration costs include the costs of issuance, preliminary inspection, and disaster and harvest inspections. These costs depend on the number of disasters reported and whether there is partial or total damage (see Velasquez 1983). In addition, there are fixed administration costs for handling, processing, and retrieving information. Some of these costs are not fixed but vary with different approaches to assessing losses and paying indemnities.

Total administration costs for most programs have generally been relatively small. This is particularly surprising in the case of Mexico, since a large number of farmers are insured under the program. However, this may be because of the minimal supervision and evaluation provided at harvest time (Aubey and Hogan 1979; Hogan 1981). In Costa Rica, the administration costs are low because the program is concentrated on a small number of large-scale farmers and because the program has very little supervision. However, inspections may have been made with more intensity in recent years (Arauz 1983). In the United States, the administration cost

TABLE 16.2 Uses and sources of funds, seven agricultural insurance programs

| Country, program, and years | Use of funds[a] | | Source of funds[a] | |
|---|---|---|---|---|
| | Indemnities | Direct costs | Premiums paid by farmers | Government contributions |
| Mexico, ANAGSA (100 million *pesos*) | | | | |
| 1963–78 | 8.186 | 1.117 | 4.171 | 5.142 |
| Costa Rica, INS (million *colones*) | | | | |
| 1970–82 | 715.054 | 49.237 | 175.589 | 588.702 |
| Panama, ISA (million dollars) | | | | |
| 1977–82 | 1.688 | ... | 1.787 | ... |
| Brazil, PROAGRO (1,000 million *cruzeiros*) | | | | |
| 1975–80 | 22.164 | 1.427 | 6.120 | 13.879 |
| Brazil, COSESP (1,000 million *cruzeiros*) | | | | |
| 1976–80 | 471.400 | 79.900 | 346.300 | 205.000 |
| United States, FCIC (million dollars) | | | | |
| 1977 | 148.944 | 23.206 | 101.797 | 12.000[b] |
| 1978 | 47.528 | 23.635 | 93.566 | 12.000 |
| Israel, IFNRA (million pounds) | | | | |
| 1967–76 | 237.568 | 15.152 | 165.038 | 165.038 |

*Source*: ANAGSA 1980, Arauz 1983, Arcia 1983, Velasquez 1983, FCIC *Annual Report* 1979, IFNRA 1978, and chapter 14 in this volume.

[a]Amounts are accumulated in current prices over the years shown.

[b]Does not include $50 million of issued capital stock.

is very large in relation to the total cost of the program, and about 65 percent of it is due to personnel costs.

Of the insurance schemes considered in table 16.2, Panama's Agricultural Insurance Institute has probably the largest average administration cost per policy issued. It has a rather intensive supervision program and, as a result, moral hazard is minimal. Furthermore, thanks to good planning, a mixed clientele of small- and medium-sized policies, and a new computerized data-management system, ISA is lowering its average administrative costs. Arcia (1982) reported that, in 1981–82, the administrative costs were between 2 and 14 cents per dollar of coverage for crops, and between 1 and 5 cents per dollar of coverage for livestock. The average administration cost for crops and livestock were, respectively, 4.5 and 1.8 cents per dollar of coverage. Variations among items are explained by the average size of policy (in terms of coverage), the distance to the farm (which affects the cost of fuel and the number of inspections that an officer can make), the number of times that disasters are reported, and so on.

The foregoing analysis suggests that the premiums needed to cover indemnity and administration costs of all-risk crop insurance should be in the order of 20 percent. This is high compared to the cost of nonagricultural insurance. It is also sufficiently high that farmers might be unwilling to buy insurance. Aggressive marketing strategies by insurers would be necessary unless government subsidies are allowed. Such marketing would in turn increase the cost of insurance. This explains in part why private companies have not entered the agricultural insurance business.

## The Finance of Agricultural Insurance

Nearly all crop insurance schemes depend on government financial support.[1] Government contributions have taken several forms: subsidies to premiums, allowances for administration costs, and subsidized reinsurance against catastrophic disasters. Reinsurance has typically been the largest government contribution, as premiums have not been sufficient to cover catastrophic losses. The exception has been the case of Panama, where private reinsurance covered the premium deficit from its inception until 1981–82. However, in that crop year, premiums plus reinsurance were not sufficient to cover losses. The Agricultural Insurance Institute had to finance its debt with the Agricultural Development Bank of Panama.

In the earlier years (1963–67) of the Mexican program, the government contribution to premiums was 40 percent. Between 1967 and 1972, it was 52 percent. From then on until 1976, the subsidy to premiums averaged 64 percent. It began declining after 1976, and, at the time of writing, was around 50 percent (based on the author's calculations using data from Aseguradora Nacional Agrícola y Ganadera, or ANAGSA). In addition, the government also finances the administration costs of ANAGSA.

The Costa Rican rice insurance program has been very heavily subsidized. Over the last twelve years, the government has financed around 77 percent of the program. This heavy subsidy, together with low-interest credit, has allowed rice production (which accounts for over 70 percent of the insurance portfolio) to increase, in spite of rather stable prices. The benefits of the program have accrued to a small number of farmers in the area of Guanacaste (see chapter 15).

The U.S. program operated by the Federal Crop Insurance Corporation (FCIC) is a voluntary all-risk insurance program that has enjoyed significant amounts of government subsidies. The government provides appropriations for administrative expenses. In 1978 and 1979 this contribution was equal to $12 million. An important source of income in 1977 was the issuance of capital stock for $50 million. This allowed FCIC

1. There are crop insurance programs in Mauritius and Chile provided by the private sector on a commercial basis. However, they are both relatively new, and it is too soon to determine whether they will survive without government subsidies.

to finance its devastating losses, which were a record high of $148 million at that time.

The most heavily subsidized insurance program is in Japan. Between 1939 and 1980, the Japanese government has financed over 90 percent of the cost of the insurance program (see chapter 13). Part of this cost was a subsidy to premiums; on the average, the treasury paid 60 percent.

## Actuarial Principles and Premium Rate Making

Premium calculations for agricultural insurance have been discussed in the literature by Halcrow (1948), Botts and Boles (1958), Dandekar (1977), Togawa and Kada (1979), and Rustagi, Lee, and Price (1983).

If we assume that an insurance program is self-financed and that no profits are distributed, then over the long run premiums plus interest earned on temporary surplus funds must equal indemnities plus administration costs. The discussion here centers on the calculation of that part of the premium required to cover indemnities (the so-called pure premium).

In principle, those farmers with the riskiest yields should pay the largest premiums. However, calculating premiums for each farmer is not possible for practical reasons. If an average premium is calculated for a group of farmers so that each farmer in the group pays the same rate, then those farmers facing less than average risks will end up subsidizing the others. They may soon realize this and abandon the program if it is voluntary (the adverse-selection problem).

Dandekar (1977) proposed his homogeneous-area approach to solve this problem.[2] Under this scheme, the crop yield for an area is insured, and all insured farmers in the area pay the same premium and receive the same indemnity. Indemnities are paid whenever the average yield for the area falls below some critical level irrespective of the actual yields obtained by individual farmers. Premiums should then be calculated on the basis of the year-to-year variations in the average crop yield for the area. The premiums should therefore be higher in areas where the year-to-year variability is larger. Dandekar also suggested that the average annual yields be estimated through crop cutting surveys. Since these are done anyway to provide agricultural statistics, the cost of these services need not be charged to the insurer.

A particularly attractive feature of the area approach is its potential to cut administration costs, particularly those associated with farm inspection. In fact, farm inspections are not even necessary with this approach. Providing a farmer pays his premium, it is not really necessary that he actually grow the crop he has insured. Indeed, he need not even be a

2. Halcrow (1948) made a similar proposal some thirty years earlier.

farmer at all.[3] The insured would simply receive indemnities for whatever crop acreage he had paid premiums. A necessary feature of the approach is that those who are insured not have the capacity to interfere with the average yield measurements each year. This may not always be an easy thing to guarantee.

The homogeneous-area approach sounds appealing, but in practice the homogeneity condition is questionable. Small variations in ground contours can significantly affect flood damage. Also, a few days difference in planting dates can lead to important differences in the effects of drought or flood. In highland farming, a few meters difference in altitude and wind direction can make a difference to the effects of frost and hail. It seems likely that homogeneous areas may often not exist beyond the farmer's plot, in which case the likelihood of high positive-yield correlations within an area will be rather small. In contrast, Dandekar (1977, p. 7) argues for positive-yield correlations, at least in the Indian context.[4]

The use of yield data has been recommended as the best alternative when previous actuarial information is not available. This approach ignores the effect of changes in the premium rates on farmers' demand for insurance, which affects the insurance portfolio. Also, even statistically pure yield data is not without its problems for premium rate making. The major problem is that the variability of yield may be due to several factors, not all of which are related to natural hazards. For example, changes in government policies from year to year can affect the use of inputs such as fertilizers. Also, the scarcity or the high price of insecticides may limit their use for controlling diseases. Under these circumstances, it is difficult to assess the yield variability attributable to the type of disaster for which coverage is to be provided.

Farm-income variability is determined by price and yield risks, and these vary among individuals. An innovative feature of the crop insurance program in the United States is that farmers can choose among three yield and price levels when calculating their premiums and expected indemnities. As the probability of getting a larger yield and a larger price diminishes, the premium is raised as a percentage of total coverage (FCIC 1980).

## Portfolio Management of the Insurer

Agricultural insurers are financial institutions and should be managed as such. However, most agricultural insurance programs do not depend on

3. Hazell (1981) has argued that the insurer could simply sell insurance tickets, which anyone could buy through vendors, rather like lottery tickets. When an indemnity is payable, it could be announced on the radio or in newspapers, and the tickets exchanged at chosen banks or post offices.

4. See chapter 2 for an alternative view.

their financial management but on their bargaining capacity to obtain government funds. Like agricultural development banks, they usually do not exploit portfolio-management principles, nor do they have a professional interest in the generation of financial resources. In this section we consider how efficient portfolio management could help insurers generate additional financial resources, protect their portfolios, and make more efficient use of their physical and financial capacities.

The occurrence of catastrophic losses in a single year can destroy an insurer. Protection against this can be achieved by diversifying the portfolio, by carrying reserves, and by reinsuring the portfolio. The insurance portfolio comprises shares of coverage provided for different crops in different regions. Each of these options has its own mean and variance of net returns and is correlated in a particular way with other items in the portfolio. The problem confronting the insurer is the selection of portfolio shares for different crops in different regions. These shares must be chosen to provide an acceptable combination of income and risk for the total portfolio (see Arcia 1982 for a formalization of these concerns). Given an expected loss ratio, the larger the share of an item in the portfolio, the greater the danger of catastrophic loss to the insurer, and therefore the greater the need to use up reserves or reinsurance.

Table 16.3 shows the total number of insured items in some of the portfolios for which information is available. A dramatic case of portfolio

TABLE 16.3 Portfolio composition of five national agricultural insurance programs (percent of total coverage)

| Item | Israel 1967–80 | United States 1948–78 | Costa Rica 1970–80 | Panama 1982 | Japan 1980 |
|---|---|---|---|---|---|
| Citrus | 31.48 | 1.27 | | | |
| Cotton | 23.06 | 3.84 | 16.26 | | |
| Vegetables | 7.78 | | | 8.61 | |
| Corn | 3.65[a] | 28.23 | 1.20 | 11.44 | |
| Apples | 4.71 | | | | |
| Poultry | 18.29 | | | | |
| Barley | | 1.44 | | | 10.00[b] |
| Sorghum | | 1.40 | 8.86 | 8.20 | |
| Tobacco | | 26.56 | | | |
| Wheat | | 18.84 | | | |
| Rice | | | 72.37 | 37.62 | 90.00 |
| Beans | | | 1.31 | | |
| Livestock | | | | 33.66 | |
| Other | 11.03[c] | 6.74[d] | | | |

[a]Includes some other grains.
[b]Wheat and barley.
[c]Includes seventeen other crops plus broiler chickens.
[d]Includes twenty-two other crops.

concentration is that of rice in Costa Rica. Rice is grown in one region and accounts for 72 percent of the total portfolio coverage. Rice has not had the largest loss ratio, but losses have nevertheless occurred every year. Because its weight in the portfolio is so large, there is no chance that these losses can be offset by premium payments from crops that do not suffer losses in the same years. A recent study of the Costa Rican insurance program blamed this concentration on rice as one of the main reasons for the high costs of the program to the government (Academia de Centroamerica 1980). The crop insurance portfolios of Israel and the United States are more diversified.

The portfolio risk is most efficiently reduced when the insurer can diversify over contracts that have negatively correlated returns. Diversification across crops and regions sometimes provides these negative correlations, but not always. For example, in the United States, Pomareda (1981) found that, although tobacco and wheat are grown in different regions, the correlation of their loss ratios is 0.418. In contrast, in Israel, the correlations between the loss ratios of apples with that of vegetables, grains, and citrus were negative (Pomareda 1981). What is also important in portfolio diversification is the different capacities of crops to respond to weather factors during different stages of their growing cycle. Therefore, insurers should diversify among planting dates and varieties of annual crops, and among cultural practices that advance or retard fructification in the case of fruit crops. Insurers could expand these options by offering different premiums and deductibles (as a percentage of total coverage) for different cultural practices.

A recent and interesting example of the benefits and costs associated with portfolio diversification is in Panama. Sorghum was the only crop that, between the creation of the program and 1981, had an average loss ratio greater than one (it averaged 2.52). Over the same period, sorghum represented only 11.2 percent of ISA's portfolio, and the regular payment of indemnities for sorghum helped to build up an image of ISA as an insurer that pays. ISA's difficult position in 1982 was to a great extent due to the effect of drought on rice, whose coverage had been increased from 32 percent to 45 percent of the total portfolio. At the same time, the loss ratio for rice increased from a weighted average of 0.47 to 1.20.[5] A closer analysis of ISA's experience with rice reveals that the loss ratio over the last five years has increased as follows:

| Crop Year | Loss Ratio |
|---|---|
| 1978–79 | 0.08 |
| 1979–80 | 0.25 |

5. The loss ratio for rice has very low correlations with corn (0.151) and sorghum (0.547). These, after rice, are the two most important crops in the portfolio.

| Crop Year | Loss Ratio |
|---|---|
| 1980–81 | 0.41 |
| 1981–82 | 0.73 |
| 1982–83 | 1.20[6] |

The reasons underlying these figures may cast some doubt on the longer-term prospects for rice insurance in Panama.

The seasonality of agriculture in many countries creates problems for the administration of insurance. Issuance of policies and preliminary inspections are done when the rains begin, creating excessive work for the staff. Later in the year the work load declines, but the staff cannot be laid off. Insurers need to diversify their portfolios to reduce this problem. For example, the portfolio might include second-season crops, some of which could be irrigated. This is done in Panama for industrial tomatoes and onions, which are grown under irrigation when no other crop in ISA's portfolio is grown. Coverage for these crops in 1981–82 represented 8.4 percent of ISA's total coverage. Because the producers of these crops are small scale, the number of policies issued accounted for 22 percent of the total.

The seasonality of policy issuance, the length of the cropping cycle, the occurrence of partial or total disasters during the cycle of each crop, and the number and coverage of policies have important implications for the inflow and outflow of funds in the insurer's account. Exploiting the structure of this stochastic net surplus provides the key to managing the maturity composition of the investment portfolio and to managing the reserves of the insurer (Pomareda and Villalobos 1983).

Agricultural insurers, like other insurers, must derive returns from investing premium receipts. It might be that this income could allow some agricultural insurers to become self-financing. If the insurer is owned by the farmers, or if it is a mutual organization, then any surplus or end-of-year dividends could be distributed. The farmer can then visualize his premium as a form of savings, for which the net return is given by the performance of all farmers and the financial-management capacity of the insurer.

## Reinsurance of Agricultural Insurers

Reinsurance is a means of risk sharing, and it generally arises when the insurer is asked to issue coverage that it cannot prudently carry entirely at its own risk. The nature of catastrophic risks in agriculture generates a

6. Preliminary estimate.

strong need for reinsurance. Yet there is a limited market for agricultural reinsurance.

Among the possible forms of reinsurance, Hanson (1980) suggested that nonproportional reinsurance is the more appropriate type for agricultural insurers. With stop-loss reinsurance, for example, the insurer pays the total amount of all claims in a specified period (say a year), up to a total limit determined in advance for that period; the limit may be a dollar amount or a percentage of earned premium. The reinsurer pays a predetermined proportion of losses in excess of the limit for the period, subject to a predetermined maximum reinsurance benefit. With catastrophe reinsurance, the reinsurer pays the insurer a predetermined proportion of all claims (in excess of a deductible) that arise from a single catastrophic event.

A reinsurer should not demand changes in the premiums charged farmers by the insurer if the program is actuarially sound—that is, if premiums cover expected indemnities. However, this is not the case with most crop insurers, and historical loss ratios have affected the terms of reinsurance contracts. In the case of Panama, for example, between 1977 and 1981 the ratio of indemnities to coverage on sorghum averaged 14 percent, but premiums were only 5 percent.[7] When negotiating the reinsurance contract, the reinsurer would not cover sorghum unless the premium rate was raised to 14 percent.

Gilboa and Maurice (1979) claim that "the threat of catastrophic losses is the single most effective deterrent to the introduction of comprehensive crop insurance programs in developing countries." They also argue that the threat of catastrophic losses is the strongest reason for agricultural insurers to rely on reinsurance, thereby prudently avoiding a dependence on excess reserves or the need for government contributions. Although reinsurance is probably necessary for self-financed agricultural insurers, there is not yet a widespread market for this type of insurance. There are few crop insurance programs that currently have reinsurance—Mauritius, Puerto Rico, South Africa, Zimbabwe, Israel, Chile, Panama, Spain (with government subsidies)—but most have only done this for short periods, and it is not known whether the terms of the contracts are improving or deteriorating over time. Other countries that do not have commercial reinsurance have managed to receive huge amounts of government reinsurance (Japan, Canada, Sweden, Costa Rica, Mexico, and the United States). The agricultural reinsurance market may only develop when agricultural insurers are better managed.

7. The indemnity-to-coverage ratio for the five growing periods were 2.02, 16.24, 5.28, 7.76, and 27.98.

## Summary and Concluding Comments

The cost of agricultural insurance is a crucial determinant of the success of an insurance program. Administration and risk costs are both important components, and they are not independent of each other. Given the high costs of insurance and the poor financial management of most programs, it is not surprising that nearly all insurance schemes have had to rely heavily on government subsidies to help cover premiums and administration costs. Governments have also had to act as a reserve in the event of catastrophic losses. It is possibly too soon to judge whether self-financed agricultural insurance programs are feasible, but the possibilities could be increased through improvement of actuarial practices, better management of insurance and investment portfolios, a lowering of administration costs, and by gaining access to reinsurance.

# Epilogue

Peter Hazell
Carlos Pomareda
Alberto Valdés

Risk is an important consideration in agriculture. Yield and price risks induce farmers to allocate their resources conservatively. Farmers pursue more diversified cropping patterns than is socially optimal, and they are sometimes reluctant to adopt improved technologies because of the increased risks associated with their use. In many regions there is also the risk of widespread catastrophic losses because of drought, flood, hail, pest, or other natural disasters. Such catastrophes can seriously set back farm development, they can lead to difficult welfare problems for farmers and other agriculturally dependent households, and they can cause widespread defaulting on loans from agricultural development banks.

Traditionally, farmers have learned to cope with risks through various management practices. Risk can be reduced through prudent husbandry techniques and through appropriate choice of cropping patterns. Strategies such as storage, credit, and off-farm employment can also help minimize the effects of serious crop losses when they occur. Rural institutions have also evolved to help farmers manage risks. Some land-tenure systems, such as sharecropping, provide a risk-sharing device between landlord and tenant. Rural moneylenders can also help tide farmers over from poor years to good, as can kin support and extended family systems. In industrialized countries, market institutions often exist whereby agricultural risks can be spread to other sectors of the economy. These include efficient credit markets, some types of insurance, and, sometimes, commodity futures markets. Such institutions are much more rudimentary in developing countries.

These practices and institutions can reduce risks for farmers, but they never fully remove them. The question of whether governments should intervene and provide comprehensive multiple-risk crop insurance for farmers is therefore a relevant one. Many governments do this (for example, the United States, Japan, Mexico, Brazil, and Costa Rica), and on a global basis, many hundreds of millions of dollars are spent each year on the public subsidization of crop insurance schemes. Recent years have also seen a growing interest in crop insurance in developing countries in Asia and Latin America, and by international agencies such as the Food and Agricultural Organization, the United Nations Conference on Trade and

Development, and the Inter-American Institute for Cooperation on Agriculture.

In this book, we have tried to put crop insurance in perspective as one of several policy instruments for managing agricultural risks. It is a special purpose instrument—it addresses only yield risks. Therefore, it is only relevant when yield risks, and particularly the possibility of disastrous yields, are the predominant source of income variability. Even then, alternative policies may still be more effective or cheaper. For example, efficient credit markets could provide most of the same benefits to farmers as crop insurance, particularly if credit is also offered for consumption purposes and repayment can be deferred in disaster years. Small-scale farmers and landless workers may also be more effectively assisted in years of natural catastrophes through food subsidy schemes or food-for-work programs.

In theory, crop insurance is an efficient way of spreading risks among farmers, among regions, across sectors of the economy, and over time. Expectations of its benefits include improved farm resource allocation and higher farm incomes, larger national supplies of important food crops, and the improved performance of agricultural development banks. In developing countries, expectations that crop insurance enhances technological innovation are particularly prevalent. Multiple-risk crop insurance is also often perceived as being one of the few politically and administratively feasible ways of selectively assisting rural families in times of distress. Also, unlike many other government relief programs, the compensation provided is a purchased right of the insured. It is not a government handout and there is less uncertainty attached to its dispensation.

Crop insurance has also proved attractive to agricultural development banks, particularly when it is tied to farm credit on a compulsory basis. In the event of an insured disaster, the indemnity is paid directly to the bank to cancel the farmer's debt. From the bank's point of view, this is an effective way to reduce loan defaults and thus protect its capital assets. The farmer, however, often perceives insurance as another cost attached to the loan; the insurance premium is simply added to the interest rate.

In practice, multiple-risk crop insurance has proved disappointing, and it has fulfilled few of its supposed objectives. A key factor is that the administration costs are generally too high relative to the benefits in risk reduction that farmers or banks receive. Typically, these costs average about 6 percent of the value of coverage, which is very high compared to normal administration costs for life insurance of about 1 to 1.5 percent. Given also that an actuarially fair premium for all-risk crop insurance is generally between 5 and 15 percent, then farmers would have to pay premiums of between 10 and 20 percent if insurance is to be self-financing. At this cost, it is not surprising that farmers have proved unwilling to purchase all-risk crop insurance voluntarily. It should also be remembered that crop insurance only covers part of the yield risks, and it makes no contribution at all toward reducing many of the other price, resource, and health risks confronting a farmer. In many cases, these other types of risk are much more important in destabilizing farm income.

The cost of multiple-risk crop insurance tends to be particularly high in developing countries. Large numbers of small farms and a wide diversity of agricultural practices greatly adds to administration and inspection costs. Poor data on actuarial risks and a lack of skilled personnel also hamper the writing and enforcement of sound contracts.

More generally, multiple-risk crop insurance is expensive because of moral hazard problems. Moral hazard arises when farmers fail to take reasonable precautions against crop losses because they can rely on yield compensation from the insurer. For example, farmers may fail to protect insured crops with adequate amounts of pesticides. They may even decide to use less fertilizer and other inputs that affect yield. These actions increase the risk confronting the insurer, and they do so in a way that is not usually allowed for in the actuarial calculations upon which the premium is based. As a result, the insurer must either incur higher administration costs by undertaking more frequent inspections of farm practices or risk unfavorable loss ratios (the ratio of indemnities to premiums). Either way, the insurer will eventually have to increase the average premium rate charged.

To make multiple-risk crop insurance viable, many governments have been willing to subsidize it. Of the larger schemes, public subsidies range from a low of 25 percent of indemnities in the United States, to 50 and 80 percent, respectively, of total payments in Brazil and Mexico. Subsidies of these magnitudes cannot be justified on purely economic grounds. Analyses of the Mexican and Japanese crop insurance programs show that there is a substantial net social loss from the subsidies. Given that such subsidies could be diverted to more productive public investments, publicly supported crop insurance programs are likely to be quite costly for most developing countries. The problem is aggravated by the scarcity of skilled manpower in such countries and the cost of its diversion to insurance activities.

That governments do subsidize crop insurance suggests other objectives than narrowly economic ones. Crop insurance provides relief to rural families in times of need. Several governments also use crop insurance subsidies as a means to transfer income to farmers. Both welfare objectives are faulted by the observation that crop insurance mostly benefits the larger-scale and more prosperous farmers, particularly when it is tied to agricultural credit. More carefully targeted relief measures, such as food for work, might prove more cost effective in attaining welfare goals.

Governments have also facilitated multiple-risk crop insurance through legislation that makes it compulsory and by providing reinsurance. But even when it is heavily subsidized, many farmers are unwilling to purchase multiple-risk crop insurance on a voluntary basis. These are often the lower-risk farmers who have less need for insurance or are unwilling to pay premiums based on average risk levels. If these farmers do not purchase insurance, then the insurer must charge higher premium rates, thereby making insurance unattractive for other farmers, too. Compulsory insurance solves this problem of adverse selection, but it effectively means that lower-risk farmers subsidize higher-risk farmers. A better alternative is to tailor premium rates to individual farm risks, but this is rarely feasible given existing data and would be very costly to administer.

Government-provided reinsurance may be essential in the early stages of development of an insurance program if it is to survive major catastrophes or a run of bad years. However, government reinsurance often introduces a moral hazard problem with the insurer. As long as the government is committed to making up any shortfalls in indemnity payments, there is little incentive for the insurer to pursue sound portfolio management or to rigorously inspect crop damage.

Overall, the findings in this book are not encouraging for crop insurance, and governments would be well advised to look carefully before embarking on large and costly multiple-risk crop insurance programs. Some lessons emerge, though, as to how crop insurance might be made more cost effective in assisting farmers.

Insured risks should be restricted to natural hazards such as hail, flood, and hurricane damage. Such risks avoid the problem of moral hazard, and they can be easily monitored and the damage assessed at reasonable cost. Much of the data necessary for actuarial calculations is also often available from local weather stations, and the risks can be evaluated at a regional level rather than the farm level. However, the Japanese experience suggests that indemnity payments must still be tailored to losses at the farm rather than the regional level.

The administrative costs of crop insurance can also be reduced through better management. Most programs are not managed efficiently, either in allocating personnel and physical resources or in selecting the insurance portfolio and managing financial reserves. These inefficiencies are in large part a result of the blanket guarantee for financial solvency provided by governments to public insurers. Mixed-capital ventures or farmer-owned cooperatives might offer more viable institutional alternatives to public programs. Governments should also seek to transfer their reinsurance functions to the international insurance market once insurance programs are well established. However, the managerial discipline that this can invoke should not be impeded by excessive government regulations on the insurance portfolio or by continued easy access to public funds when serious losses occur.

Administrative costs might also be reduced through new approaches to crop insurance. Insurance based on homogeneous areas rather than on individual farms has not fared well, but logical extensions to the area approach, such as regional hail or rainfall lotteries, have yet to be explored. Schemes of these kinds could be very cost effective, but they would obviously be far less effective in matching indemnities to the needs of individual farmers. Nevertheless, they might provide a satisfactory degree of covariation between indemnities and income shortfalls for a large part of the rural populace. However, such insurance should not be compulsory.

Finally, there is considerable scope for the development of other types of risk-specific insurance for farmers in developing countries. These might include accident and life insurance, theft insurance for livestock and machines, fire insurance for buildings, and so forth. These types of insurance are best provided by the private sector, but government has a key role to play in improving the policy and legislative climate for the development of such private contracts.

# Bibliography

Academia de Centroamérica. 1980. "El Seguro de Cosechas en Costa Rica: Evaluación y Propuesta de Reforma." San Jose, Costa Rica: IICA.

Adams, D. W., G. Douglas, and J. D. Von Pischke. 1984. *Undermining Rural Development with Cheap Credit.* Boulder, Colo.: Westview Press.

*Agricultural Finance Review.* Various issues. Washington, D.C.: U.S. Department of Agriculture.

Ahsan, Syed M. 1981. "Public Crop Insurance for Developing Countries: The Lessons from the Japanese Experiment." In *The Rural Challenge*, edited by Margot A. Bellamy and Bruce L. Greenshields. Hampshire, England: Gower.

Alvarado, M., T. S. Walker, and H. E. Amaya. 1979. "Comparación de las Recomendaciones de Parcelas Demonstrativas de Maíz y Frijol con la Tecnología Utilizada por los Agricultores de las Regiones Occidental y Oriental de El Salvador." Miscellaneous paper. San Andres, El Salvador: CENTA.

ANAGSA. 1980. Información Estadística, Departamento de Operación Agrícola, Sección de Programación. Mexico, D.F.: ANAGSA.

Anderson, Jock R., J. L. Dillon, and J. B. Hardaker. 1977. *Agricultural Decision Analysis.* Ames, Iowa: Iowa State University Press.

Arauz, G. 1983. "Aspectos Economicós Financieros Vinculados con el Seguro Agrícola en Costa Rica." Paper presented at ALIDE/IICA Latin American Seminar on Agricultural Credit and Insurance, Panama, January 31 to February 3, 1983.

Arcia, G. 1982. *El Seguro Agropecuario en Panama.* San Jose, Costa Rica: IICA Agricultural Credit Insurance Project.

———. 1983. *El Proyecto Agropecuario en Panama.* San Jose, Costa Rica: IICA Agricultural Credit Insurance Project.

Arrow, K. J. 1962. "Economic Welfare and the Allocation of Resources for Invention." In *The Rate and Direction of Inventive Activity: Economic and Social Factors*, National Bureau of Economic Research. Princeton: Princeton University Press.

———. 1963. "Uncertainty and the Welfare Economics of Medical Care." *American Economic Review* 53:941–73.

———. 1974. "Limited Knowledge and Economic Analysis." *American Economic Review* 64:1–10.

Arrow, Kenneth J., and Robert C. Lind. 1970. "Uncertainty and the Evaluation of Public Investment Decisions." *American Economic Review* 60:364–78.

——. 1972. "Reply." *American Economic Review* 62:171–72.

Aubey, R., and A. J. Hogan. 1979. "Mexican Crop Insurance: A Research Report on Financial Aspects." San Jose, Costa Rica: IICA Agricultural Credit Insurance Project.

Baker, C. B. 1974. "An Economic Alternative to Concessional Farm Interest Rates." *Australian Journal of Agricultural Economics* 18:171–92.

Banco de Desarrollo Agropecuario de Panama. *Memoria Annual.* Various issues. Panama.

Barah, B. C., and Hans P. Binswanger. 1982. "Regional Effects of National Stabilization Policies: The Case of India." Progress Report 37, ICRISAT Economics Program. Patancheru, India: ICRISAT.

Barber, Lloyd E., and Philip J. Thair. 1950. "Institutional Methods of Meeting Weather Uncertainty in the Great Plains." *Journal of Farm Economics* 32:391–410.

Bassoco, L. M., and R. D. Norton. 1983. "A Quantitative Framework for Agricultural Policies." In Roger D. Norton and Leopoldo M. Solís, 1983.

Bassoco, Luz María, and Teresa Rendon. 1973. "The Technology Set and Data Base for CHAC." In *Multi-Level Planning: Case Studies in Mexico*, edited by Louis M. Goreux and Alan S. Manne. Amsterdam: North-Holland.

Baumol, W. J. 1963. "An Expected Gain-Confidence Limit Criterion for Portfolio Selection." *Management Science* 10:174–82.

Beeson, Bennie E. 1971. "Management of Insurable Risk by East Tennessee Tobacco Farmers." Ph.D. diss., University of Tennessee.

Behrman, J. R. 1968. *Supply Response in Underdeveloped Agriculture.* Amsterdam: North-Holland.

Benedict, Murray R. 1953. *Farm Policies of the United States, 1950–1970: A Study of their Origins and Development.* New York: Twentieth Century Fund.

Benito, Carlos. 1976. "Peasants' Response to Modernization Projects in Minifundia Economies." *American Journal of Agricultural Economics* 58:143–51.

Bhatnagar, V. S., and J. C. Davies. 1981. "Pest Management in Intercrop Subsistence Farming." *Proceedings of the International Workshop on Intercropping, Hyderabad, India, January 10–13, 1979.* Patancheru, India: ICRISAT.

Binswanger, H. P. 1980. "Attitudes Toward Risk: Experimental Measurement in Rural India." *American Journal of Agricultural Economics* 62:174–82.

Binswanger, Hans P., and Mark S. Rosenzweig, eds. 1984. *Contractual Arrangements, Employment and Wages in Rural Labor Markets in Asia.* New Haven: Yale University Press.

Binswanger, Hans P., and James G. Ryan. 1977. "Efficiency and Equity Issues in Ex Ante Allocation of Research Resources." *Indian Journal of Agricultural Economics* 32:217–31.

Binswanger, Hans P., and Donald A. Sillers. 1983. "Risk Aversion and Credit Constraints in Farmers' Decision Making: A Reinterpretation." *Journal of Development Studies* 20:5–21.

Bliss, C. J. 1979. "Risk Bearing in Indian Agriculture." *In Risk, Uncertainty and Agricultural Development*, edited by J. A. Roumasset, J. M. Boussard, and I. Singh. Laguna, Philippines: Southeast Asian Regional Center for Graduate Study in Agriculture and the Agricultural Development Council.

Botts, Ralph R., and James N. Boles. 1958. "Use of Normal-Curve Theory in Crop Insurance Ratemaking." *Journal of Farm Economics* 40:733–40.

Brainard, William C., and Richard N. Cooper. 1968. "Uncertainty and Diversification in International Trade." *Food Research Institute Studies* 8:257–85.

Bray, Norman R. 1963. "Performance of Federal Crop Insurance in Western Nebraska." Master's thesis, University of Nebraska.

Browning, D. 1971. *El Salvador: Landscape and Society.* London: Oxford University Press.

Campbell Committee. 1981. *Report of the Committee of Inquiry into the Australian Financial System.* Canberra: Australian Government Publishing Service.

Carter, H. O., and G. W. Dean. 1960. "Income, Price, and Yield Variability." *Hilgardia* 30:175–218.

Charnes, A., and W. W. Cooper. 1963. "Deterministic Equivalents for Optimizing and Satisficing Under Chance Constraints." *Operations Research* 11:18–39.

Clendenin, J. C. 1942. "Federal Crop Insurance in Operation." *Wheat Studies of the Food Research Institute* 18:228–90.

Collinson, M. P. 1972. *Farm Management in Peasant Agriculture.* London: Praeger.

Colmenares, J. H. 1975. "Adoption of Hybrid Seeds and Fertilizers Among Colombian Corn Growers." Mexico, D.F.: CIMMYT.

Corden, W. M. 1974. *Trade Policy and Economic Welfare.* Oxford University Press.

Cutie, J. 1975. "Diffusion of Hybrid Corn Technology: The Case of El Salvador." Ph.D. diss., University of Wisconsin.

Dandekar, V. M. 1977. "Crop Insurance for Developing Countries." Teaching and Research Forum 10. New York: Agricultural Development Council.

Delvo, Herman W., and L. D. Loftsgard. 1967. *All-Risk Crop Insurance in North Dakota.* Bulletin 468. Fargo: Department of Agricultural Economics, North Dakota State University.

Demsetz, H. 1969. "Information and Efficiency: Another Viewpoint." *Journal of Law and Economics* 12:1–22.

Diaz, H. 1974. "An Institutional Analysis of a Rural Development Project: The Case of Puebla Project in Mexico." Ph.D. diss., University of Wisconsin.

Dillon, John L., and Pasquale L. Scandizzo. 1978. "Risk Attitudes of Subsistence Farmers in Northeast Brazil: A Sampling Approach." *American Journal of Agricultural Economics* 60:425–35.

Duloy, John H., and Roger D. Norton. 1973. "CHAC: A Programming Model of Mexican Agriculture." In *Multi-Level Planning: Case Studies in Mexico*, edited by Louis M. Goreux and Alan S. Manne. Amsterdam: North-Holland.

———. 1975. "Prices and Incomes in Linear Programming Models." *American Journal of Agricultural Economics* 57:591–600. Reprinted with extensions in Norton and Solís 1983.

Durham, William H. 1979. *Scarcity and Survival in Central America: Ecological Origins of the Soccer War.* Stanford: Stanford University Press.

El Salvador, Directorate General of Statistics and the Census. 1974. *Third Na-*

*tional Agricultural and Livestock Census 1971*, vols. 1 and 2. San Salvador: Government of El Salvador.

Farm Credit Administration. 1978. *Agricultural Situation Report*, May 8. Washington, D.C.: U.S. Department of Agriculture.

———. 1980. *The New All-Risk Crop Insurance Program—The Farmer's Silent Partner.* Washington, D.C.: U.S. Department of Agriculture.

———. *Annual Report.* Various issues. Washington, D.C.: U.S. Department of Agriculture.

Federal Crop Insurance Corporation Task Force. 1970. *A Study of the Federal Crop Insurance Corporation.* Washington, D.C.: U.S. Department of Agriculture.

Galbis, V. 1981. "Manejo de las Tasas de Interes." *Monetaria* 4:263–302.

Gardner, Bruce L. 1979. *Optimal Stockpiling of Grain.* Lexington, Mass.: Lexington Books.

Gerhart, J. 1975. "The Diffusion of Hybrid Maize in Western Kenya." Ph.D. diss., Princeton University.

Gilboa, D., and N. Maurice. 1979. "The Reinsurance of Comprehensive Crop Insurance Programs." Paper presented at FAO, October 1979, Rome, Italy.

Gladwin, C. H. 1977. "A Model of Farmers' Decisions to Adopt the Recommendation of Plan Puebla." Ph.D. diss., Stanford University.

Goldberger, Arthur S. 1964. *Econometric Theory.* New York: John Wiley and Sons.

Green, Roy M. 1938. "An Evaluation of Crop Insurance Possibilities." *Journal of Farm Economics* 20:214–20.

Griliches, Z. 1957. "Hybrid Corn: An Exploration in the Economics of Technological Change." *Econometrica* 25:501–22.

Grisley, William. 1980. "Effect of Risk and Risk Aversion on Farm Decisionmaking: Farmers in Northern Thailand." Ph.D. diss., University of Illinois.

Guillet, David. 1981. "Surplus Extraction, Risk Management and Economic Change Among Peruvian Peasants." *Journal of Development Studies* 18:3–24.

Gustafson, R. L. 1958. "Carry Levels for Grains: A Method for Determining Amounts that Are Optimal under Specified Conditions." Technical Bulletin 1178. Washington, D.C.: U.S. Department of Agriculture.

Halcrow, Harold G. 1948. "The Theory of Crop Insurance." Ph.D. diss., University of Chicago.

———. 1949. "Actuarial Structures for Crop Insurance." *Journal of Farm Economics* 31:418–43.

Hanson Inc. 1980. "Review of ISA's Crop Credit Insurance Program." Washington, D.C.: IICA Agricultural Credit Insurance Project.

Haswell, M. R. 1973. *Tropical Farming Economics.* London: Orient Longman.

Hazell, Peter B. R. 1971. "A Linear Alternative to Quadratic and Semivariance Programming for Farm Planning Under Uncertainty." *American Journal of Agricultural Economics* 53:53–62.

———. 1981. "Crop Insurance—A Time for Reappraisal." *IFPRI Report* 3:1–4.

———. 1982. "Application of Risk Preference Estimates in Farm-Household and Agricultural Sector Models." *American Journal of Agricultural Economics* 64:384–90.

Hazell, P. B. R., R. D. Norton, M. Parthasarathy, and C. Pomareda. 1983. "The Importance of Risk in Agricultural Planning Models." In Norton and Solís, 1983.

Hazell, P. B. R., and P. L. Scandizzo. 1974. "Competitive Demand Structures Under Risk in Agricultural Linear Programming Models." *American Journal of Agricultural Economics* 56:235–44. Reprinted with extensions in Norton and Solís 1983.

Heckman, J. 1974. "Shadow Prices, Market Wages, and Labor Supply." *Econometrica* 42:679–94.

Heisig, Carl P. 1946. "Income Stability in High-Risk Farming Areas." *Journal of Farm Economics* 28:961–72.

Hoffman, G. Wright. 1925. "Crop Insurance—Its Recent Accomplishments and Its Possibilities." *American Academy of Political and Social Science Annals* 117:94–120.

Hogan, A. J. 1981. "The Role of Crop Credit Insurance in the Agricultural Credit System in Developing Economies." Ph.D. diss., University of Wisconsin.

Hogan, A. J., J. G. Morris, and H. E. Thompson. 1981. "Decision Problems under Risk of Chance Contrained Programming: Dilemmas in the Transition." *Management Science* 27:698–716.

ICRISAT. 1980. *Annual Report 1979/80.* Patancheru, India: ICRISAT.

———. 1981. *Proceedings of the International Workshop on Intercropping, Hyderabad, India, January 10–13, 1979.* Patancheru, India: ICRISAT.

IFNRA. 1978. "A Description of IFNRA." Tel Aviv: Insurance Fund for Natural Risks in Agriculture Ltd.

Industries Assistance Commission. 1978. *Report on Rural Income Fluctuations.* Canberra: IAC.

Jabara, Cathy L., and Robert L. Thompson. 1980. "Agricultural Comparative Advantage Under International Price Uncertainty." *American Journal of Agricultural Economics* 62:188–98.

Jessup, Paul F. 1980. *Modern Bank Management.* St. Paul: West.

Jodha, N. S. 1975. "Famine and Famine Policies: Some Empirical Evidence." *Economic and Political Weekly* 10:1609–23.

———. 1978. "Effectiveness of Farmers' Adjustments to Risk." *Economic and Political Weekly (Review of Agriculture)* 13(25):A38–A48.

———. 1981a. "Agricultural Tenancy: Fresh Evidence from Dryland Areas in India." *Economic and Political Weekly (Review of Agriculture)* 16:A118–A128.

———. 1981b. "Role of Credit in Farmers' Adjustment Against Risk in Arid and Semi-Arid Tropical Areas of India." *Economic and Political Weekly* 16:1696–1709.

———. 1981c. "Yield Stability and Economics of Intercropping in Traditional Farming Systems." *Proceedings of the International Workshop on Intercropping, Hyderabad, India, January 10–13, 1979.* Patancheru, India: ICRISAT.

———. 1982. "A Study of Traditional Farming Systems in Selected Villages of Tanzania." *ICRISAT Economics Program Progress Report.* Patancheru, India: ICRISAT.

Jodha, N. S., M. Asokan, and J. G. Ryan. 1977. "Village Study Methodology and

Resource Endowments of the Selected Villages." ICRISAT Economics Program Occasional Paper 16. Patancheru, India: ICRISAT.

Johnson, D. Gale. 1947. *Forward Prices for Agriculture.* Chicago: University of Chicago Press.

Jones, Lawrence A., and Donald K. Larson. 1965. *Economic Impact of Federal Crop Insurance in Selected Areas of Virginia and Montana.* Agricultural Economic Report no. 75. Washington, D.C.: U.S. Department of Agriculture.

Just, Richard E. 1975. "Risk Response Models and Their Use in Agricultural Policy Evaluation." *American Journal of Agricultural Economics* 57:836–43.

Kent, M. A., and A. G. Lloyd. 1983. "Coping with Rural Income Instability: Some Estimates of Probability of Default Under Various Loan Repayment Arrangements." Paper presented at Annual Conference of Australian Agricultural Economics Society, Brisbane, February 1983.

King, Robert, and George Oamek. 1981. "Federal All-Risk Crop Insurance and Disaster Assistance as Risk Management Tools for Colorado Dryland Wheat Farmers." Paper presented at Western Agricultural Economics Association Annual Meeting, Lincoln, Nebraska, July 1981.

Knight, F. H. 1921. *Risk, Uncertainty and Profit.* Boston: Houghton Mifflin.

Kramer, Randall A., and Rulon D. Pope. 1982. "Crop Insurance for Managing Risk." *Journal of the American Society of Farm Managers and Rural Appraisers* 46:34–40.

Lee, Ivan M. 1953. "Temperature Insurance—An Alternative to Frost Insurance in Citrus." *Journal of Farm Economics* 35:15–28.

Lipton, Michael. 1979. "Agricultural Risk, Rural Credit, and the Efficiency of Inequality." In *Risk, Uncertainty and Agricultural Development*, edited by James A. Roumasset, Jean-Marc Boussard, and Inderjit Singh. Laguna, Philippines, and New York: Southeast Asian Regional Center for Graduate Study and Research in Agriculture and the Agricultural Development Council.

Lloyd, A. G. 1977. "Farm Income Stabilisation—Some Options." Paper presented at Annual Conference of Australian Agricultural Economics Society, Brisbane, February 1977.

Loftsgard, Laurel D. 1967. "Attitudinal Reactions to the FCIC Program." In *Crop Insurance in the Great Plains.* Bozeman: Montana Agricultural Experiment Station Bulletin 617.

Maddala, G. S. 1977. *Econometrics.* Tokyo: McGraw-Hill Kogakusha.

Mann, Charles K. 1977. "Packages of Practices: A Step at a Time With Cluster?" Paper presented at American Agricultural Economics Association Meeting, San Diego, July 31 to August 3, 1977.

Markowitz, Harry M. 1959. *Portfolio Selection—Efficient Diversification of Investments.* Cowles Foundation Monograph 16. New Haven: Yale University Press.

Massell, Benton F. 1969. "Price Stabilization and Welfare." *Quarterly Journal of Economics* 83:284–98.

Mayet, P. 1893. *Agricultural Insurance in Organic Connection with Savings-Banks, Land-Credit, and the Computation of Debts.* London: Swan Sonnenschein.

Mexico, Ministry of the Presidency. 1973. *Lineamientos de la Politica Economica y Social del Sector Agropecuario* (December). Reprinted in English in Norton and Solis 1983.

Miller, Thomas A., and Warren L. Trock. 1979. *Disaster Assistance to Farmers—Needs, Issues and Programs.* Great Plains Agricultural Council Publication 88. Fort Collins: Colorado State University.

Miller, Thomas S., and Alan S. Walter. 1977. "An Assessment of Government Programs that Protect Agricultural Producers from Natural Risks." *Agricultural Food Policy Review* 1:93–103.

Mishan, E. J. 1975. "The Folklore of the Market: An Inquiry into the Economic Doctrines of the Chicago School." *Journal of Economic Issues* 9:681–752.

Moscardi, B. R. 1976. "A Behavioral Model for Decision Making Under Risk Among Small-Holding Farmers." Ph.D. diss., University of California.

Myrick, Dana H. 1970. *All Risk Crop Insurance: Principles, Problems, and Potentials.* Montana Agricultural Experiment Station Bulletin 640. Bozeman: MAES.

Navarro, L. A. 1977. "Dealing with Risk and Uncertainty in Crop Production: A Lesson From Small Farmers." Paper presented at Symposium on Risk and Uncertainty in Decision Processes of Small Farmers in Less Developed Countries, AAEA-WALA Joint Annual Meeting, San Diego, July 1977.

Nerlove, Marc. 1958. *Distributed Lags and Demand Analysis for Agricultural and Other Commodities.* Washington, D.C.: Agricultural Marketing Service, U.S. Department of Agriculture.

Newbery, D. M. G. 1975. "Tenurial Obstacles to Innovation." *Journal of Development Studies* 11:263–77.

Newbery, D. M. G., and J. E. Stiglitz. 1979. "Sharecropping, Risk Sharing, and the Importance of Imperfect Information." *In Risk, Uncertainty and Agricultural Development*, edited by J. A. Roumasset, J. M. Boussard, and I. Singh. Laguna, Philippines: Southeast Asian Regional Center for Graduate Study in Agriculture and the Agricultural Development Council.

———. 1981. *The Theory of Commodity Price Stabilization: A Study in the Economics of Risk.* Oxford: Clarendon.

Norman, D. W. 1974. "Rationalising Mixed Cropping Under Indigenous Conditions: The Example of Northern Nigeria." *Journal of Development Studies* 11:3–21.

Norton, Roger D., and M. Leopoldo Solís. 1983. *The Book of CHAC: Programming Studies for Mexican Agriculture.* Baltimore: Johns Hopkins University Press.

Oi, W. 1961. "The Desirability of Price Instability Under Perfect Competition," *Econometrica* 29:58–64.

O'Mara, G. T. 1971. "A Decision Theoretic View of the Microeconomics of Technique Diffusion." Ph.D. diss., Stanford University.

Ootsuka, K., and Y. Hayami. 1982. "Social Costs of Rice Policy in Japan." Paper presented at the Second Western Pacific Food Trade Workshop, Jakarta, Indonesia.

Papendick, R. K., P. A. Sanchez, and G. B. Triplett. 1976. *Multiple Cropping.* Madison, Wis.: American Society of Agronomy.

Pasour, E. C., and J. Bruce Bullock. 1975. "Implications of Uncertainty for the

Measurement of Efficiency." *American Journal of Agricultural Economics* 57:335–39.

Pauly, Mark V. 1968. "The Economics of Moral Hazard: Comment." *American Economic Review* 58:531–37.

Pearce, I. 1975. "Resource Conservation and the Market Mechanism." In *The Econometrics of Natural Resource Depletion*, edited by D. W. Pearce and J. Rose. New York: Macmillan.

Peck, Anne E. 1977. "Implications of Private Storage of Grains for Buffer Stock Schemes to Stabilize Prices." *Food Research Institute Studies* 16:125–40.

Pengra, Ray F. 1947. "Crop Production in the Semi-Arid Regions on Insurable Risk." *Journal of Farm Economics* 29:567–70.

Perrin, Richard, and Don Winkelmann. 1976. "Impediments to Technical Progress on Small Versus Large Farms." *American Journal of Agricultural Economics* 58:888–94.

Pomareda, C. 1981. "Portfolio Composition and Financial Performance of Agricultural Insurers." AGROCRED 14. San Jose, Costa Rica: IICA Agricultural Credit Insurance Project.

———. 1984. "Financial Policies and Management in the Growth of Agricultural Development Banks." Boulder, Colo.: Westview.

Pomareda, C., and A. Villalobos. 1983. "Seasonality of Agriculture and Implications for Management of the Insurance and Investment Portfolio of an Agricultural Insurer." San Jose, Costa Rica: IICA Agricultural Credit Insurance Project.

Pope, Rulon D., and Richard Prescott. 1980. "Diversification in Relation to Farm Size and Other Socioeconomic Characteristics." *American Journal of Agricultural Economics* 62:554–59.

Pratt, J. M. 1964. "Risk Aversion in the Small and in the Large." *Econometrica* 32:122–36.

Quiggin, John C., and Jock R. Anderson. 1981. "Price Bands and Buffer Funds." *Economic Record* 57:67–73.

Rao, R., and R. W. Willey. 1980. "Evaluation of Yield Stability in Intercropping Studies on Sorghum Pigeonpea." *Experimental Agriculture* 16:105–16.

Ray, P. K. 1967. *Agricultural Insurance: Theory and Practice and Application to Developing Countries.* Oxford: Pergamon.

Rodewald, Gordon E. 1960. "Farmers' Attitudes Toward and Evaluation and Use of Insurance for Income Protection on Montana Wheat Farms." Master's thesis, Montana State University.

Rodriguez, R., M. Alvarado, and H. E. Amaya. 1978. "Estudio Agrosocioeconomico de Pequenos Agricultores en La Zona Oriental." Paper presented at SIADES Conference, San Salvador, February 1978.

Rothschild, Michael, and Joseph Stiglitz. 1976. "Equilibrium in Competitive Insurance Markets: An Essay on the Economics of Imperfect Information." *Quarterly Journal of Economics* 90:629–49.

Roumasset, James A. 1976. *Rice and Risk: Decision Making Among Low-Income Farmers.* Amsterdam: North-Holland.

———. 1978. "The Case Against Crop Insurance in Developing Countries." *Philippine Review of Business and Economics*, March:87–107.

Rowe, William H., and Leroy K. Smith. 1940. "Crop Insurance." *Yearbook of Agriculture.* Washington, D.C.: U.S. Department of Agriculture.

Rustagi, N. K., W. F. Lee, and E. C. Price. 1983. "Crop Insurance Premium Determination—The Indian Case." Paper presented at Special Seminar, IRRI, Los Banos, Philippines, March 1983.

Ruthenberg, Hans. 1976. *Farming Systems in the Tropics.* 2d ed. Oxford: Clarendon.

Ryan, J. G. 1972. "A Generalized Crop-Fertilizer Production Function." Ph.D. diss., North Carolina State University.

Samuelson, P. A. 1952. "Spatial Price Equilibrium and Linear Programming." *American Economic Review* 42:283-303.

Sanderson, Fred H. 1943. "A Specific-Risk Scheme for Wheat Crop Insurance." *Journal of Farm Economics* 25:759-76.

Schultz, Theodore W. 1979. "The Economics of Research and Agricultural Productivity." IADS Occasional Paper. New York: IADS.

Shipley, John. 1967. "Role of Federal Crop Insurance in a Changing Agriculture." *Crop Insurance in the Great Plains.* Montana Agricultural Experiment Station Bulletin 617. Bozeman: MAES.

Sillers, Donald A. 1980. "Measuring Risk Preferences of Rice Farmers in Nueva Ecija, Philippines: An Experimental Approach." Ph.D. diss., Yale University.

Singh, R. P., and T. S. Walker. 1982. *Determinants and Implications of Crop Failure in the Semi-Arid Tropics of India.* ICRISAT Economics Progress Report 40. Patancheru, India: ICRISAT.

Sistema Alimentario Mexicano. 1979. *Notas Analíticas y Lineamientos Metodológicos para el Proyecto Sistema Alimentario Mexicano.* Mexico, D.F.: Oficina de Asesores del C. Presidente.

Sistema Alimentario Mexicano/IFPRI. 1982. *Consideraciones Económicas en Relación con las Políticas del SAM de Aseguramiento Agrícola y Riesgo Compartido.* Mexico, D.F.: SAM.

Starr, Gayle David. 1963. "The Federal Crop Insurance Program in Eastern Nebraska: Saunders County, A Case Study." Master's thesis, University of Nebraska.

Stigler, G. J. 1967. "Imperfections in the Capital Market." *Journal of Political Economy* 75:287-92.

Stiglitz, Joseph E., and Andrew Weiss. 1981. "Credit Rationing in Markets with Imperfect Information." *American Economic Review* 71:393-410.

Togawa, T., and R. Kada. 1979. *Actuarial Method in Crop Insurance Through the Experience of Japan.* Bangkok, Thailand: FAO Regional Office for Asia and the Far East.

Tsujii, Hiroshi. 1982. "Comparison of Rice Policies Between Thailand, Taiwan, and Japan: An Evolutional Model and Current Policies." In *A Comparative Study of Food Policy in Rice Countries—Taiwan, Thailand, and Japan*, edited by Hiroshi Tsujii. Kyoto, Japan: Kyoto University.

Turnovsky, Stephen J. 1978. "The Distribution of Welfare Gains from Price Stabilization." In *Stabilizing World Commodity Markets: Analysis, Practice and Policy*, edited by Gerard Adams and Sonia A. Klein. Lexington, Mass.: Lexington Books.

U.S. Congress. 1923. Senate Select Committee on Investigation of Crop Insurance. *Investigation of Crop Insurance.* Hearings, 67th Cong., 4th sess.

U.S. General Accounting Office. 1976. *Alleviating Agricultural Producers' Crop Losses: What Should the Federal Role Be?* Washington, D.C.: GAO.

———. 1977. *The Federal Crop Insurance Program Can Be Made More Effective.* Washington, D.C.: GAO.

———. 1981. *Analysis of Certain Operations of the Federal Crop Insurance Corporation.* Washington, D.C.: GAO.

Valgren, V. N. 1922. *Crop Insurance: Risks, Losses, and Principles of Protection.* USDA Bulletin 1043. Washington, D.C.: U.S. Department of Agriculture.

Velasquez, V. 1983. Diseno Institucional, Manejo Financiero y Viabilidad del Seguro Agropecuario. Paper presented at ALIDE/IICA Latin American Seminar on Agricultural Credit and Insurance, Panama, January 31 to February 3.

Villa Issa, M. 1976. "The Effect of the Labor Market in the Adoption of New Production Technology in a Rural Development Project: The Case of Plan Puebla, Mexico." Ph.D. diss., Purdue University.

Vincent, D. P. 1976. "Economic Aspects of Farm Poverty." *Australian Journal of Agricultural Economics* 20:103–18.

Virmani, Arvind. 1981. *The Nature of Credit Markets in Less Developed Countries: A Framework for Policy Analysis.* Domestic Finance Study 71. Washington, D.C.: Development Economics Department, World Bank.

Walker, Thomas Steven. 1980. "Decision Making by Farmers and by the National Agricultural Research Program on the Adoption and Development of Maize Varieties in El Salvador." Ph.D. diss., Stanford University.

———. 1981. "Risk and Adoption of Hybrid Maize in El Salvador." *Food Research Institute Studies* 18:59–88.

Walker, T. S., R. P. Singh, and N. S. Jodha. 1983. *Dimensions of Farm-Level Diversification in the Semi-Arid Tropics of Rural South India.* ICRISAT Economic Program Progress Report 51. Patancheru, India: ICRISAT.

Walker, T. S., R. P. Singh, M. Asokan, and H. P. Binswanger. 1983. *Fluctuations in Income in Three Villages of the Semi-Arid Tropics of Peninsular India.* ICRISAT Economics Program Progress Report 57. Patancheru, India: ICRISAT.

Waugh, F. V. 1944. "Does the Consumer Benefit from Price Instability?" *Quarterly Journal of Economics* 58:602–14.

Weiss, A. 1980. "Job Queues and Layoffs in Labor Markets with Flexible Wages." *Journal of Political Economy* 88:526–36.

Willey, R. W. 1981. "A Scientific Approach to Intercropping Research." *Proceedings of the International Workshop on Intercropping, Hyderbad, India, January 10–13, 1979.* Patancheru, India: ICRISAT.

Willey, R. W., M. R. Rao, and M. Natarajan. 1980. "Traditional Cropping Systems with Pigeonpea and Their Improvement." *Proceedings of the International Workshop on Pigeonpeas, December 15–19, 1980.* Vol. 1. Patancheru, India: ICRISAT.

World Bank. 1982. *World Development Report 1982.* New York: Oxford University Press.

Wrather, S. E. 1943. "Adaption of Crop Insurance to Tobacco." *Journal of Farm Economics* 25:410–18.

Yamauchi, Toyoji. 1964. "Consideration on Farmers' Demand for Crop Insurance in Japan." *Rural Economic Problems* 1.

———. 1973. *The Theory and Practice of Crop Insurance in Japan.* Technical Bulletin 18. Taipei City, Taiwan: Food and Fertilizer Technology Center.

# Contributors

Gustavo Arcia is an agricultural economist with the Research Triangle Institute in North Carolina. At the time this volume was prepared he was based in Panama as an economics research specialist with the Inter-American Institute for Cooperation on Agriculture.

Luis Avalos is an insurance specialist with the Inter-American Institute for Cooperation on Agriculture, in Quito, Ecuador.

Luz María Bassoco, now with the Secretaría de Programacíon y Presupuesto, was formerly with the Sistema Alimentario Mexicano, Mexico City, Mexico.

Hans P. Binswanger is head of the Research Unit, Agriculture and Rural Development Department at the World Bank, Washington, D.C.

Celso Cartas, now with the Secretaría de Programacíon y Presupuesto, was formerly with the Sistema Alimentario Mexicano, Mexico City, Mexico.

Guilherme Leite da Silva Dias is with the Instituto de Pesquisar Economicas, Universidade de Sao Paulo, Brazil.

Bruce L. Gardner is professor of agricultural economics at the University of Maryland, USA.

William M. Gudger is head of the Crop Credit Insurance Project at the Inter-American Institute for Cooperation on Agriculture, San Jose, Costa Rica.

Peter B. R. Hazell is director of the Agricultural Growth Linkages and Development Policy Program at the International Food Policy Research Institute, Washington, D.C.

N. S. Jodha is an agricultural economist with the International Crops Research Institute for the Semi-Arid Tropics, India.

Randall A. Kramer is professor of agricultural economics at the Virginia Polytechnical Institute and State University, USA.

Alan G. Lloyd is professor of agricultural economics at the University of Melbourne, Australia. He was formerly a commissioner with the Industries Assistance Commission.

Mauro de Rezende Lopes is director of the Comissao de Financiamento de Producao, Brasilia, Brazil.

ROGER G. MAULDON is commissioner, Industries Assistance Commission, Canberra, Australia.

JOHN W. MELLOR is director of the International Food Policy Research Institute, Washington, D.C.

FRANCISCO MORILLO is director general of the Inter-American Institute for Cooperation on Agriculture, San Jose, Costa Rica.

ROGER D. NORTON is professor of economics at the University of New Mexico, USA.

CARLOS POMAREDA is visiting professor at North Carolina State University. At the time this volume was prepared he was an economics research specialist at the Inter-American Institute for Cooperation on Agriculture, San Jose, Costa Rica.

AMMAR SIAMWALLA is executive director of the Agriculture and Rural Development Program at the Thailand Development Research Institute in Bangkok. At the time this volume was prepared he was a research fellow at the International Food Policy Research Institute, Washington, D.C.

HIROSHI TSUJII is associate professor of agricultural economics at Kyoto University, Japan.

ALBERTO VALDÉS is director of the International Food Trade and Food Security Program at the International Food Policy Research Institute, Washington, D.C.

J. D. VON PISCHKE is senior financial analyst with the Agriculture and Rural Development Department at the World Bank, Washington, D.C.

THOMAS S. WALKER is an associate of the Agricultural Development Council stationed at the International Crops Research Institute for the Semi-Arid Tropics, India.

TOYOJI YAMAUCHI formerly a professor at the College of Agriculture, University of Osaka Prefecture, is now a professor at the Osaka University of Commerce, Japan.

# Index

## Index